JASON MORAN

JASON MORAN

____

Edited by   Adrienne Edwards

____

With contributions by   Philip Bither
Adrienne Edwards
Okwui Enwezor
Alicia Hall Moran
Danielle A. Jackson
George E. Lewis
Glenn Ligon
Jason Moran

Walker Art Center   Minneapolis

CONTENTS

FOREWORD
Olga Viso

Jason Moran is the first museum exhibition to investigate the interdisciplinary work of pianist, composer, and visual artist Jason Moran, whose art, while grounded in music, bridges the visual and performing arts. He challenges traditional forms of musical composition, aligning objects with sound in an effort to underscore their inherent theatricality. Moran's work–often produced in collaboration with prominent visual artists, including Stan Douglas, Theaster Gates, Joan Jonas, Glenn Ligon, Julie Mehretu, Lorna Simpson, and Kara Walker–embraces the essential tenets of jazz music. This volume and exhibition consider the artist's solo and collaborative works as generative investigations that further the fields of experimental jazz, performance, and visual art. Moran's compositions, whether executed through the medium of sculpture, drawing, or sound, rest between classifications; taken together, they are the embodiment of interdisciplinarity. In this, Moran joins a cohort of artists who have a similar impulse, from Joseph Beuys to Adrian Piper. Considering the Walker's long-standing interdisciplinary focus, a presentation of this scale fits perfectly, joining projects such as *Art Performs Life: Merce Cunningham/Meredith Monk/Bill T. Jones* (1998), *Trisha Brown: So That the Audience Does Not Know Whether I Have Stopped Dancing* (2008), *Eiko and Koma: Naked* (2010), *Ralph Lemon: Scaffold Room* (2014), and *Merce Cunningham: Common Time* (2017). To date, *Jason Moran* is the most ambitious project under the Walker Art Center's three-and-a-half-year Interdisciplinary Initiative, supported by a generous $1 million grant from the Andrew W. Mellon Foundation. The initiative is meant to ignite and support rigorous scholarship and deepen our understanding of boundary crossing artistic practices, particularly those that are time based and performance driven.

The Walker has been fortunate to enjoy a long and meaningful history with the artist. Our seventeen-year relationship traverses two directors and includes six engagements, three commissions, and a residency. This history began under the curatorial leadership of the Walker's McGuire Director and Senior Curator of Performing Arts, Philip Bither, who has maintained an ongoing conversation with the artist throughout the years, continually lending support to his groundbreaking investigations. Moran appeared with his trio, the Bandwagon, and Sam Rivers in 2001; with Greg Osby + String in 2002; and again with the Bandwagon for the premiere of *Milestone* in 2005. He was onstage in 2007 for his production *In My Mind: Monk at Town Hall, 1959*, and in 2015 with his contemporary and longtime friend Robert Glasper. He returned in 2018 to premiere *The Last Jazz Fest*, a collaboration with DJ Ashland Mines (aka Total Freedom), with visual artists Ryan Trecartin and Lizzie Fitch. The work, commissioned by the Walker on the occasion of this exhibition, underscores our institutional commitment to affirm Moran's significance not only within the field of music but also in the realm of contemporary visual arts.

Observing *Jason Moran* as it unfolded over several years has unearthed many discoveries that point to the Walker Art Center's long and exceptional relationship with presenting and supporting experimental jazz. In 1964, the museum, under the leadership of performing arts coordinator John Ludwig, initiated the yearlong series Jazz at the Guthrie, which featured Thelonious Monk, John Coltrane, Charles Mingus, Dizzy Gillespie, and Duke Ellington. Miles Davis performed in May 1968. After the launch of this seminal series, the Walker's occasional but keen interest in jazz experimentalists became formalized with the establishment of the Performing Arts Department in 1970, spearheaded by Suzanne Weil (1969–76). Under Weil's leadership, Davis played again in 1971 and 1973, and Herbie Hancock appeared in 1974. Performing Arts director Nigel Redden (1976–82) showcased legendary avant-gardists Cecil Taylor (1979), Julius Eastman (1980), the Art Ensemble of Chicago (1980), Amiri Baraka (1980), Sun Ra and His Arkestra (1980), Max Roach (1980), and Archie Shepp (1981). Ornette Coleman's first concert at the Walker was in 1984, when Charles R. Helm, technical director for Performing Arts and later music programmer, organized the Walker's concerts and events. During Philip Bither's twenty-year tenure at the museum, the Walker has presented programs with Butch Morris and IMP ORK in March 1998; Cassandra Wilson with Bill T. Jones/Arnie Zane Dance Company in 2009; Vijay Iyer in 2005, 2012, and 2018; Burnt Sugar and Vernon Reid in 2013; Craig Taborn in 2013, as well as many others. Over the past fifty years, the Walker has convened more than two hundred jazz experimentalists–a breathtaking history and illustration of a community to which Moran wholeheartedly belongs.

The exhibition *Jason Moran* presents a compelling argument that treads a fine line between group and solo show. Resistant to the categorization of the white cube or black box, the show is rather a gray space, indicated by its carpeted floors, painted walls, and theatrical lighting, thoughtfully reflective of Moran as an artist. Local musicians (and the artist himself) perform live on Moran's 2015 "set sculptures"–*STAGED: Savoy Ballroom 1* and *STAGED: Three Deuces*, and the newly commissioned *STAGED: Slugs' Saloon*–in the galleries throughout the run of the show.

The exhibition is curated by the Walker's former curator at large Adrienne Edwards, whose cross-disciplinary curatorial approach and oversight of the Walker's Interdisciplinary Initiative with Philip Bither has activated the institution's experimental platforms with newfound energy and rigor. I am extraordinarily grateful for Adrienne's ambitious aims in conceptualizing this exhibition and catalogue, bridging the fields of visual arts and performing arts, and challenging exhibition practice. In her new role at the Whitney Museum of American Art, which she assumed shortly after the exhibition's Minneapolis premiere, she will continue to advance this important work. Assisting Adrienne, Interdisciplinary fellow Danielle A. Jackson has been an essential partner in the realization and development of the exhibition. Adrienne joins me in thanking the artists, individuals, and institutions that have generously lent artworks and other materials to this project (page 275). Many of them have allowed video works to be exhibited in new ways, specifically as a composed synchronized loop arranged by Moran on projection screens. The result of this and other in-gallery presentations merges artworks, performance documentation, video, and sound to foreground the collaborative nature of the artist's practice and also to offer alternative contexts and in-depth readings of critically acclaimed works, among them Glenn Ligon's *The Death of Tom*, Stan Douglas's *Luanda-Kinshasa*, Lorna Simpson's *Chess* (2013), and Kara Walker's *National Archives Microfilm M999 Roll 34: Bureau of Refugees, Freedmen and Abandoned Lands: Six Miles from Springfield on the Franklin Road* (2009). Significantly, the Walker has its own resonant history of exhibiting and collecting works by Moran's collaborators.

An exhibition and catalogue of this scale required the partnership of key funders who have our eternal gratitude. We are particularly thankful to the Andrew W. Mellon Foundation for its support of the Jason Moran project, and thank Earl Lewis, former president; Elizabeth Alexander, president; Mariët Westermann, executive vice president; and Susan Feder, program officer, for their significant support of artists working at the intersection of performance, installation, and visual arts. We are also grateful for the generous support provided by the National Endowment for the Arts, the William and Nadine McGuire Commissioning Fund, National Advisory-Board and Producers' Council members Mike and Elizabeth Sweeney, and Steinway & Sons. We are also ever thankful for the leadership of the Walker's Board of Trustees (page 275), who encourage the vision of the institution. Their affirmation of the mission to serve artists, their confidence in our staff, and their reinforcement of our commitment to excellence is key to the success of our ambitious interdisciplinary art programs and exhibitions.

I am exceptionally grateful for the partnership of the Walker's extraordinary team of senior leaders, including Christopher Stevens, chief of advancement; Mary Polta, chief financial officer; Annie Gillette Cleveland, former director of marketing and strategic communications; Rishi Donat, director of human resources; Nisa Mackie, director and curator of Education and Public Programs; Emmet Byrne, design director and curator; Mike Bettison, director of technology and digital strategies; and Siri Engberg, Visual Arts senior curator and director of exhibitions management. Their leadership has supported the Walker's exemplary staff in working together to bring the exhibition to realization. I join Adrienne in thanking those listed in the acknowledgments and the many staff members who have made meaningful contributions to this project from its inception to its presentation. It is our great pleasure to be able to share this exhibition with audiences in Boston; Columbus, Ohio; and New York through our tour partners at the Institute of Contemporary Art/Boston, the Wexner Center for the Arts, and the Whitney Museum of American Art. We are grateful to ICA/Boston director Jill Medvedow; Wexner director Sherri Geldin; and Whitney director Adam Weinberg and Scott Rothkopf, deputy director for programs and chief curator, for their partnership on this exhibition, and to their dedicated staffs, including curatorial coordination by the Wexner's senior curator Michael Goodson, the ICA/

Boston's curatorial associate Jeffrey De Blois, and Adrienne Edwards at the Whitney, in her new role there. We also thank the Wexner's director of Performing Arts Lane Czaplinski and former director Charles R. Helm for their support of the commissioned performance and production residency.

Lastly, we extend our warmest thanks to Jason Moran, whose spirit has touched the Walker throughout the years. His dedication to the project and generosity at every turn have been truly remarkable—we are immensely grateful.

ACKNOWLEDGMENTS
Adrienne Edwards

A catalogue of this magnitude and complexity requires the contributions and talents of many individuals both inside and outside the walls of the Walker Art Center. Book making is, of course, a group undertaking, whereby its composers and collaborators commit to bringing the imagined to life.

First, I must express my profound gratitude to the brilliant artists who contributed to the exhibition: The Bandwagon (Tarus Mateen and Nasheet Waits), Stan Douglas, Lizzie Fitch, Theaster Gates, Alicia Hall Moran, Joan Jonas, Glenn Ligon, Julie Mehretu, DJ Ashland Mines, Adam Pendleton, Adrian Piper, Robert Pruitt, Lorna Simpson, Ryan Trecartin, Kara Walker, Carrie Mae Weems, and Jason Moran, who brings this creative group of visionaries together. It has been a true pleasure to work with dedicated artists to realize this ambitious project of Moran's work, particularly, through the lens of collaboration. There would, of course, be no book without its exceptional authors. I thank Philip Bither, Okwui Enwezor, Alicia Hall Moran, Danielle A. Jackson, George E. Lewis, Glenn Ligon, and Jason Moran for original, thought-provoking, and deeply invested contributions. Each brought expertise to cast into language a phenomenal intellectual, artistic, and personal history with Jason's work. The authors and artists whose content graces the pages of this book allowed the project to move beyond documentation of an exhibition and to become a compelling record of investigations and new scholarship in music, performance, and contemporary art at large.

Thanks also to the image providers and photographers for their visionary pictures of Jason's works, artistic inspirations, and powerful archival material: AP Press; Archives Leloir, Sarl; Archives of American Art, Smithsonian Institution; Art Resource; Artists Rights Society; Leslie Parks Bailey; Isabella Balena; Estate of Jean-Michael Basquiat; Dawoud Bey; Brant Foundation; Ole Brask/Jan Persson Archive/ CTS images; Marta Buso; Estate of E. Simms Campbell; Cornell Capa/Magnum Photos; Castelli Gallery; Chicago Symphony Orchestra; Joáquin Cortes/Román Lores; Paula Court; Da Camera of Houston; Stephen Daiter Gallery; Kevin Davies; Melvin Edwards; Adama Delphine Fawundu; Ella Fitzgerald Charitable Foundation; Galen Fletcher; Estate of Lona Foote; Getty Images; Jeff Gold; Lévy Gory Gallery; William P. Gottleib/Ira and Leonore S. Gershwin Fund Collection, Music Division, Library of Congress; Estate of Alex Hansen; Alexei Hay/Trunk Archive; Brenda Hutchinson; Danielle A. Jackson; Joan Jonas Studio; KADIST; Jean-Pierre Leloir; Ralph Lemon; Guy Le Querrec/Magnum Photos; Glenn Ligon Studio; Pin Lim/Forest Photography; Luhring Augustine; Ari Marcopoulos; Roberto Marossi; Julie Mehretu and Sarah Rentz (Julie Mehretu Studio); Manfred Montwé; Estate of Peter Moore; Jason Moran and Alicia Hall Moran; Robert Morris; Museo Nacional Centro de Arte Reina Sofía, Madrid; Museum of Contemporary Art Chicago; Nasher Sculpture Center, Dallas; Senga Nengudi; Oddball Films; Office of Contemporary Art Norway; Farzad Owrang; Estate of Nam June Paik; Performa; Adrian Piper Research Archive; Gene Pittman; Quaku/Roderick Young; Moira Ricci; Bobby Rogers; John Rogers; Elizabeth Campbell Moskowitz; Todd Rosenberg; Raymond Ross Archives/CTS images; Nate Ryan; Don Schlitten; Schomburg Center for Research in Black Culture, New York Public Library; Jack Shainman; Sikkema Jenkins & Co; L. Simpson Studio; Estate of Marvin and Morgan Smith; Ming Smith; Wadada Leo Smith; Sprüth Magers; Kevin Todora; VAGA, New York; VG Bild-Kunst, Bonn; Walker Art Center, Minneapolis; Kara Walker; Robert Wedemayer; Yale University Beinecke Rare Book & Manuscript Library; and David Zwirner Gallery.

Jason Moran is an ambitious interdisciplinary project that runs across our institutional platforms. Nothing short of a team effort, it is characteristic of the Walker's risk-taking program. It could not have been achieved without the generosity of many individuals, galleries, and organizations that have lent artworks and supported the artist's practice. I offer my sincere gratitude to Luhring Augustine, particularly senior director Lauren Wittels, who attentively and enthusiastically provided support and resources whenever needed. Additional thanks go out to: L. Simpson Studio; Joan Jonas Studio; Hauser and Wirth; Sikkema Jenkins & Co; Glenn Ligon Studio; David Zwirner; Stan Douglas Studio; Performa; and Sarah Rothenberg, Ab Sengupta, and Leo Boucher of Da Camera Chamber of Music and Jazz.

At the Walker, I thank archivist Jill Vuchetich and visual resources librarian Barb Economon for their eager and sincere assistance in supporting the research needs for this project and gathering archival materials, many of which appear in this publication. I also thank board member Michael Peterman for his research assistance and stalwart support. Former Visual Arts department administrator Remy Mason attended to the logistical aspects of the project, including the artist's visits to Minneapolis. She additionally provided early coordination for the catalogue production, which was expertly led to completion by design studio manager Alanna Nissen. The design of the catalogue is the work of graphic design studio 12:01—Office of Hassan Rahim, whose groundbreaking visuals and art direction heighten the work displayed on its pages. Additional art direction was facilitated by Walker design director Emmet Byrne. Its extraordinary images have come to life with the expertise of senior image specialist Greg Beckel; his attention to detail is unparalleled. Cathy Lebowitz, our magnificent editor, treated every word in and component of the book with care. I am grateful for her curiosity, dedication, and diligence. The meticulous attention of Pamela Johnson was vital to the catalogue. In developing this publication, we were also ever grateful for the artist's involvement and enthusiasm about the project.

In addition to the Walker's senior leaders that Olga Viso mentions on the previous pages, I am truly thankful for the work of the many staff members who have been instrumental to the success and realization of the project. Interdisciplinary fellow Danielle A. Jackson provided key assistance with loan and image requests, interpretation, and installation. She has been an asset and a partner, managing various aspects of the exhibition, performance, and publication. I also had the pleasure, in the initial phases of this project, of working with former curatorial fellow Jordan Carter. Registrar Bryan Stusse extraordinarily coordinated the loans and shipping. The exhibition's installation planning was begun by Cameron Zebrun, and the process completed by Ben Geffen and Doc Czypinski. The exhibition benefited greatly from the expertise of the program services team, in particular Kirk McCall, David Dick, and lead technician Peter Hannah, who were responsible for executing the curatorial team's vision of an immersive gallery. Audiovisual specialist Peter Murphy, exhibition media technician Jeffrey Sherman, and consulting sound engineer Sascha von Oertzen demonstrated their media expertise effortlessly. Media producer Andy Underwood-Bultmann skillfully handled every detail related to the exhibition's documentation needs. I also thank the Public Relations and Marketing staff members: Michelle Wood, associate director of strategic marketing; Rachel Joyce, public relations associate director; and Paul Schmelzer, web editor. Chris Cloud, former social media and community manager, engaged various social media platforms to highlight the artist's work, reaching beyond the walls of the institution. Senior curator Siri Engberg provided logistical and operational guidance and support throughout the process; her words and knowledge were invaluable.

The interpretation of the exhibition brilliantly bridged accessibility and criticality thanks to the contributions of Nisa Mackie, director and curator of Education and Public Programs; interpretation fellow Alexandra Nicome; and Walker senior editor Pamela Johnson, with assistance from Annie Jacobson, who immersed themselves in the project's content. Ryan Gerald Nelson, the exhibition's graphic designer, translated the show's concept into visual form and created a stunning video guide and wall mural for gallery visitors.

An interdisciplinary exhibition that champions performance, such as this one, could not be possible without the efforts of the Walker's stellar Performing Arts department. Performing Arts coordinator Molly Hanse and senior program officer Julie Voigt lent key support to the Walker's interdisciplinary initiative. The performances, both in the gallery and on the stage of the McGuire Theater, have greatly benefited from the work of Doug Benidt, associate curator; Danielle A. Jackson; and Philip Bither, William and Nadine McGuire Director and Senior Curator of Performing Arts. I must also thank the talented Events Production and Visitor Services team, in particular Christian Gaylord, Ben Geffen, David Goldstein, Ella Kampelman, Jon Kirchhofer, Claire Lindsey-McGinn, Doug Livesay, and Pearl Rea.

The myriad administrative details related to the exhibition's internal planning, tour, and opening at the Walker were coordinated with the assistance of exhibitions administrator Erin McNeil. Kerstin Beyer, Alycia Anderson, Kirstin Tracy, and Michelle Poss from Development and Membership expertly oversaw the opening celebration. An exhibition of this scope requires strong support, and I am enormously grateful to Marla Stack, director of special projects fundraising, and Megan Dunn, development associate, for their fundraising efforts. Lastly, I want to thank former executive director Olga Viso for her unwavering enthusiasm and support throughout the exhibition's life. It is a privilege to work with an institution that champions artists' experimentation at every level.

CLOSER

It's Christmas morning and I'm staring at a beetle slowly making its way across the window shades. For the past two weeks, I've noticed this beetle's silhouette, holding stubbornly steady in one position. Even when a breeze rocks the shades, the beetle is unmoved. Though this morning, I noticed the beetle had moved two inches to the right. Two inches closer to something. What is it? Two weeks, two inches.

Somehow this beetle reminds me of a conversation I had with composer Henry Threadgill. He spoke about a new piece of his that was built on short versus long sounds and phrases. Threadgill said the phrases mimicked Morse code, and that even if the "short" phrase of music had a duration of a calendar year, the "long" phrase could be one year plus a minute. Two years, two phrases.

When I'm in the midst of a solo, I like to play phrases of music "over the bar line." This means that I resolve the phrase far past where/when the original resolution occurs. I stack the phrases, kind of like run-on sentences. That tug on the music also pulls the musicians and the listener, so we all tilt together. Eventually the phrase breaks and resets. The comedian Franklyn Ajaye once said to me that performing for jazz audiences was great, because the audience was capable of following a joke for longer stretches of time. He thought it allowed the comedian more room for abstraction before resolving with a punch line.

The night before I moved to New York I sat in a car and cried. The anxiety was overwhelming, but the anxiety did not outweigh the thrill of what I could encounter in New York. At eighteen years old, I was moving to the city of my dreams, where the music lived every hour of the day. Two years after my arrival, I met my wife, Alicia Hall, the bold feminist mezzo-soprano and composer. Her Barnard wit and intellectual precision defined our dating style. She'd take me to see Abbey Lincoln and Cassandra Wilson. She'd tell me that the woman's story was often erased in jazz history. These conversations defined our futures. Our goal was to make new space on the stage.

As artists in the 2012 Whitney Biennial, we created *BLEED*, a five-day performance gathering with more than ninety performers, including Kara Walker, Joan Jonas, Esperanza Spalding, Adam Pendleton, Lorraine O'Grady, Bill Frisell, Rashida Bumbray, and many more. We put the music and the practice—i.e., the execution of it and the work on it—up close to the audience.

In 2015 we presented *Work Songs* at the Venice Biennale. At the invitation of curator Okwui Enwezor, the forty-minute piece was performed daily in the Giardini. The performers' stamina to deliver a set of African American work songs on a constantly shifting backing track was the "work." The performance was on a blood red stage designed by David Adjaye. Bleed for real.

So, as this exhibition approaches, I ask that you come up close. These pieces emerge from my performance practice. My body in relationship to the piano and to the bodies in the audience. In Slugs', the audience was three feet away from the band. In the Savoy Ballroom, the musicians were elevated and on top of the dancers. In the Three Deuces, the audience was on the same level as the musicians, shoved into a corner of a 52nd Street basement. Where do we sit to be moved? I sit up close.

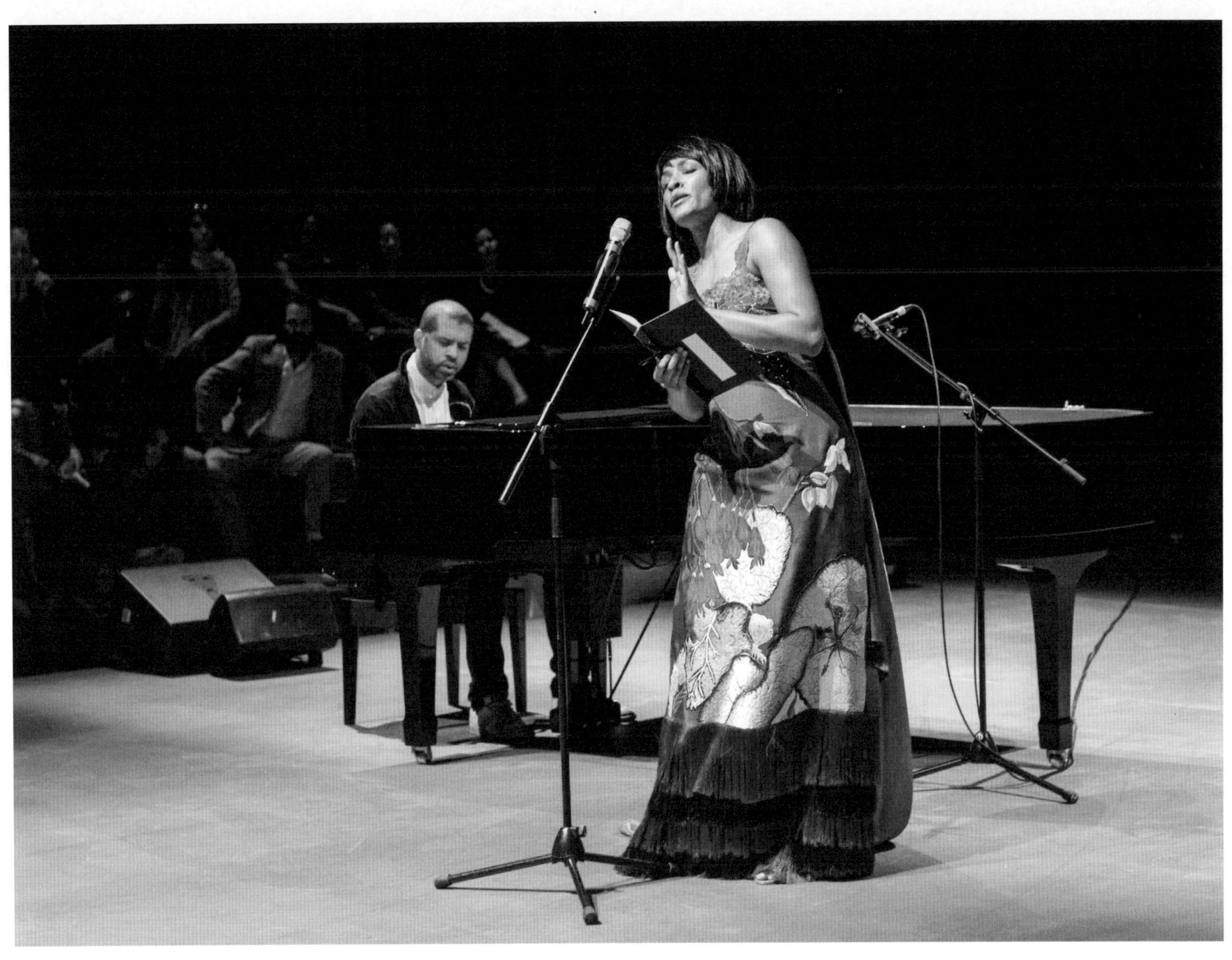

Jason Moran and Alicia Hall Moran performing *Work Songs* at the Arena, Central Pavilion, Giardini, as part of the exhibition *All the World's Futures* at the 56th Venice Biennale, 2015

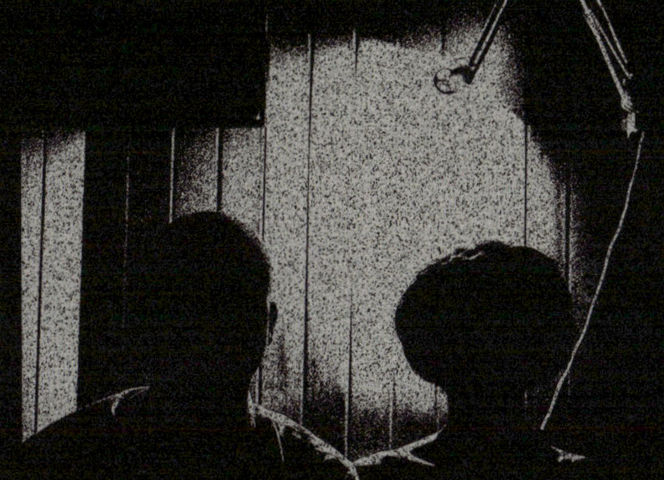

ALICIA
HALL MORAN
13——26
I'LL SAY
"SOUND
COMES AT YOU
IN   WAVES"

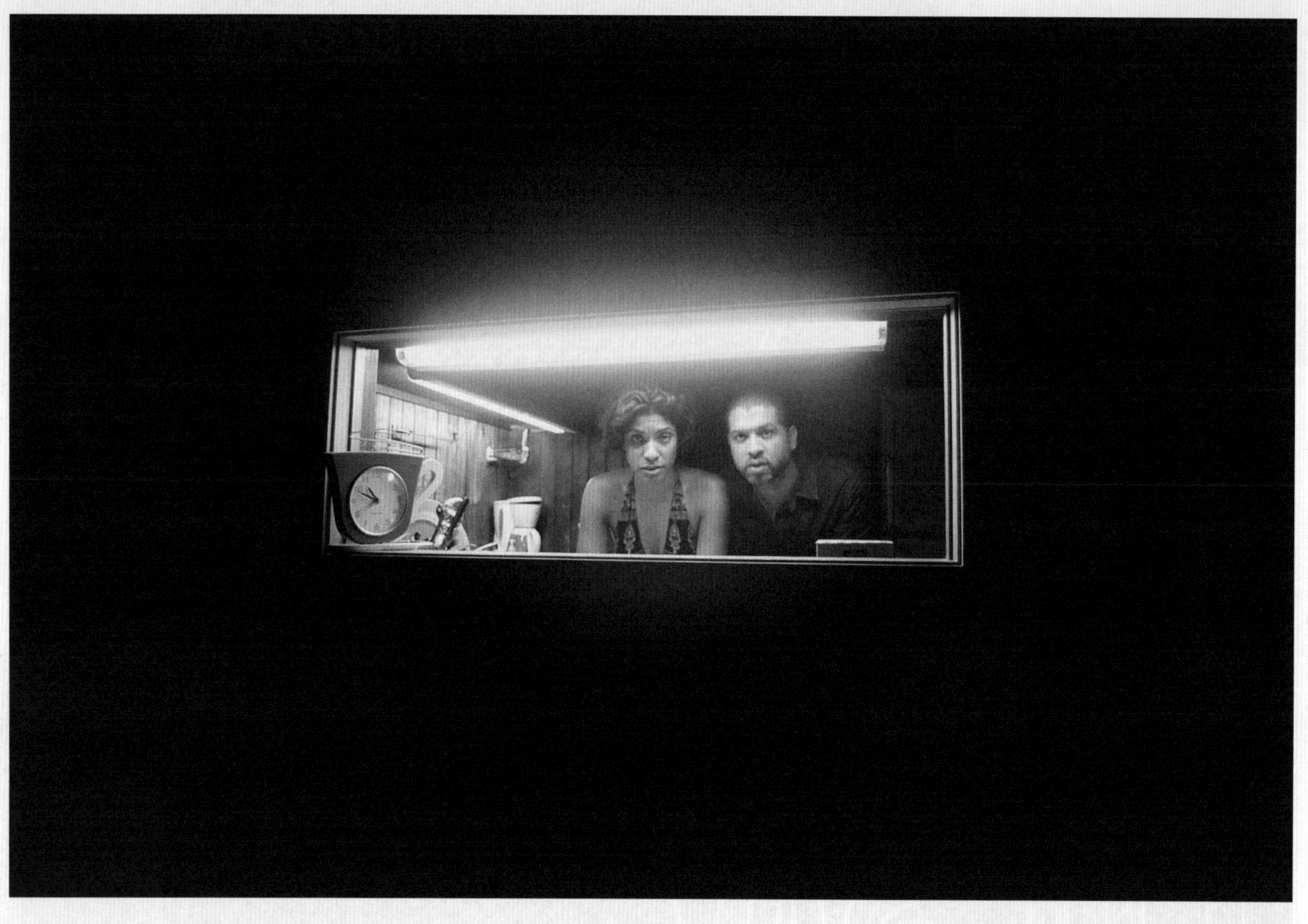

Alicia Hall Moran and Jason Moran at Acadia Summer Arts Program (Kamp Kippy), Maine, 2014

 ALICIA HALL MORAN

Sound comes at you in waves. What you hear is for you. Your hearing will never be duplicated ever again. Did you know that? That's how it is. Listen. Jason is playing a luncheon at the Kennedy Center, and he's the tribute artist to the late great pianist Dr. Billy Taylor. Jason makes his music, and he gives a speech; tells the story of Dr. Taylor giving him sound advice as an eager high school student, and some people begin to cry. I can't say why other people cried, but to me something I had forgotten to hold was restored in his waves of sound. I found a little hope for myself at a luncheon. Jason Moran is just that good.

Toward evening, my husband and I, we dress up for a very big dinner with a lot of the very same folks from lunch. When we get to our table, Jason is seated next to Sonny Rollins, the Saxophone Colossus. "You know why I like you?" Mr. Rollins asks Jason. "Because you don't smile."

Now I don't know how Mr. Rollins parsed Jason's utterly bifocal attitude of sacrificial devotion and unilateral nofucksgiving to a jazz audience, and I don't know the thoughts of the people who cried when Jason played and spoke about Dr. Taylor, but I know what happened to them. He moved them all. They began in one place and got deposited in another. That is the artist's job. To bring new perspective.

If the actress Meryl Streep, remembering Jason from the luncheon, recognizes him standing in the doorway after dinner, then places her hands on his shoulders, squares her eyes with his and says "YOU ARE MAGIC," in the Oscar-worthy way, then that is only to make a point. She remembered him because his sound became hers. That is, sound comes at you in waves, and what you hear is for you, and because your hearing will never be duplicated ever again, it has a value. So you hold on to it. Because it is yours.

I know Jason loved me immediately because I listened to what he had to say. Early in our relationship he'd say to me, "Stop listening to what I say!," because he wanted me to operate on the basis of what he meant (you know what I'm sayin'?). But I listen to what people say and what they say matters to me. What they say shows me what they think. "You think too much" was a frequent review when I started out as a classical vocal performance major at the conservatory. I'd ask Jason, "Who are they, these other people who don't think?" He would always say, essentially, something like, "Everybody doesn't think as much as you." And that's how it's been for the past couple decades: explaining the world to one another, alternately leading one another through darkness.

And that brings me to playing in the dark. We are exceptional in this. It has gotten to the point that if an area is too filled with light, then we may just step aside and happily allow someone else to occupy that space. We are looking for questions, trying for answers in ourselves, genuinely searching for a solution for our People. And who are our People? The people who want to be. Simple as that.

Alicia Hall Moran
April 21, 2017
New York City

"I'll say."
—Mary Lou Moran

"For all of those who wanna profile and pose. Rock you in your face, stab your brain with your nose bone. You all alone in these streets, cousin. Every man for they self in this land we be gunning. And keep them shook crews running like they supposed to. They come around, but they never come close to. I can see it inside your face you're in the wrong place. Cowards like you just get their whole body laced up. With bullet holes and such. Speak the wrong words, man, and you will get touched. You can put your whole army against my team and I guarantee you it will be your very last time breathing."

Oh, Lord.

"Your simple words just don't move me. You're minor, we're major. You all up in the game and don't deserve to be a player." Ok, I'm ready. You recording?

Of course.

Oh, I'm sorry.

Tell me about hip-hop and visual art.

Well, one of the first things that made sense to me from a kind of design perspective was the group Public Enemy's main image: a man in a hip-hop stance, inside the crosshairs of a scope. The lead rapper of the group is Chuck D and he designed that logo: his music, his politics, and his image.

Who were you quoting when I started the recording?

The rapper Prodigy from the group Mobb Deep. He died today. Sickle cell anemia. That song "Shook Ones" moves me with the lyric, "If I die I couldn't choose a better location, getting closer to God in a tight situation."

The location, right. His environment …

… is the instrument. But any artist who plays an instrument is collaborating with that instrument, because it's the thing that makes sense out of what the performer believes they hear. It does the translating. I have much affection for what the piano brings to me, what it allows, and I'm sensitive to how I touch it too. The forces it can withstand.

top (left to right): Big Noyd, Prodigy, and Havoc (Mobb Deep) with producer Scarface Twin at Queensbridge Projects, New York, 1995

bottom: Chuck D and Flavor Flav (Public Enemy), New York, 1987

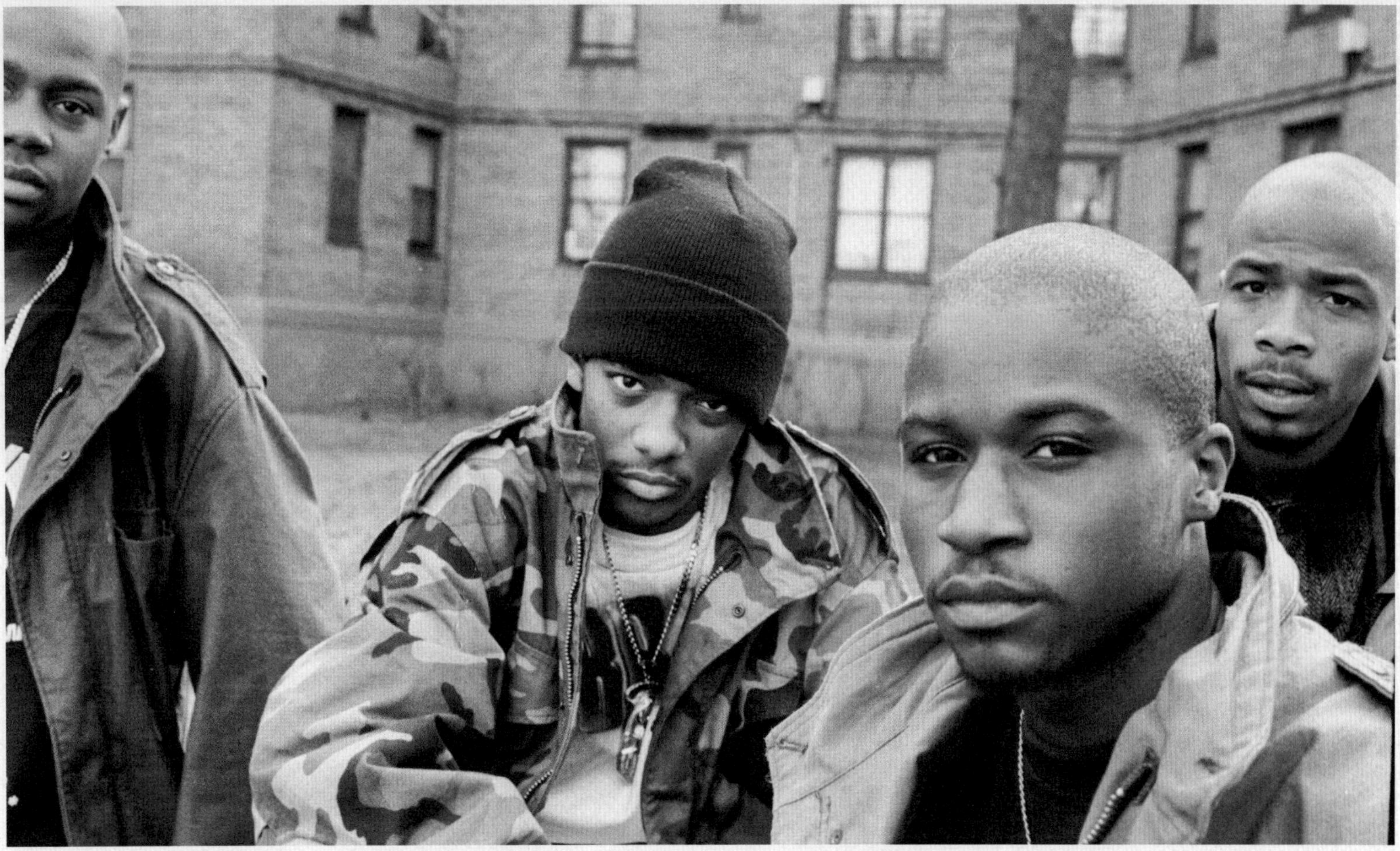

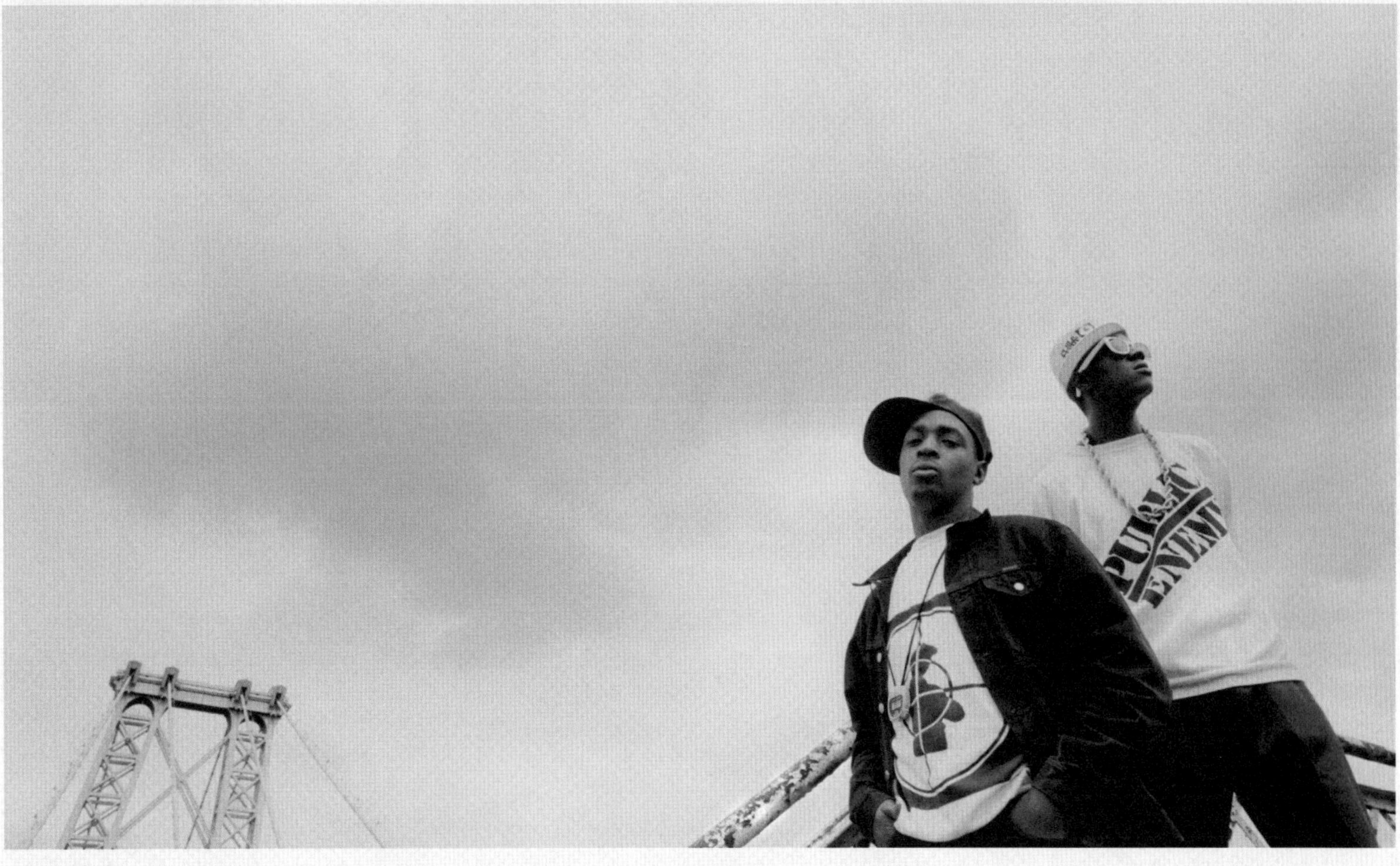

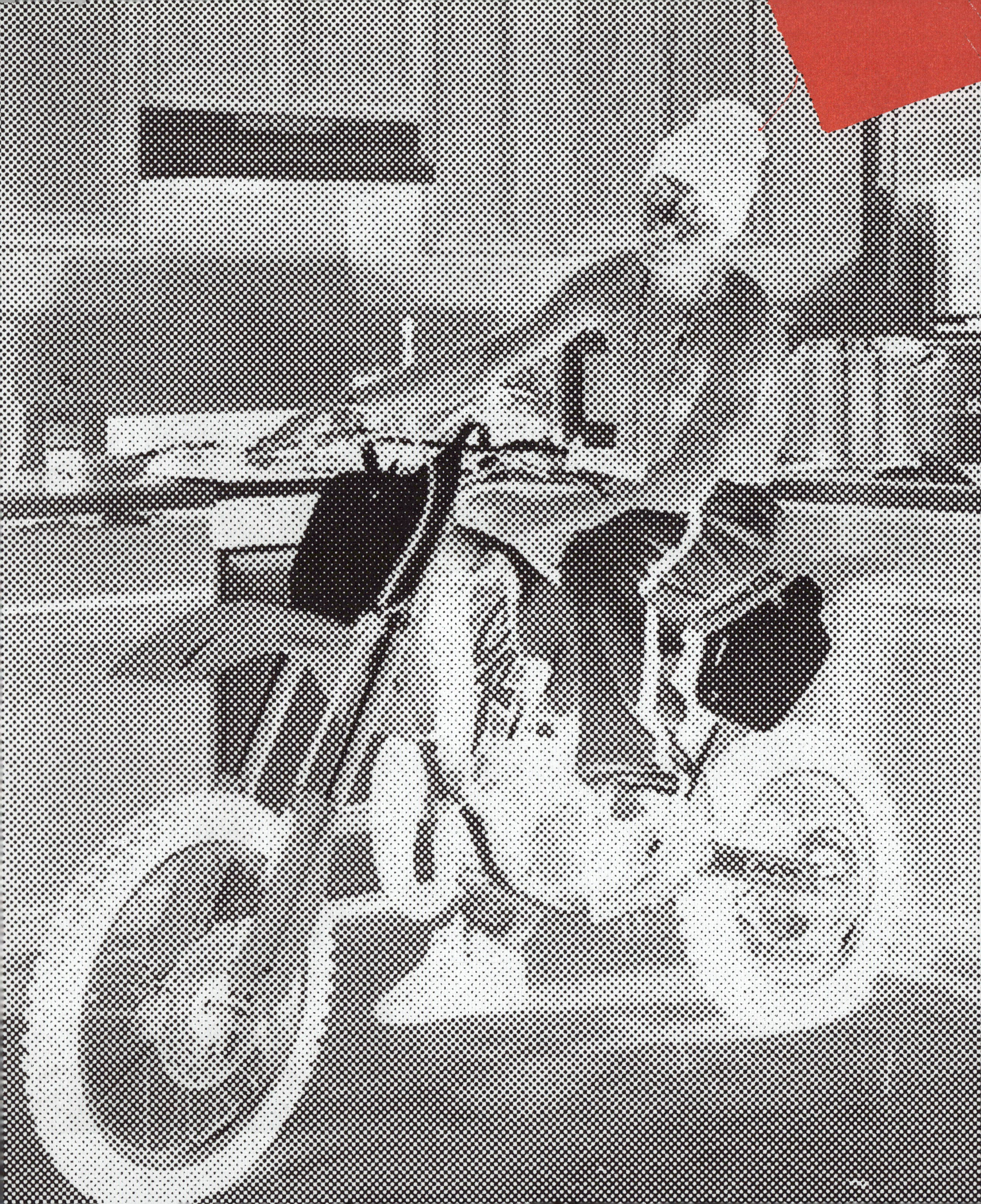

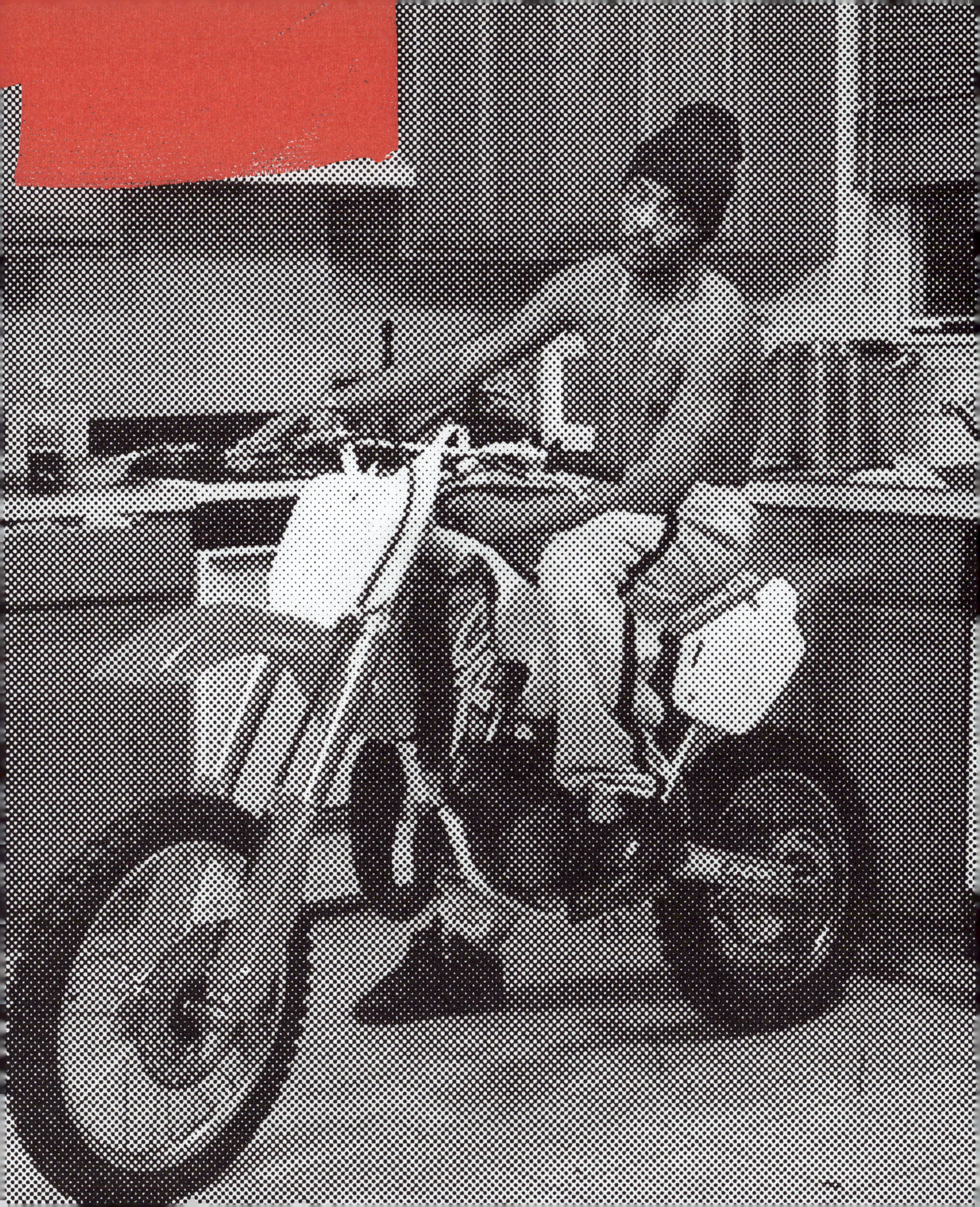

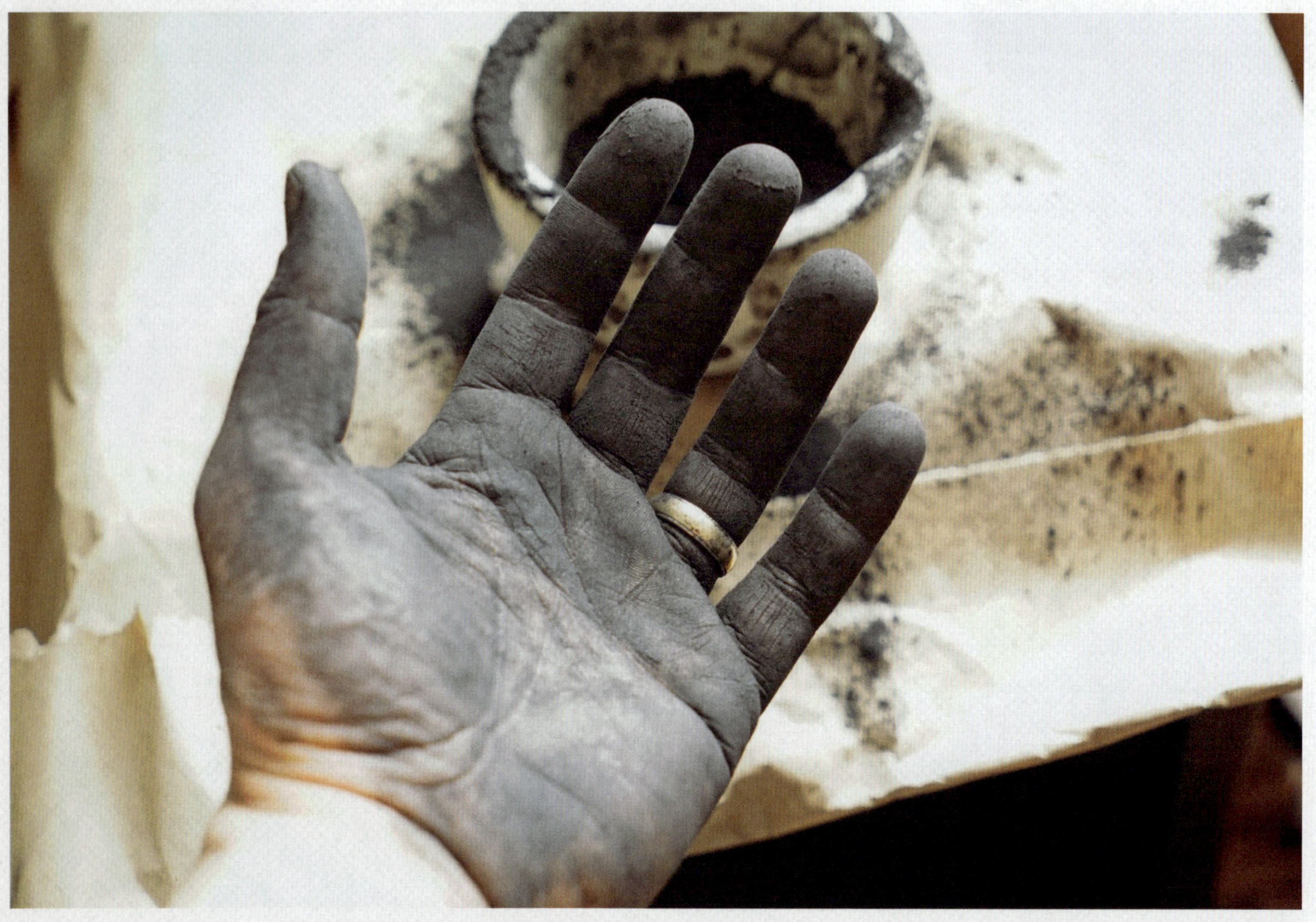

ALICIA HALL MORAN

Do you think this translates to jazz?

Jazz is a music of recovery. Say when Duke Ellington's band was at the height of its soul and precision. There'd be these solos, and Paul Gonsalves, the tenor saxophone player, was totally drunk onstage. Duke noticed this, called him to solo on every song; put him on blast. Gonsalves did OK but that stuff—those relationships, personal battles, social battles, music battles—those tensions arise in every performance. It's what attracts us to Billie Holiday sharing her voice the way she did, or to Nina Simone's timbre and her pianistic technique. There are always layers.

Layers?

Yeah.

Do you think of your works on paper as layers of the *Savoy* and the *Three Deuces*?

I think about them as remnants of a performance, or a mapping of the performer, an interrogation of the performer. Another way I think about them, because of conversations I've had with Joan Jonas and other people who talk about music and its residue, is as the residue of the performance. But these aren't public performances. They are me in my art studio making these paper pieces.

Some of them are on player piano rolls, which are an interesting part of music history. Player pianos were like early karaoke machines. They'd be in bars, and the lyrics were printed on the side of the piano roll. As they'd roll up, people sang along. A Fats Waller song. A George Gershwin song. Since they recorded James P. Johnson or Fats Waller as pianists, I also see them as kind of "snapshotting" through a machine. Snapshotting blackness into a machine.

Why blackness? Didn't they record white people?

Yeah, they did [laughs]. I always wondered if the player piano was threatening to musicians, like stereo was to Carnegie Hall. There's something about its ability to mimic the pianist's spacing. Seeing their spacing in all those perforations on the page. The holes. Player piano rolls are so beautiful to look at. I used to collect them as part of my jazz ephemera. Then I started to think of them as paper, just paper that reacts to charcoal dust, or whatever dust I use to put my fingers onto those pages, onto my piano.

Charcoal dust?

That's what I dip my hands into when I play on top of these pieces of piano paper.

Jason Moran's hand covered in charcoal dust
in the studio, 2016

Previous pages:
Portrait of Prodigy (from Mobb Deep) on bike
in kitchen, 1999; originally published in
Vibe magazine, January 2001

I'm trying to figure out how you got to that medium—charcoal on paper. What was your process?

Well, I worked with charcoal like twenty years ago. I used to sketch whatever with charcoal and watercolors when I was on the road. I've always liked what charcoal does on white paper. It's basic and immediate. I was thinking of all the times I've played the piano, but now perspective is flipped. What do the piano keys see when my fingers come down and hit them?

Mm-hmm. It's very interesting to think of your process as an attempt to give the instrument a point of view …

And the stage, to consider its point of view—not just the performer's.

I recently told a woman, "I sing concerts," and she said, "In the context of concerts, I'm very much in the audience." It hadn't ever really occurred to me that by saying I perform, I had already named her. She was telling me where she was in that scenario. I think you're playing around with that.

Yeah.

Your stages seem vulnerable to me in that they face open. They ask to be read. You haven't put them in any kind of shadows. In highlighting the details, you take away some of the mystique. Do you think the way a stage looks affects how people play?

Definitely. The way the stage is built sets up a relationship. Does the audience encircle you? Is the audience only in front of you? Does the stage look down on its audience, or are you going to play eye to eye? You have to raise your eyes to talk to the people at the top of the Apollo, and you know those people at the top, that's where any youthful energy is at too. They're all hype.

The Blue Note in New York has weird, striped vinyl siding, a mirror pattern all around the room, and a tiny, high stage. Village Vanguard is this odd, skinny diamond with a low ceiling. It's one-fourth wood flooring, three-quarters carpet, and a velvet curtain in the back. The first table is right behind the piano player's bench, like two feet away. You can't run backstage.

Jason Moran performing in *STAGED: Three Deuces* at the Arsenale, 56th Venice Biennale, June 20, 2015

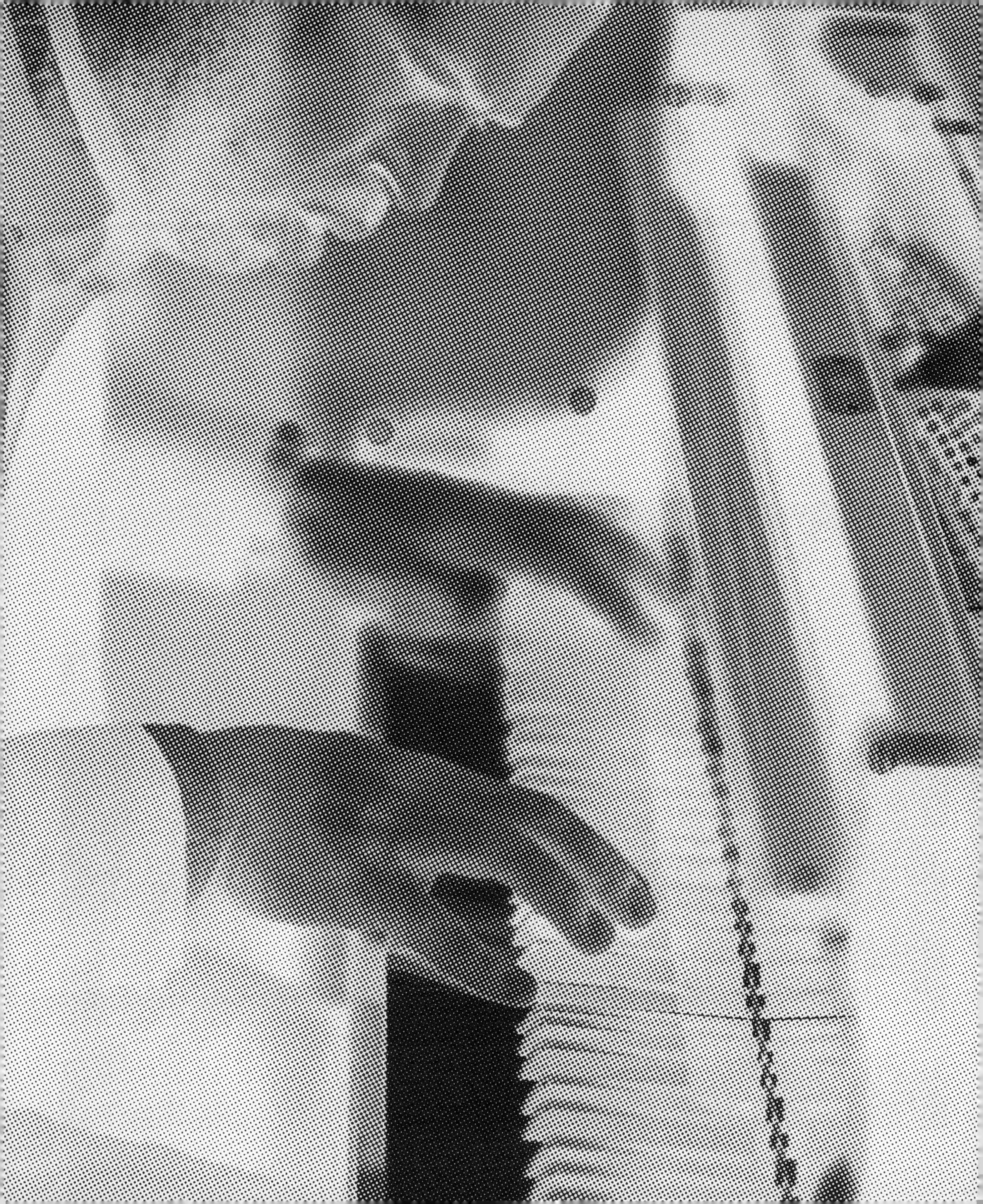

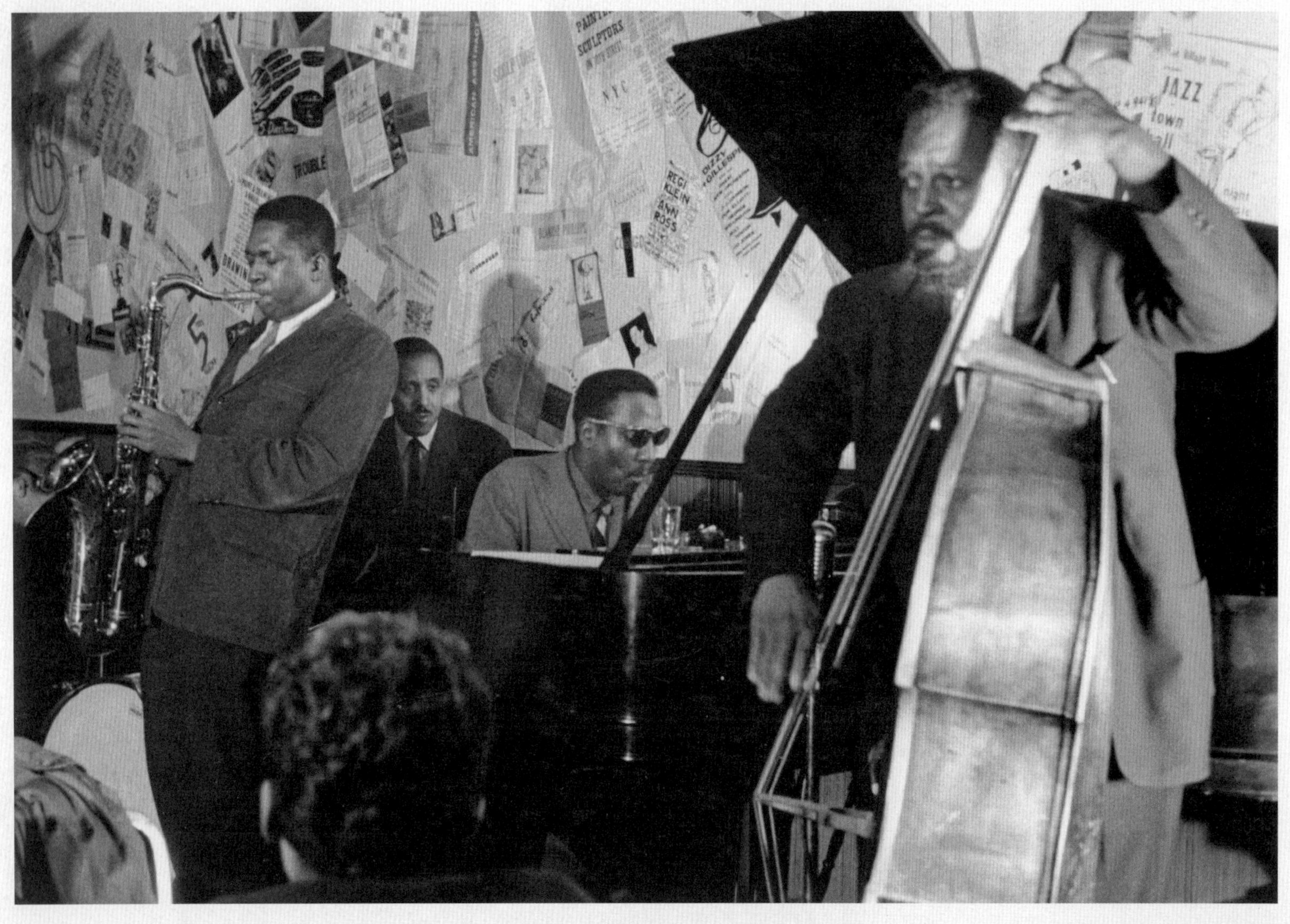

ALICIA HALL MORAN

How is it to play for an audience in the *Three Deuces*?

It's been interesting. We played in Venice ten or so times [*All the World's Futures*, 56th Venice Biennale]. We played at the gallery in Bushwick about eight times [*STAGED*, Luhring Augustine gallery], and we played in Cambridge [Ethelbert Cooper Gallery of African and African American Art, Harvard University]. Usually people have stood or sat on the floor. In Cambridge, there were chairs and tables like a club, and it was kind of deep to have that feel in a small room. In Bushwick, I brought in special guests. They started playing on the *Savoy Ballroom* stage as we played on the *Three Deuces*. Then they joined us at the *Three Deuces*, as if the set Uptown was finished, and it was time to come to Midtown and sit in.

Slugs' Saloon is the third stage in the series. The stages don't have a historical read but are extremely personal, about my ambition to sit among eras. How I would have loved to play in that place—Five Spot or Fillmore East. I look for the chance to make the stage into something else, bringing skateboard ramps and tents into the concert hall. I had thirty-five kids on the Chicago Symphony Center stage with Theaster Gates's sculptures.

The country's changed, but none of these things are unlocked from any of the others. Jazz is not sitting out there on an island by itself. The music is affected, and jazz is one of those forms of music that maps America's progress. I say progress.

(left to right): John Coltrane, Shadow Wilson, Thelonious Monk, and Ahmed Abdul Malik at the Five Spot, New York, 1957

JASON MORAN: PUSH ALL THE BUTTONS, SHAVE THE EDGES, OR ALL STRAIGHTEN THEM OUT

ADRIENNE EDWARDS

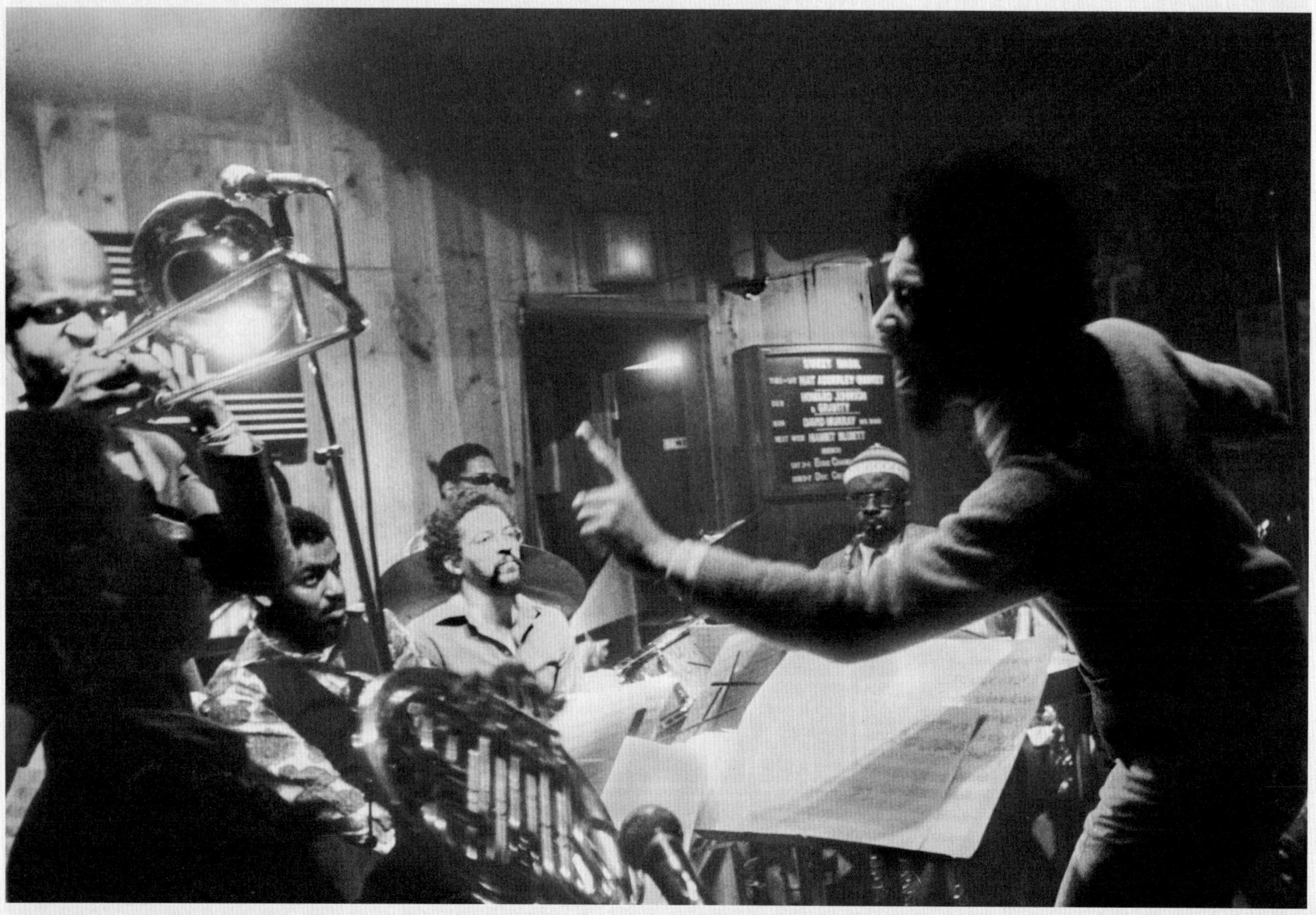

     ADRIENNE EDWARDS

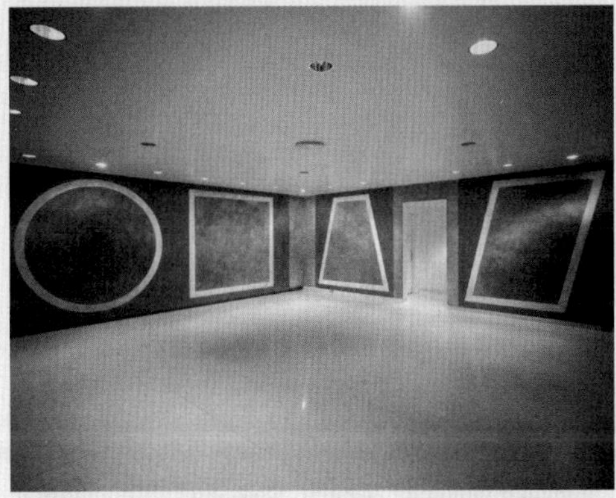

Sol LeWitt, *Four Geometric Figures in a Room*, 1984, ink on latex paint on gypsum board, 101½ x 1,107½ in. (256.8 x 2813 cm)

SET: PRELUDE

The "set," for which musicians come together to collaboratively improvise, riffing off of one another to create the musical experience, underlies every aspect of Jason Moran's first solo museum exhibition, which aims to encapsulate his varied output as an interdisciplinary artist. Already a renowned jazz musician, playing all the big festivals and venues, and recording on Blue Note Records—as well as being an avid collector, photographer, and jazz journal publisher—Moran entered into an investigation of a certain way of being conceptual around the turn of the century, coming to coalesce what Sol LeWitt described as the "paramount idea" with technical virtuosity. It was in 2001 at the Walker Art Center that Moran encountered a 1984 wall work by LeWitt titled *Four Geometric Figures in a Room*.[1] "There was something that had just started setting into my mind around Conceptualism. … I was having my first Sol LeWitt experience and what it meant to see those lines and feel myself within those lines, you know, and the freeness that I felt in relationship to that," he said.[2] Soon after, my colleague Philip Bither invited Moran to create a stage commission for the Walker's theater that would engage with the institution's collection.[3] Moran found his motivation in Adrian Piper's *Mythic Being* works, in particular the photo- and text-based series *The Mythic Being; I/You (Her)* (1974), ten images that are part of a larger project featuring groundbreaking performances and classified advertisements. Piper's distinct and destabilizing combination of sly humor, formal innovation, and sharp critique is a prescient example of Conceptual art incorporating identity and the social world by playing with and subverting racial and gender stereotypes. Piper's approach instigated Moran's commitment to reveal his process as a musician.[4] For the commission, Moran created and produced *Milestone* (2005) with Alicia Hall Moran, an artist performing and composing between the genres of opera, art, theater, and jazz—who is his wife and first collaborator—and his trio, the Bandwagon. *Milestone* probes his attraction to the force of formal abstraction, departing from LeWitt and Piper, as means to "pinpoint emotion, pinpoint narrative, pinpoint history" within the framework of a jazz concert.[5]

Moran's conceptual turn meaningfully aligns the themes of his works with the long history of conceptual thought about blackness. For blackness is always already conceptual. In harnessing the tenets of Conceptual art, the system of race and how it expresses itself as jazz and the blues are dematerialized. As I have written elsewhere,[6] it is useful to invoke what French literary theorist Gérard Genette describes in *The Work of Art: Immanence and Transcendence* (1997) as "the conceptual state." For Genette, a conceptual work does not exist exclusively and exhaustively in an object. The conceptual state is, rather, multivalent, both informing and informed by the context of its making and viewing. In relation to Moran's art, we are reminded of the conceptual state's performative nature, looking from the object to the gesture that realized it, then to the idea from which it evolved, and ultimately to the sensual events—which is also to say lived experience—that imbue its proposition, whether they're "critical, paradoxical, provocative, polemical," or perhaps even traumatic.[7]

SET: OBJECTS

Moran is known for jazz styles, from stride piano to free music. His approach to these idioms has less to do with working "authentically" by attending to tradition or taking refuge in nostalgia. Rather Moran's investment is in history's potential for innovation, to which these sonic expressions testify—the force of their affective patina arising from their cultural, social, political, and economic constraints. For his aim is always the alchemical possibility of creation, evinced in his use of digital sampling and recirculation of hip-hop as well as in his sculptures.

Moran's *STAGED* works are three-dimensional homages to the now-gone edifices of seminal jazz venues in New York City. The way Moran fabricates these pieces allows them to be easily understood as monuments to a lost and under-valued past. The Walker Art Center exhibition features *STAGED: Savoy Ballroom I* and *STAGED: Three Deuces* (both of which received critical acclaim in artistic director Okwui Enwezor's exhibition *All the World's Future* at the 2015 Venice Biennale), and *STAGED: Slugs' Saloon*, a new commission premiering in the show. When one stands in front of Moran's fragmented abstraction of Harlem's Savoy Ballroom, which operated between the mid-1920s and late 1950s, the work's strange, gravity-defying arch pitches toward you; the gleaming gilded portion leading to the ornamental overhang feels threatening, as though one could be caught in the undertow of its very artifice were it to reach the end of the trajectory it optically asserts. The pristine veneer of this sculpture is seduc-tively impenetrable, creating a fierce dissonance heightened by the repetitive, droning sounds and enunciations of the recorded black work songs emanating from the work.

Moran correlates the alienated labor of black beings in the agricultural and industrial landscapes of the United States to the alienated scene of enter-tainment—out of the fields and factories and onto the stage. The works in the *STAGED* series are strange environments that are each integrally connected to the social history and real politics of the venues for which they are named. These important sites of invention in jazz were also testing grounds of American policies of nondiscrimination at the height of the Jim Crow period of segregation. The very Americanness of jazz and its origination in the blues seems on display and also up for questioning, as the dazzling beauty of the *STAGED* objects and their ability to entertain and satisfy are countered by their "staged" sounds.

For his take on midtown Manhattan's legendary Three Deuces club, where avant-garde jazz of the mid-1940s and '50s was incubated, Moran works with and against a feeling of quiet agitation, which is established by the object and the choice of music. There is something subversive to an entertainment space decked out in the style of a padded cell, with walls more common to psychi-atric hospitals than music venues. However, Moran's use of vinyl padding, compressed under a ceiling only eight feet tall, is true to the original venue. A ghostly player piano increases the sense of strangeness. The curious quality of this set is also located in its focus on the corner of a room, a topic poignantly explored in Enwezor's essay in this catalogue. In this respect, Randy Williams's installation *Homage to the Edge of a Corner* (1977) comes to mind. Shown at the groundbreaking Just Above Midtown Gallery, founded by Linda Goode Bryant to exhibit interdisciplinary work by black American artists, Williams's work included a column of razor blades in the corner and a structure of open frames that cre-ated an interplay between geometric forms. Similarly, Moran depends upon reduction and isolation, the appearance and disappearance of differing lines and forms. Importantly, at the Three Deuces, musicians were no longer beholden to entertaining audiences, inciting them to dance. Rather, here the music attained a highly cerebral level in the way the melodies functioned to exhaust the song.

Arcing along the evolution of jazz, the third set is based on Slugs' Saloon. More dive than club, it was a spot in New York's seedy Alphabet City from the early 1960s to 1972, where musicians went to play after their paying gigs. The experimentalists of free jazz often could be found, including Albert Ayler, Ornette Coleman, Keith Jarrett, and Charlie Mingus as well as Sun Ra and his Arkestra, who had weekly gigs. It acquired infamy when trumpeter Lee Morgan was shot dead by his wife-manager, Helen Moore. Unlike the venues that inspired the other *STAGED* works, there is little that is architecturally distinct about Slugs' Saloon. The long narrow space had exposed brick walls, sawdust covering the floor, col-orful light orbs in a line down the middle, and a mural by artist Bob Thompson,

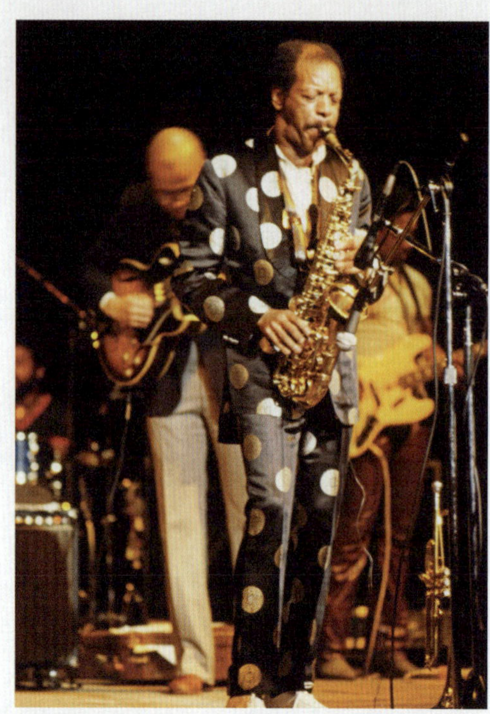

Ornette Coleman and Prime Time performing at the Guthrie Theater as part of a Walker Art Center music program, Minneapolis, February 4, 1982

　　　　ADRIENNE EDWARDS

Keith Jarrett performing at the Guthrie
Theater as part of a residency sponsored
by the Walker Art Center and the Saint
Paul Chamber Orchestra, Minneapolis,
December 22, 1974

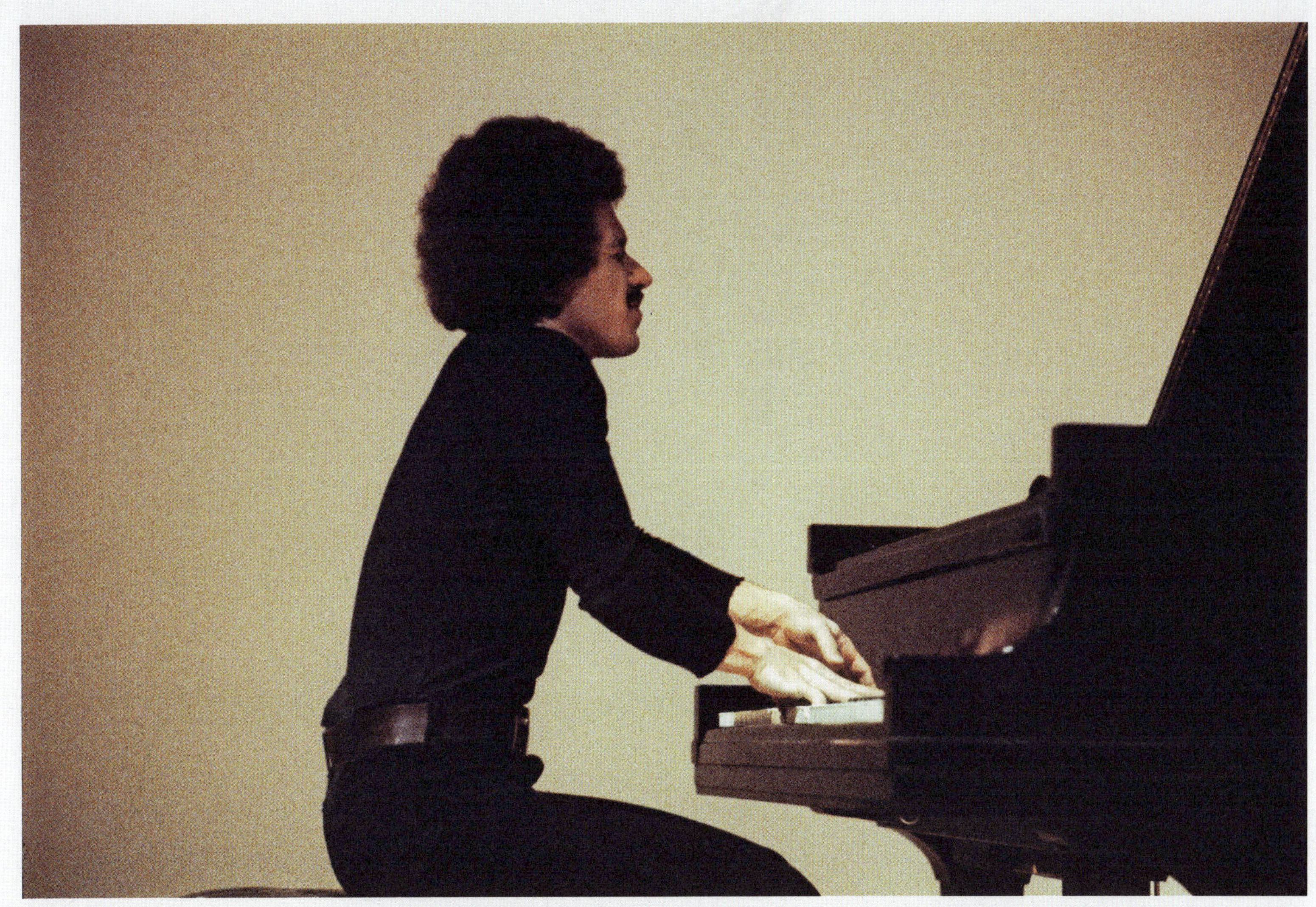

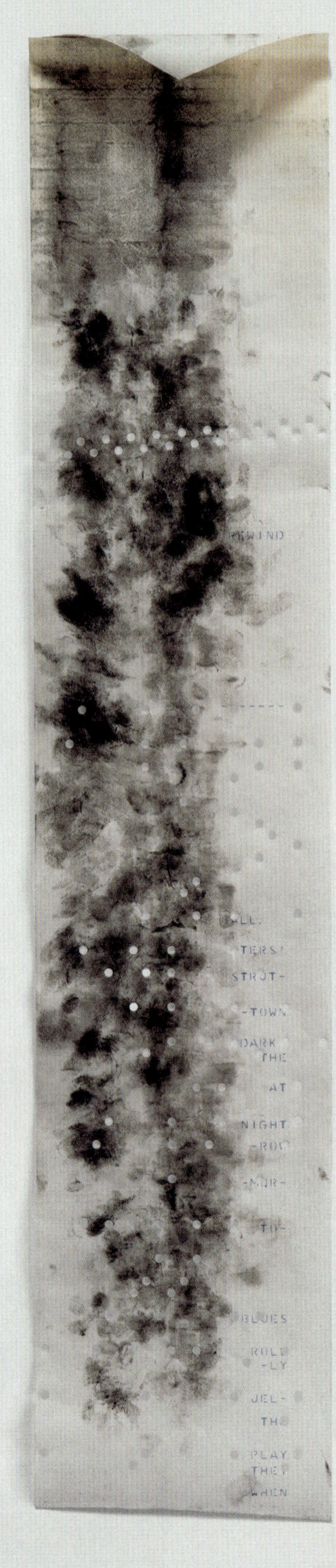

Jason Moran, *Strutter's Ball*, 2016, charcoal
on paper, 34½ x 6¾ in. (87.6 x 17.1 cm)

ADRIENNE EDWARDS

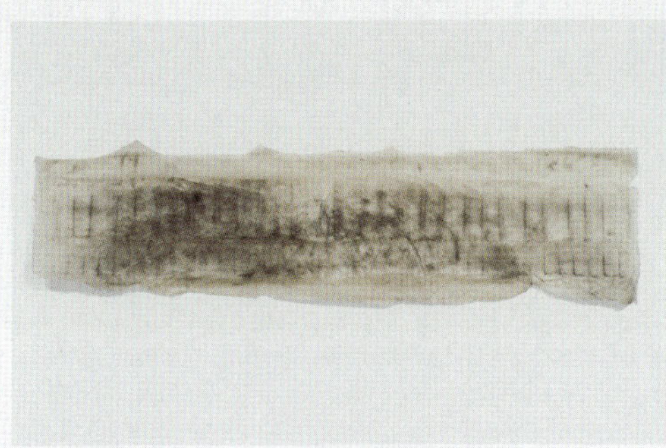

Jason Moran, *Run 2*, 2016, charcoal on paper,
9½ x 37¾ in. (24.1 x 95.9 cm)

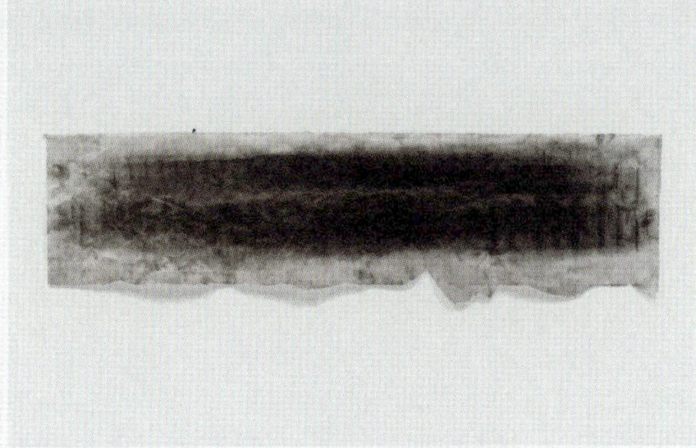

Jason Moran, *Run 6*, 2016, charcoal on paper,
10 x 36½ in. (25.4 x 92.7 cm)

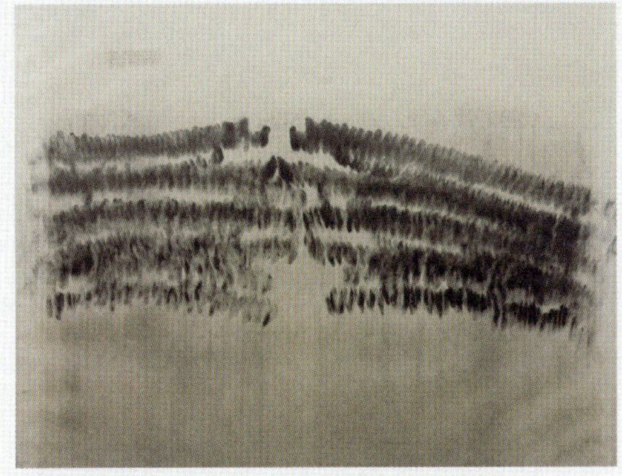

Robert Morris, *Blind Time XXII*, 1973,
graphite pigment on cardboard, 34½ x 45¼ in.
(87.5 x 115 cm)

who was a regular. Moran's new sculpture draws upon these disparate and fragmented architectural, functional, and spatial elements to create an atmospheric scene that summons a feeling of the club and the experimental music made in it.

Moran's drawings from the ongoing *Run* series—shown at Luhring Augustine in 2016 in his first gallery exhibition—are intimate and immediate, while still privileging the residue of history. They give sculptural presence to sound by rendering in dark matter what is regarded as ephemeral, offering highly gestural entrees into the artist's process. Moran tapes elongated pieces of paper on the keys of a piano or keyboard, and caps his fingertips with charcoal. The paper catches the movements of his playing. As curator Naomi Beckwith notes in *Parkett*, Moran's drawings bring to mind the text paintings of Glenn Ligon, the basketball drawings of David Hammons, and the sculptural works of Terry Adkins that use black American culture as artistic material.[8] So too they relate to the impromptu drawings Joan Jonas creates during performances and to a range of artistic approaches using body impressions as painting and drawing devices, including Hammons's body prints. Perhaps most resonant is a series that Robert Morris started in the '70s and continued to develop over some forty years. For his *Blind Time* drawings, Morris works with his eyes closed, enveloping himself in darkness as his hands touch, stroke, and rub graphite onto paper. The soft yet intense blackish accumulations mark passed time, as Morris puts it.[9] While Moran does not assume a kind of blindness, his drawings do arrive under the veil of blackness, affectively and temporally tracing the process of making jazz music in private. Their embodiment of the art-making event results in visual notations achieved through acts of repetition and presented in serial, which is to say systematic, forms. In this way, Moran uses the body, as scholar Eve Meltzer describes in relation to Morris's *Blind Time* works, "to administer the mechanisms of a system: the pressure, pace, pattern, and direction of its touch, the capacity of its breath, its physical memory of making a mark."[10]

SET: INTERLUDE

A digression into the blues dances of Ralph Lemon, a choreographer, dancer, and visual artist who defines himself as a conceptualist, assists in examining the conceptual state that Moran entered into around the turn of the millennium. Twenty years older than Moran, Lemon replaces the cool sterility for which Conceptualism is historically known with the sonic force of blackness in music. His travels in the Mississippi Delta, in part along the route of the Freedom Bus Rides, which began in 1961, produced private and semiprivate dances. Talking to people and learning about places, he danced improvisationally in the living rooms of jazz musicians' families, in motel rooms and cemeteries, at the Blue Front juke joint in Bentonia, and in the driveway of civil rights activist Medgar Evers (which was the site of his assassination in 1963), among other locales. These dances in the Delta, collectively called the Living Room dances, culminated in the multimedia theatrical performance *Come home Charley Patton* (2004).

Lemon's 2012 book of the same name—simultaneously a diaristic account, a collection of drawings, an analytical study, and an ethnographic memoir—reflects on the project. In it, the artist recounts an incident about a man named Minnifield who was lynched in a swamp clearing by a mob. Lemon describes himself dancing alone in a derelict theater in Yazoo City, Mississippi, on Thanksgiving Day in 2002:

> Empty bleachers and a little stage inside the shell of an old building with no front façade or roof on Main Street. I danced on the stage, occasionally falling through the decaying plywood, to Mississippi John Hurt's 1928 recording "Louis Collins." … The song seems appropriate, somebody mourning somebody else, its simple and hypnotic tone a sublime activation. Cars speeding by on Main Street, my audience. A three-minute blues

dance, twice, a prayer maybe, to Mr. Minnifield, and to all those who had to run away, in truth or fiction. And then one more dance, but this time a freer movement experiment to the Pretenders' "Chain Gang," a hurling body dance just for me, bringing the episode a little more forward in time, while staying backward, I hope. The sky is a radiant blue. And not a single car nor person stops to watch.[11]

Lemon's mental and somatic processes involve eerie correlations to the crime. Minnifield in the swamp clearing corresponds to Lemon alone in the remains of a bygone edifice. A hole was dug into the ground to burn Minnifield; Lemon's feet dig fissures as he dances. The selected songs make up a lyrical counterpoint to the hurling body dance, which is shaped by gestures simulating running, being hosed down with water, and being thrown over a bridge. In all these instances, Lemon uses his body, as Moran employs his stage sculptures, to generate a kind of speculative knowledge, a resonance between past and present. Like Moran's drawings, the language and gestures are delivered simply; Lemon attends to unspeakably quotidian violence with the most ordinary inflection. In so doing, he does not conjure history merely to allow it to hang in the air as a toxic mood; rather, his simple actions and words seem to be seismically impelled into the very ground, as though historical circumstances are being suspended in the banal character of the landscape. Lemon feels the blues, sussing out significant events to highlight the ways in which it is irreducible to one thing or object. The blues, in this instance, inheres in the narrative and movements through which these events circulate; each recitation, each act has the power to emanate the blues.[12]

SET: COLLABORATIONS

As a memorial to free jazz, Moran's *STAGED: Slugs' Saloon* (and Lemon's exploration of the Delta blues, one of free jazz's antecedents) brings to mind histories of experimentation exemplified by the Association for the Advancement of Creative Musicians (AACM). This collective of musicians from the South Side of Chicago was founded in 1965 at the height of social and political upheavals in the United States. Music scholar and contributor to this catalogue George E. Lewis discusses its seminal role in his book on the collective,[13] illuminating the importance and vital quality of being together through music as one of the ways in which the concept of blackness expresses itself. As was common at the time, the collective's aesthetic interests were bound to distinct political, social, and economic objectives as strategies of resistance. The influence of AACM extended beyond the genre of jazz, influencing the development of what is considered to be experimental music in general.[14] Lewis observes:

> The insistence by blacks that music has to be 'saying something' becomes part of a long history of resistance to the silencing of the black voice. Indeed, as might be expected from a people whose genetic, historical, and cultural legacies were interrupted through strained, systematized violence, every effort was made by the musicians to recover rather than disrupt historical consciousness.[15]

Moran's numerous collaborations with visual artists align with what Trinidadian Marxist scholar C. L. R. James described as "creative social power," which is realized through the shared labor of the assembly.[16] It is important to note here that, for James, the social bonds developed by capitalism in the context of work are contradictory. On the one hand, a mutual consciousness arises from the interactions, and this has the potential to nurture the development of individuality through creativity. On the other hand, the extreme antagonism endemic to the system itself negates such a possibility by generating alienation, or the illusion of an unbridgeable gap between individuals and the institutions sustained by their participation. For James, this alienation was most severe in the United States,

ADRIENNE EDWARDS

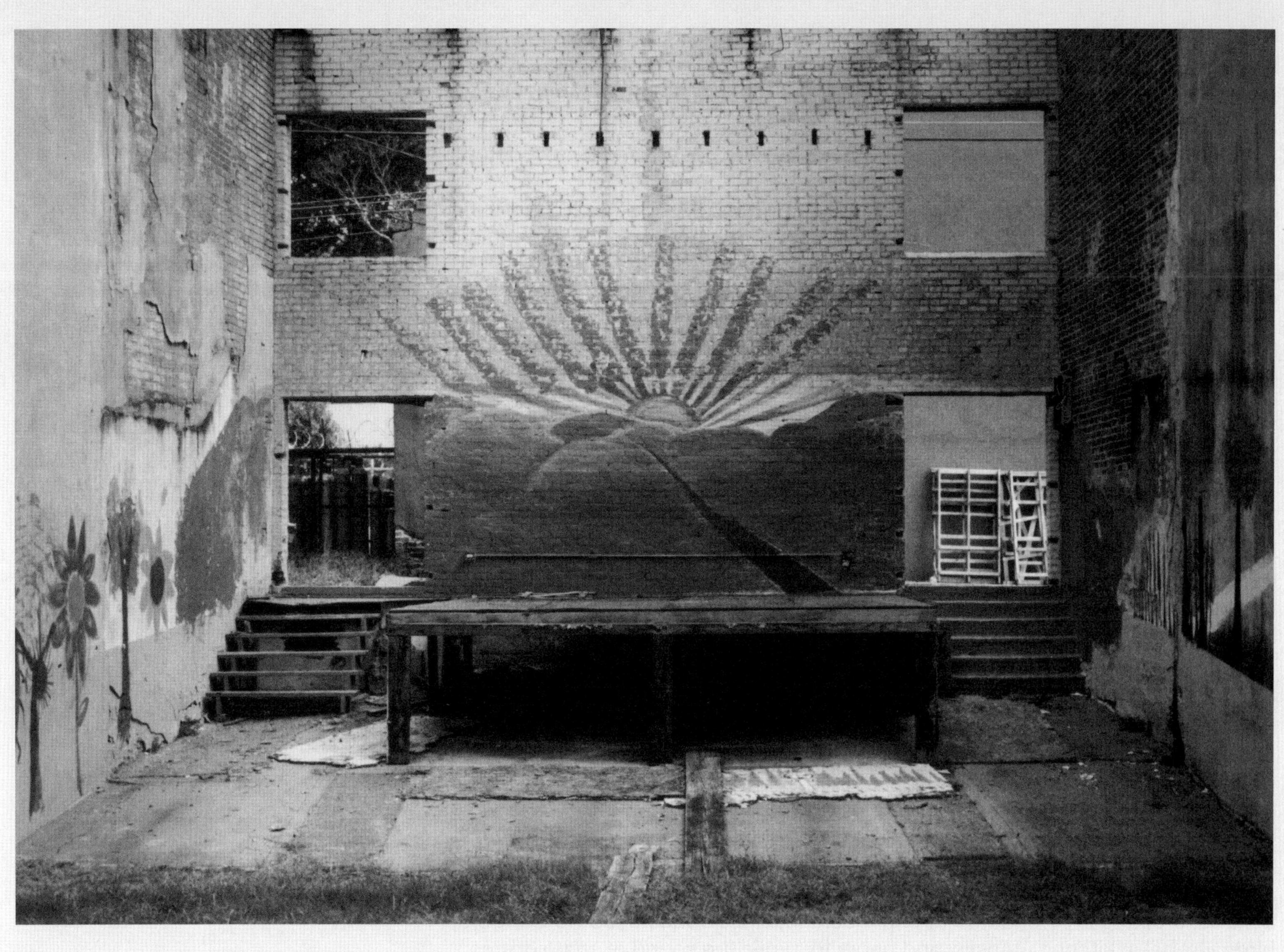

Ralph Lemon, *Yazoo City Theater, Mississippi,*
2002, digital image, dimensions variable

precisely because it obviously contradicted its founding ideals, doubly so regarding blackness. Moran's collaborations with visual artists are thus both evidence of and antidote for alienation. As James indicated, there is no better evidence of creative social power than black cultural expressions in the United States.[17]

James suggests that the blackness of certain cultural expressions, encounters, and alliances have historically enabled a feeling of freedom, no matter how fleeting, as a sustaining factor in art-making. Therefore, the notion of "freedom" implied in free jazz or as a characteristic of improvisation in general is proposed as a radical ideology that challenges formal conventions through stylistic approaches rooted in and routed through blackness. As anthropologist John Szwed notes:

> The esthetics of jazz demand that a musician play with complete originality, with an assertion of his own musical individuality. ... At the same time jazz requires that musicians be able to merge their unique voices in the totalizing, collective improvisations of polyphony and heterophony. The implications of the esthetic are profound and more than vaguely threatening, for no political system has yet been devised with social principles which reward maximal individualism within the framework of spontaneous egalitarian interaction.[18]

Accordingly, this exhibition coalesces a set of Moran's relationships with other artists to excavate and explicate his creative approaches, conceptual sedimentation, and evolution of ideologies across fields. It includes projects with some of the most important artists working today, all of whom are substantially represented in the Walker's collection.

Moran has completed four collaborations with pioneering video performance artist Joan Jonas, whose multimedia works borrow from folk traditions and ritual, and incorporate costumes, live drawing, video projections, movement, and text: *The Shape, the Scent, the Feel of Things* (2005), *Reading Dante* (2007–10), *Reanimation* (2012), and *They Come to Us Without a Word II* (2015). For the first, a commission by Dia: Beacon, Moran and Jonas rehearsed seven hours a day for five days a week during an entire summer, developing the score together as the project evolved. Over the years, they have employed unlikely objects to make music. On several occasions, Moran placed a Pellegrino bottle, paper, and cowbells inside a piano, creating an orchestral sound machine, while Jonas used Kerbangers, birdcalls, bells, kitchen utensils, and paper to mimic the sound of snare drums.[19] One can track aspects of Moran's evolution through his work with Jonas, such as his extension of performance techniques to the process of drawing, integrating visual elements like masks and costumes into his presentations, and transposing traditional cultural forms onto contemporary art. Ultimately, Jonas and Moran's trusting yet critical exchanges center on their approaches to improvisation, since both understand that rigor and structure are required to make magic.

Employing the format of a religious convening, Adam Pendleton created *The Revival* in 2007 for the Performa biennial.[20] Moran and Hall Moran codirected the music for this live event, which featured a twenty-eight-person choir. The performance mimed the structure of religious revivals such that there were pivotal moments in which the figure of repetition could be meaningfully located as a call-and-response or as a simultaneous summoning and deployment of the collective, the plural in relation to the singular. As the choir entered the darkness of Stephan Weiss Studio in New York and took its position on two-part, multitiered plywood platforms, the audience heard Pendleton reciting a text he had composed in a measured, methodical cadence, meandering through repetitions of phrases about ethical and political values relating to black and gay life and history. The space gradually became illuminated as Pendleton spit out what he named as "symbols," or vernacular, hate-filled speech acts common to the "dozens," a game of spoken words aimed to insult with the greatest flair. Then he emerged, austerely dressed in a white suit jacket and oxford shirt, gleaming black pants, and florescent yellow sneakers, walking into the center of the space to ascend a square, raised platform,

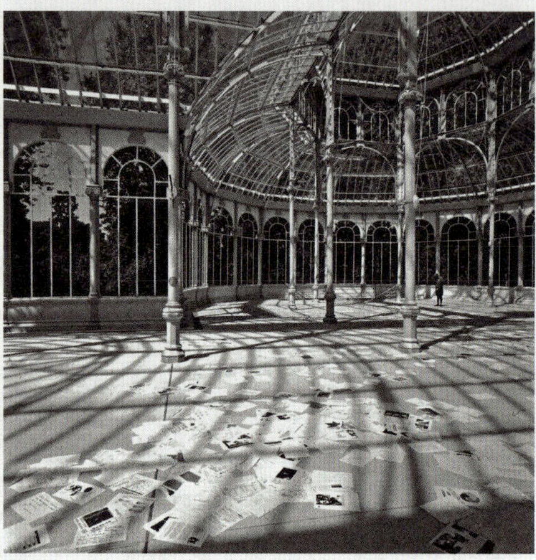

Installation view of David Hammons's *Global Fax Festival* project at the Palacio de Cristal, Parque del Retiro, Madrid, 2000

ADRIENNE EDWARDS

also of plywood, as Moran played the piano. Pendleton repeated the phrase he articulated at the start of performance: "we lived on a small island stone nation, love without sound, without color, without stone." Ten minutes into the piece, the choir swelled with the sonic beauty of a hymn that typically demarcates the beginning of a church service, and Pendleton reminded the audience that language "occurs in real time." As the artist articulated words such as "fat chance" and "erotic," the choir responded in a cappella "glory," the infelicitous congruence of these verbal offerings creating a tension between the profane, or the mundane, and the sacred. In Pendleton's sacrilege sermon, he tells us "the experience of language is not isolated. It is an act taking place in the world like all else. It is not the act, separate, describing the world. It is, it occurs, in real time."[21]

Glenn Ligon's first foray into filmmaking, *The Death of Tom* (2008), allowed him to explore his interest in performance while experimenting with text in a different medium. Working with a cinematographer, Ligon focused on re-creating a scene from Edwin S. Porter's fourteen-minute silent film *Uncle Tom's Cabin* (1903), which was based on Harriet Beecher Stowe's 1852 abolitionist novel of the same name. Porter made the film for Edison Manufacturing Company, employing Thomas Edison's technology. In keeping with this, Ligon shot the re-creation on a hand-cranked camera, using 16mm film with a double exposure.[22] As it turned out, Ligon's film had not been properly loaded in the camera, resulting in what he called "blurry, fluttery, burnt-out black and white images, all light and shadows."[23] Through the greater force of chance, Ligon realized that only abstraction could redress the profound subject matter of the novel and the film. The result is an abstract film about disappearance and presence, about what W.E.B. Du Bois described as the "illogical trends and irreconcilable tendencies" of the race concept that dominated his life and the systems through which it circulated, such as chattel slavery and Jim Crow. Knowing a film made for Edison would have been accompanied by piano music during its theatrical presentation, Ligon invited Moran to improvise a score based on "Nobody," the signature song of Bert Williams, a vaudeville blackface performer and the first black person to take a lead role on Broadway. Moran honed in on the failed moving images and played, as he describes it, "to the shadows."[24] In reflecting on the stakes of his collaboration with Ligon, Moran explained:

> Bert Williams was kind of like Michael Jackson one hundred years ago. He sold millions of copies of this song "Nobody." He's also one of the early conceptualists. He hated the song "Nobody" so much that he recorded a song called "Somebody," and then he recorded another song called "Everybody."... I started to perform this song "Nobody," and it's a difficult song to perform because of all the layers of baggage: it is a minstrel song and as a jazz performer, you're already kind of tampering with a lot of layers that just come up when you enter through the back door to come into the theater.[25]

Kara Walker's *National Archives Microfilm M999 Roll 34: Bureau of Refugees, Freedmen and Abandoned Lands: Six Miles from Springfield on the Franklin Road* (2009) developed out of her research into the US Department of War's Bureau of Refugees, Freedmen, and Abandoned Lands. Established in 1865 to aid former slaves in the transition to freedom, the Freedmen's Bureau kept detailed records of the brutal violence inflicted on African Americans during the Reconstruction era. In this film, Walker depicts one example of such terrorist acts as described in interviews with members of a family who were attacked or sexually assaulted and whose home was burned by a mob of angry white men. Part of the artist's larger series titled *The Bureau of Refugees*, the work also alludes to the tradition of puppetry and incorporates handmade set constructions. Glimpses of Walker's hands and face appear as she manipulates the puppets, while Moran and Hall Moran's original score animates the narrative sequences with sound that intensifies as the plot thickens. At one point, glimmering red, yellow, and orange pieces of Mylar flicker and signal flames, layered atop a silhouette of a home.

Senga Nengudi, *Ceremony for Freeway Fets*
with Studio Z members Maren Hassinger,
David Hammons, Kenneth Severin, Roho,
Joe Ray, and Franklin Parker, 1978 (detail),
chromogenic print, 12 x 18 in.
(30.5 x 45.7 cm)

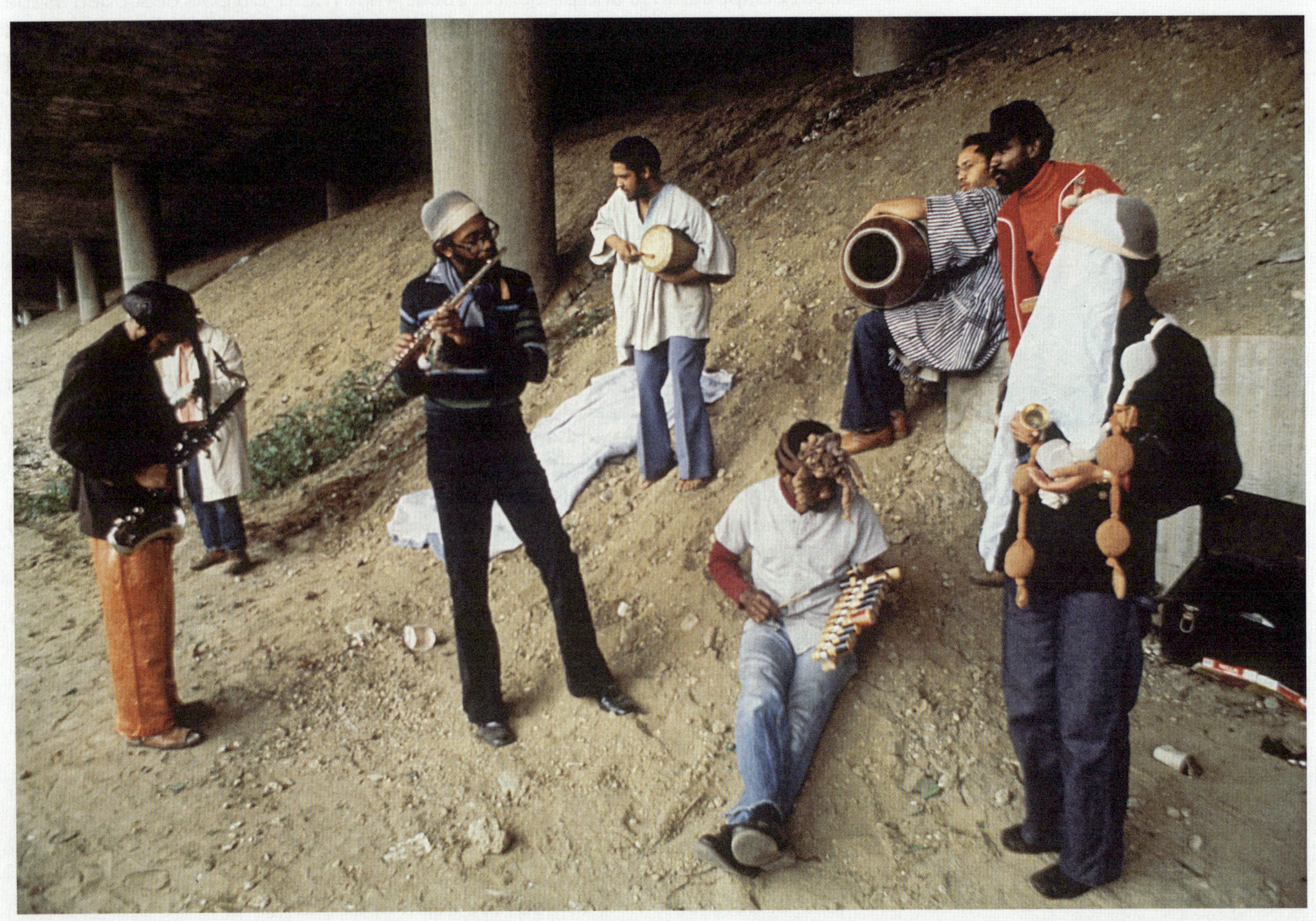

In the months following the 2016 US election, Julie Mehretu temporarily moved her studio to a former neo-Gothic church in Harlem in order to create a pair of monumental paintings for the atrium of the San Francisco Museum of Modern Art. Titled *HOWL, eon (I, II)* (2017) the massive abstractions explore contradictory narratives of westward expansion through layers of color and marks. On the balcony of this cavernous decommissioned church, Mehretu invited Moran to join her, which he did regularly. Over the winter and spring months of 2017, on an electric piano, he composed and improvised a set of phrases and gestures that respond to the sonic residue within the church: fragments of hymns, erasure, and repetitions.

These sounds appear and disappear throughout *MASS (HOWL, eon)*, Moran and Mehretu's Performa 17 commission that took place at the old parish this past November. With Moran on piano, Jamire Williams on drums, and Graham Haynes on cornet, an hour-long score was performed live, accompanied by video projections of methodically expanding and contracting details from the two works Mehretu had created in the space.

Mehretu's paintings are based on distorted images of recent land and racial protests (following the extrajudicial killings of young black men in London, Ferguson, and Baltimore) as well as on mid-nineteenth-century depictions of the American West. Her attention to light in transforming these subjects into abstractions resonates with Moran's emotional soundtrack, which is concerned with light as a way to register and experience time while moving in space.

Carrie Mae Weems's video installation *Lincoln, Lonnie, and Me—A Story in 5 Parts* (2012) is an ambitious piece that employs the nineteenth-century Pepper's Ghost technology to lend an eerie three-dimensionality to moving images. The spectral figures she captures include a Playboy bunny, President Lincoln, and a civil rights protester, some of whom are played by Weems herself. The soundscape, arranged by Moran, includes pop music, recitations of the Gettysburg Address, reflections of a minstrel performer, and electronic-infused blues.

For Lorna Simpson's *Chess* (2013), a three-channel video installation, Moran takes one of Johannes Brahms's fifty-one piano exercises—short, difficult compositions meant to hone musical skills—as the basis for improvising. Simpson employs a hinged mirror, commonly used in early twentieth-century studio photography, to develop a five-way image, capturing herself playing chess and Moran's hands gliding across the piano keys.[26] Moran and Simpson discussed the idea of opposition within one person as a conceptual verve for the work.

Moran recalls Stan Douglas's process for creating the six-hour, intricately composed jazz film *Luanda-Kinshasa* (2013), which references the origins and history of jazz in Africa. Dividing the room in two, Douglas shot half of the film during on session and the other half the following day. In order for this approach to work musically, Moran made the songs interchangeable, formulating a way for the parts of different songs to intersect. Moran, who played the band leader, and Douglas selected the cast of ten musicians to simulate a 1970s experience—somewhat of a challenge since it required a kind of time travel, musically and visually. Moran recently described his impression of Douglas's charge: "Let's go back to the mid-1970s when Miles Davis was making his records. And let's say he kept going on a certain track after the record *Live-Evil*. What would he make?"[27]

A collaboration between Jason Moran and Theaster Gates, *Looks of a Lot* (2014) explores themes of violence, absence, loss, and the resilience of the human spirit. Working with Chicago's Kenwood Academy Jazz Band as well as jazz composer Ken Vandermark and vocalist Katie Ernst, Moran created a layered multimedia and jazz improvisation project, commissioned by the Chicago Symphony Orchestra. The stage was set with Gates's sculptural objects made from salvaged materials, which doubled as music stands. Another sculpture, his multitiered shoe shine chair, was used by Moran as he played a hand-cranked music box with a prepunched musical score. Utilizing traditional and nontraditional instruments, including vintage minstrel windup toys and horns, to produce a procession of sound, *Looks of a Lot* brings together narratives that resonate with the Chicago scene.

Collaboration has been a frequent mode of working for artists invested in interdisciplinary experimentation. Like Moran and Hall Moran—who have partnered on projects for the Venice Biennale, the Whitney Biennial, the Walker Art Center, Performa, and the Philadelphia Museum of Art, among others—Romare Bearden and choreographer Nanette Rohan Bearden often collaborated. And Bearden contributed to three Alvin Ailey Dance Company works, including slide projections of his jazz paintings at a performance of the ballet *Night Creatures* in August 1976.

In an interview, Senga Nengudi, speaking of her experience with Studio Z—a loose collective of artists working in Los Angeles in the 1970s and '80s that included Greg Edwards, David Hammons, Franklin Parker, and Maren Hassinger—remarked on the importance of improvisational jazz: "I would say we were interested in applying performative interactions to our practices. We wanted to break with the exclusive studio solo relationship between an artist and their work. We were really interested, again, in jazz. Sun Ra's Arkestra and the Chicago Art Ensemble ... were moving in a direction that captivated us. We were interested in this total theater kind of thing."[28]

Experimentalist Lawrence "Butch" Morris was a horn player, arranger, and composer known for his dismantling of bebop and for devising Conduction, an improvisatory and intuitive compositional technique for leading a fluid ensemble of musicians. He collaborated with Nengudi and also worked with Hammons. For Hammons's *Global Fax Festival* (2000), a performance at the Palacio de Cristal, in Madrid, organized by the Museo Nacional Centro de Arte Reina Sofía, the artist installed numerous fax machines on the ceiling, while Morris reacted improvisationally to the downward flutter of hundreds of faxed pages.

Video art pioneer Nam June Paik's forays into artistic collaboration illumine meaningful exchanges between musicians and visual artists committed to cross-disciplinary experimentation. Paik's deep creative engagement with classically trained musician Charlotte Moorman instigated a profound artistic feedback loop between the two artists that led to some of his best known works, including *Opera Sextronique* (1967), *TV Bra for Living Sculpture* (1969), and *TV Cello* (1971). As curator Joan Rothfuss points out, "their creative process was based on an exchange of ideas *during performance*, and the results depended as much on her performative energy, ideas, and audacity as they did on Paik's concepts."[29] Paik's earliest public media experiment was *Hommage à John Cage*, "music for audiotapes and piano," at Jean-Pierre Wilhelm's gallery in Düsseldorf in 1959. Joseph Beuys attended the event, launching a series of artistic collaborations and a lifelong friendship.[30] Beuys spontaneously destroyed a piano in Paik's first solo exhibition *Exposition of Music – Electronic Television* (1963). They collaborated in 1984 on the concert *Good Morning, Mr. Orwell*. Though from very different backgrounds, Paik and Beuys shared an interest in the extreme aggression, destruction, and aftereffects of war, believing shamanism could counter the devastation of such events upon society.

SET: POST-SCRIPT

Moran's art is individual and polyvocal, in as much as it has evolved from the modes and means of jazz. Coming of age in the aftermath of the civil rights and Black Power movements, Moran presupposes the falsehood of jazz's perceived marginality within mainstream institutions and the canon of Western music. For creative expressions of blackness have not focused on such validation, but instead on necessary contradictions, abandoned territories, and convenient mergers.

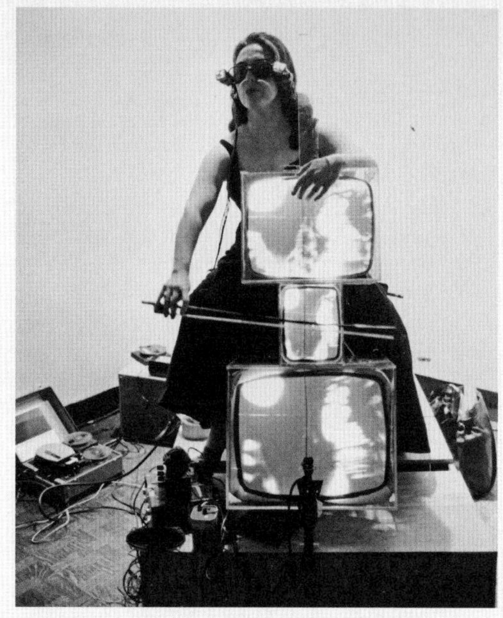

Peter Moore, *Charlotte Moorman performing Nam June Paik's "Concerto for TV Cello and Videotapes,"* 1971, gelatin silver print, 10 x 8 in. (25.4 x 20.3 cm)

ADRIENNE EDWARDS

Manfred Montwé, *Nam June Paik, Exposition of Music, Galerie Parnass 1963. Installation View After Joseph Beuys Action*, 1963, digital image, dimensions variable

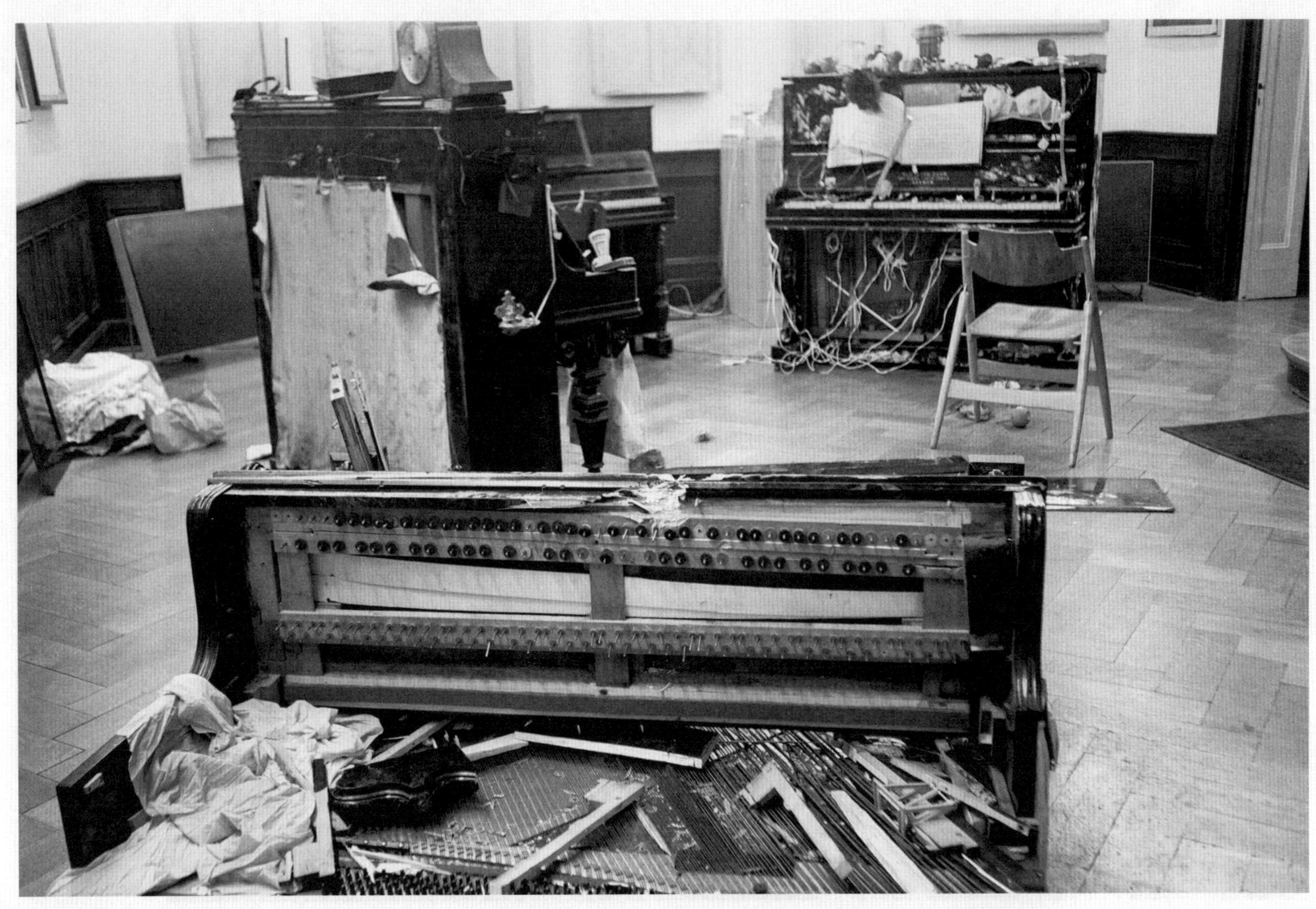

Demonstrators protesting the fatal shooting
of 15-year-old African American James Powell
by a white officer flee club-wielding police in
Harlem, New York, July 20, 1964

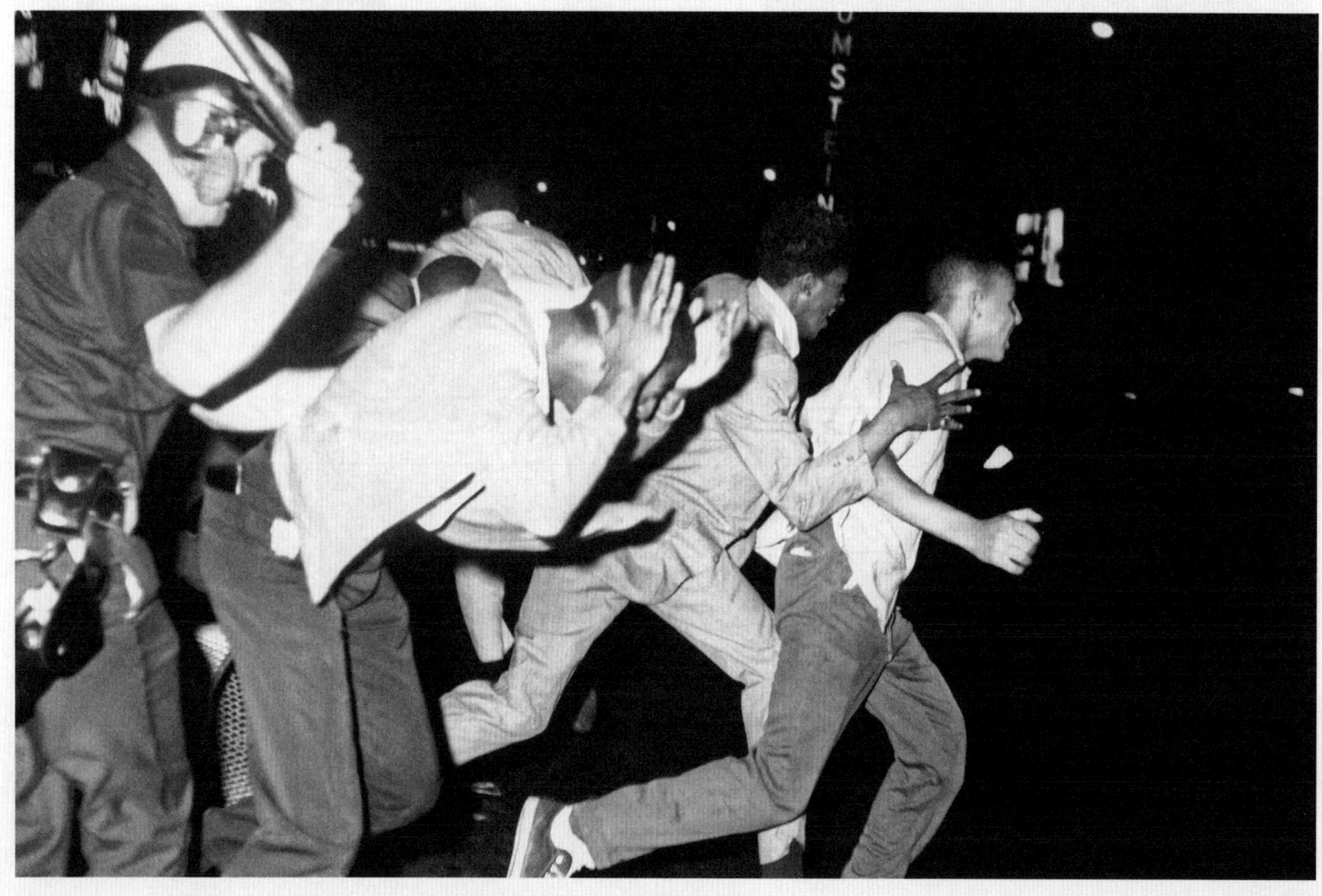

     ADRIENNE EDWARDS

Violence as affective force and matter for experimental art is compounded when exposed to the proximity of blackness. A compelling historical case is Steve Reich's *Come Out* (1966), an audiotape composition featuring the voice of Daniel Hamm, one of the so-called Harlem Six, giving testimony in court. James Baldwin, in response to this incident, in which police gravely beat six youths who were charged with the murder of a storekeeper in 1964, published a stirring critique of police violence against black beings in *The Nation*. Baldwin calls for an account by way of a reflection upon the stakes at hand:

> This means that I also know, in my own flesh, and know, which is worse, in the scars borne by many of those dearest to me, the thunder and fire of the billy club, the paralyzing shock of spittle in the face, and I know what it is to find oneself blinded, on one's hands and knees, at the bottom of the flight of steps down which one has just been hurled. I know something else: these young men have been in jail for two years now. Even if the attempts being put forth to free them should succeed, what has happened to them in these two years? People are destroyed very easily. Where is the civilization and where, indeed, is the morality which can afford to destroy so many?[31]

This appeal resonates strongly. From the recording of Hamm's testimony, Reich extracted the statement "I had to, like, open the bruise up, and let some of the bruise blood come out to show them." It is repeated three times, and then reduced to the last words "come out to show them."[32] According to Reich, *Come Out*, an early tape piece, involved "one tape loop going and another identical loop slipping slightly behind the first one."[33] Such an approach brings to mind Moran's remark about his compositional style in his artist's statement in this catalogue: "I like to play phrases of music 'over the bar line.' This means that I resolve the phrase far past where/when the original resolution occurs. I stack the phrases, kind of like run-on sentences." For Reich, his two channels are initially in accord but eventually dissolve into reverberations—irrational, opaque, chaotic noise. The rhythmic cadence of the speech act is deconstructed and transformed into sound that is imbued with the intense violence of the experience.

In the mid-1960s, Reich repeatedly demonstrated a fascination with blackness in language. "It's Gonna Rain" (1965) features the voice of Brother Walter, a black Pentecostal preacher, and "Oh Dem Watermelons" (1965) samples nineteenth-century minstrel songs. Reich's scores are painstakingly arranged so that the sounds correlate with and thereby express their structure through the repetition of a rhythmic pulse, an elemental quality of West African music and jazz, and in that blackness was his means to innovation. Yet his minimalist approach, contracting and isolating the vocality of blackness, fails. Instead, the unwieldy sense of unraveling mimics lived blackness itself—precarious, unstable, uncertain, undermined. As Baldwin tells us "the ways of being, the ways of life of the despised and rejected, nevertheless, contain an incontestable vitality and authority."[34]

The fact that Ligon showed a set of paintings titled *Come Out* (2014) affirms the constellation of histories in which Moran's work is enmeshed. Blackness as conceptual material is a vital force—an oblique, obscure, and defiant mode of resistance that we know because it returns to us again and again, somehow as an invariably different-same. I write this conclusion as a storm looms on the horizon under an alt-right banner. Yet the phenomenon of totality eclipses all, arching over and enrapturing us in total darkness. We are mindful of our salve for the realities of living the concept of blackness today, abiding by their terms and purpose for existence: polyphony, accumulation, repetition, innovation, opacity, fungibility, and so on.

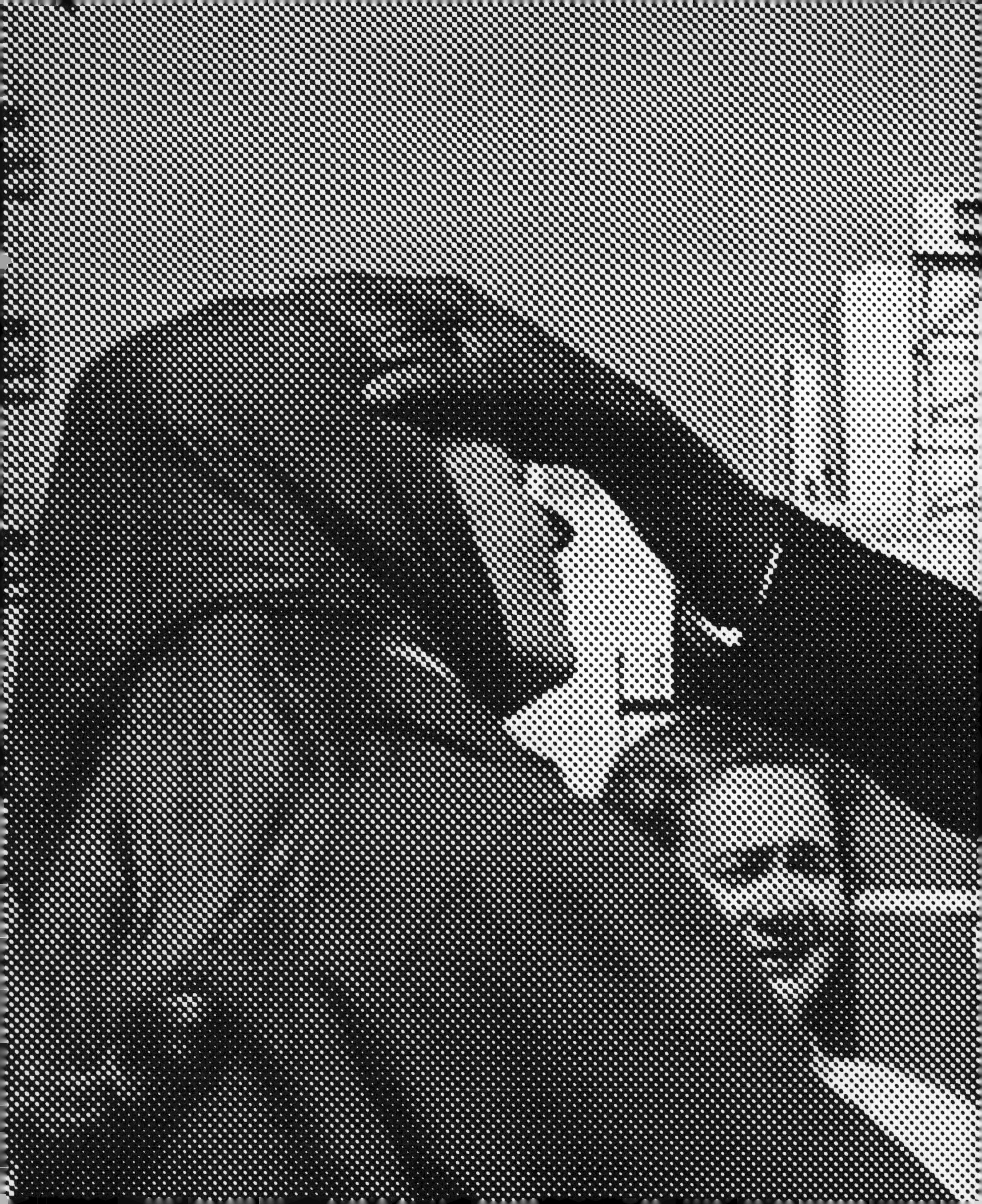

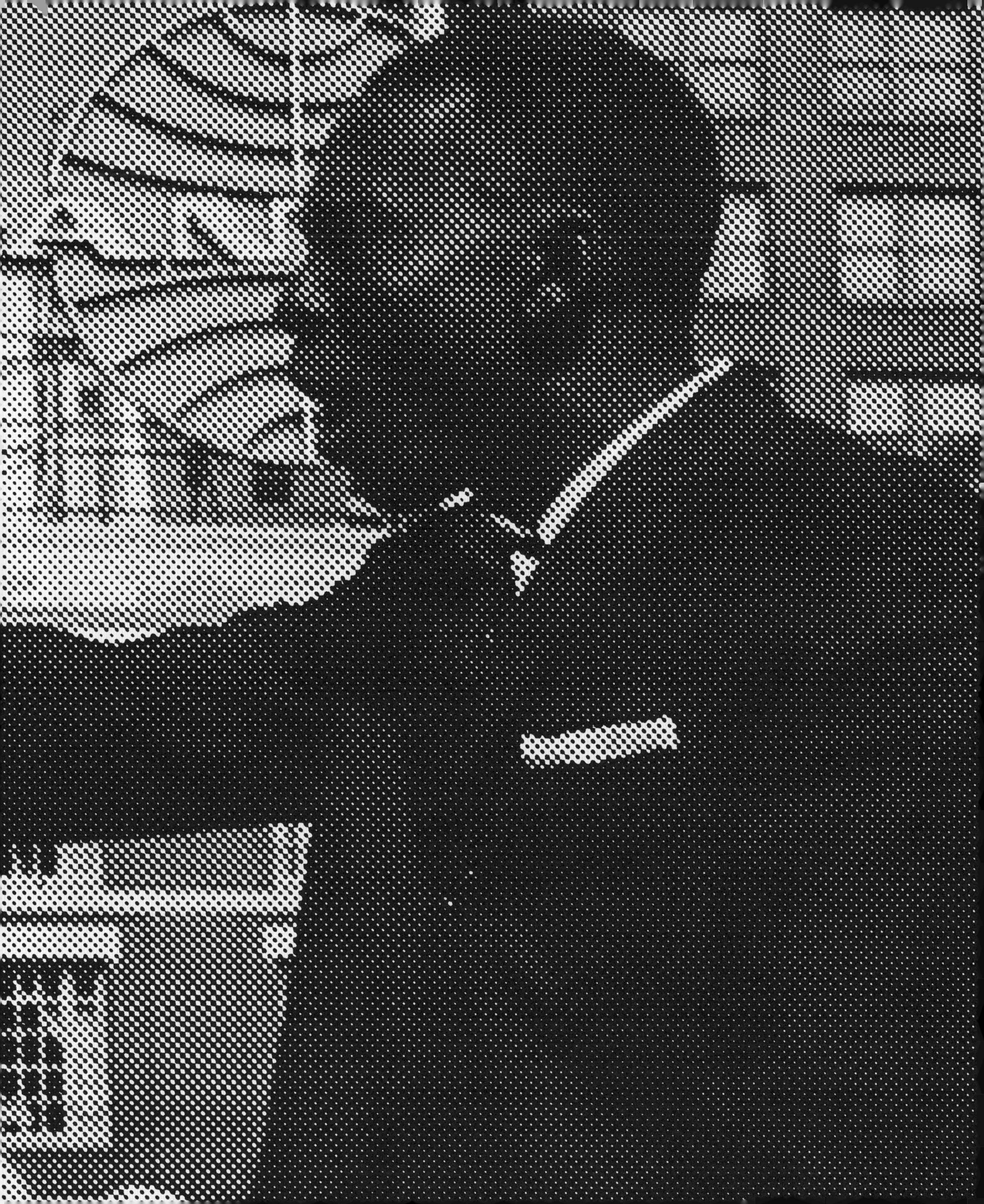

Glenn Ligon, *Come Out Study #3*, 2014,
silkscreen on canvas, 35⅜ x 48⅜ in.
(90.5 x 123.5 cm)

Previous pages:
Still from a film documenting Brother Walter,
the Pentecostal preacher who inspired Steve
Reich's *It's Gonna Rain*, giving a sermon in
Union Square Park, San Francisco, circa 1960

ADRIENNE EDWARDS

NOTES

The title of this essay quotes musician and composer Lawrence "Butch" Morris referring to Sun Ra. See Butch Morris, interview by David Henderson, *Bomb*, No. 55 (Spring 1996): 32–36.

1. LeWitt's artwork was commissioned for the Walker Art Center by then-director Martin Friedman.
2. Jason Moran, interview by the author at the artist's studio, New York, May 26, 2017.
3. Philip Bither is the McGuire Director and Senior Curator of Performing Arts at the Walker Art Center and a contributor to this catalogue.
4. Jason Moran, interview by the author at the Walker Art Center, April 25, 2017.
5. Moran interview, April 25, 2017
6. See Adrienne Edwards, "Blues as the Conceptual State," in *On Value*, ed. Ralph Lemon and Triple Canopy (New York: Triple Canopy, 2016), 83-92.
7. Gérard Genette, *The Work of Art: Immanence and Transcendence* (Ithaca, NY: Cornell University Press, 1997), 147.
8. Naomi Beckwith, "Aural Traditions: The Art of Jason Moran," *Parkett* 99 (2017): 8.
9. Robert Morris, quoted in Eve Meltzer, *Systems We Have Loved: Conceptual Art, Affect, and the Antihumanist Turn* (Chicago: University of Chicago Press, 2013), 100.
10. Meltzer, 106.
11. Ralph Lemon, *Come home Charley Patton* (Middletown, CT: Wesleyan University Press, 2013), 113.
12. See Edwards, "Blues as the Conceptual State."
13. George E. Lewis, *A Power Stronger Than Itself: The AACM and American Experimental Music* (Chicago: University of Chicago Press, 2008).
14. Lewis, x.
15. Lewis, 41.
16. C.L.R. James, *American Civilization* (Cambridge: Blackwell Publishers, 1993), 209.
17. For more on the subject, see Adrienne Edwards, "The Struggle for Happiness, or What Is American About Black Dada," in *Black Dada Reader*, ed. Adam Pendleton (London: Koenig, 2017).
18. Jon Szwed, "Josef Skvorecky and the Tradition of Jazz Literature," *World Literature Today* 54, no. 4 (1980): 588.
19. Joan Simon, "In the Studio: Joan Jonas and Jason Moran." *Art in America*, May 1, 2015, http://www.artinamericamagazine.com/news-features/magazine/in-the-studio-joan-jonas-and-jason-moran/.
20. *The Revival* took place at Stephan Weiss Studio, New York, on November 1, 2007, as part of the Performa 07 biennial and was viewed by the author in documentary form. Curator: RoseLee Goldberg; musical direction: Jason Moran, Adam Pendleton, Alicia Hall Moran, and Vaneese Thomas (choir director); testimonies: Jena Osman, Liam Gillick, Charles Sandison (computer-generated data projection).
21. See Adrienne Edwards, "There for (him) to pick it up when (he) come(s) back to get it," in *Repetition in Adam Pendleton's Time-based Art* (New York: Friends of Education of the Museum of Modern Art, 2014).
22. Glenn Ligon, "Interview with Jason Moran," in *Yourself in the World: Selected Writings and Interviews*, ed. Scott Rothkopf (New Haven, CT: Yale University Press, 2011), 176.
23. Ligon, 176.
24. Ligon, 176.
25. Jason Moran, interview by the author at the Walker Art Center, April 25, 2017.
26. Beckwith, "Aural Traditions," 7.
27. Jason Moran, interview by the author at the Walker Art Center, April 25, 2017.
28. Senga Nengudi, interview by Elissa Auther at the University of Colorado for the Archives of American Art, Smithsonian Institution, July 9, 2013.
29. Joan Rothfuss, "The Ballad of Nam June and Charlotte: A Revisionist History," in *Nam June Paik* (Liverpool: Tate, 2011), 146.
30. Stephan von Wiese, "'You MARTYR of July 20, 1964': Paik and Beuys in a Media Duet," in *Nam June Paik*, 127.
31. James Baldwin, "A Report from Occupied Territory," *The Nation*, July 11, 1966.
32. Siarhei Biareishyk, "Come Out to Show the Split Subject: Steve Reich, Whiteness, and the Avant Garde," *Current Musicology*, No. 93 (Spring 2012): 87.
33. Jonathan Cott, "Interview with Steve Reich," SteveReich.com http://www.stevereich.com/articles/Jonathan_Cott_interview.html (accessed July 25, 2017).
34. Baldwin, "A Report from Occupied Territory."

UNIVERSE

Jason Moran's "universe," depicted on the following pages, is a visual narration of the artist's world. Conveying the breadth and depth of the inspirations, journeys, and relationships that inform his interdisciplinary body of work, the collages are composed of a variety of scanned materials and manipulated photographs, many of which were taken by Moran while on tour at music festivals or working on projects with his long-standing collaborators. Another manifestation of the set, Moran's universe traces the history of his conceptual turn, illustrated by candid snapshots of friends, fellow musicians, influences, moments, and scenes.

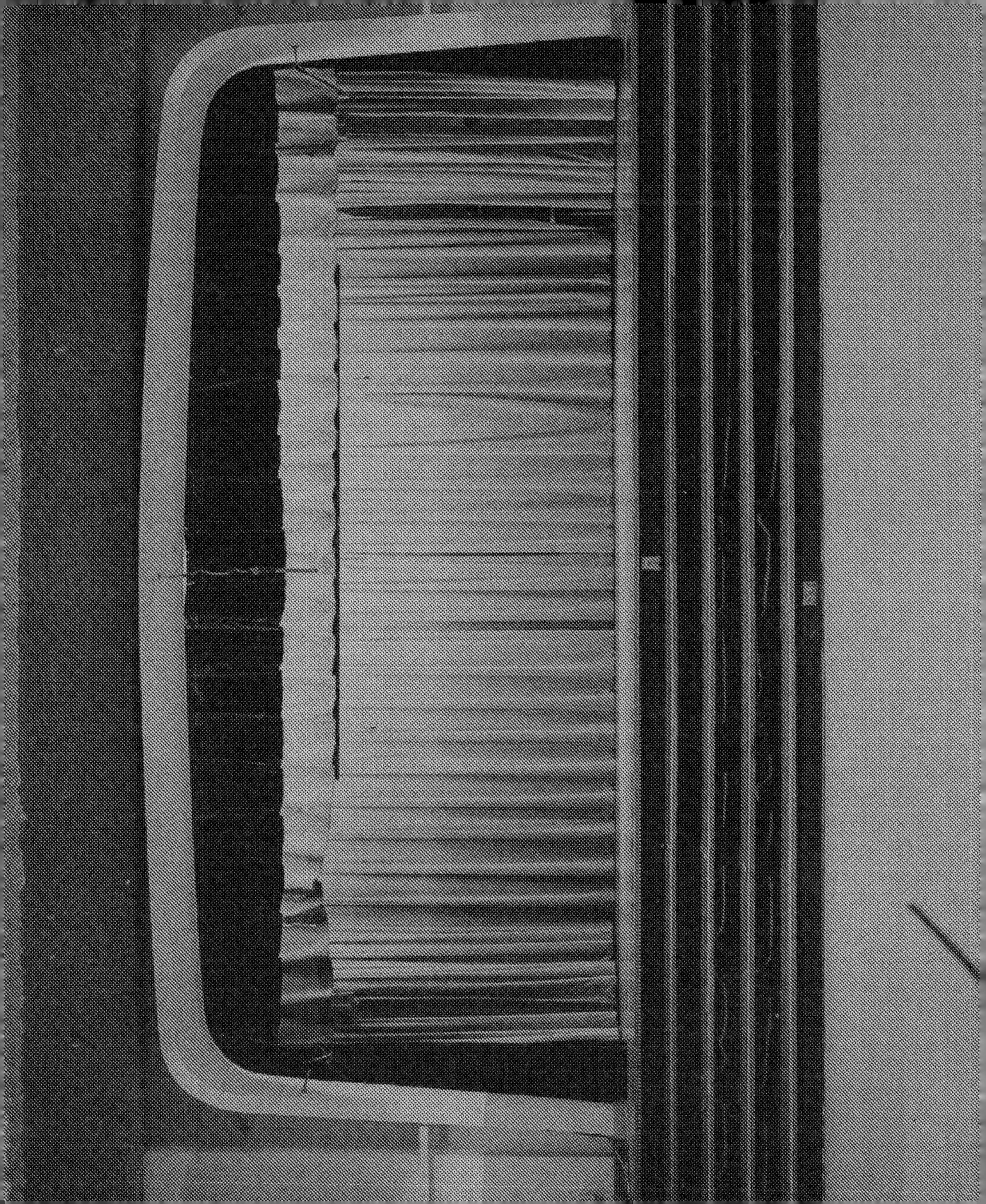

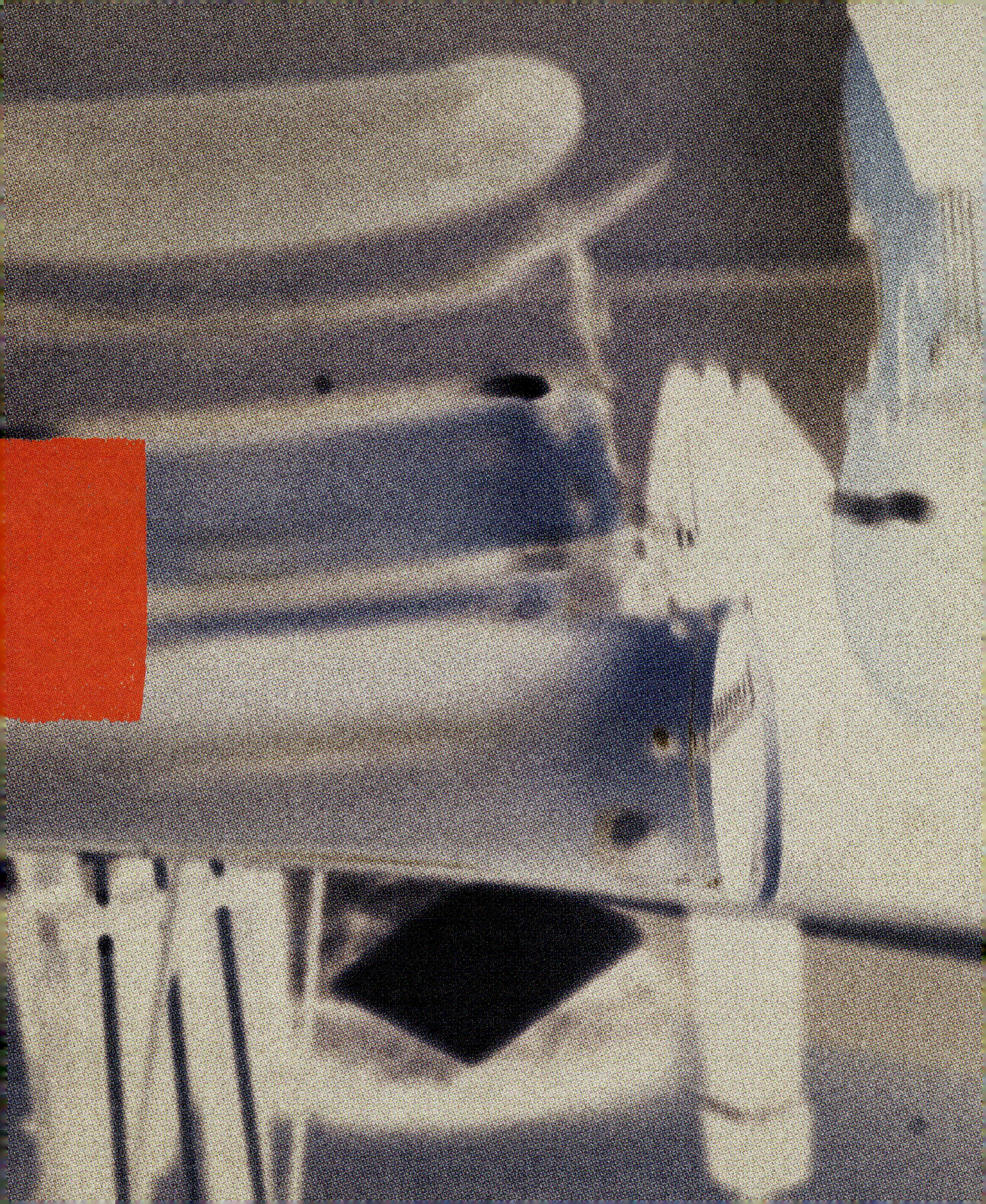

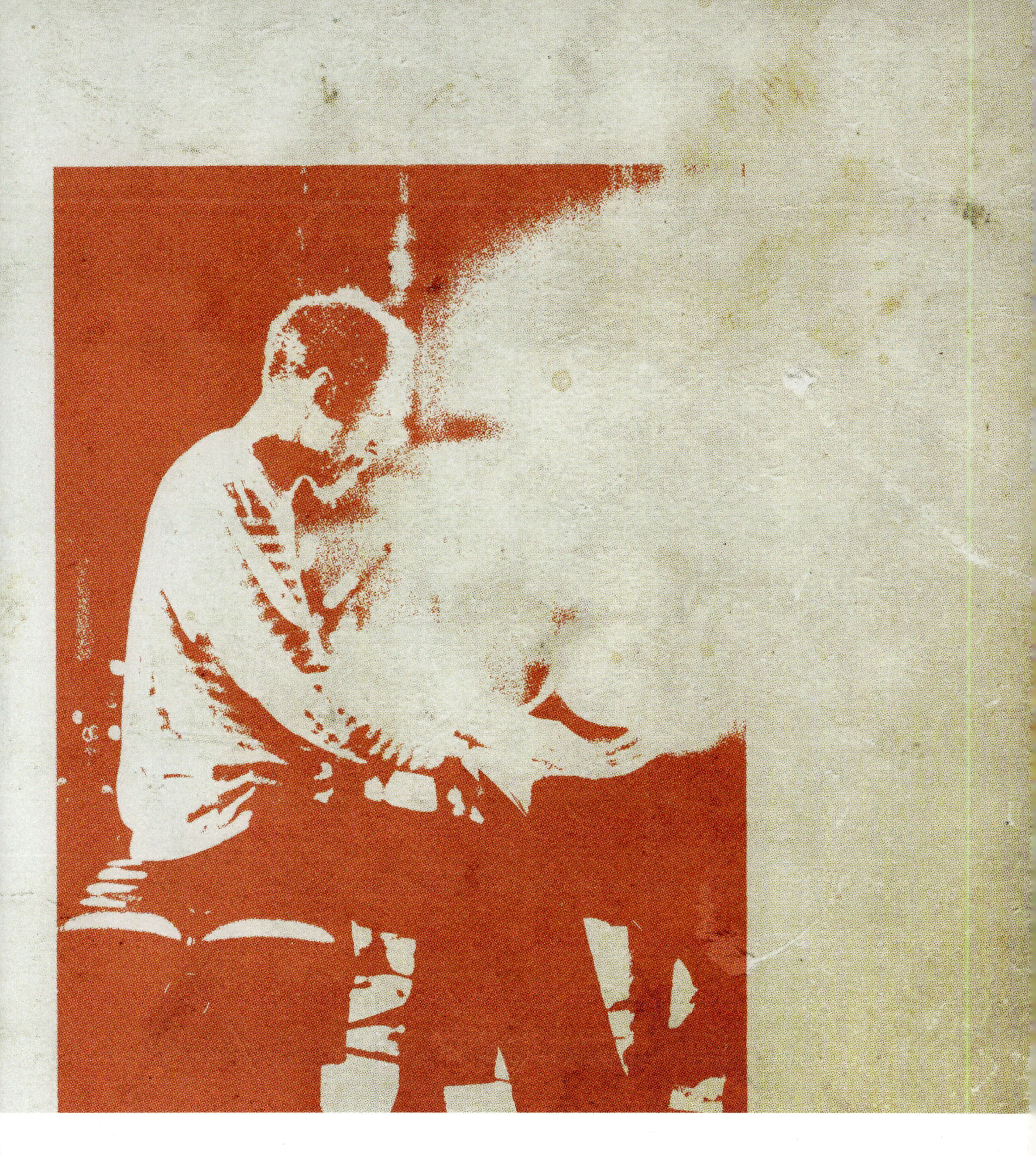

12/11/05

Dear Jason,

Please forgive me. I'm obviously losing my marbles. Check with signature enclosed.

It was wonderful to meet you. I was very glad to read your card — I'd worried afterwards that my own fascination with hard reality, my obsession with seeing clearly even if it's painful, my desire not to deceive myself even if it's pleasant — all that and more might have come off as some sort of Debbie Downer syndrome. I'm glad it didn't, because I'm VERY excited by your work and the directions it's taking (I've been playing all three of your albums ever since; "A Gentle Shift South" makes me cry every time). I'm going to try to be at the Knitting on May 21st.

I'm here now to thank _you_, Jason, for weaving my work into your magic.

Best,
Adrian

With All Good Wishes for a

HAPPY NEW YEAR
HAPPY NEW MONTH
HAPPY NEW WEEK
HAPPY NEW DAY
HAPPY NEW HOUR
HAPPY NEW MINUTE
HAPPY NEW SECOND
HAPPY NEW NOW

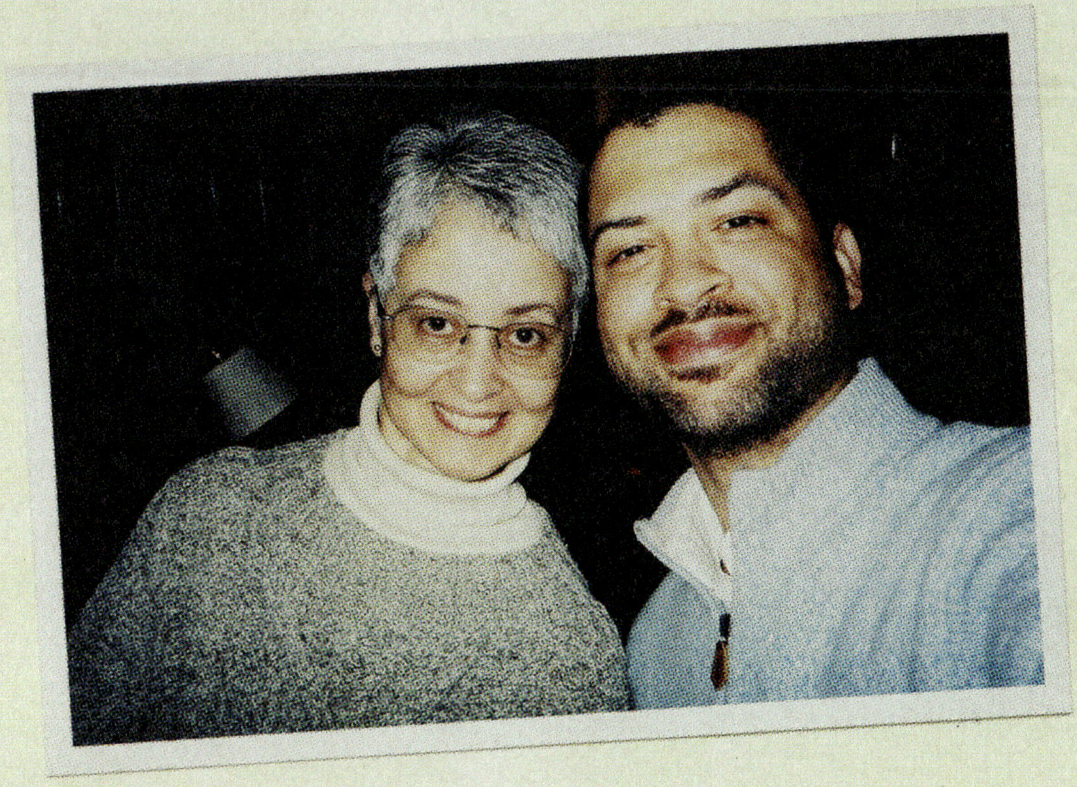

No Red.

PLAYLIST

How can an abstract jazz artist say clearly how they
stand? The sequence of these pieces often states the
recent work centers around exploring possible answer

format: by

01

"Other Than Art's

02
Alicia writes some of the greatest melodies I've ev
the "jazz wife" musing on the whereabouts of the t
Brussels, Köln . . ."

03

04
When I was a kid my mother used to sit in on my
played. The loud sound of her pencil scratching aga
my early years at the piano. This song is in honor o
answer to Adrian Piper's directive that follows on t

05

nd make an audience under–
em. But in all seriousness, my
e question.

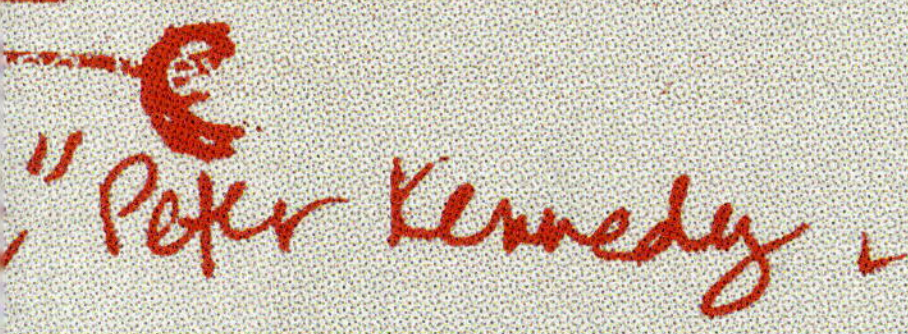

"Peter Kennedy"

ard. Here she's on vocals as
g husband – "London, Paris,

Publishing.
essons and take notes as I
aper accompanied much of
nemory as much as it is my
that Artists ought to be writing."

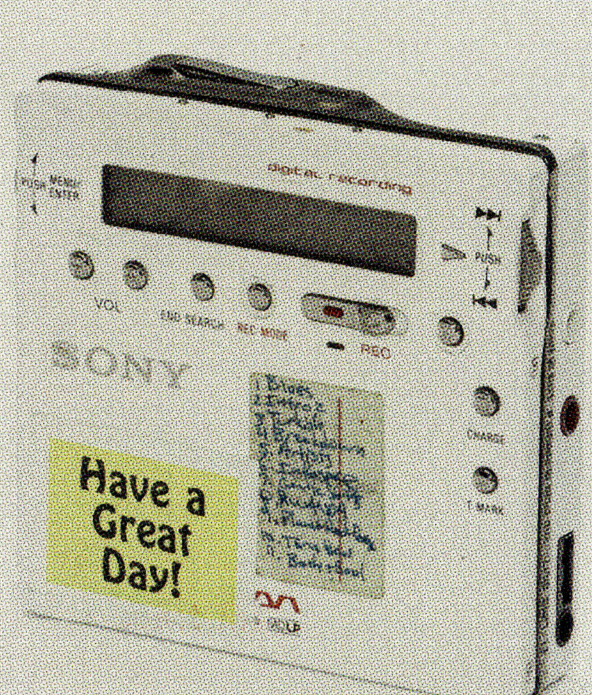

make
even
bottom, specially.

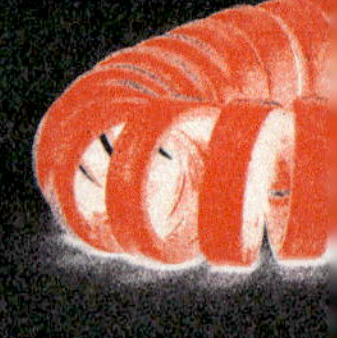

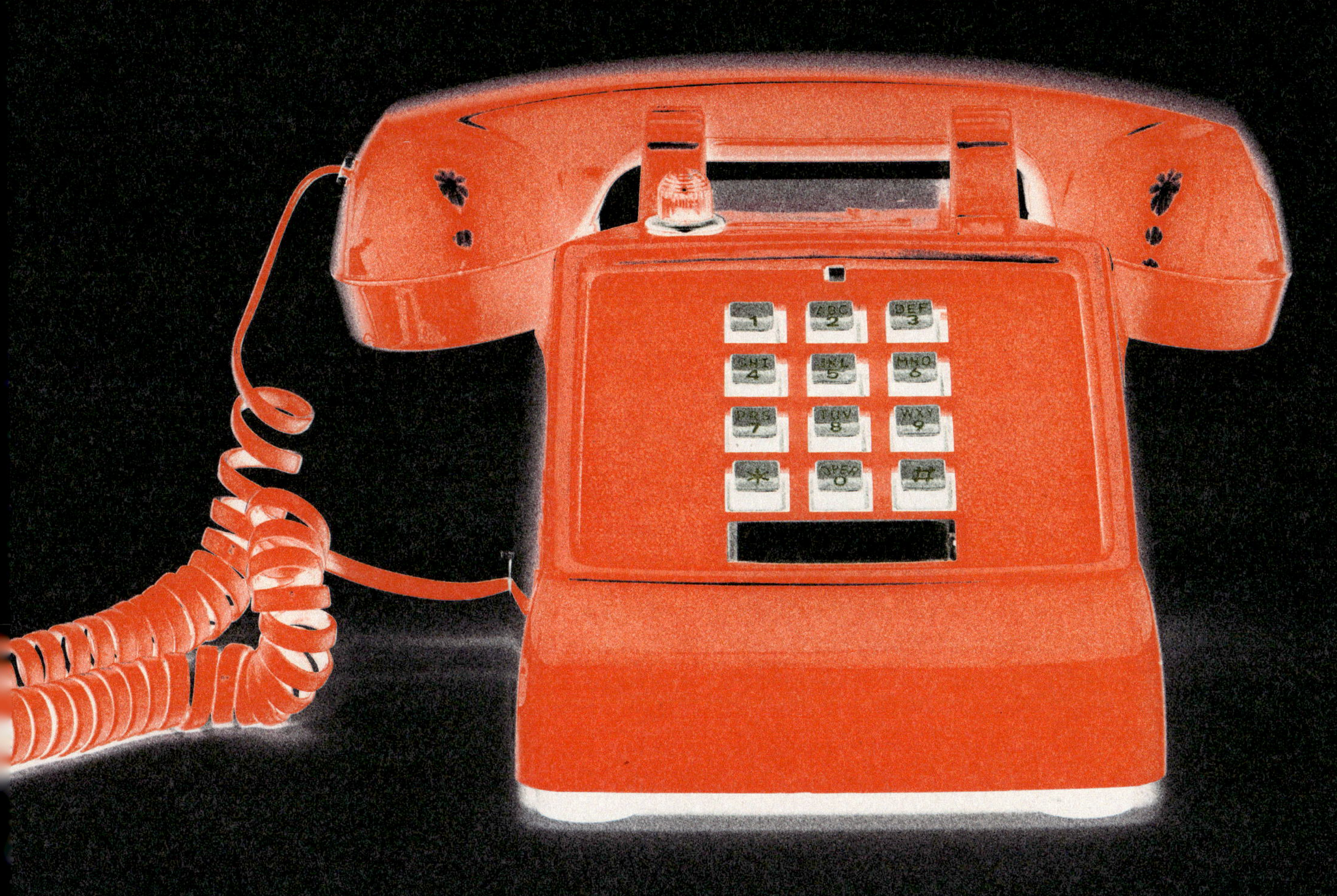

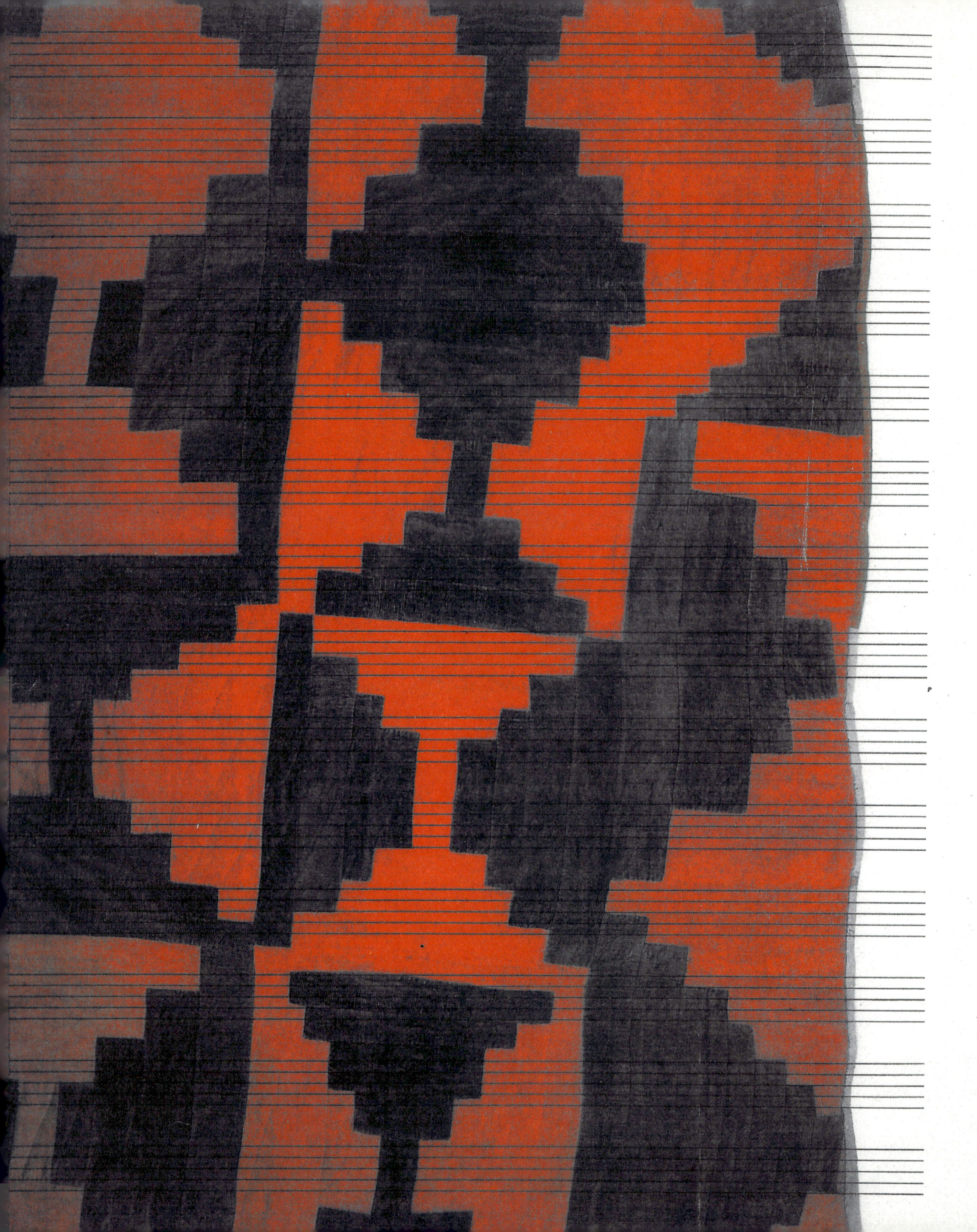

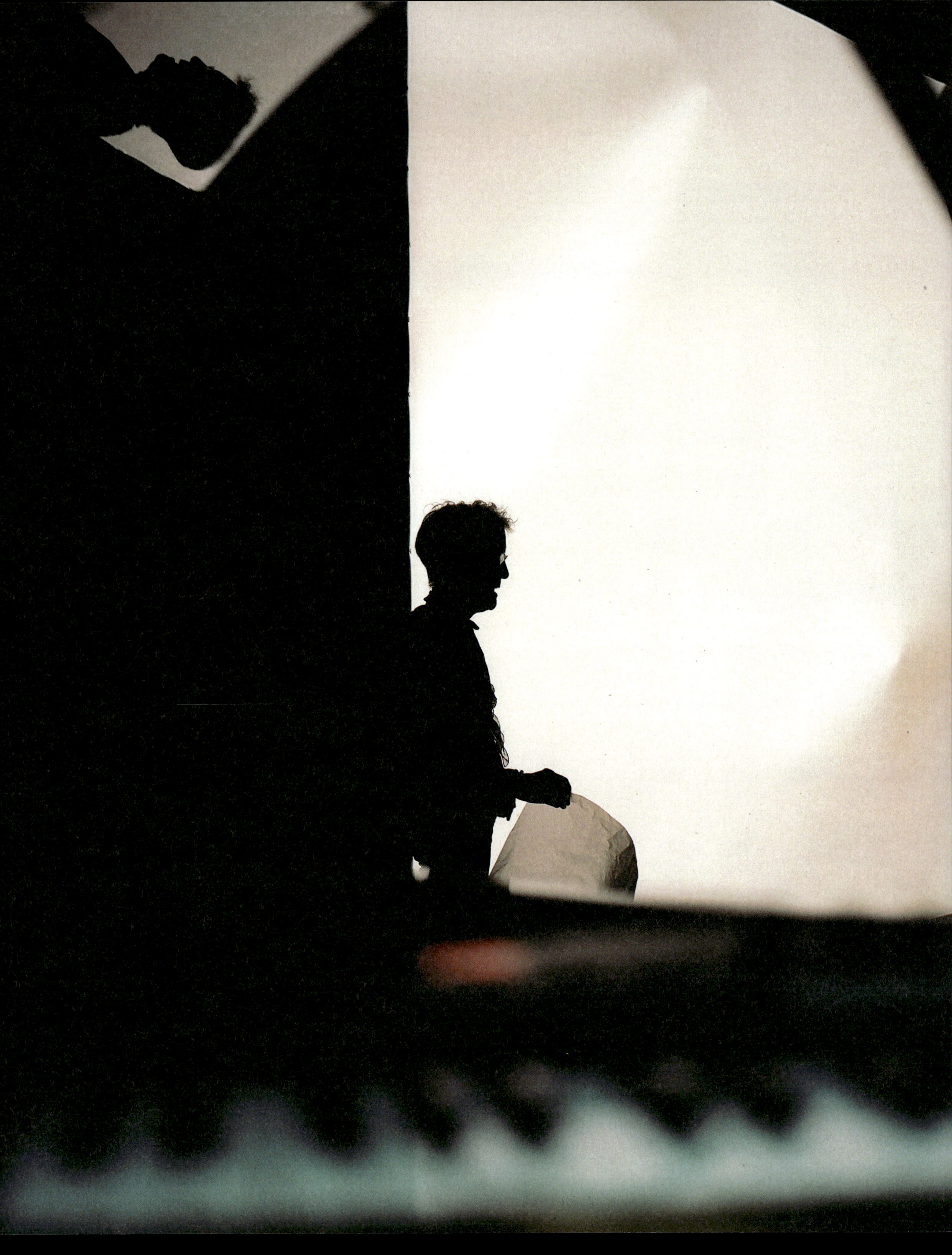

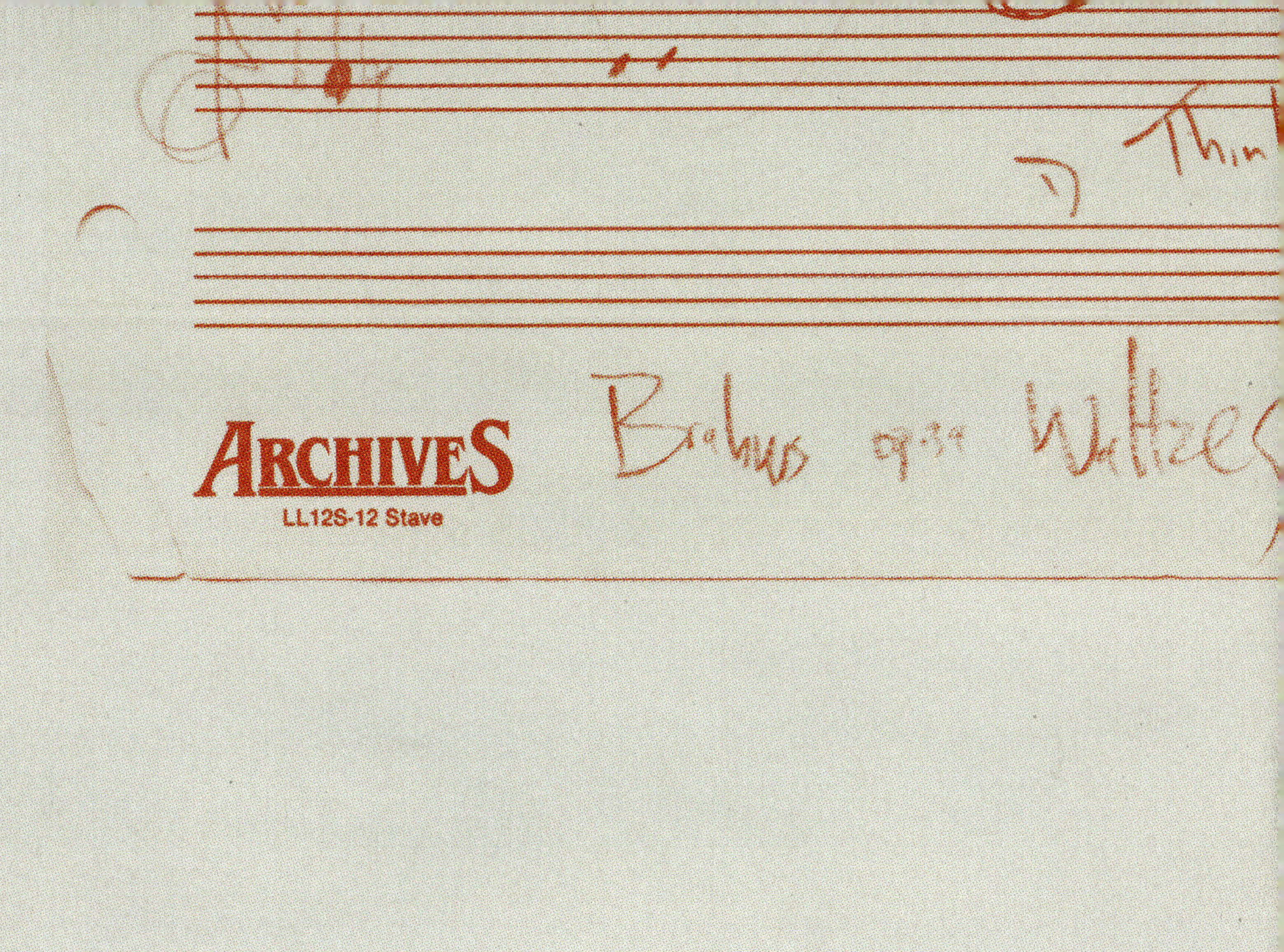

Thin
ARCHIVES
LL12S-12 Stave
Brahms op.39 Waltzes

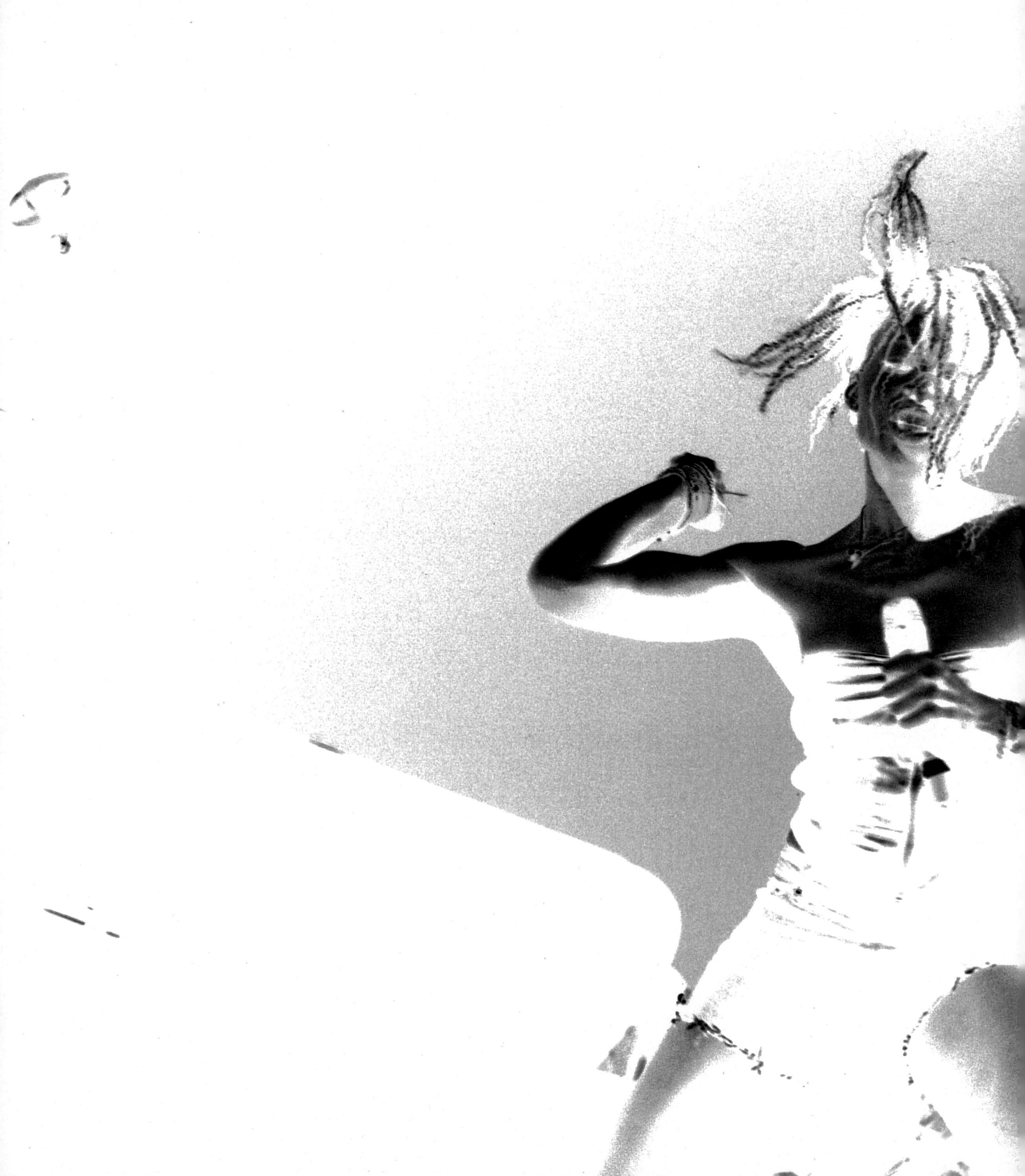

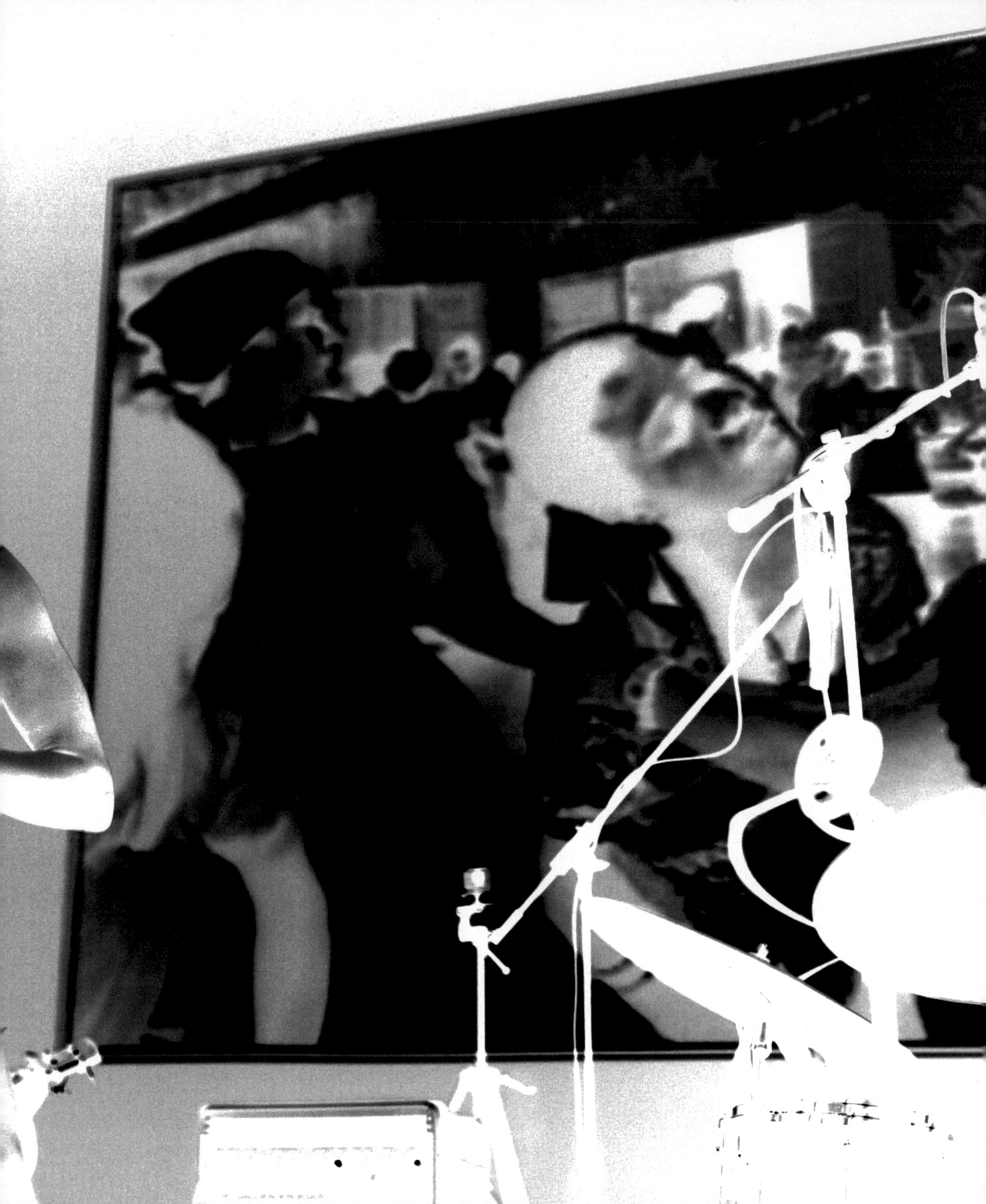

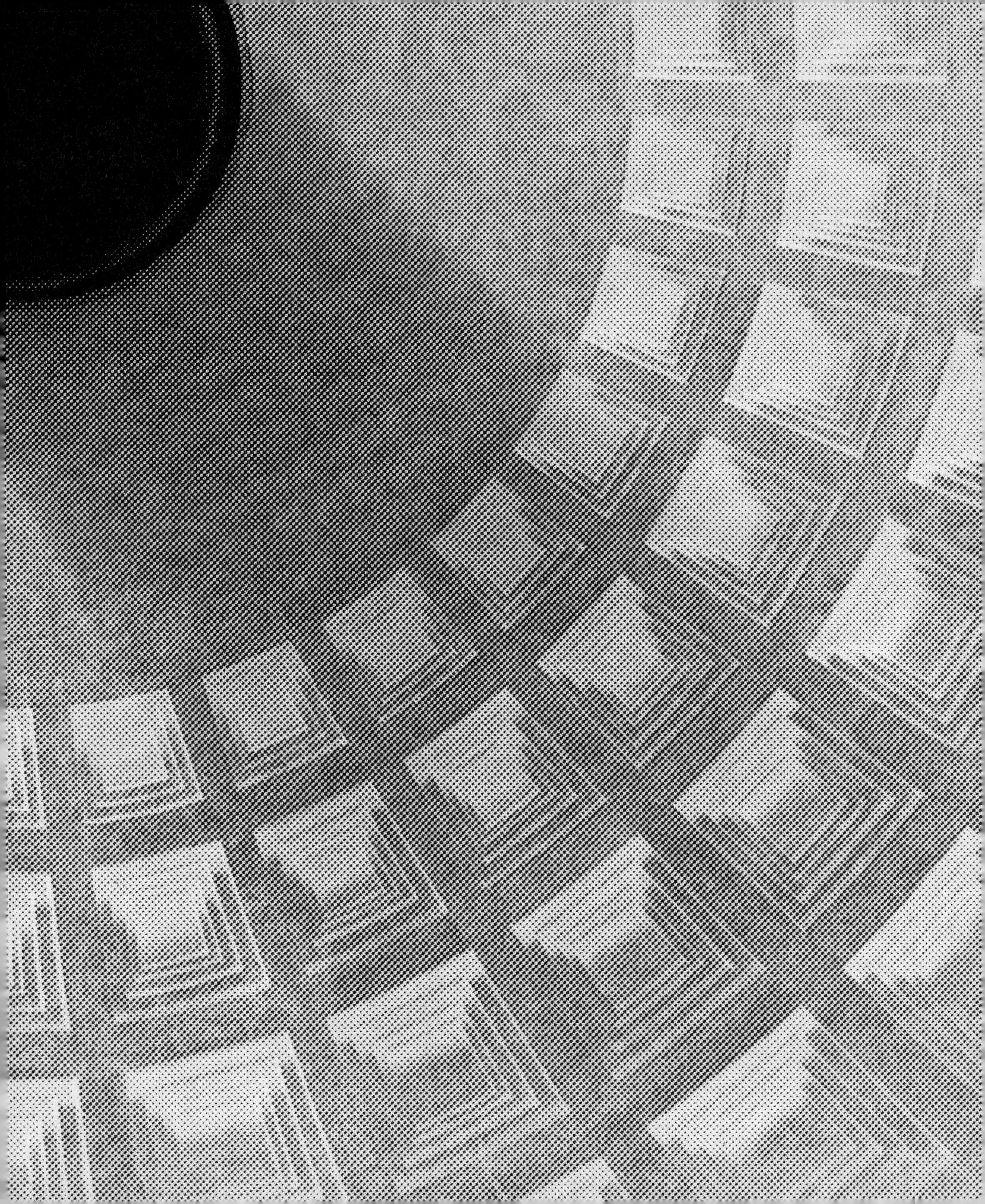

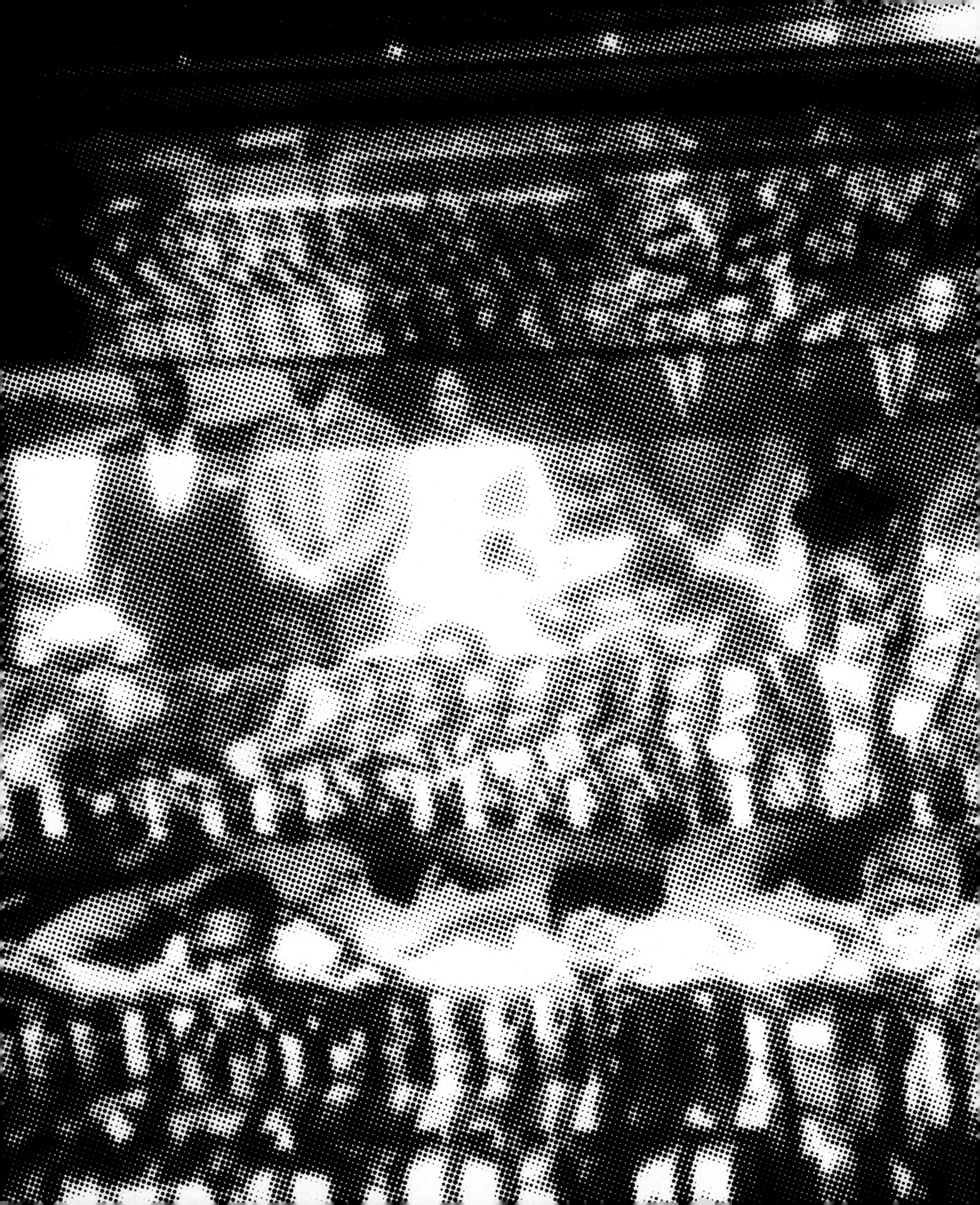

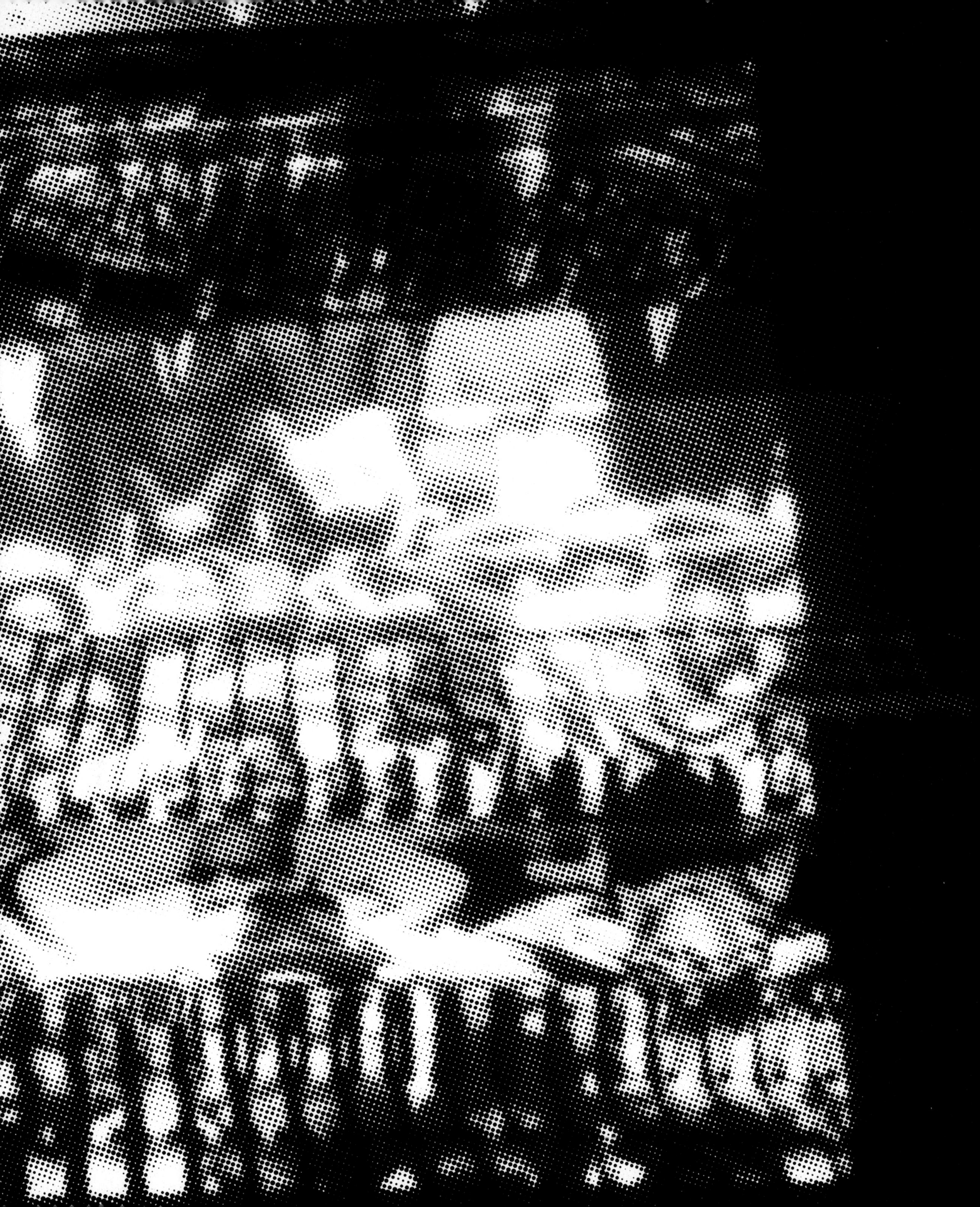

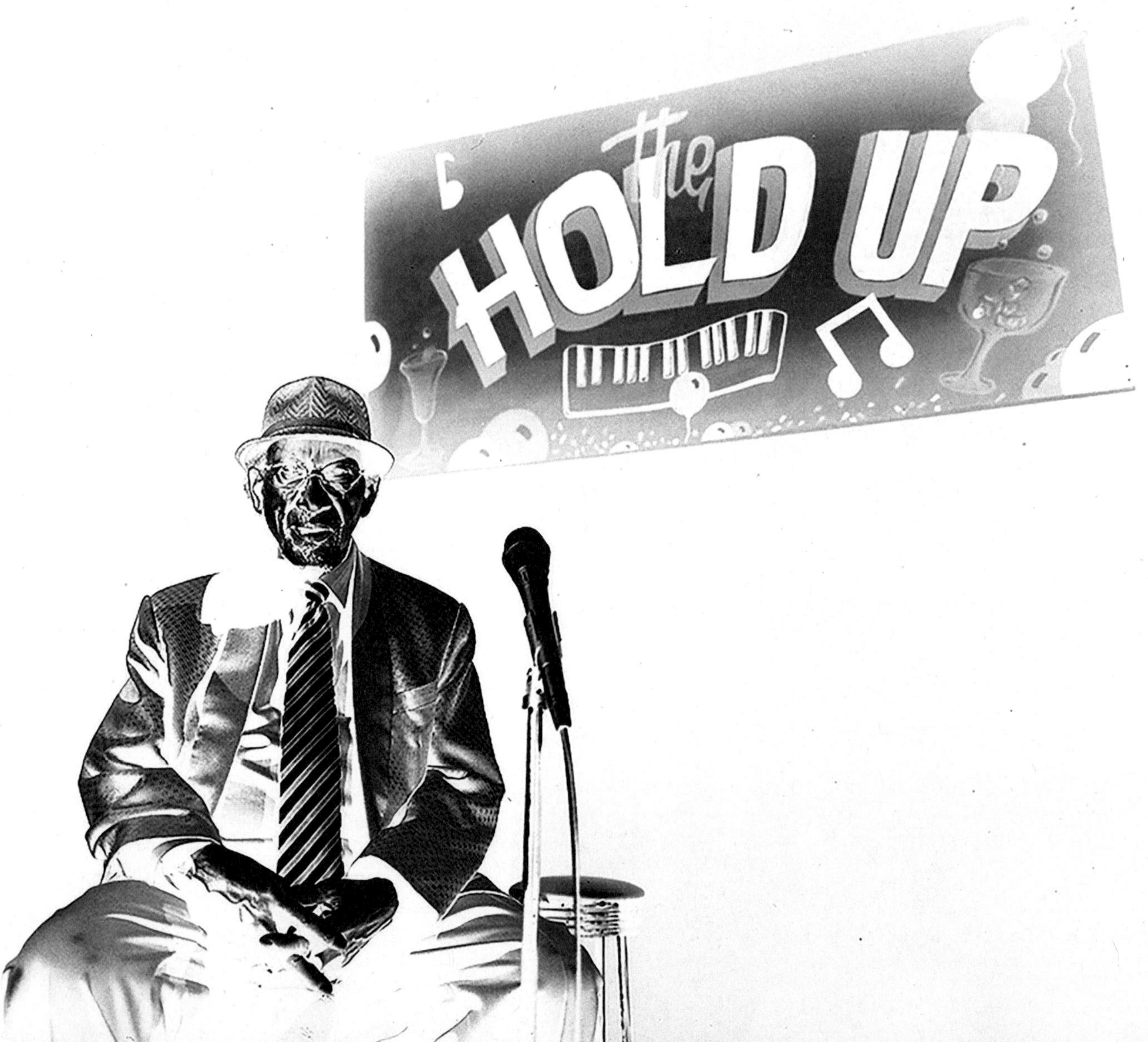
the
HOLD UP

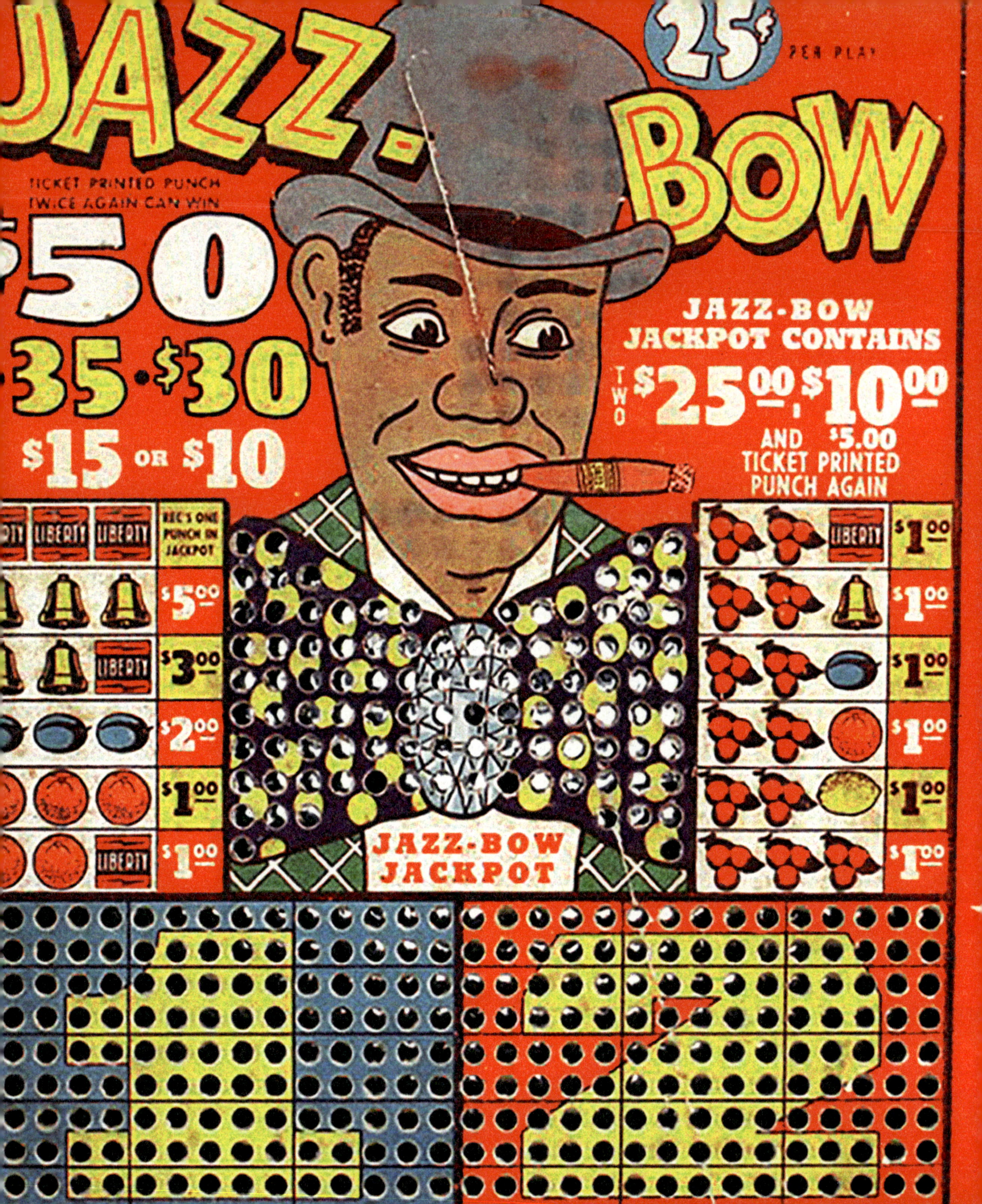

JAZZ-BOW
25¢ PER PLAY
TICKET PRINTED PUNCH TWICE AGAIN CAN WIN
$50
$35 · $30
$15 OR $10
JAZZ-BOW JACKPOT CONTAINS
TWO $25.00 $10.00
AND $5.00
TICKET PRINTED PUNCH AGAIN
REC'S ONE PUNCH IN JACKPOT
LIBERTY LIBERTY LIBERTY
$5.00
LIBERTY $3.00
$2.00
$1.00
LIBERTY $1.00
JAZZ-BOW JACKPOT
LIBERTY $1.00
$1.00
$1.00
$1.00
$1.00
$1.00

THU, JUN 18, 2015

Jason Moran
G72FVF

JFK ▸ VCE

NYC - Kennedy (JFK) ▸
Venice (VCE)
FLIGHT DL474

*Gates may change. Check

Ticket#: 006 7595092484

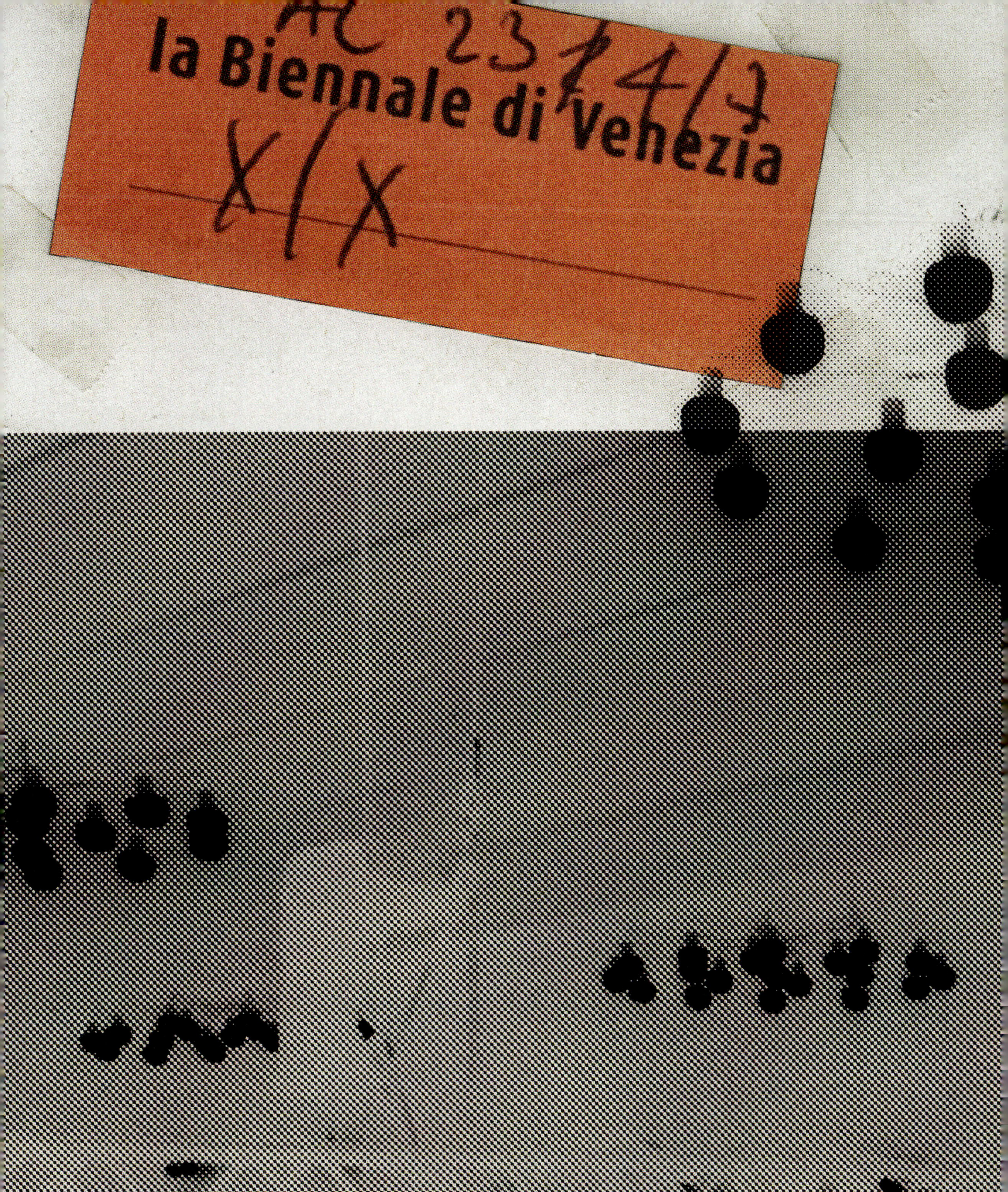
la Biennale di Venezia

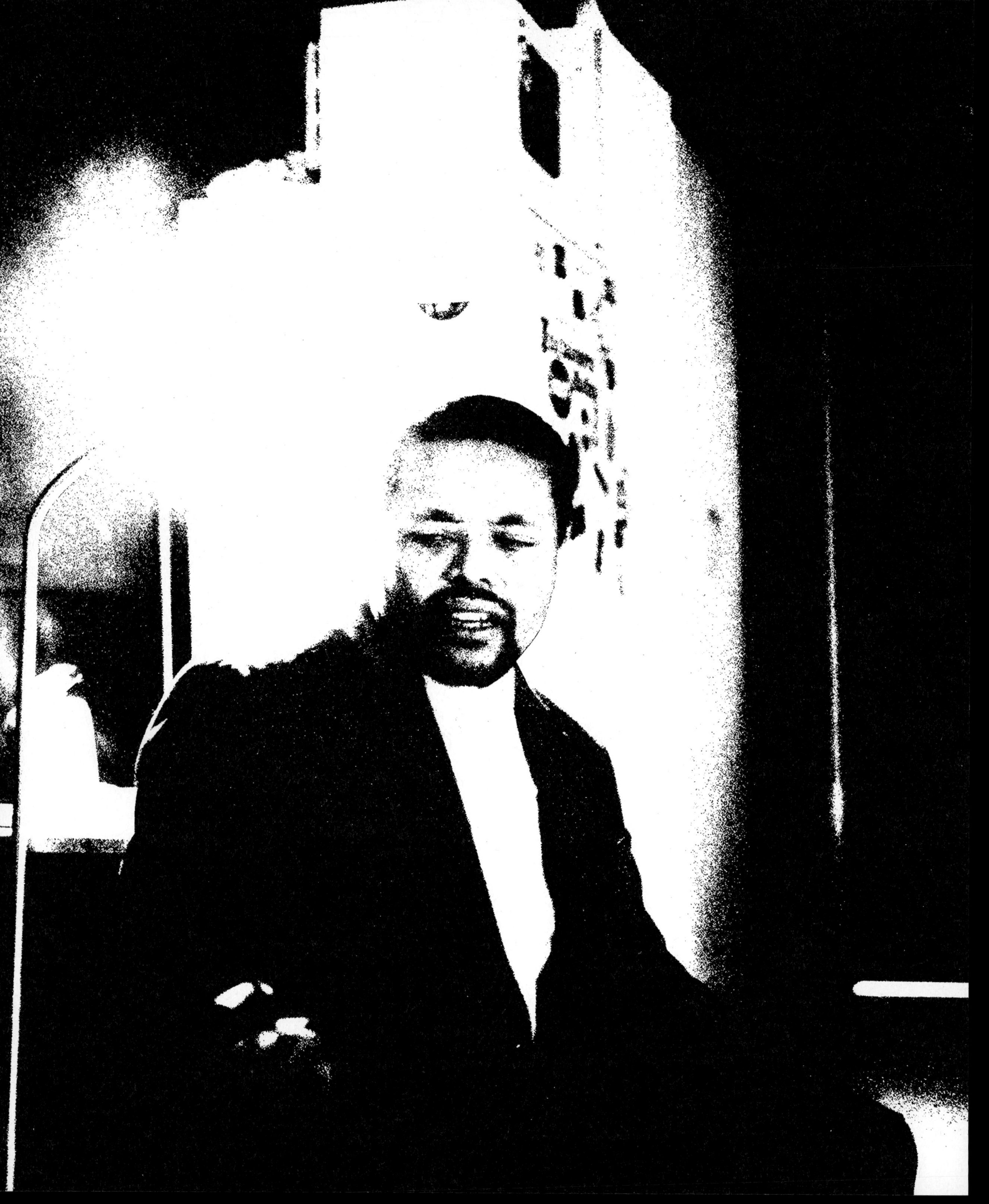

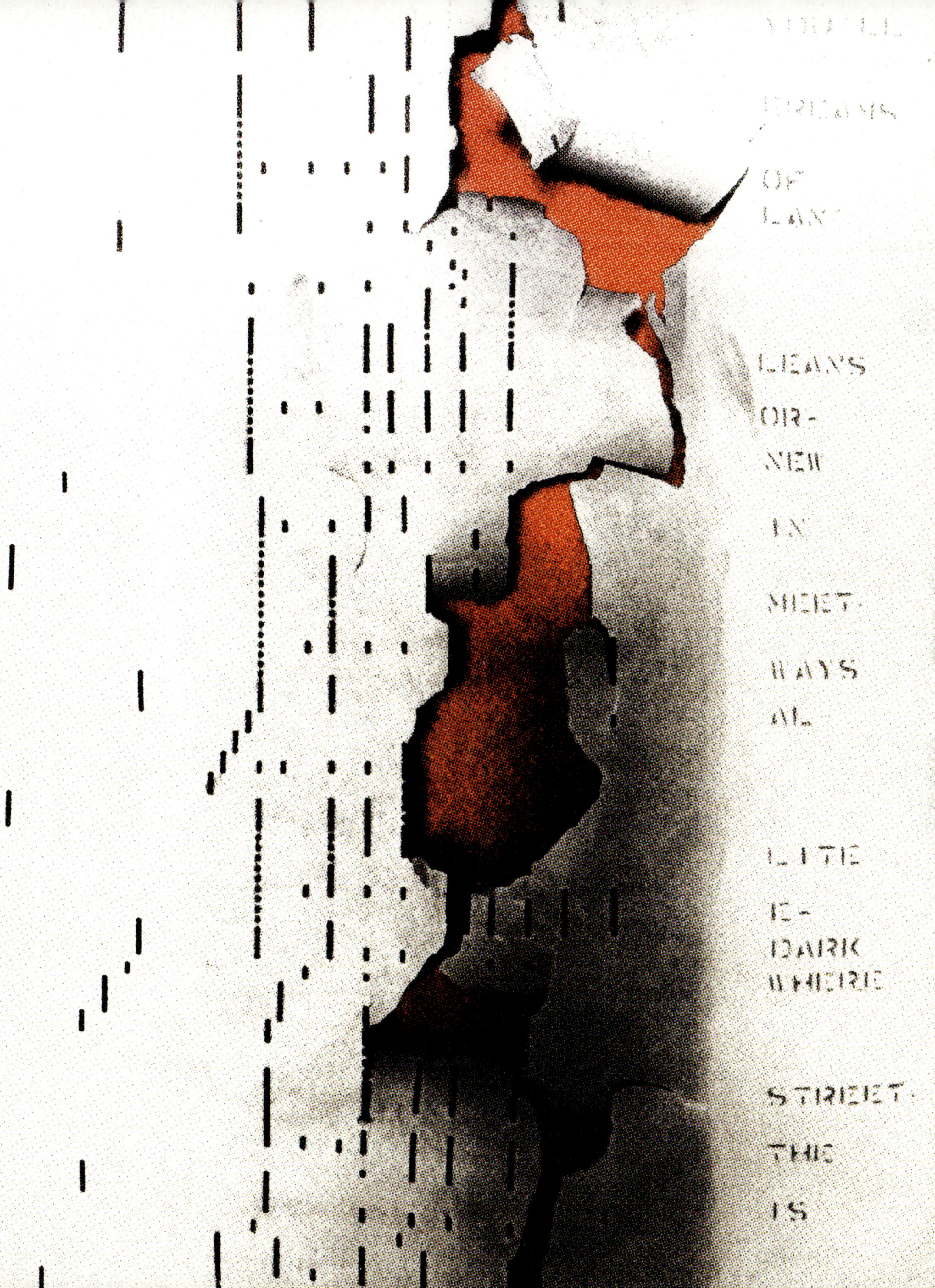

YOU'LL
DREAMS
OF
LAN-
LEAN'S
OR-
NEW
IN
MEET-
WAYS
AL-
LITE
E-
DARK
WHERE
STREET-
THIS
IS

LOOP

ISSUE NO. 1 — FALL 2016

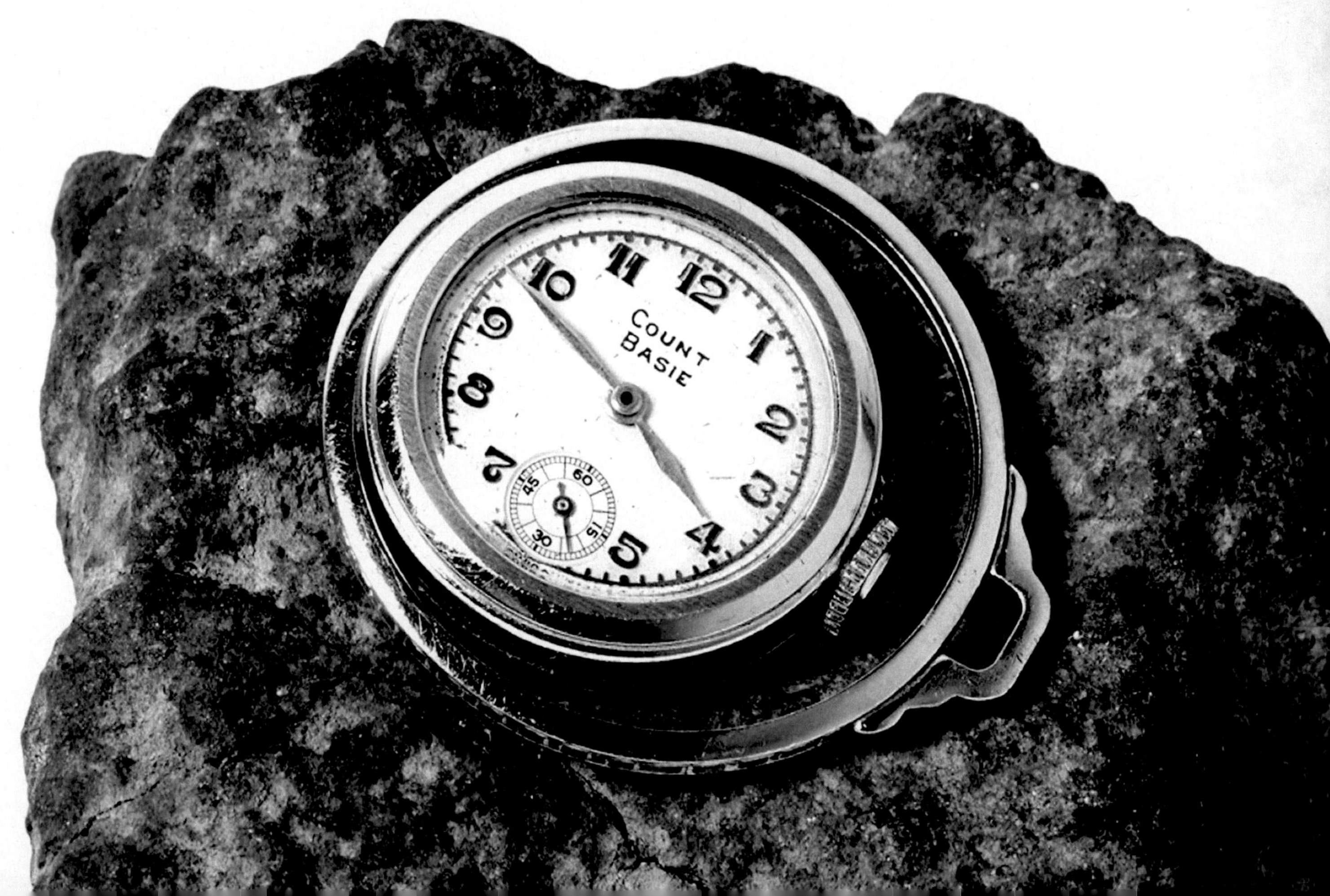

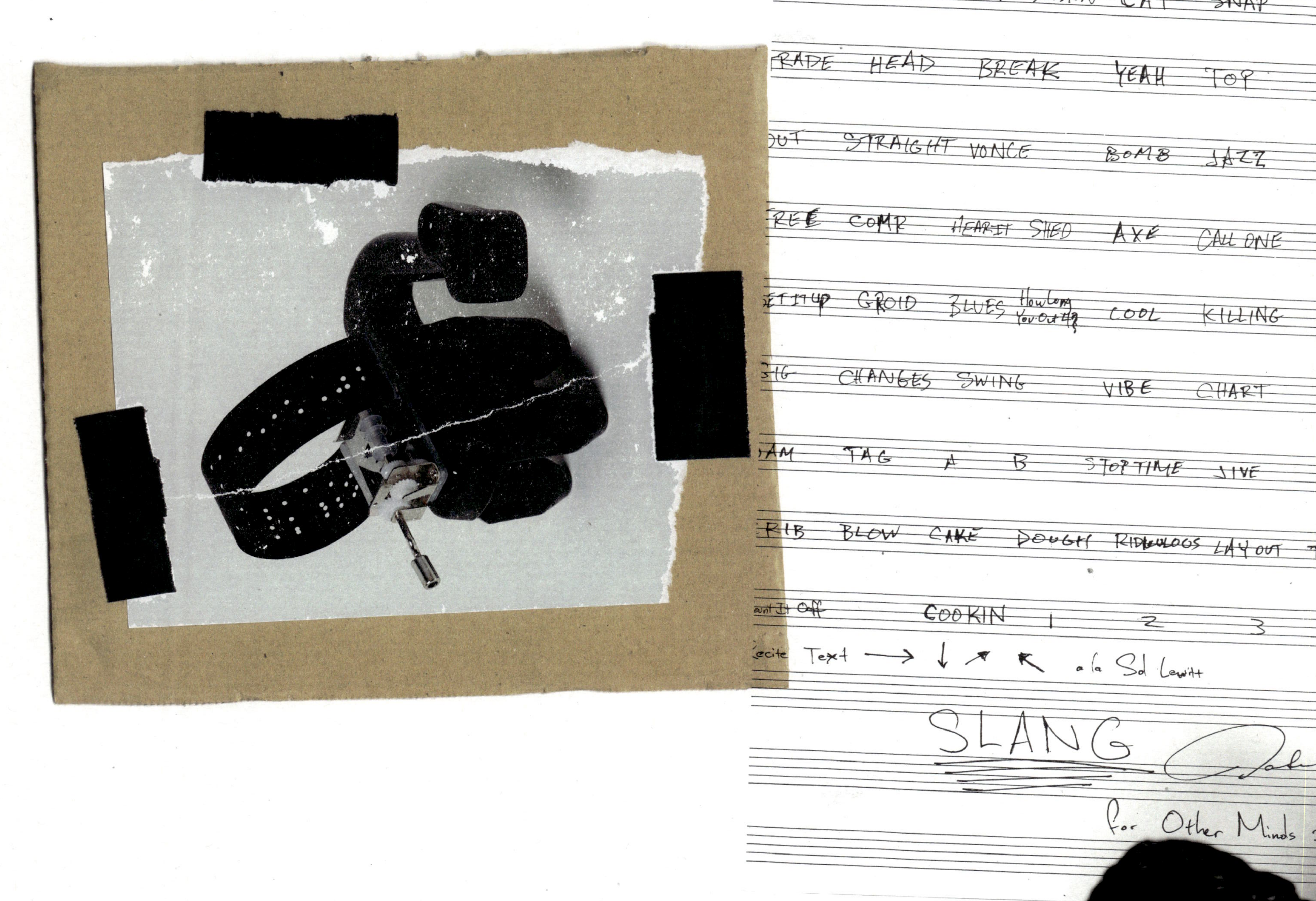
AG SOLO LOOP SESSION CAT SNAP
RADE HEAD BREAK YEAH TOP
OUT STRAIGHT VONCE BOMB JAZZ
REE COMP HEAR-IT SHED AXE CALL ONE
ET IT UP GROID BLUES How Long You Out #? COOL KILLING
SIG CHANGES SWING VIBE CHART
AM TAG A B STOP-TIME JIVE
RIB BLOW CAKE DOUGH RIDICULOUS LAYOUT TR
ount It Off COOKIN 1 2 3
Recite Text → ↓ ↗ ↖ a la Sol Lewitt
SLANG
for Other Minds 20

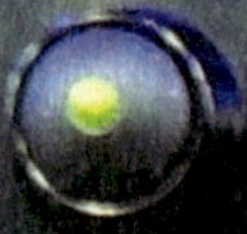
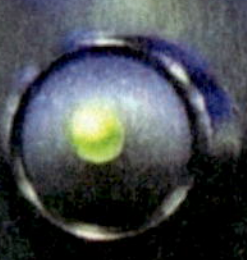
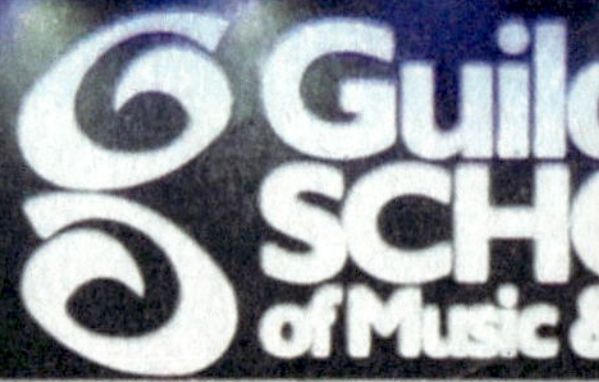

DOWN
BLUES
UP
Guild
SCH
of Music &

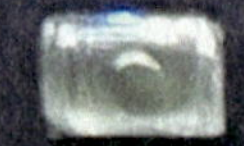

datavideo
A

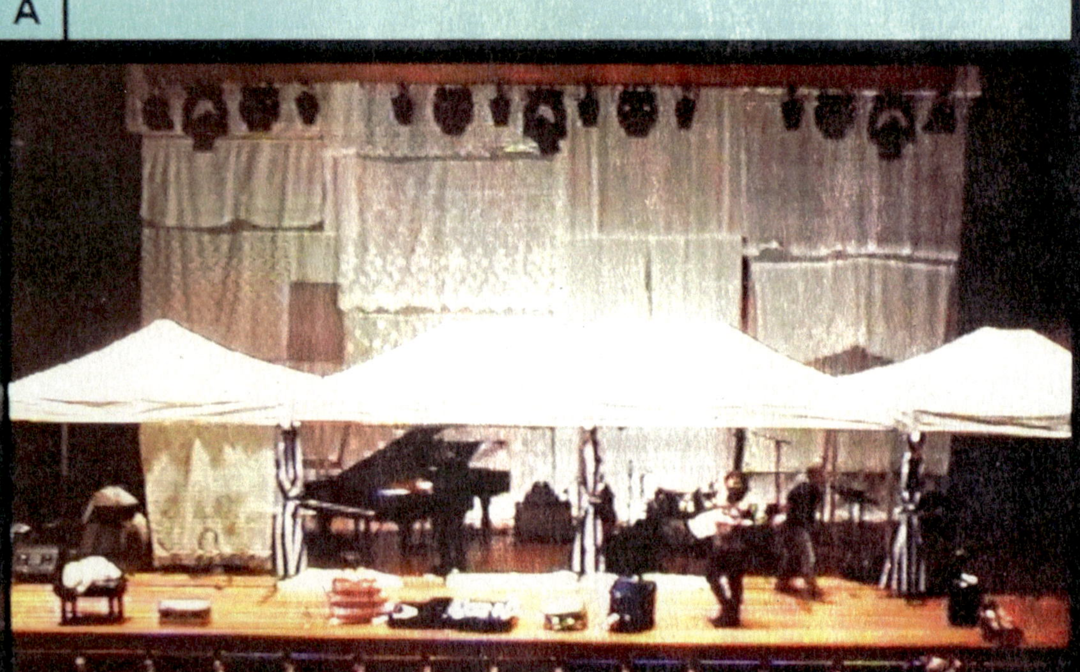

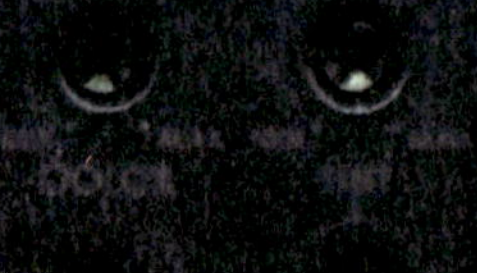

BRIGHTNESS   CONTRAST

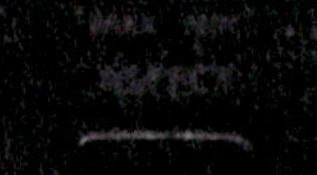

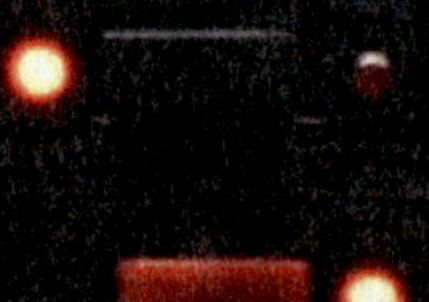

AMX

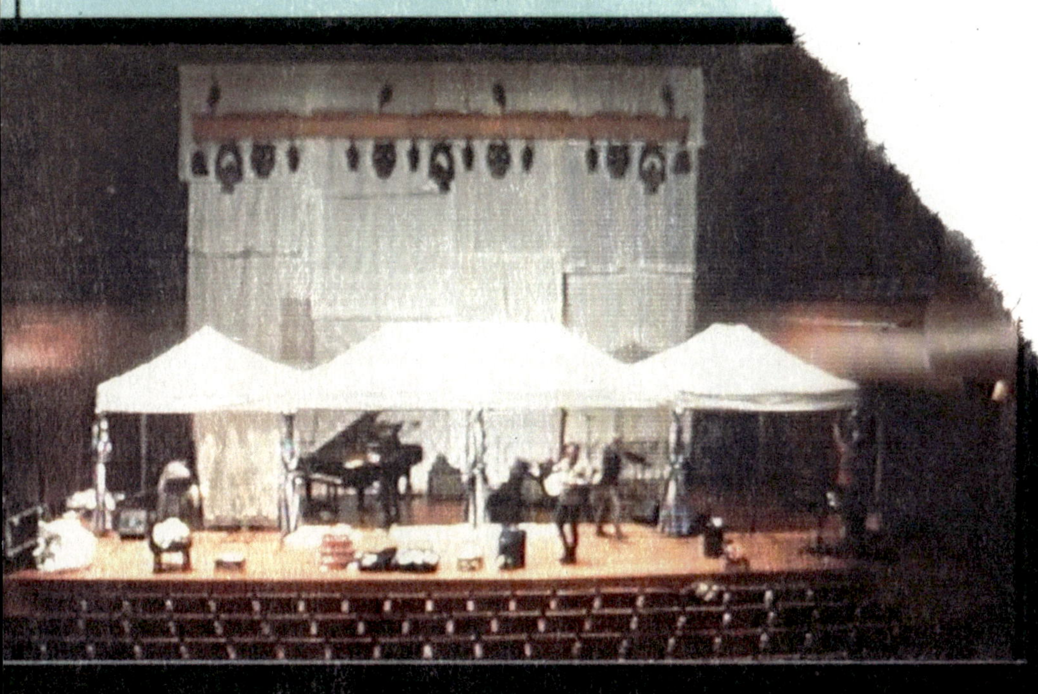
DOWN
WHIT
VOL
END SEARCH
REC MODE
REC
CLOCK
14:4548

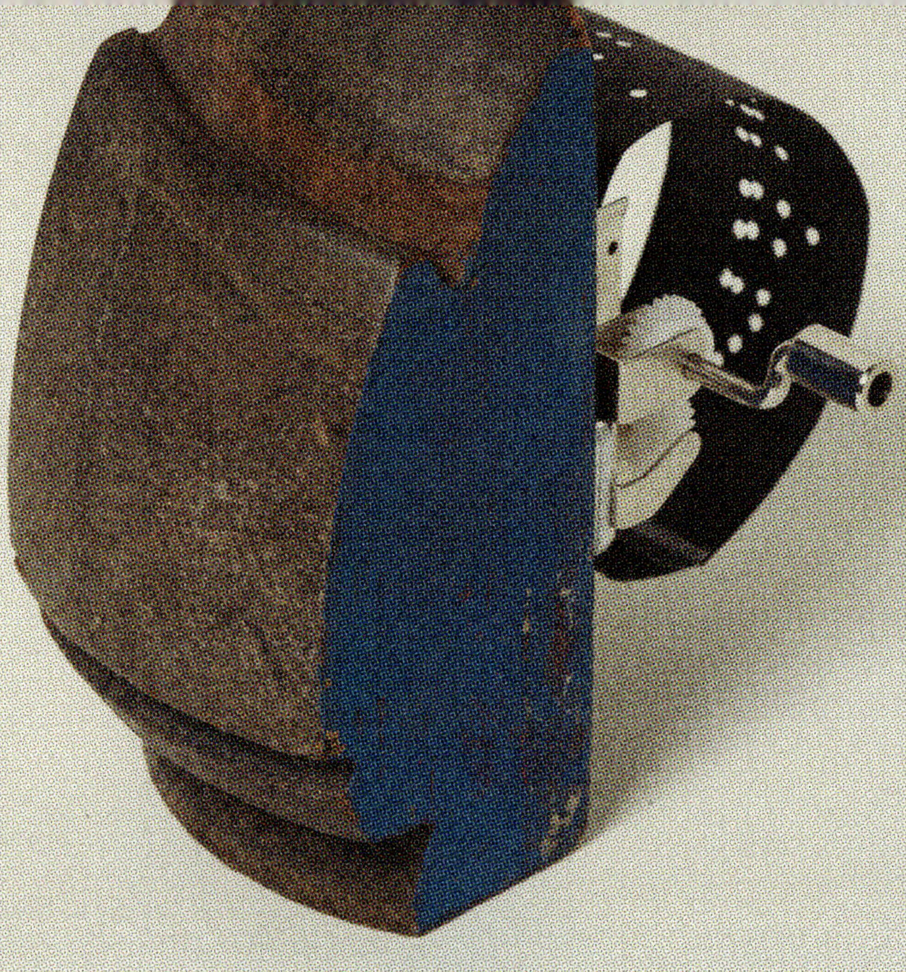

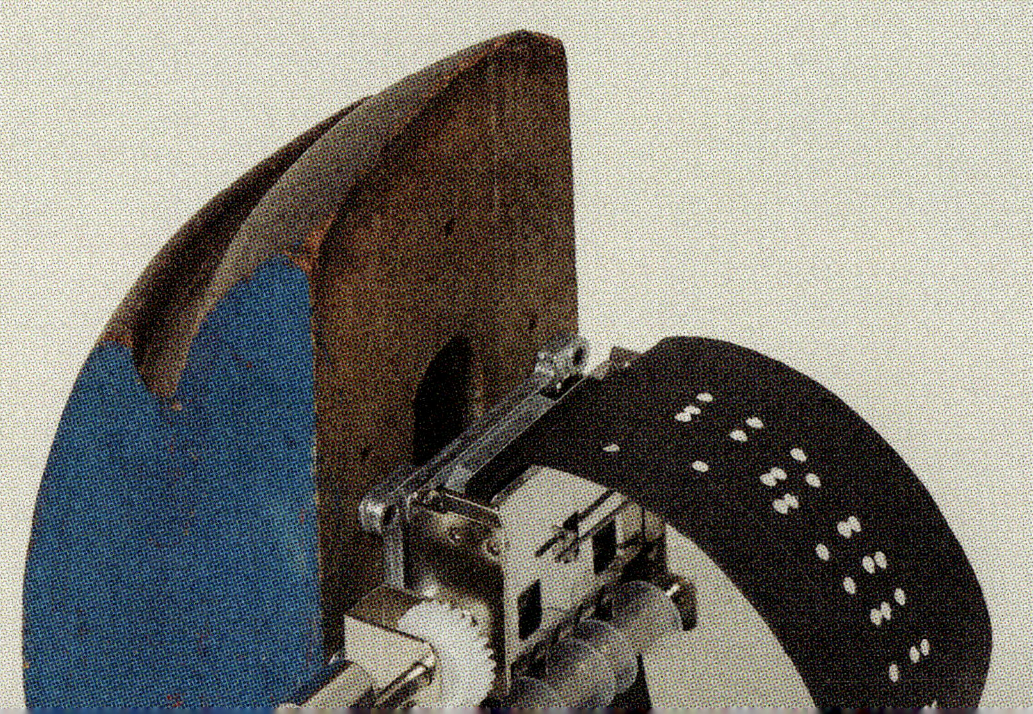

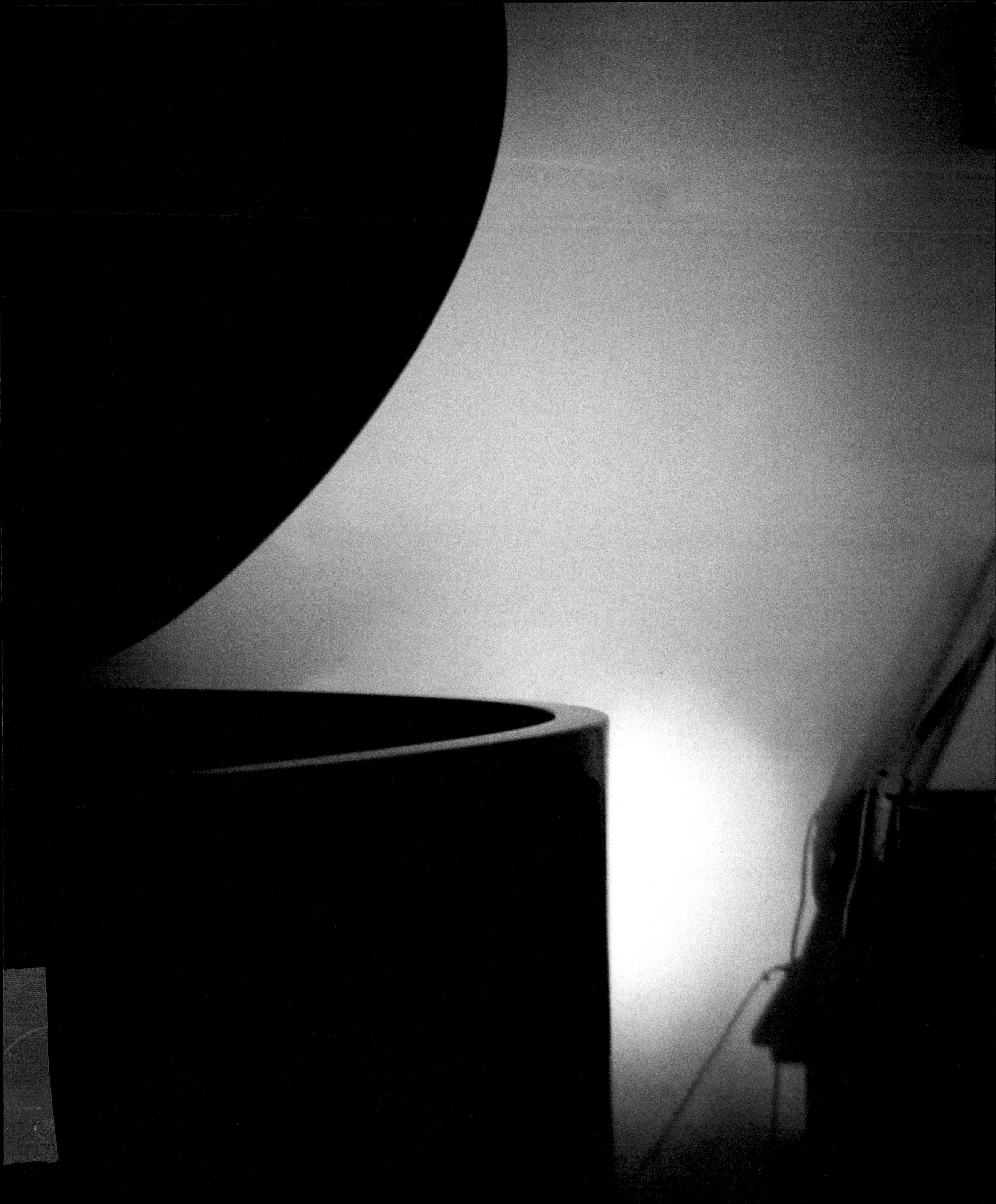

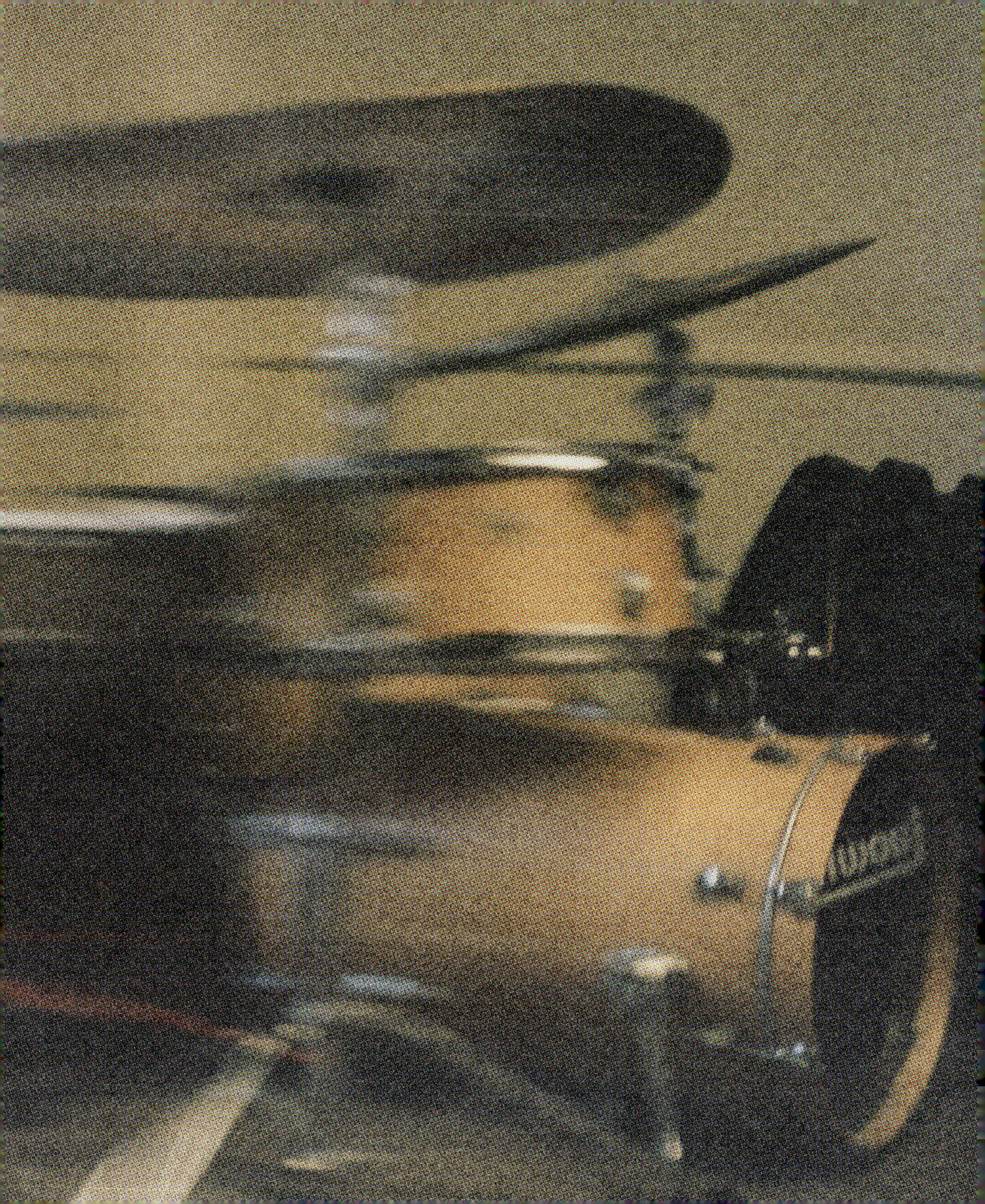

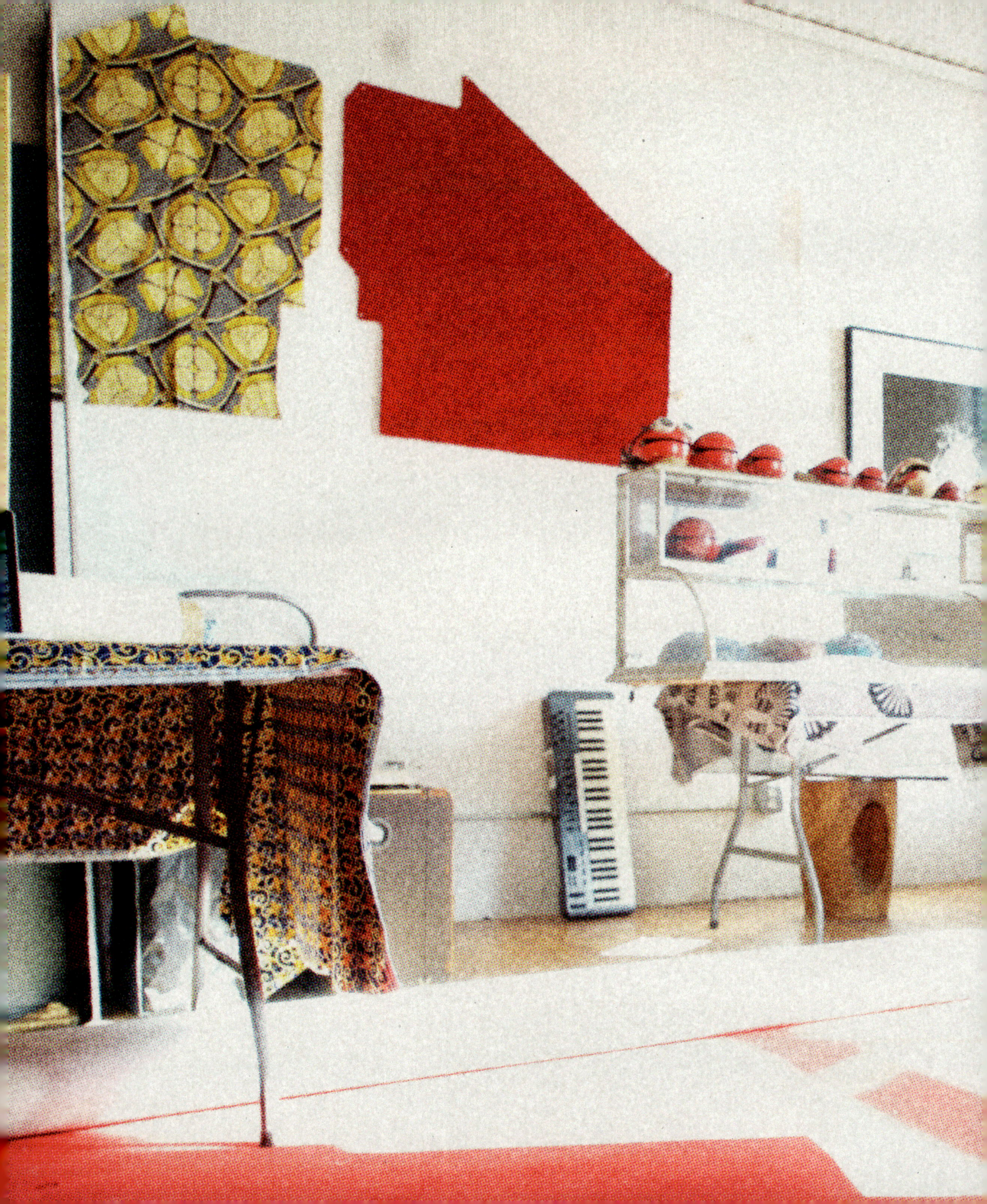

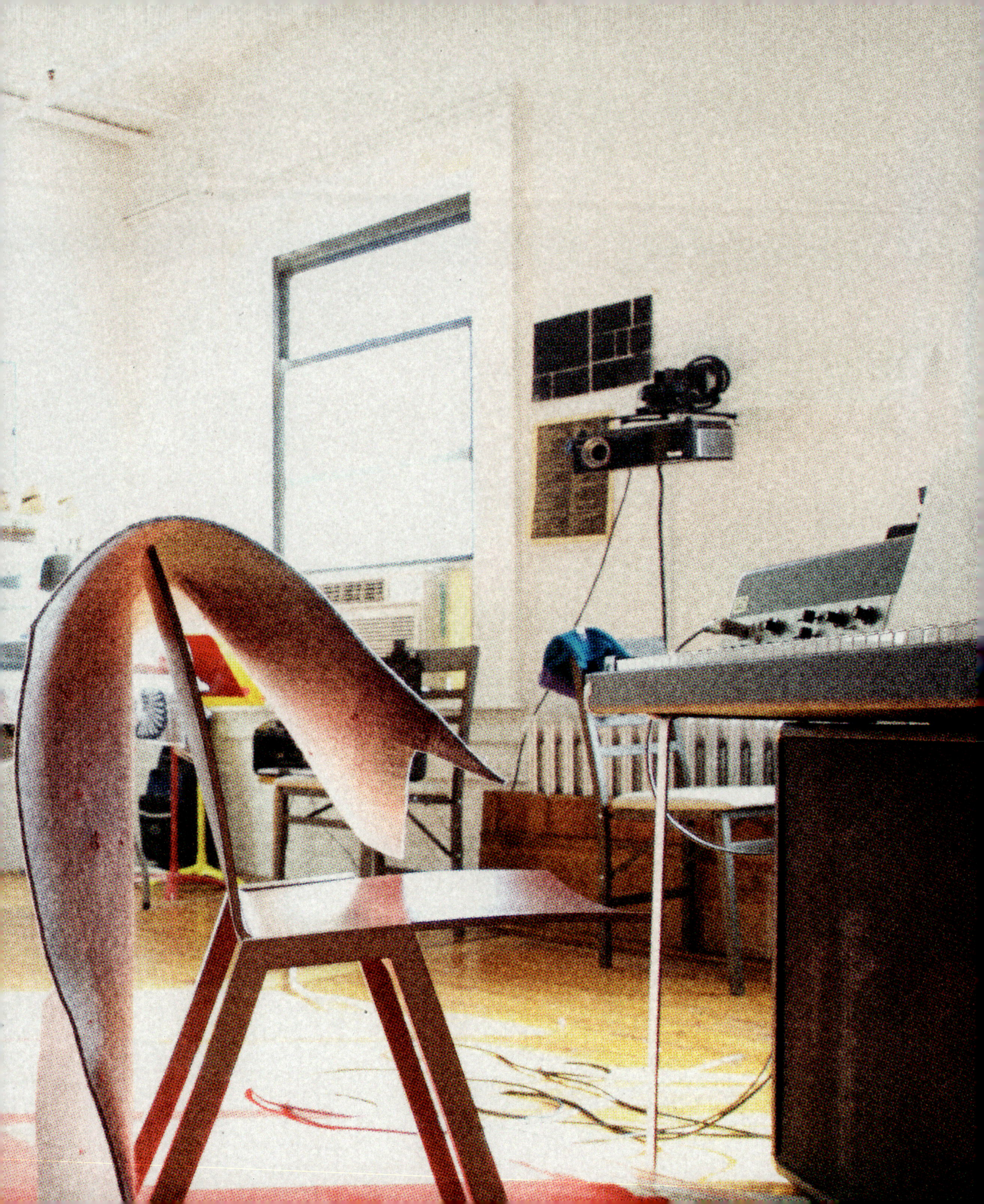

Ag 9.6 pb
Au ... .98
...2018 ...1-193 pb Hu 477 OBI
...gh 244-234 to
...AMZN 125 pb OBI Au 1652 OBI
...7 pb Ag 31.52 - 29.79 MUX
... AEM 31.42 88 - 30 → 20.87
... Ann wt gold 74 1553 -
3? OB Nem 21.5 130 - 126.34 euro
...1563 - 1525 range OBI Xg 5.24 pb
...53 - 1.43 gold 15 pb Mar 2009 pt Au
... - 15.36 5.71 - 1081 - 8.91 Au 1540 - 1528 pB
gld 163.10 - 165 or if 153 ↓ 160.55 resis Au
...570 - 558 pb ? Pot 36 pb 575.4 gap 568.18 Aapl
17.42 - 46.7 pb area Aapl 486? OBI vsh pb David 11.04 -
...pl 363 11-23-11 pdln 637 pb free Loc - 1.01 - .99 - 2.18
...M 80.54 sell sht TwM 31.12 TZA 18.99 SDS 15.51 - 16.18 SL

 75.14 - 75.4 ibm 173 pb Au 1580 Larry Pb 1300 Ag
Aapl 555 - 620 range 594 pb 1620 — if 1500 Au 1622 pb
50 - 355 - Au 1681 bounce OBI SNE 15.64 Voi-4m 1625 mus
CMg 317 HMY 8.8 ANR 75 - 8 Dec 16 new KATE OMN 7 - 7.5 pb
Kate → rf 6.6? Wal 6.95 - Arsd 10.34 Aapl 555 gap PC 4.5
AEM 34.61 - 31.42 2 650z gg 600 - 700 oz

Soux 52 pb - 38 SLv 25 65 MXWL 9.6 - 14 1yr
Jtg 1.85 pb vol XAU 137 pb Hui 926 OBI? AMZN 193 - 12
Ecx 34 → 48 consolidation gg/2 - 2.43 SL 1.74 MNST = hansen
XAU 146 pb Hui 398 pb OBI? Ag 16.02 gg .72 SL .56 Ag 16.
SL 15.04 3.32 Hi Vol Iapl
CMR 9.84 pb Basil Au 1649 - 1613 sup 1680 resis OBI gmer

108 pb MA 394 pb May 2010 pt pm OBI SNE 15.64 yen 78
Blk Sp. 2 + SLW 27.96 pb Basil 25.84 - 25.21 - 31.41 bounce? 77
sht 39.78 - 35 - 37 SL 40.94 exM 152 - 1.43 17? Aapl 550 -
AZN 196 - 179 pb euro 126 pb? OBI 119 VZ pb exM 152 - 1.
X 17.27 pb OBI gg 13.84 - if 33.85 holds ok Aapl 529

29.6 - 28.54 euro 126 pb $ 82 - 89 SLW 21 - 20 pb
hold out 1.19 Au 1530 - 1450 - 1200 pb
136.33 Amex pb OBI gld 148 - 145 Aapl 526 pb
230 ft Soux 47 vol (40 - 66 run) Abx 17.27 pb
40 gg 33.85 - 13.84
...DAY B pt 89.8 - 75.12 pb SPY 116 - 82

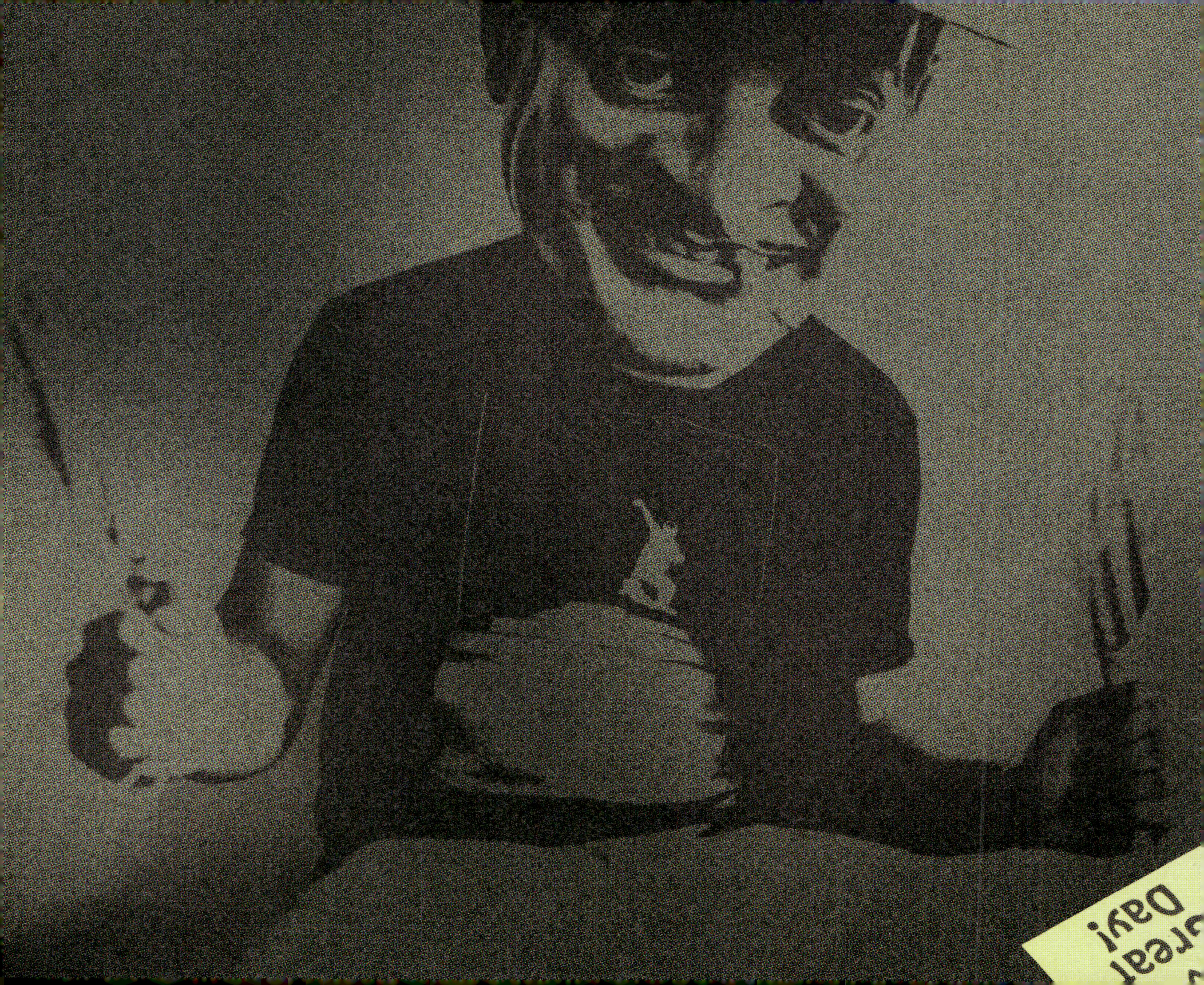
Great
Day!

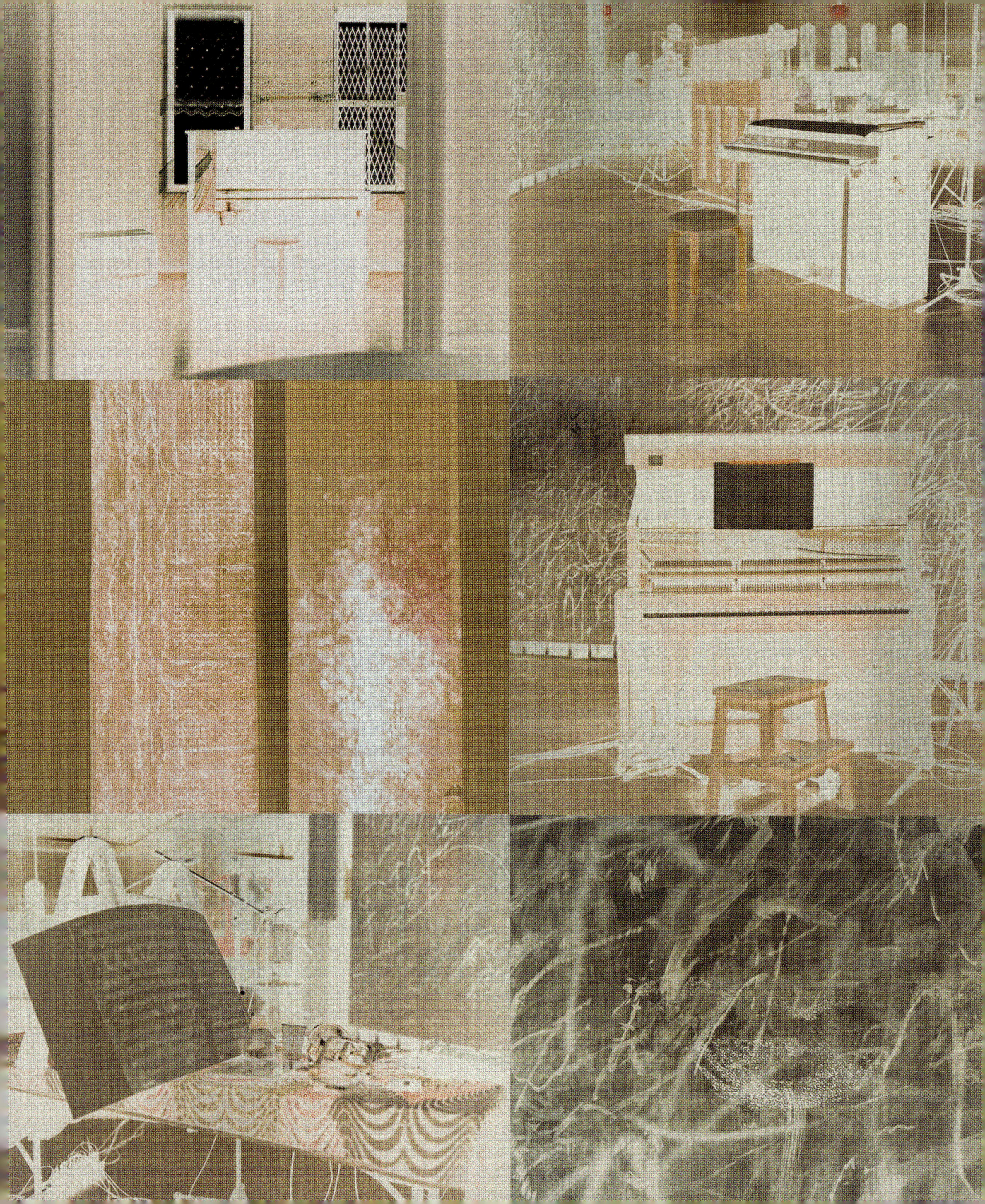

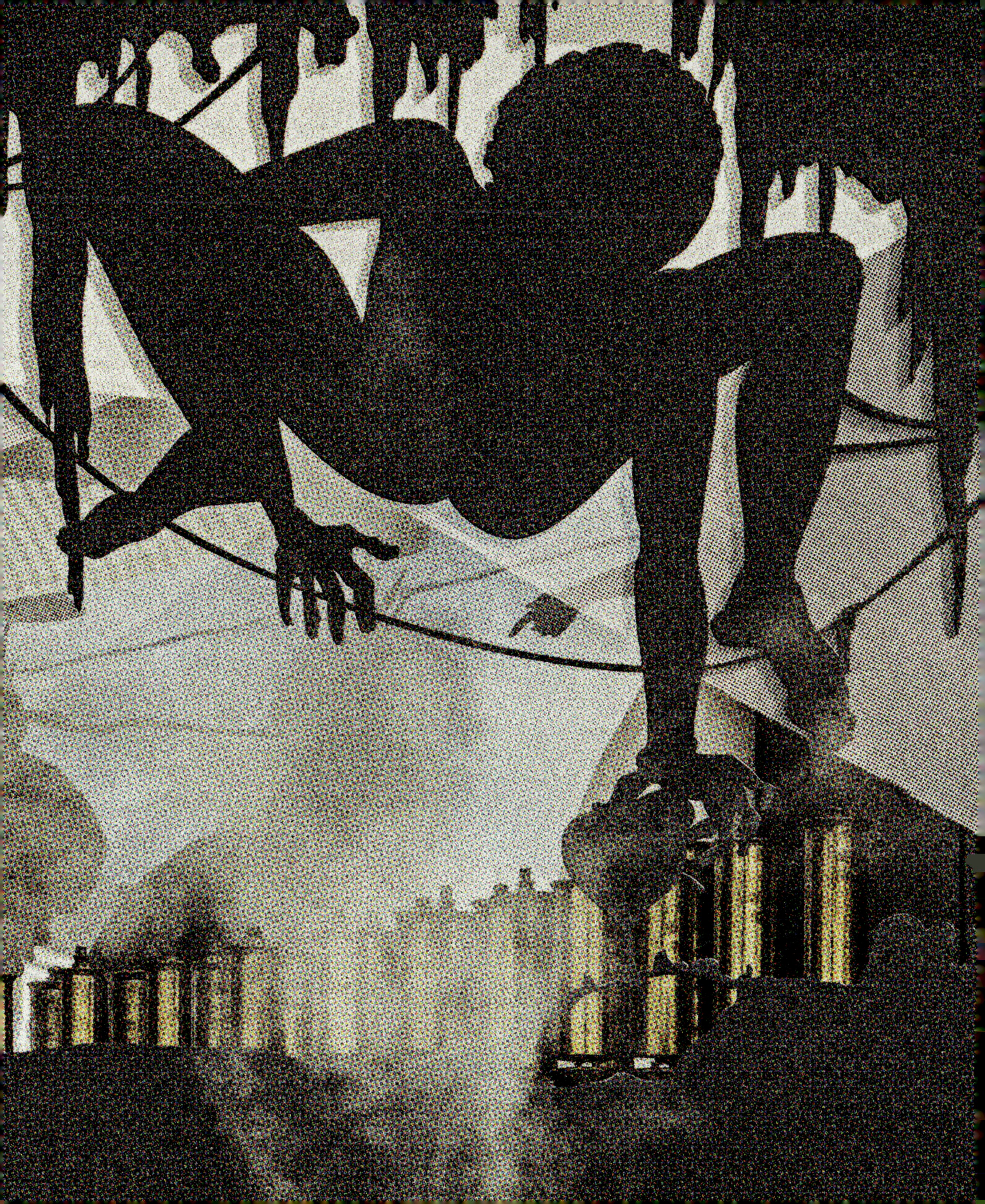

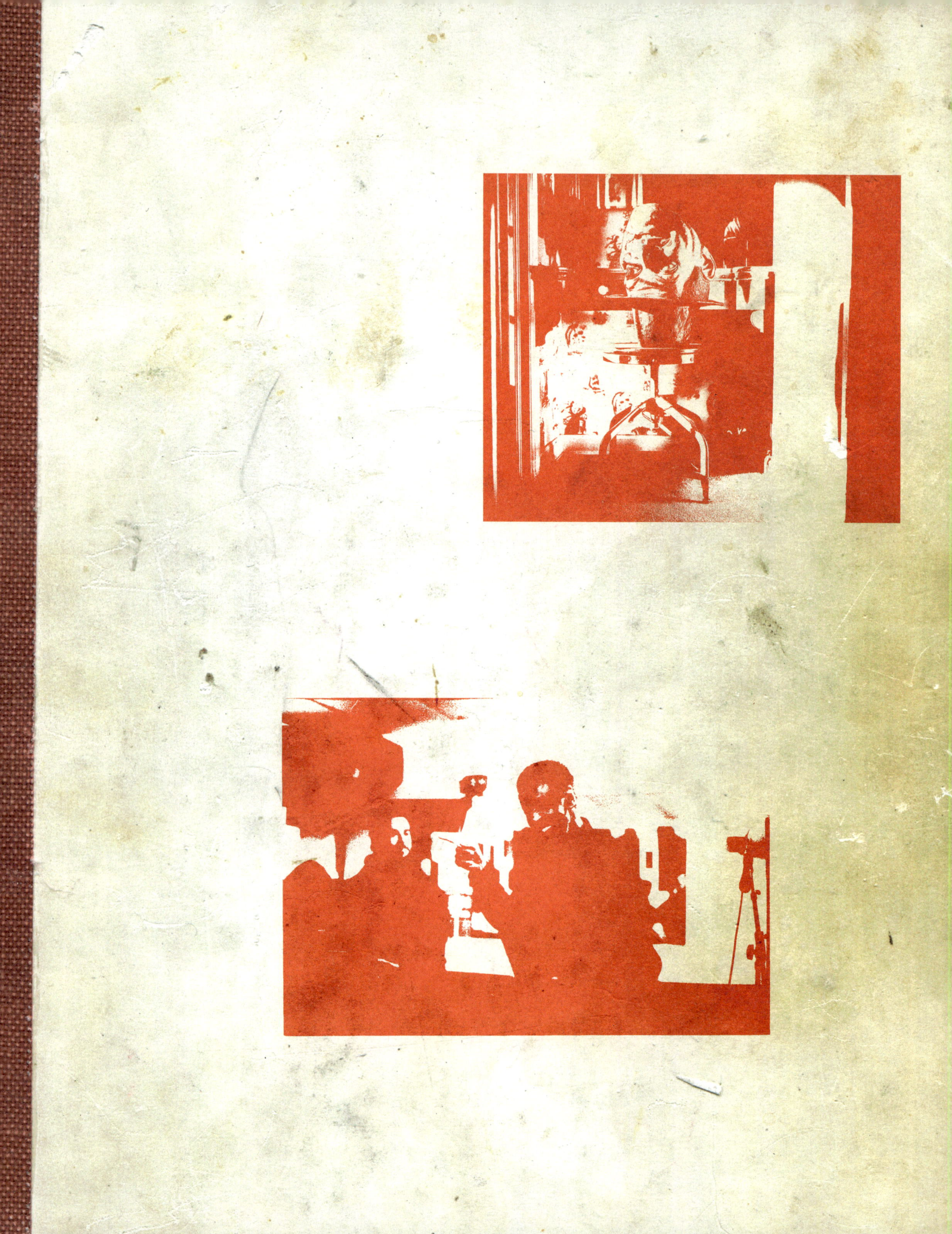

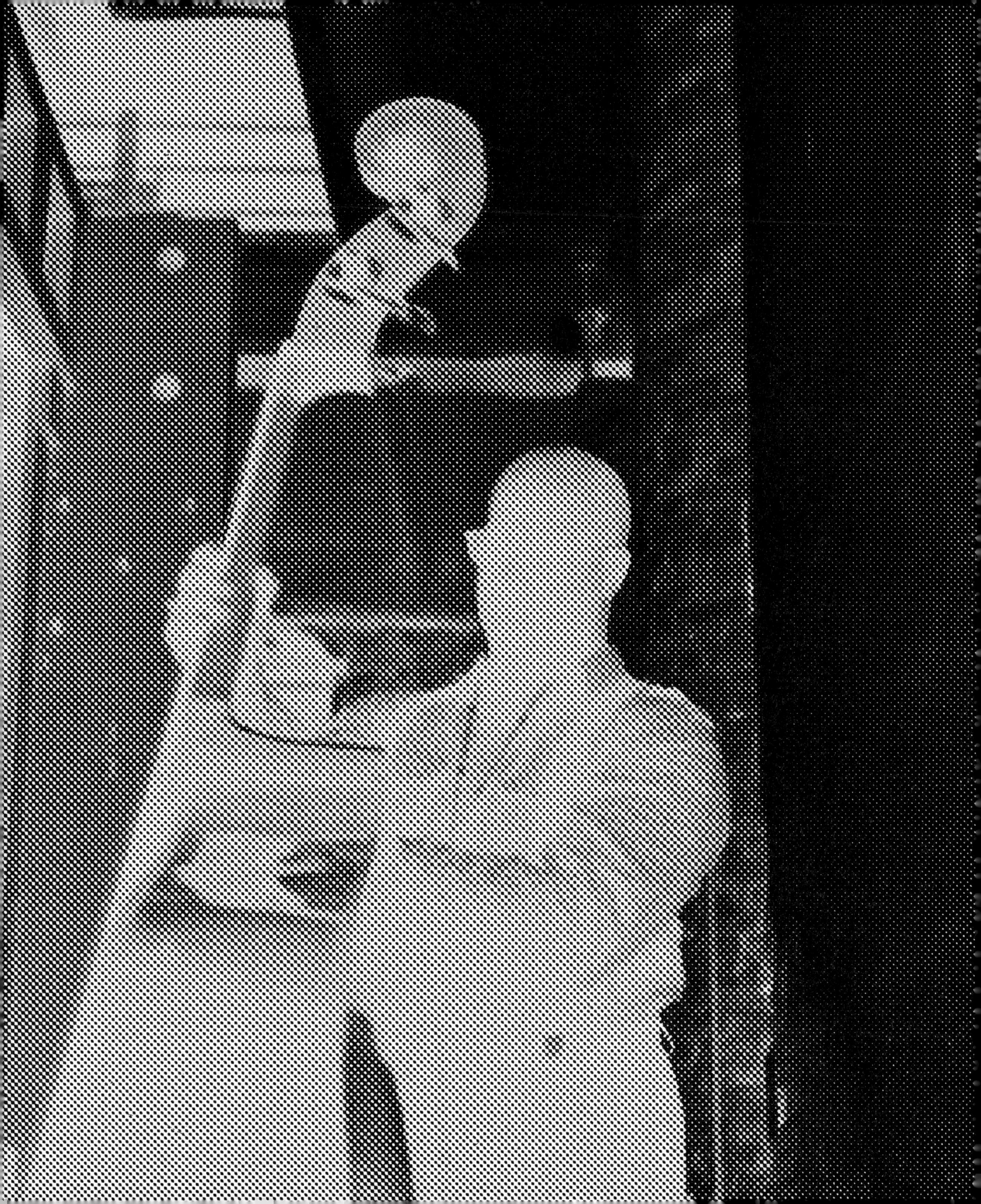

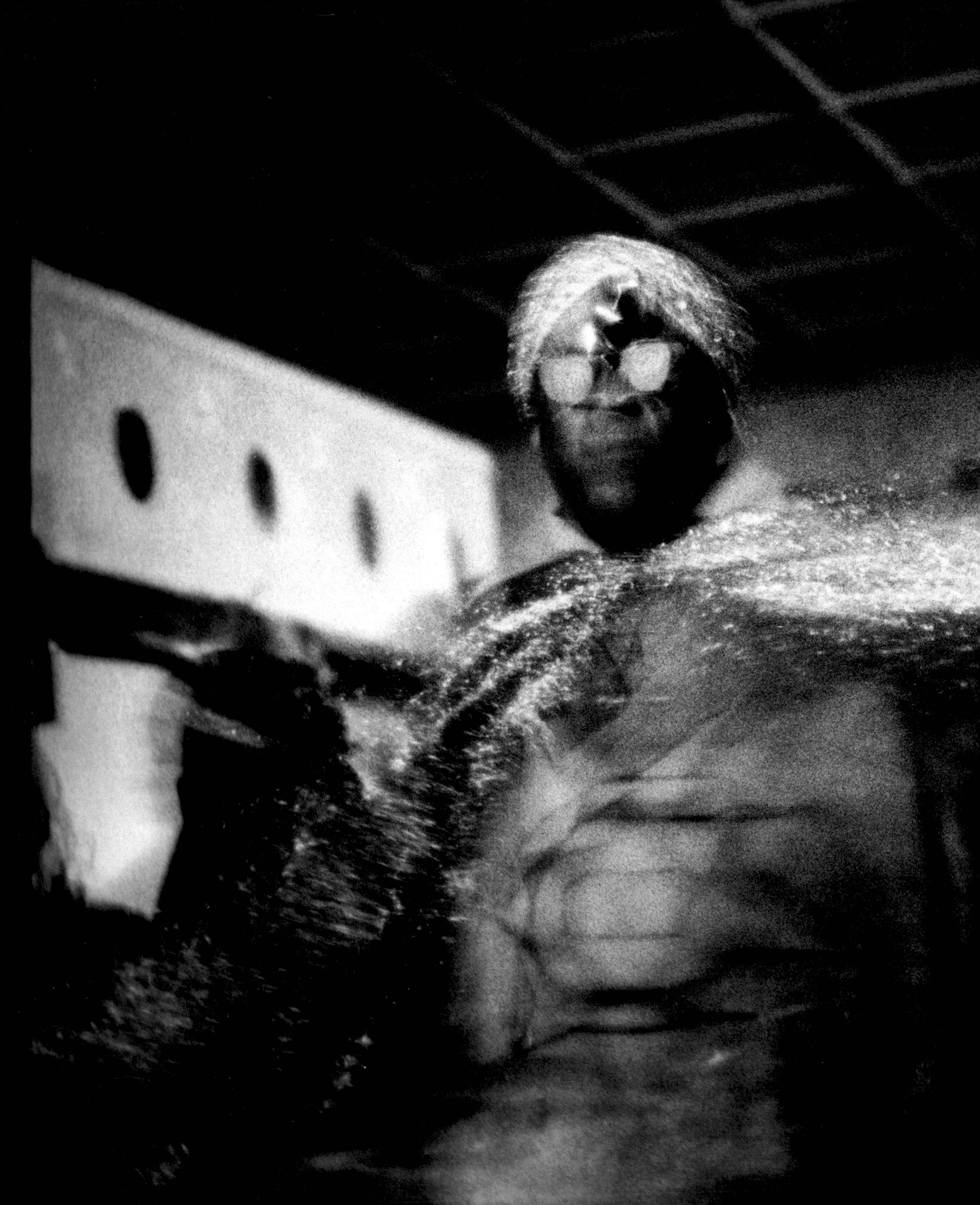

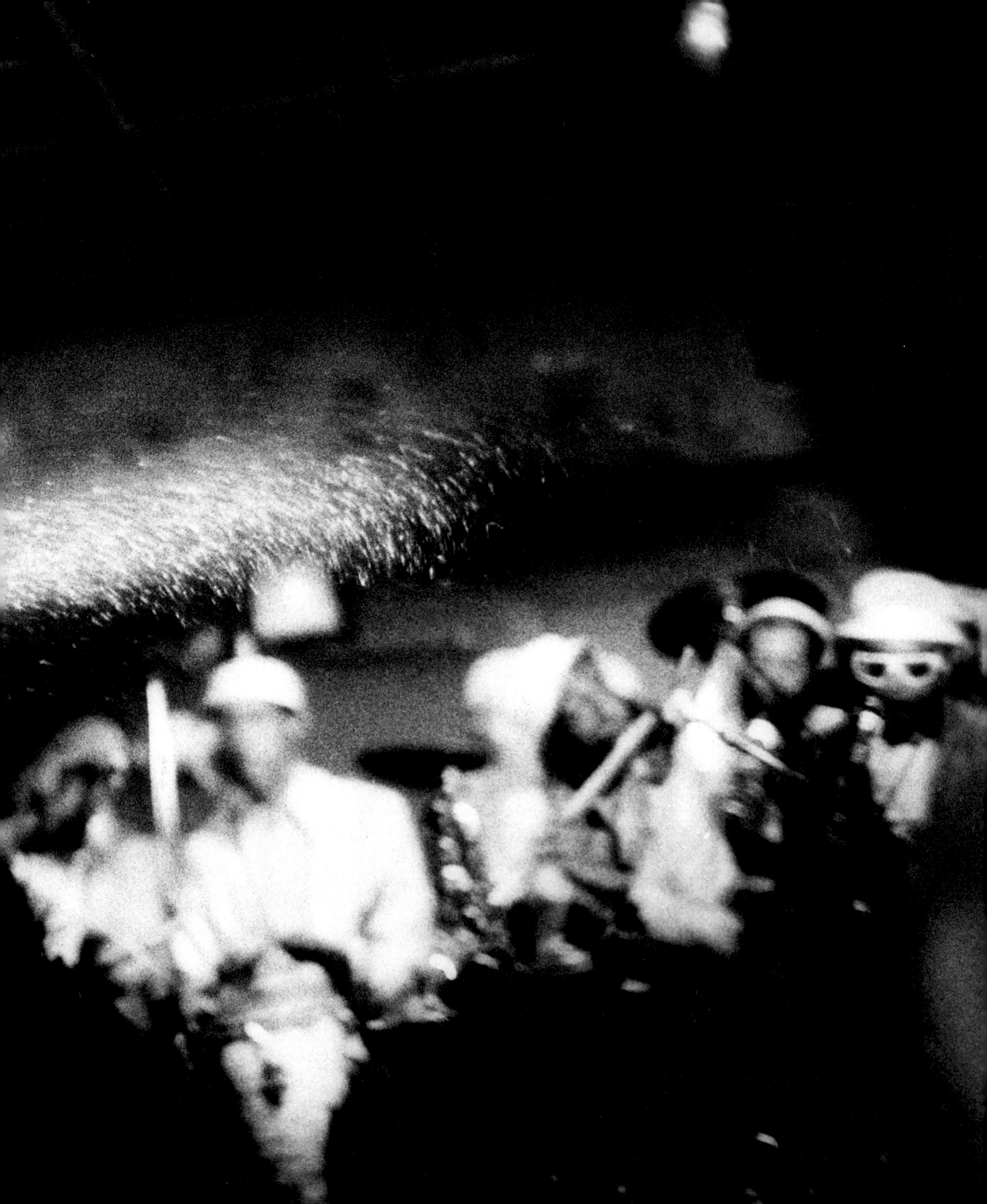

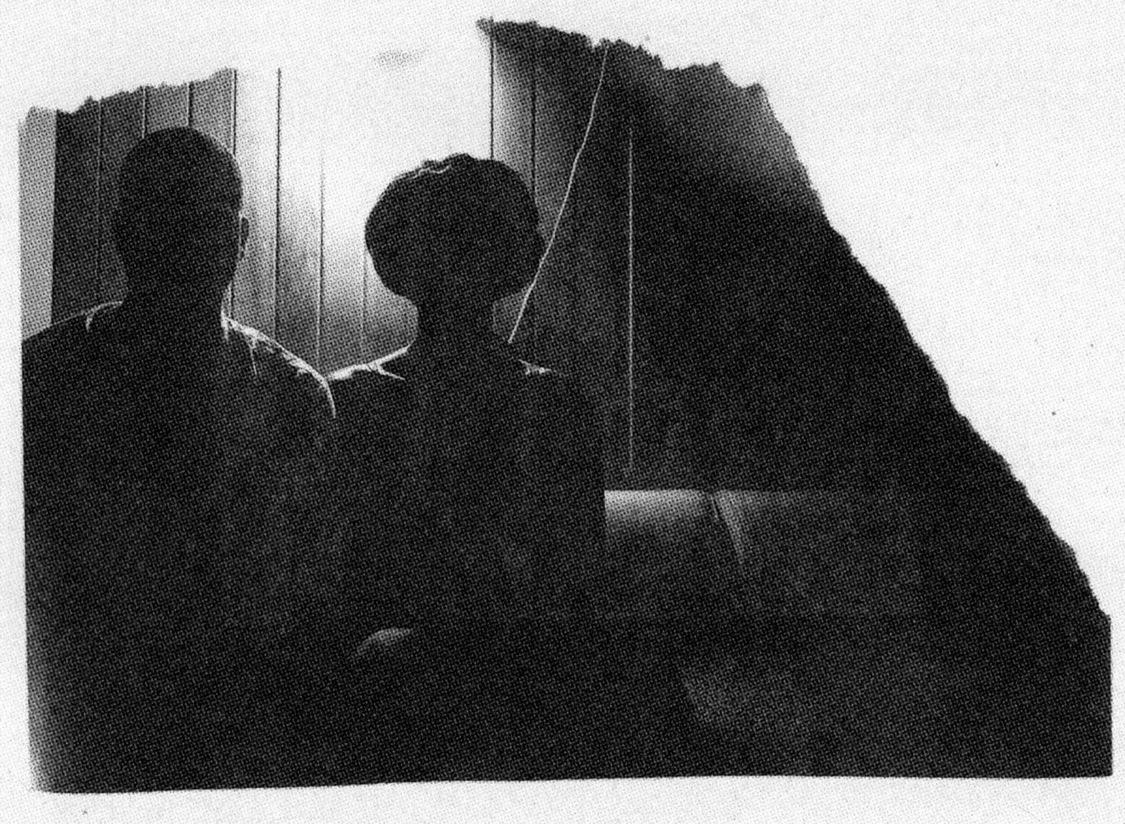

50–51: MacGregor Elementary school stage, Houston, 2015

52–53: Drum Set at New England Conservatory, 2015; Henry Threadgill at Judson Church, 2014

54–55: Adrian Piper Happy New Year card, 2005; Adrian Piper and Jason Moran at her home in Cape Cod, 2004

56–57: Editing notes for the album *Artist in Residence*, 2006; Sony Minidisc, unofficial 4th member of the Bandwagon

58–59: Red telephone from the performance *Milestone*, 2005

60–61: Score for *LIVE: TIME*, about the quilts/quilters of Gee's Bend, Alabama, 2008; Combine of manuscript paper and a transparency quilts by Mary Lee Bendolph, 2007

62–63: *Reanimation* rehearsal with Joan Jonas at the Louvre Theater, 2014; Manuscript paper

64–65: Kara Walker as "Karaoke Walkrrr" in her piece *Improvisation with Mutually Assured Destruction featuring Jason Moran & The Bandwagon*, during performance of *BLEED* at the Whitney Biennial, New York, 2012

66–67: The Pantheon, Rome, 2017

68–69: Piano with *Selma* projection, Kamp Kippy, Maine, 2014

70–71: Horace Grigsby in *HOLD UP*, Houston, 2015; Jazz pegboard

72–73: Plane ticket for Venice Biennale opening; Lights in theater in Copenhagen

74–75: Nasheet Waits at *Moods* in Zürich, 2015; Piano roll for "Darktown Strutters Ball" on red carpet

76–77: *LOOP* Magazine, Issue No. 1, with *Atomic Count Basie* image on cover, 2016; *She Cares–Slang*, music box on stove valve, 2016; Score for *Slang*, 2011

78–79: *WIND* stage manager's desk, London, 2016

80–81: *She Cares–Hill*, music box on hat stand, 2016; Piano opening, American Academy in Rome, 2017

82–83: Drum set, New England Conservatory, 2015

84–85: Jason Moran studio, New York, 2016

86–87: *LOOP* Magazine, Issue No. 2, with cover by Charles Lloyd, 2018; Jason Moran in Fats Waller mask, 2015

88–89: Piano portrait, New York, 2016; Julie Mehretu, *MASS (HOWL, eon)* recording (Harlem), 2017; Player piano rolls (Rome), 2017; Detail of Kara Walker's The *Katastwof Karavan* calliope, New Orleans, 2018

90–91: Fats Waller mask portrait Los Angeles, 2014; Henry Threadgill rehearsal, 2014; Tarus Mateen behind *STAGED: Three Deuces*, Venice, 2015

92–93: Ming Smith, *Sun Ra space II, New York, NY*, 1978, gelatin silver print, 28 $\frac{3}{16}$ x 39 $\frac{7}{8}$ in. (71.6 cm x 101.3 cm)

94–95: Jason and Alicia Moran self-portrait in Maine (Kamp Kippy), 2014

OKWUI ENWEZOR

The corner: a limit space,   a zone of confinement,
the metaphorical non-place from which black subjectivity
must seek its   liberation.

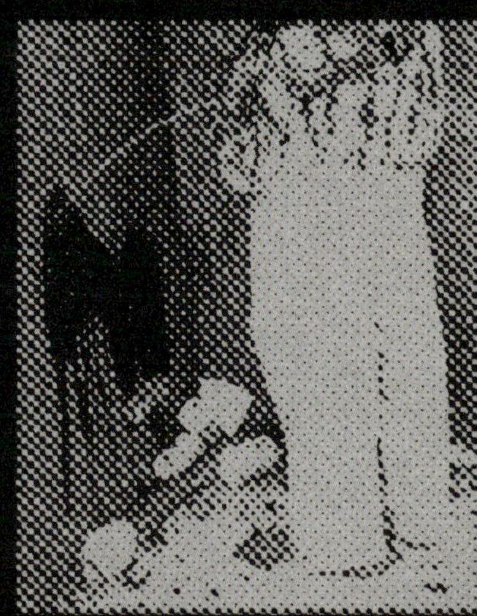

IMAGINATION

CORNERS, FIELDS, PORTALS: HAUNTED SPACES OF THE BLACK

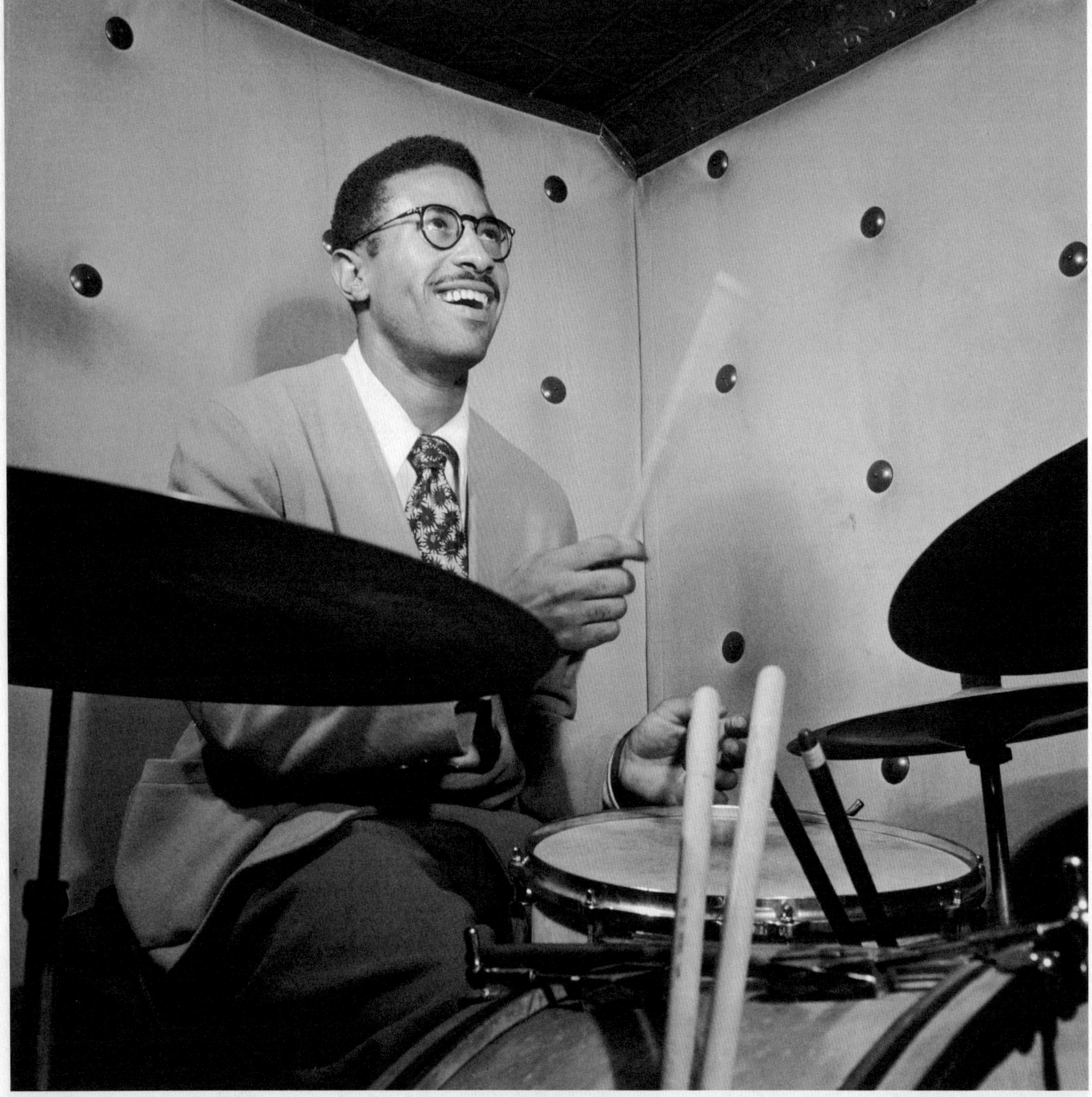

OKWUI ENWEZOR

Blackness—the extended movement of a specific upheaval, an ongoing irruption that anarranges every line—is a strain that pressures the assumption of the equivalence of personhood and subjectivity.[1]

META-SPACES

From early field songs sung by slaves to Negro spirituals, from blues to gospel, ragtime to jazz, R&B to soul, funk to hip-hop, the history of African American music in the United States, and its relationship to structures of subjection and the battle for social emancipation, is part of the unique encounter between white power and black bodies. Out of that encounter emerged a canon of musical forms that has been fundamental for modern and contemporary music. It is for this reason that Jason Moran's exhibition at the Walker Art Center opened a process of thinking in which to explore spatial practices that accompany the creation of music. The serendipitous arrival at my desk of Roscoe Mitchell's elegiac *Bells for the South Side* (ECM, 2017) as I was beginning to write this essay further accentuated the relationship between spatiality and music. In the last decade Moran has insistently inserted his work as a composer and pianist into the reciprocal and cross-disciplinary rubric of contemporary art without succumbing to the pretentious contrivances of "art music." Moran's collaborations with artists have yielded cross-genre productions in film, video, and live, participatory performances that are no less serious than those made within the conventional jazz music economy.

Mitchell's mournful, soulful, tinkling, suspiring, hissing, incantatory, propulsive, and orchestratedly discordant walls of sound, created with four rotating trios of musicians brought together in a concert at the Museum of Contemporary Art Chicago, disclose how the music-event is not only structured by time but also fills spaces to the degree that sound becomes physical, three-dimensional—an inhabited environment. Each of the rotating trios of Mitchell's double CD was shaped around compositions that followed a pattern of notations, on the one hand, and, on the other, produced capacious open forms that were not necessarily limited to improvisation. The opening piece, "Spatial Aspects of the Sound," contains barely audible, intermittent passages that continuously touch the edge of a vast oceanic silence. Listening to the recording—with its alternating swings of fulsomeness and sparseness—keens the ears to the anticipatory moment when silence is as much a sound as a space of potentiality. One is made aware of this anticipatory potential as the harmonic progression of chords shifts from destructured spatiality to the creation of social space. Perhaps this is what Mitchell was alluding to in the title of this first piece, a wordless, shimmering fugue with an expansive environment open to the elements of nature and culture.

As I listened to *Bells for the South Side*, ideas of liminality and spatial constraint, and the emancipatory possibilities of the sonic, stimulated the sense of an open field, creating all sorts of meta-spaces of discovery for how black experimental music articulates new kinds of locations for individual and collective freedoms. Such freedoms become even more manifest when you know that Mitchell was a founding member of the avant-garde collective Association for the Advancement of Creative Music (AACM). At the height of the civil rights and Black Power movements, the loose network of musicians, composers, and performers came together in Chicago around the avant-garde pianist and composer Muhal Richard Abrams to create music that was as compositionally complex and sophisticated as it was socially relevant. Mitchell was also one of the principal leaders of the Art Ensemble of Chicago, a group that grew out of the ethos of experimentation propagated by the AACM and whose motto was "Great Black Music: Ancient to the Future." This is

Adrian Piper, *Cornered*, 1988, video
installation: video (color, sound): table;
chairs; monitor; two framed birth certificates
for Adrian Piper's father, Daniel R. Piper;
lighting, dimensions variable

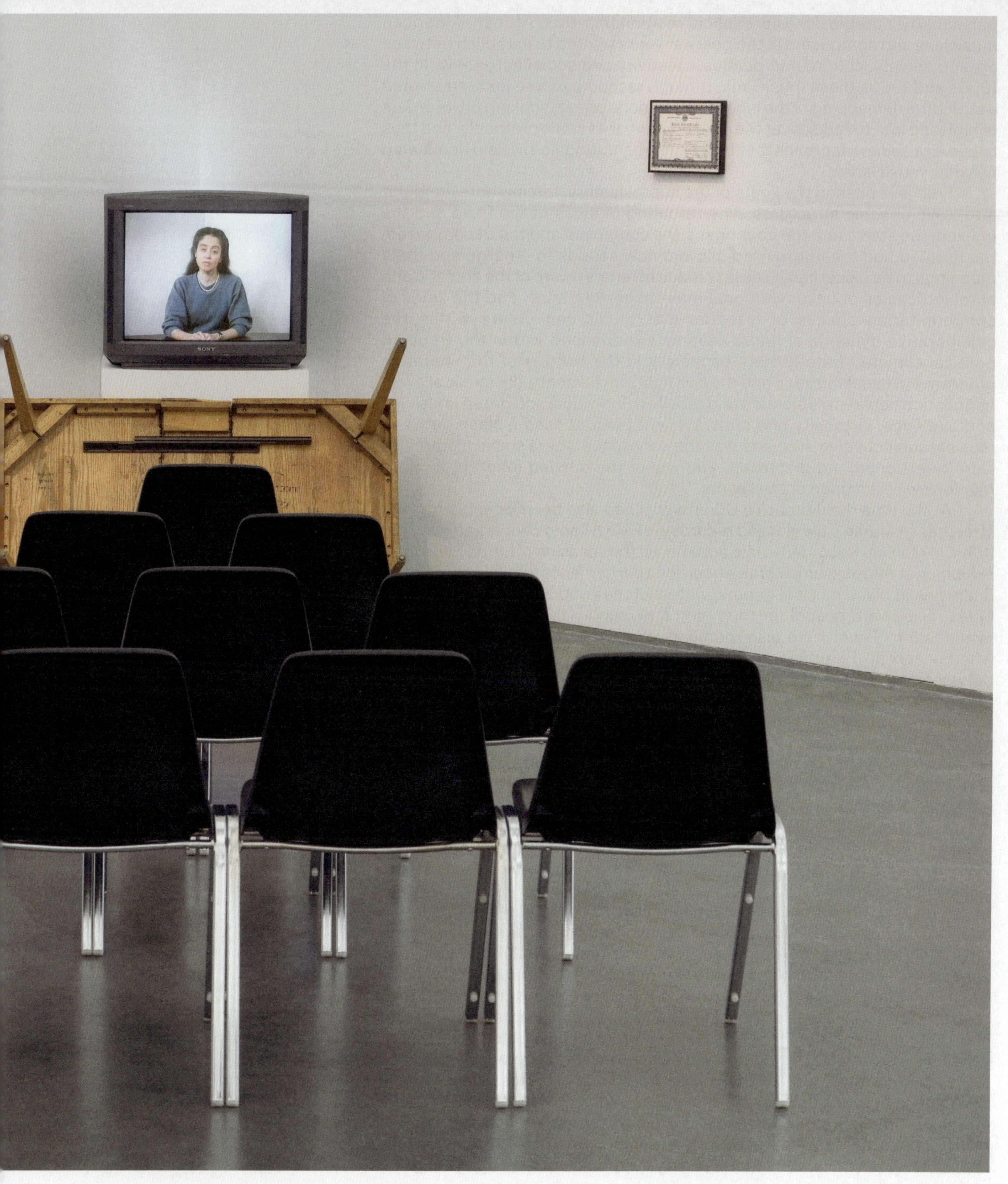

particularly notable for the explicit relationship that African American musicians and composers in the postwar years wanted to establish between art and society, culture and politics, creativity and social autonomy. In the 1950s and 1960s these musicians, through recourse to free jazz, attempted a structural demapping of the inherited traditions of jazz, shaking up its orders of high and low, to rediscover the aleatory root of its sonic protocols, and thus to carve out a new approach for black experimental music in a field dominated by white musicians.

Free jazz pushed the limits of the improvisatory, forcing notes to burst into wails of sonic structures. The rerouting of ideas of the fixed and the unfixed, the stable and the contingent, the composed and the decomposed, the notated and the improvised allowed new sounds to emerge and fresh meanings to be discerned. Free jazz made listeners aware of the somatic and aural intricacies of unconventional musical performance, and the kinds of communitarian spaces of freedom that music can create within the collaborative dynamic of improvisation. Experienced within the troubled political climate of the 1960s—especially in the context of the liberation processes of decolonization and the civil rights movement—the music allowed negotiation between subjection and rebellion, individual and group, musician and audience, virtuosity and craft. While it presupposed a clash between musical subjectivities, free jazz was the very space where social hierarchies were questioned and disturbed, and where the tension inherent in class relations was laid open at the seams.

At the time that Mitchell's CD arrived, I had also been listening for long stretches to Moran's unreleased recording of a 2013 solo concert at Haus der Kunst in Munich. Recorded in late autumn, on the occasion of Lorna Simpson's exhibition at the museum, Moran's hour-long performance felt like a tour across the plains of black musical genres, with stretches populated by melancholic blues mixed with gospel, or thumping funk sandwiched between hip-hop syncopation. There were also moments of syncretism in Moran's playing, whether mixing European new music with garrulous hard bop or shifting between the twelve-bar blues and Viennese twelve-tone serialism. For Simpson's *Chess* (2013), a meditative, three-channel, black-and-white video projected onto parallel walls, he responded to her use of mirroring and to mirroring in music, especially in the compositions and performance of maverick pianist Cecil Taylor. The percussive, jangling, growling, and clattering sounds that emanated from Moran's object-filled piano cavity framed and deframed passages of tension and release, with subtle glissando changes that enabled him to create spatial analogies. What one hears are improvisational chord and pitch changes that require foreknowledge of how the instrument obeys and distorts such effects and awareness of how the audience experiences them with a sense of immediacy.

Similarly, I had begun listening seriously to the young composer and multi-instrumentalist Tyshawn Sorey's committed and unclassifiable work. I repeatedly returned to Sorey's album *That/Not* (Firehouse 12 Records, 2007), especially the extended piano piece "Permutations for Solo Piano" and the capacious "Seven Pieces for Trombone Quartet," two compositions that extend spatiality to a vanishing point. Both Moran and Sorey, born five years apart (1975 and 1980, respectively) are great shape-shifters within contemporary jazz, insofar as black musical traditions and new music are concerned. That Sorey is also featured in *Bells for the South Side* made the cross-generational communion between musical experimentation and improvisation all the more intriguing. Mitchell's famous percussion cage, an installation-like cube of mallet-driven percussion instruments, which Sorey played, is especially apposite for the sensorial, multidisciplinary experiments in sonic modeling that

   OKWUI ENWEZOR

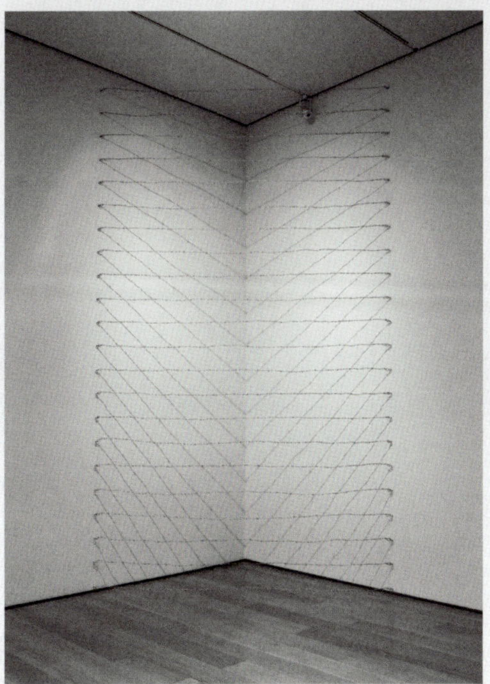

Melvin Edwards, *Corner for Ana,* 1970 (reconstructed 2015), barbed wire environmental sculpture, dimensions variable; installed as part of the exhibition *Melvin Edwards: Five Decades* at the Nasher Sculpture Center, Dallas

Moran, a leading figure of the new generation of composers and pianists, was realizing through his collaborations with a broad range of contemporary artists.

Over the years Moran has been steadily blurring the lines between genres while maintaining a rigorous focus as a composer and bandleader in musical performance. His expansion and collapse of genres has resulted in the *STAGED* sculptures, which were first presented at the 56th Venice Biennale. Part anthropological artifacts and part architectural objects, Moran's constructions are like spirit catchers, meta-spaces where African American emancipatory struggles for political autonomy, social wholeness, and creative rebellion are evoked and memorialized. The stages are not merely empty or vacated bandstands awaiting the infusion of sonic plenitude. As meta-spaces, they represent scripted fields of artistic will that mark and define black musical subjectivity, especially its trans-Atlantic worldliness. Each of the stages is analogical and affirmative, hovering in the gap between history and consciousness, artist and subject. So how is free space created within music beyond improvisation? What kind of creative agency does it hold and how is that agency deployed within the realpolitik of social deprivation?

STAGED AND CO

These questions were prompted by a moment in the image archive of postwar jazz culture in the United States. The backdrop of the depthless photograph from 1947 describes two planes of tufted beige satin meeting in a tight corner. Severely cropped, so as to almost obliterate the features of the room within which this spatial fragment exists, the image's foreground, crammed with a drum set, is dominated by a whirl of cymbals that float out of the edges of the picture. In the middle of this scene sits the drummer Max Roach, a bespectacled, ecstatic figure dressed in formal suit and tie—but with barely enough space to perform. This image, set in the legendary Three Deuces jazz club on West 52nd Street in Midtown Manhattan, portrays more than a performance venue. Its isolated sparseness evokes both the cultural economy of the midcentury jazz club and the notion that musicians, in order to escape the spatial limitations of such venues, had to play themselves out of the corner. The corner here is more than physical. It concerns an entire psychological and disciplinary structure, an apparatus of power and control that required different strategies of self-emancipation from the forces of production.

This photograph, with Roach at its center, furnished the spatial reference for *STAGED: Three Deuces* (2015). In a note on the project, Moran suggestively describes the relationship of the performer to the corner in which he is confined in terms of the subjection of the body within the field of production, and thus to the site of its appropriation by capital and disciplinary power.[2] This was dialectically extended to the cycle of "work songs," composed to be performed live during the run of the Biennale. While he did not explicitly relate the compositions to the emancipatory as such, the references to social diminution and resistance in the work songs evoked concretely the dilemma of the incarcerated body within the context of labor and production:

> The work songs I'll investigate in *STAGED* map the lyrics and the tempos of work songs sung in prisons, fields, houses. In a sampling of work songs sung in a Louisiana prison (Angola), the tempos range from fifty-seven to 190 beats per minute. The subjects of the songs range from a woman's bangs to the power of a plowing mule. The tempos fluctuate from beat to beat. The repetition of the rhythm (with a hammer, foot stomp, an axe) is as much a way of marking the time, as it is a way of masking it. The work songs untether the worker from the boss' clock by making their own internal clock, which functions on a different time scale. Mapping these

work songs both conceptually and emotionally is the task. Jason Moran and the Bandwagon will perform newer work songs composed within the past ten years that focus on the instrumental side of work songs. We will focus on the melodic content embedded in these work songs to expose the mantras that have assisted workers everywhere. The stage is a portal. The field is a portal.[3]

The spatial rubric of the two sculptures presented in the Biennale—*STAGED: Savoy Ballroom I* and *STAGED: Three Deuces*—involved the construction of two architectural fragments, each re-creating two historical performance stages linked to the history of black dance music and jazz in New York from the 1920s to the 1940s. *Savoy* was modeled on the cavernous stage of the renowned, block-long Savoy Ballroom on Lenox Avenue in Harlem, between West 140th and 141st Streets. (The legendary Cotton Club was just one block away on Lenox and 142nd Street.) The Savoy, which opened in 1926, was an attempt to create a social space where African American audiences could meet for entertainment and mass dancing Uptown. The second stage, the cramped corner of the intimate Three Deuces jazz club—a cube of no more than nine feet per side—focuses purely on the music and the kinds of spaces in which musicians played.

The corner can be understood as a disciplinary apparatus, a limit space, a zone of confinement. In the Three Deuces picture, we witness Roach pressed into this liminal zone. He must thus liberate himself from it. For the purposes of this essay, therefore, it would be constructive to explore the resonance that this spatial-cum-disciplinary device has acquired in artistic production by a host of contemporary artists. While the corner has been used to frame sculptural investigations in Richard Serra's *Strike: To Roberta and Rudy* (1969–71); Robert Smithson's Non-Site sculpture *Red Sandstone Corner Piece* (1968); and Martin Kippenberger's *Martin, Into the Corner, You Should Be Ashamed of Yourself* (1988/92), I believe that the use of that frame has a different purchase in the work of African American artists.

The corner seen in the photograph of Roach at Three Deuces and Moran's elaboration of that image in *STAGED: Three Deuces* functions as a spatial non-place, conveying an entirely sinister effect on subjectivity in the way it limits, controls, and traps the black body. The idea of playing out of the corner recalls the way a trapped boxer, cut off from access to the middle of the ring, must fight in order to gain equal footing within the arena of combat. Adrian Piper's installation *Cornered* (1988) makes this zone actual. With the shift from the noun (corner) to the adjective (cornered), she forms a barricade around the dialectic of defensiveness and hostility rather than a rectilinear frame within which to organize the operations of Post-Minimalist sculpture. The sculptural intentions of Melvin Edwards's *Corner for Ana* (1970) are not dissimilar from those of Serra and Smithson. However, Edwards's work, a curtain of barbed wire joined at perpendicular angles and meeting at a vertical joint, exposes the opposing, conflictual elements of physical and psychological threat. The notion of aggression and disobedience inherent in Piper's and Edwards's reworkings of the spatial parameters of the corner is further probed by David Hammons's public urination performance, *Pissed Off* (1981), for which he received a police summons. *Pissed Off* can be read as both the desanctioning of public decorum and the illumination of policing tactics and their impingement on subjectivity. The performance, deliberately orchestrated to provoke legal sanction, can also be read as an act of public protest against practices of social repression. Jean-Michel Basquiat's painting *St. Joe Louis Surrounded by Snakes* (1982) utilizes the corner to frame the dilemma of the great boxer, trapped in the midst of various handlers to whom his laboring body has been subordinated. The corner then

Dawoud Bey, *David Hammons, Pissed Off*, 1981, resin-coated print, 10 x 8 in. (25.4 x 20.3 cm)

 OKWUI ENWEZOR

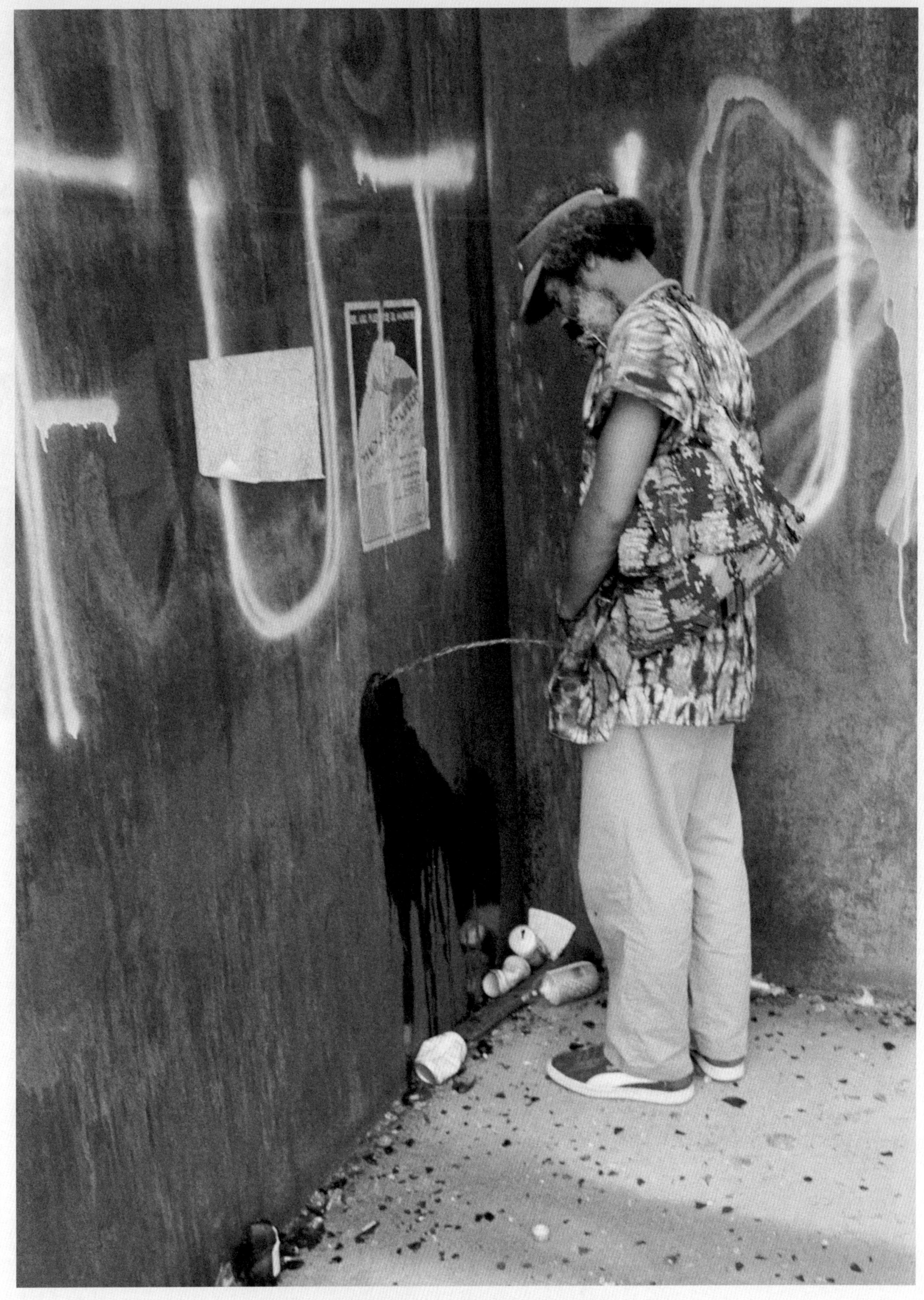

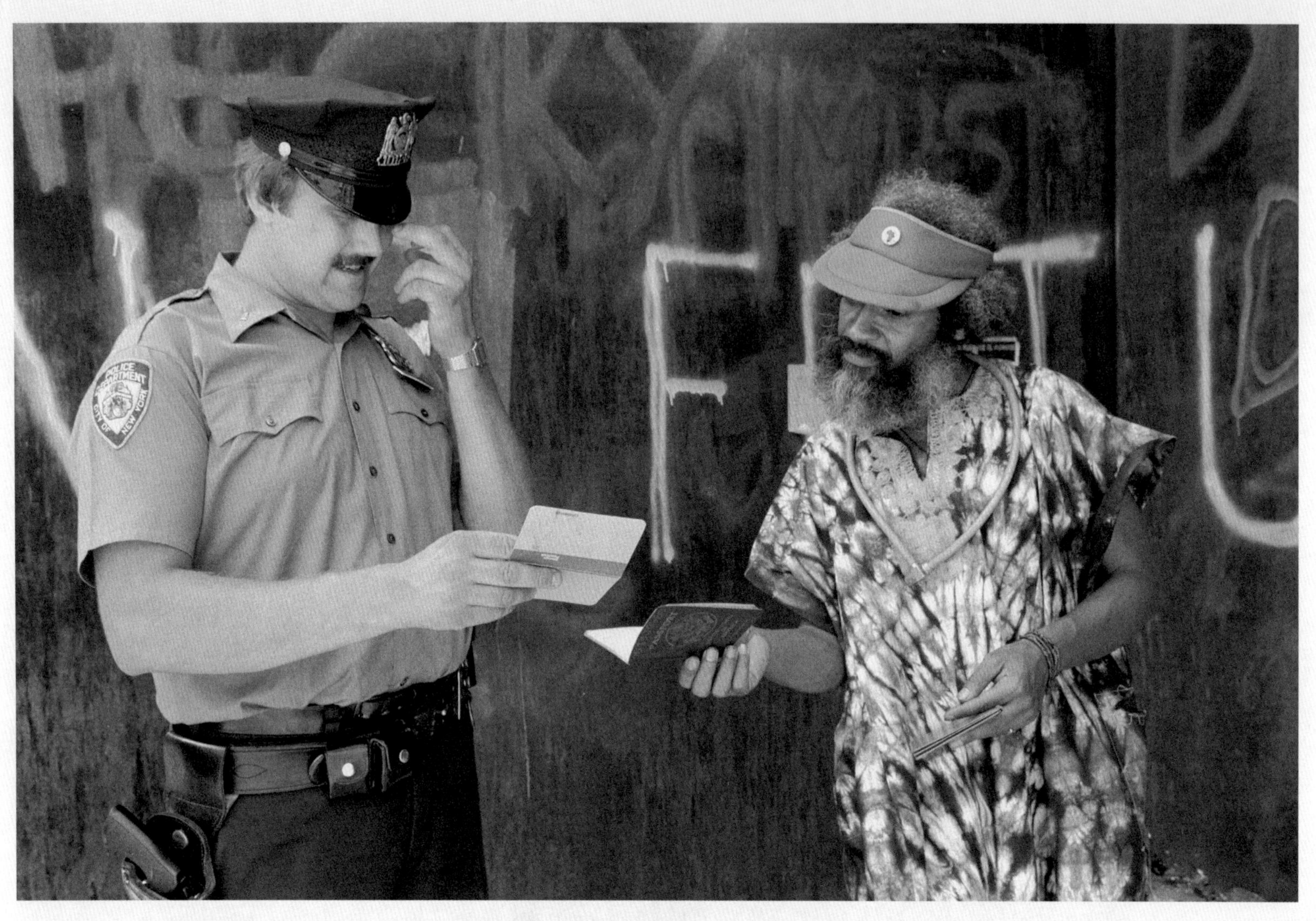

Dawoud Bey, *David Hammons, Pissed Off*, 1981,
resin-coated print, 8 x 10 in. (20.3 x 25.4 cm)

   OKWUI ENWEZOR

becomes the metaphorical non-place from which black subjectivity must seek its liberation.

OPEN FIELD

I have dwelled on some of these examples to articulate how the emancipatory ideals of radical black subjectivity have organized what I am calling Moran's spatial practices.[4] I therefore wish to shift from jazz in order to introduce a second signpost of spatiality related to funk. If jazz was the site for black creative affirmation within the canons of American culture, funk functioned as a space of intersubjective and ludic experience, where the dance floor became a democratic sphere, an open field of performative and participatory release. The group dynamics of funk music are located within black popular culture and are thus linked to culturally specific modes of subjective expression of pleasure and social autonomy. Piper explored these relationships in her piece *Funk Lessons* (1983), a series of collaborative performances staged with large and small groups. In her essay "Notes on Funk I" (1985), Piper articulates the social impetus of the music:

> Funk constitutes a language of interpersonal communication and collective self-expression that has its origins in African tribal music and dance and is the result of the increasing interest of contemporary black musicians and the populace in those sources elicited by the civil rights movement of the 1960s and early 1970s (African tribal drumming by slaves was banned in the United States in the nineteenth century, so it makes sense to describe this increasing interest as a "rediscovery").[5]

In his note on *STAGED*, Moran concludes "the stage is a portal. The field is a portal." The statement delineates that the fields of music and performance mark beginnings, not endings, entry points not termini. Performative space can, therefore, be read in terms of the collapse of the fourth wall. The field as portal—as horizontal rather than vertical surface—thus supercedes its role as a strategy of reanimation, becoming a probing mechanism for the rediscovery of the trans-genre, intersubjective, and collective experience. Moran's observation follows the expansion of performance, the choreographic, and the theatrical into contemporary art spaces. Dance, in particular, is making a resurgence inside the white cube and the museum. Its programs of movement and liveness are organized in the interplay between horizontality and verticality. In other words, they engage the sculptural spaces asserted by the Cartesian rationality of Minimalist sculpture.

Contemporary artists, from Tino Sehgal to Maria Hassabi, from Alexandra Bachzetsis to Anne Imhof, are exploiting the exhibition space to open up the social space of the museum. Yet paradoxically, the exciting proposals of these artists remain stubbornly set in the foreclosed separation between the performer and the audience. In some ways, there is something that is mercilessly middle class and middlebrow about these performative and theatrical incursions into the exhibition space and the way they are set within the decorous environment of Western cultural canons. Hardly, if ever possible, does one glean a sense of the fact that these artists are operating within a transcultural and transnational public sphere.

Piper, who took dance—in its ecstatic, dehierarchized mode of collective participation in her *Funk Lessons* performances—into the museum and exhibition space, makes a point when she writes that dance as a medium of expression has been largely inaccessible to white culture, in part because of its different social role:

> Whereas social dance in white culture is often viewed in terms of achievement, social grace or competence, or spectator-oriented entertainment, it is a collective and participatory means of self-transcendence and social union in black culture along many dimensions, and so is often much more fully

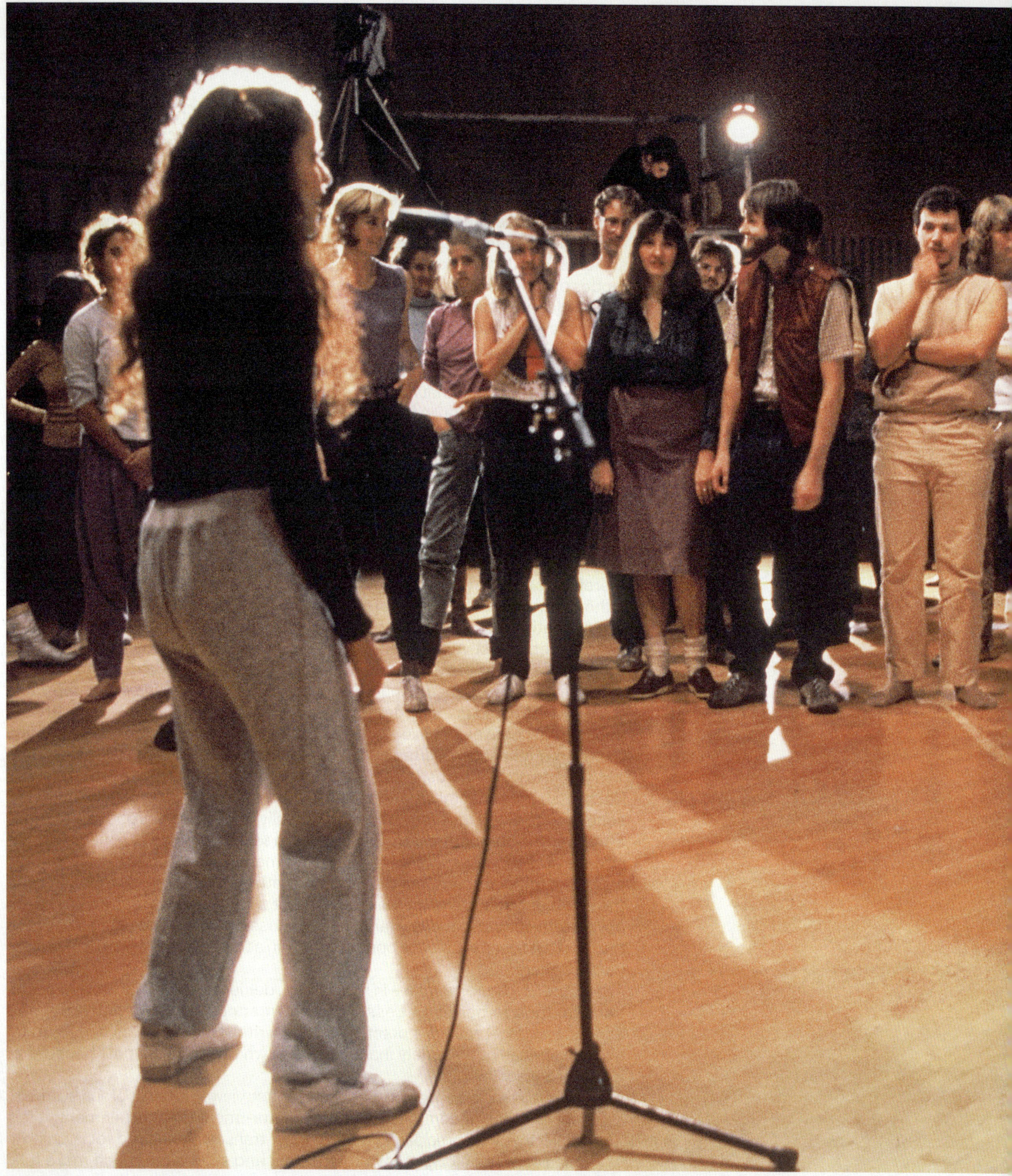

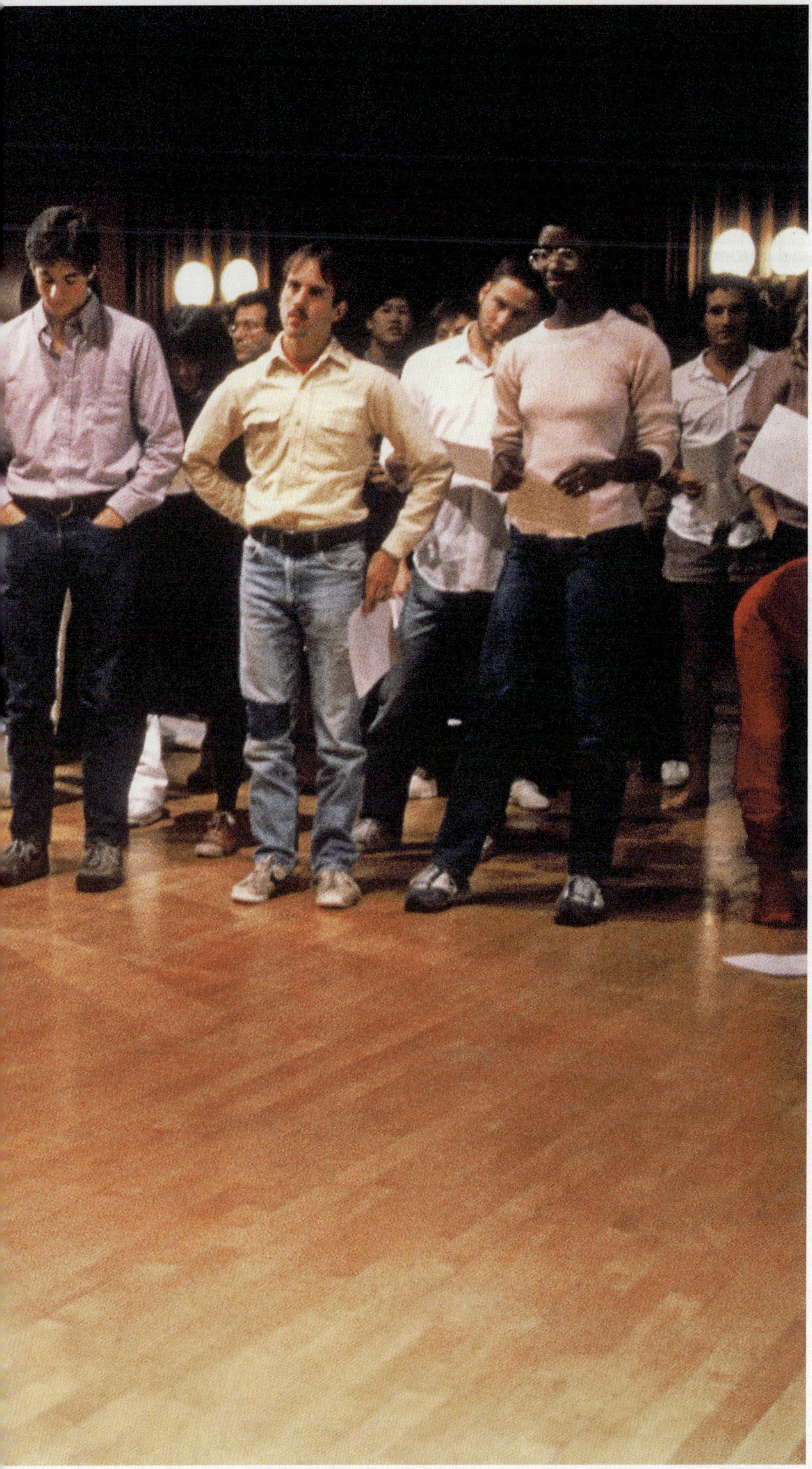

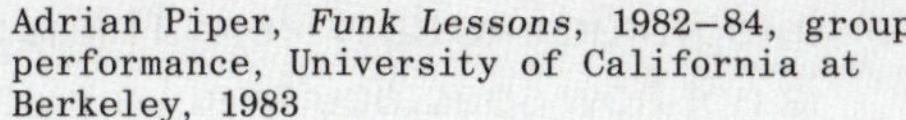

Adrian Piper, *Funk Lessons*, 1982–84, group performance, University of California at Berkeley, 1983

integrated into daily life. ... This is particularly true in funk, where the concern is not how spectacular anyone looks but rather how completely everyone participates in collectively shared, enjoyable experience.[6]

If Piper's point is true, what then do we make of the classically trained Moran's practice? Certainly, the idioms of funk were available to him, as can be seen in his collaboration with Stan Douglas in the video *Luanda-Kinshasa* (2013). This reimagining of Miles Davis's funk-inflected and poorly received album *On the Corner* (Columbia Records, 1972) demonstrates that Moran's versatility reaches beyond his classical jazz background. Before coming to contemporary art, Moran had already established himself as a serious and lauded pianist in jazz, a genre that afforded him a deep insight into the group dynamics of improvisation and the call-and-response of the blues.

From jazz to blues to funk to hip-hop, Moran's musical range is unquestionably about more than mastery and has everything to do with his interest in crossing and extending genres. His current practice employs music as a spine for his collaborations with artists. With his roots in black musical traditions, and the quest for reimagining social and exhibition spaces, he blends music, art, performance, installation, and event scores into structures of mnemonic recovery. In these collaborations, he explores how different types of space shape the imagination and reflects on actively placing them next to one another in order to disrupt the division between the static nature of an exhibition and the dynamic temporality of liveness. In Moran's work within the exhibition space, the corner is annihilated. The stage and field now serve the double spatial function of the liberatory and the collective, continuously commingling with, intermittently dissolving into, and regularly haunting each other.

Jean-Michel Basquiat, *St. Joe Louis Surrounded by Snakes*, 1982, acrylic and pastel on canvas, 42 x 40 in. (106.7 x 101.6 cm)

OKWUI ENWEZOR

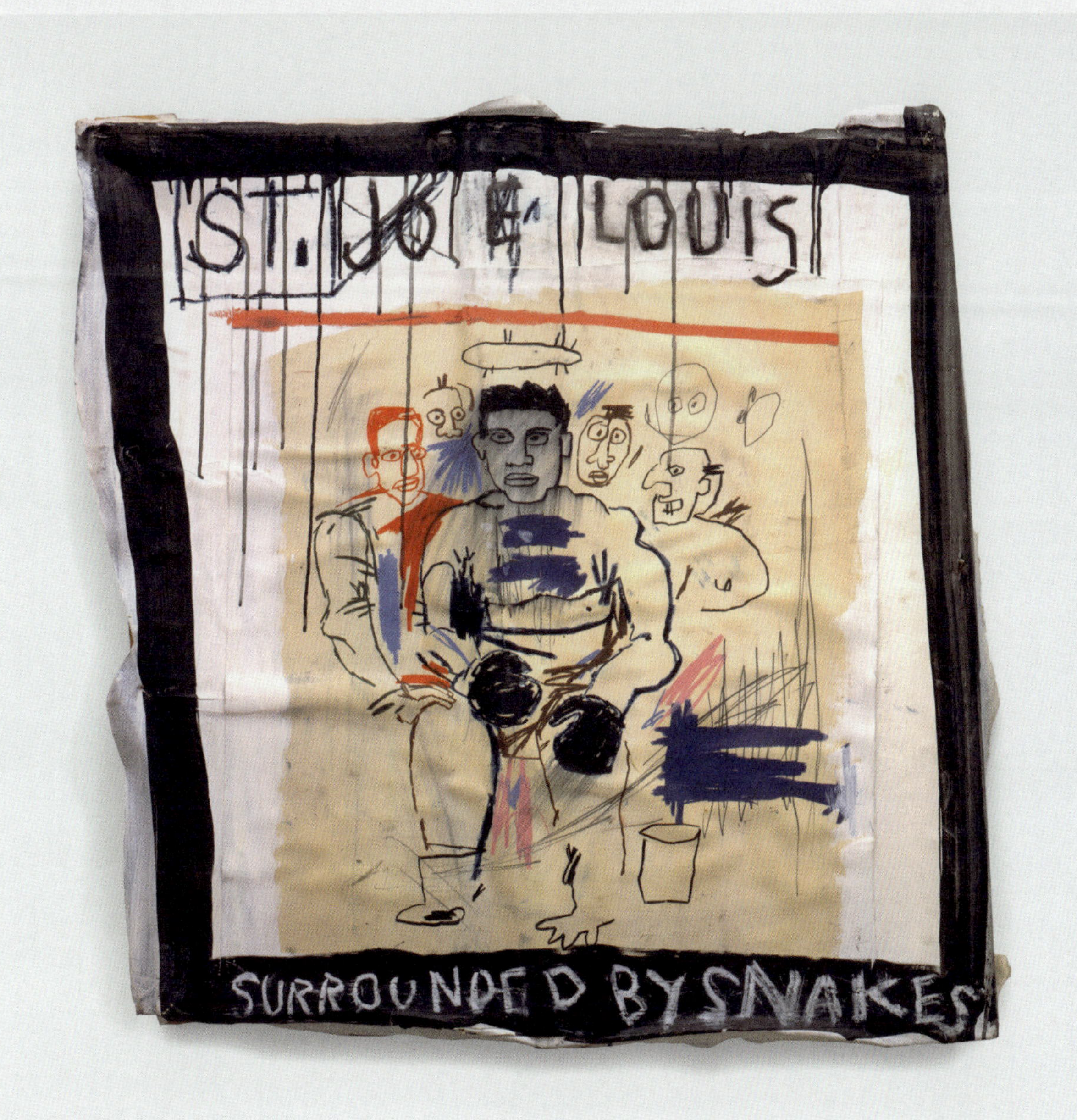

NOTES

1. Fred Moten, "Resistance of the Object: Aunt Hester's Scream" in *In the Break: The Aesthetics of the Black Radical Tradition* (Minneapolis: University of Minnesota Press, 2003), 1.
2. Jason Moran, unpublished note sent to the author.
3. Moran, unpublished note.
4. See Fred Moten, *In the Break: The Aesthetics of the Black Radical Tradition* (Minneapolis: University of Minnesota Press, 2003).
5. Adrian Piper, "Notes on Funk I," in *Out of Order, Out of Sight, Volume I: Selected Writings in Meta-Art 1968–1992* (Cambridge, MA: MIT Press, 1996), 195.
6. Piper, "Notes on Funk I," 195.

ROOTS/ROUTES

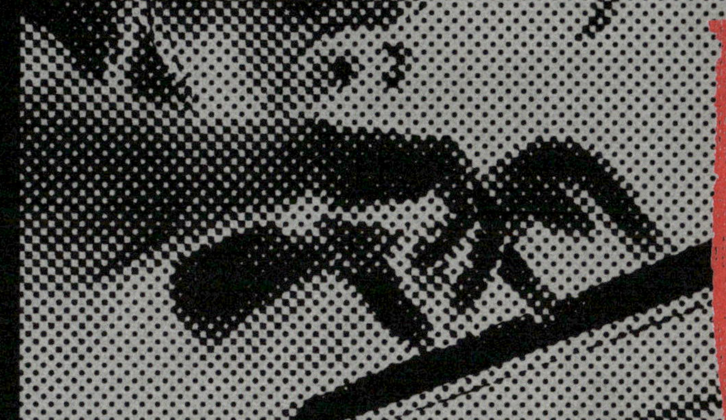

"WE TURNED THAT BASEMENT INTO A CITADEL"

GLENN LIGON

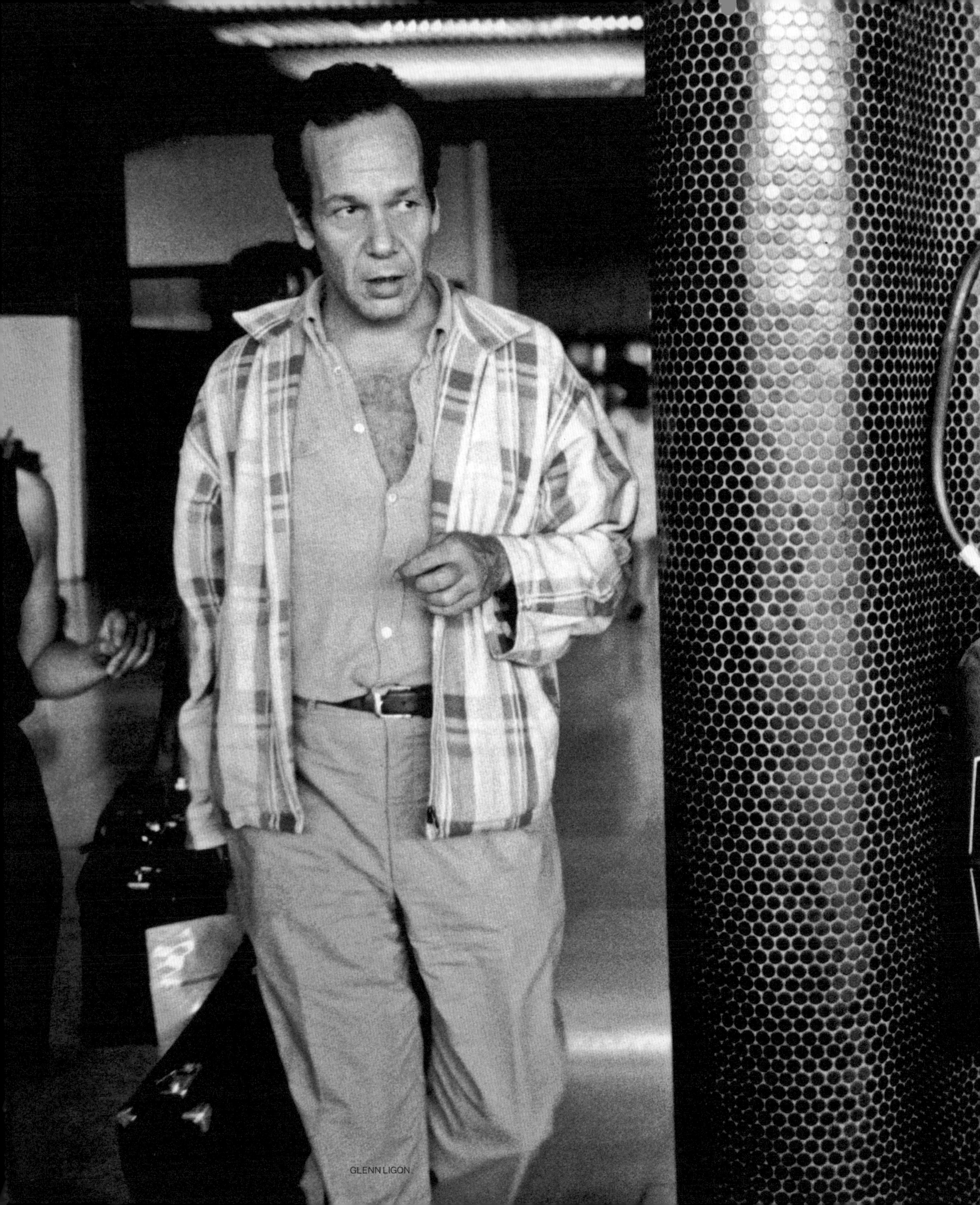
GLENN LIGON

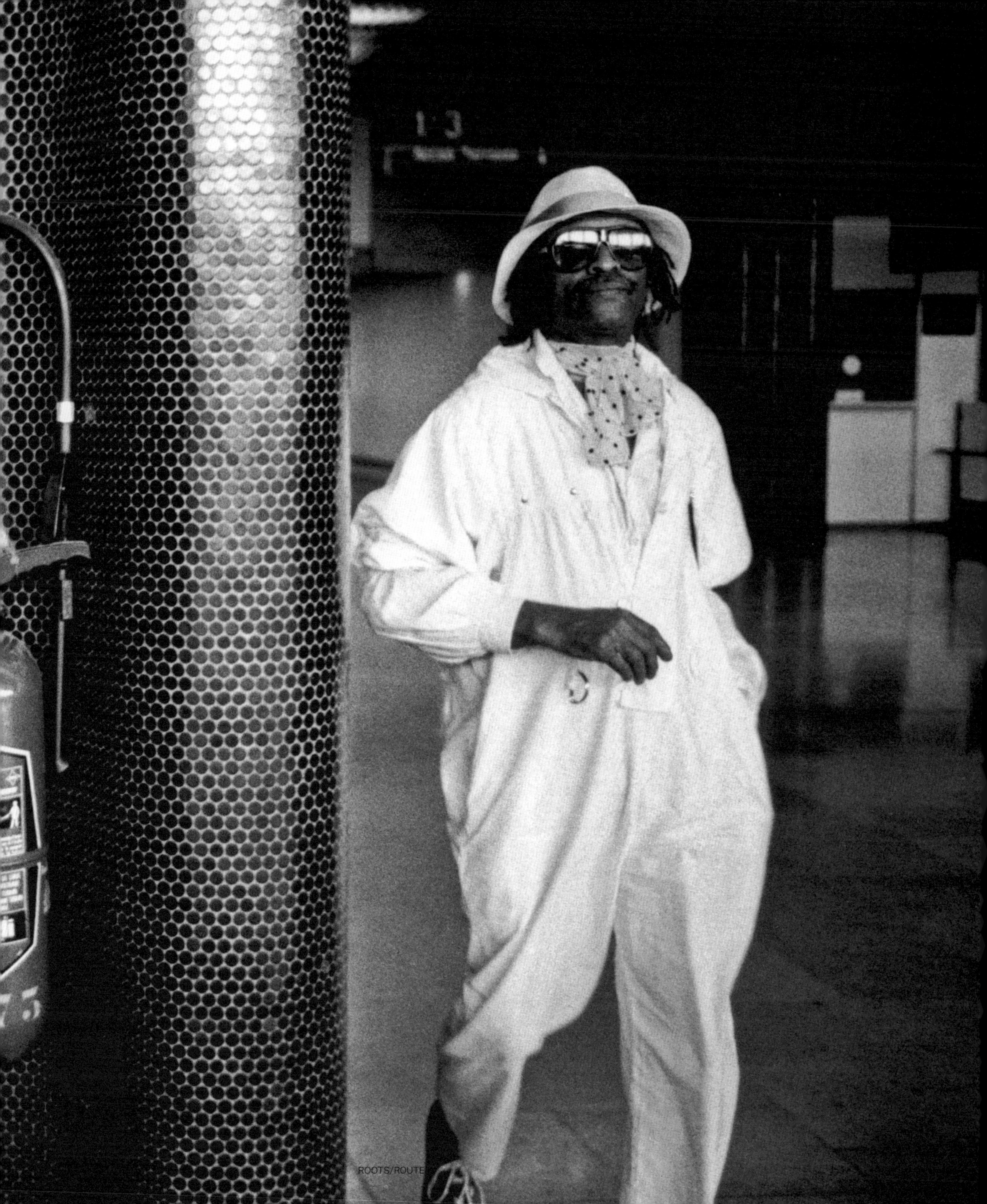

ROOTS/ROUTE

Oscar Dennard performing at the La Chat Qui
Pêche, Paris, March 9, 1959

Previous pages:
Steve Lacy and Cecil Taylor arriving at
Marseille-Marignane Airport before heading
to Vitrolles for the festival Jazz sous les
Platanes, July 1984

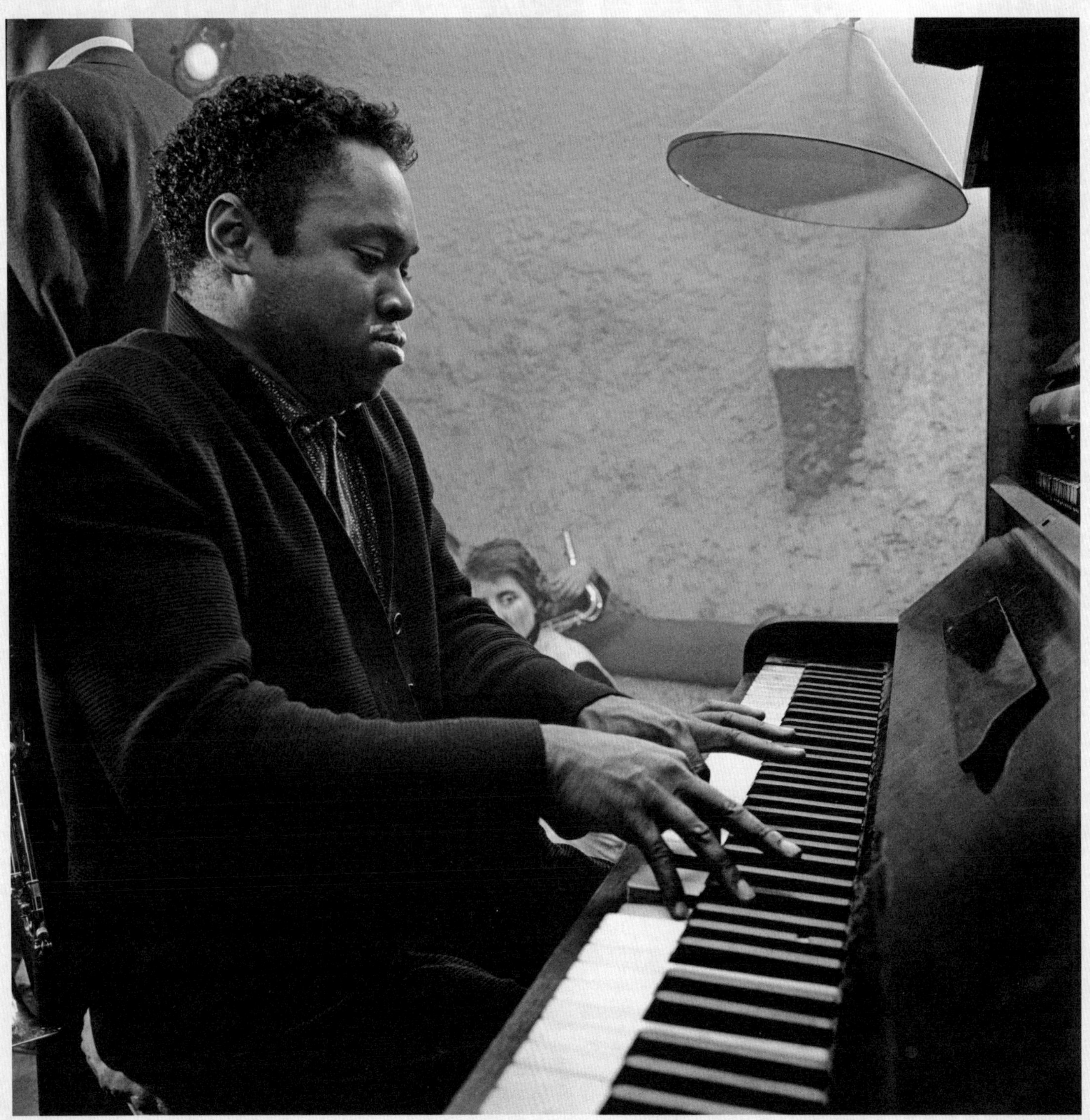

GLENN LIGON

TWELVE O'CLOCK TALES.

Cecil Taylor was in a mood. It was late August 2009, and the then-eighty-year-old pianist and his trio had just performed a ferocious set at the Highline Ballroom, a cavernous music venue in New York's Meatpacking District. I was backstage in the cramped green room with Jason Moran, who had been invited to meet him by the pianist's longtime promoter, Jill Newman. Taylor sat in a lounge chair, a dressing gown covering the white sweatpants and black mesh tank top he wore onstage. Cigarette in one hand, glass of champagne in the other, he looked Jason up and down. "People have been speaking about you," he purred. This was the prelude to a half hour monologue about musicians and singers he liked and musicians and singers he didn't like. At some point, I was introduced to Taylor, but he just gave me a cursory glance. This performance was for Jason. A friend described the experience of listening to Taylor as akin to "taking a warm bath," and, indeed, I became so immersed in the tone and flow of his words that I ceased to pay attention to their content. After our encounter, I e-mailed Jason to see what he recalled. His response bears quoting at length:

> A few things come to mind. Of course, Cecil is smoking in the room, in an establishment where you aren't allowed. He's sipping champagne. We are standing, he is sitting. His voice is the most original, craggy voice. It's like each word is crawling out of his throat. I remember we began talking about obscure pianists, and he mentioned a man called Oscar Dennard. I have a tape of Oscar that I listen to incessantly, because Oscar never really made any solo recordings. This tape was made in another musician's house and was played on the radio, and it shook my world. No one ever talks about this pianist. So, that evening, when Cecil said, "have you heard of a pianist Oscar Dennard?" I was like "HELL YES." We talked briefly about pianists who know much more than the others. … Cecil talking about Oscar reminded me that he likes to talk about what is real in the world: pianists with a lot of knowledge.

I can't recall how our conversation ended, as conversations with Cecil can go on forever. I mostly remember the smoke, the champagne, and the intense listening we were doing. After hearing Cecil play, your mind is already in another state, because he makes the most original sounds. To hear him speak also requires focused listening.

As our visit was winding up, Jason mentioned he had an upcoming gig at the Village Vanguard, a legendary jazz club in Greenwich Village where John Coltrane, Charles Mingus, Thelonious Monk, and Miles Davis had all played. Although Taylor had performed and recorded albums there, he clearly had no affection for the venue. "The Vanguard," he sniffed, annoyed even at the mention of the name. "We turned that basement into a citadel."

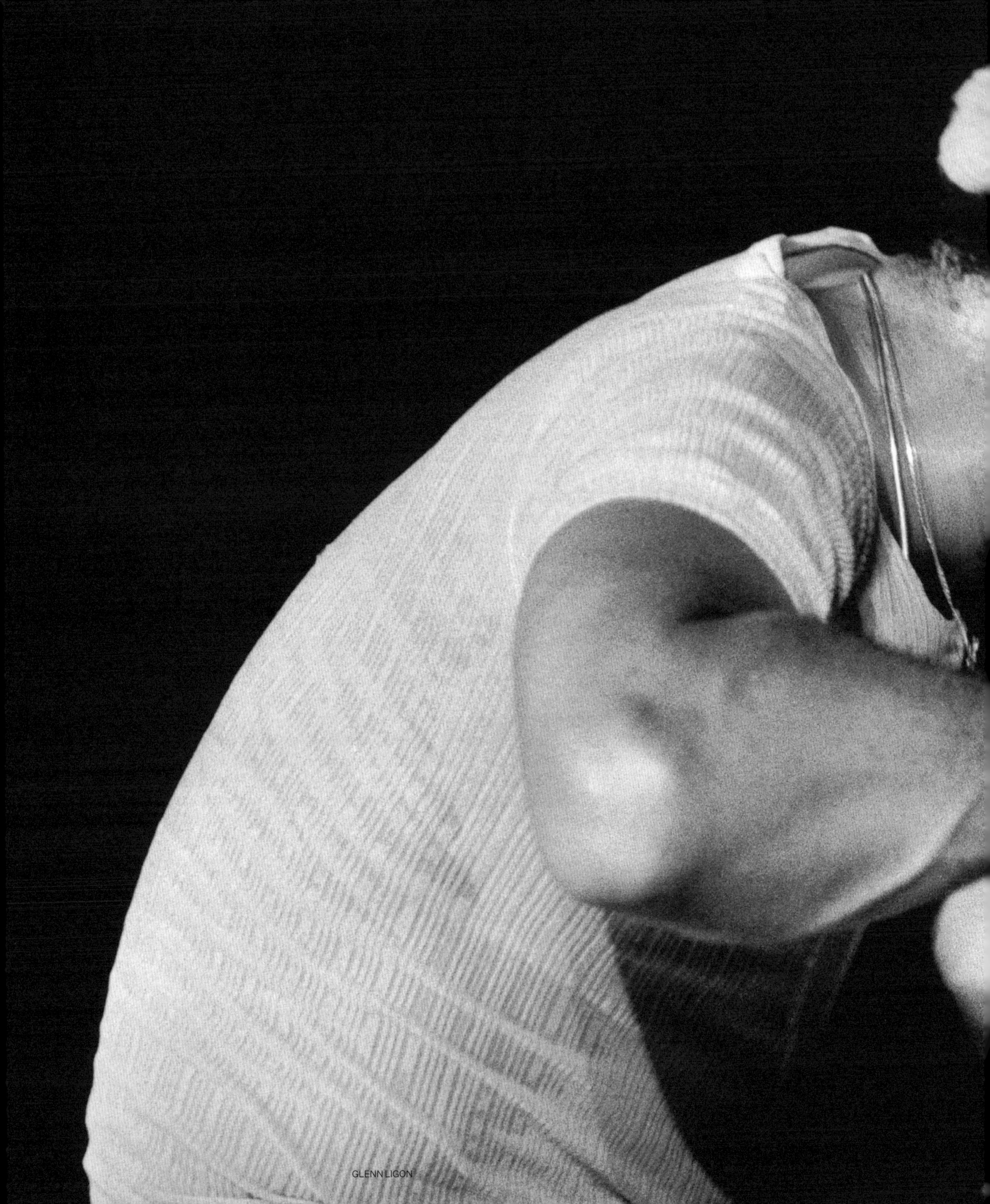
GLENN LIGON

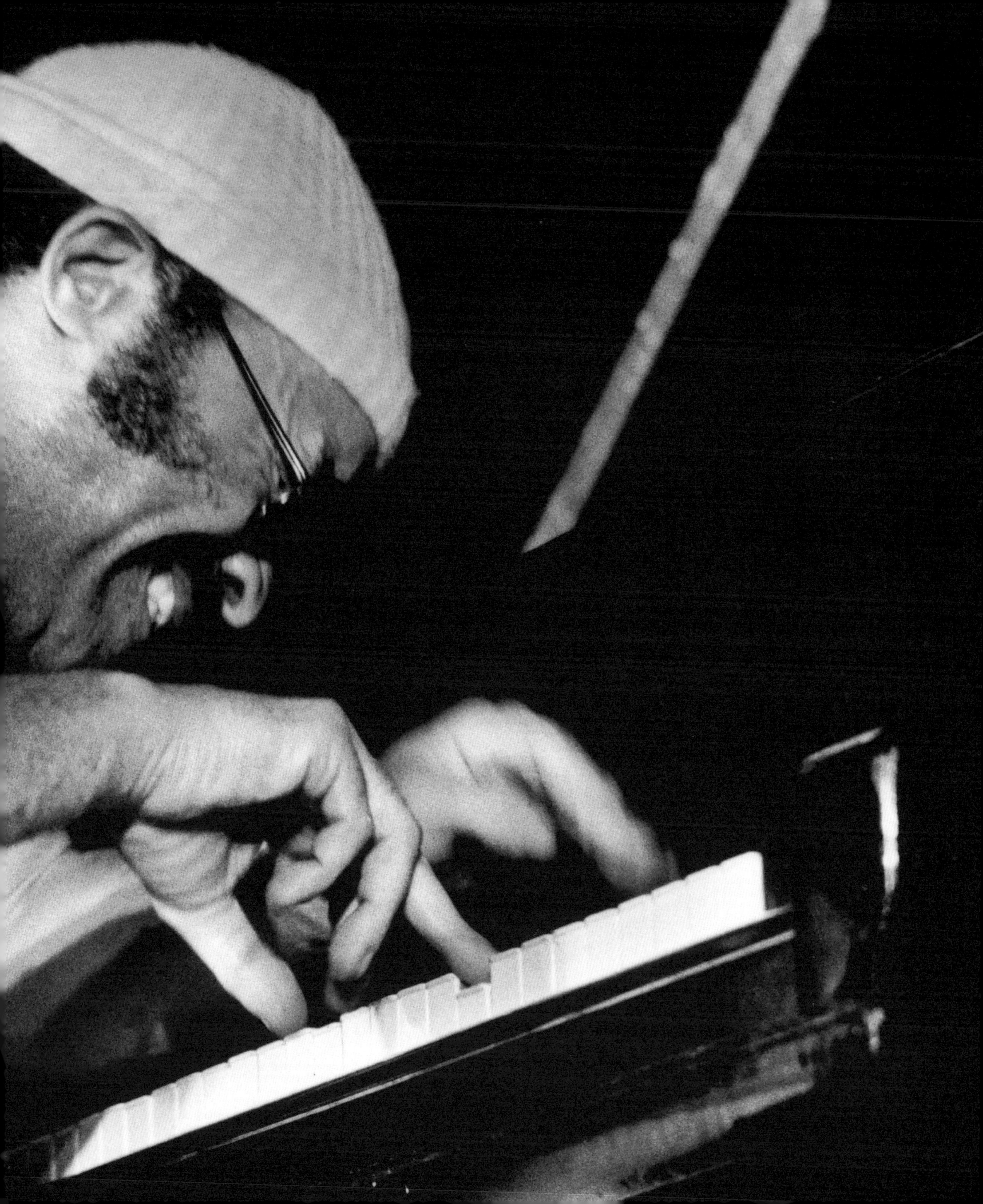

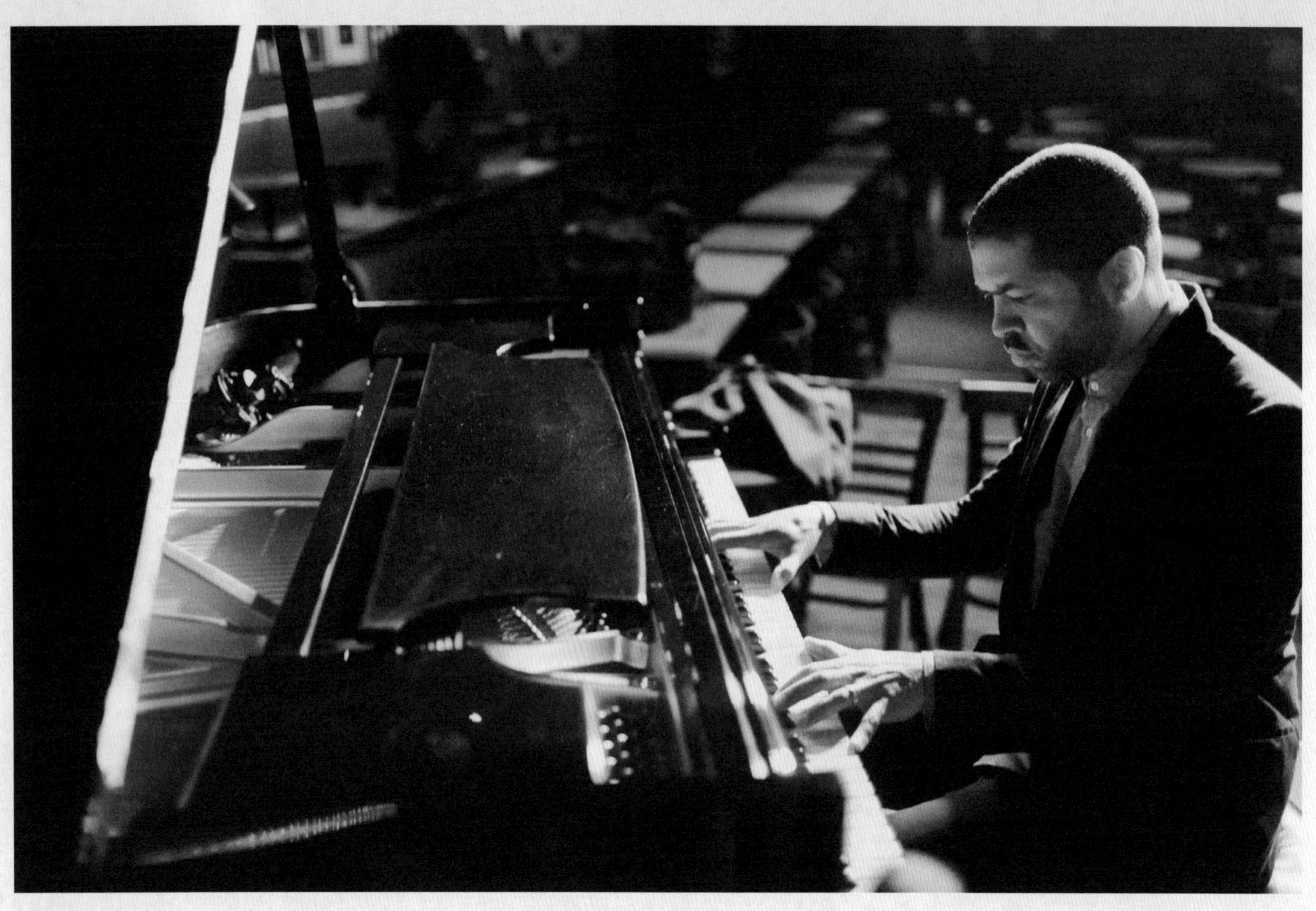

Jason Moran at the Village Vanguard,
New York, 2015

Previous pages:
Cecil Taylor performing at the
Nimes Jazz Festival, France, 1976

     GLENN LIGON

NOTES FROM THE UNDERGROUND.

In November of 2012, not long after Hurricane Sandy had caused major flooding in parts of New York City, I went to the Vanguard to hear Jason and the Bandwagon perform one of their now annual Thanksgiving-week concerts. To get into the club, you descend a set of narrow, red-painted stairs and enter a large room with pool-table felt-green walls covered with framed photos of musicians. The audience sits at long banquettes or little tables that go right up to the edge of the stage, which is a tiny, slightly raised platform backed by a red velvet curtain. The club has low ceilings, is triangular in shape, and has a seating capacity of 120—attributes that undoubtedly contribute to its phenomenal acoustic qualities. The night I was there, Jason, along with drummer Nasheet Waits and bassist Tarus Mateen, began their set by snaking through the audience single file from the rear of the club. Once seated onstage, Jason produced a small flashlight, which he trained on the images of musicians lining the walls. While this gesture was an homage to his musical antecedents, it was also about the room itself, whose survival during the hurricane he had not taken for granted. Indeed, it was a minor miracle that the band played at all that night. Nasheet had lost most of his drum sets to flood damage in a building only a few blocks from the Vanguard, and the only set he was able to salvage was the one he had onstage.

"So I started flashlighting the room again," Jason said, "because it's a place that we're lucky we didn't lose, considering what happened. For the people who were in the space, I was asking, 'Okay, so what do you think about all these faces on the wall?' Besides them being beautiful portraits by great photographers. 'Who the hell is that? Who's Hank Jones? Who's Thelonious Monk?' I shined the light on Nasheet's drum set. ... I shined it on Thelonious Monk. I shined it on John Coltrane. I just talked about the people. 'Okay, so we're in a room; let's also remember that, as listeners.' Because I'd never done that as a performer. I'm aware of it, because it's also part of my history, but at that moment, I wanted to reawaken it not only in myself but in the people who were in the space."[1] Jason and his band turned us out that evening. Now I have never seen them have an off night, but the events leading up to the gig, along with a heightened awareness of the sonic history of the room, seemed to propel their playing to another level. The Vanguard isn't church, but it is spiritual, and that night we got lifted up.

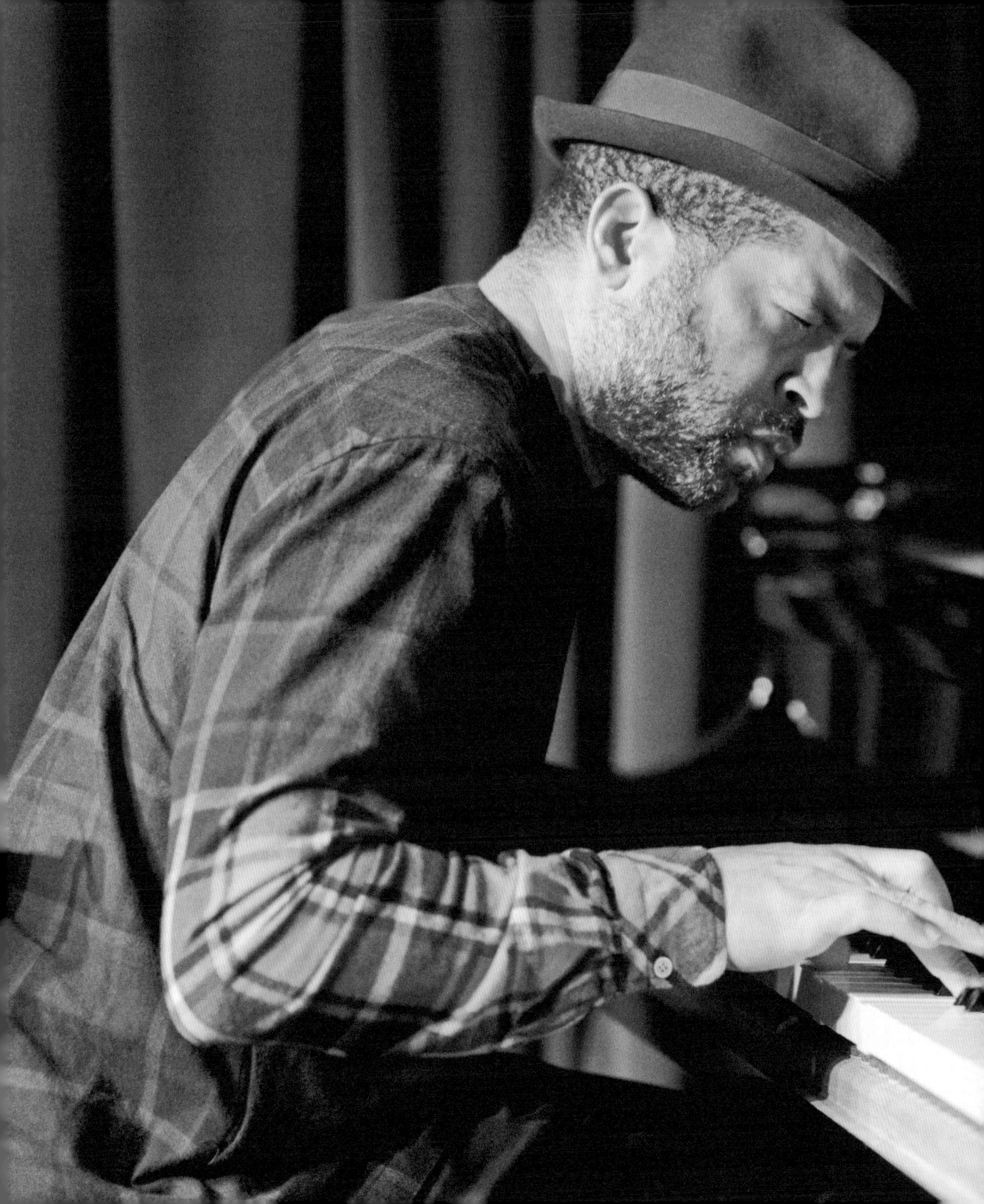

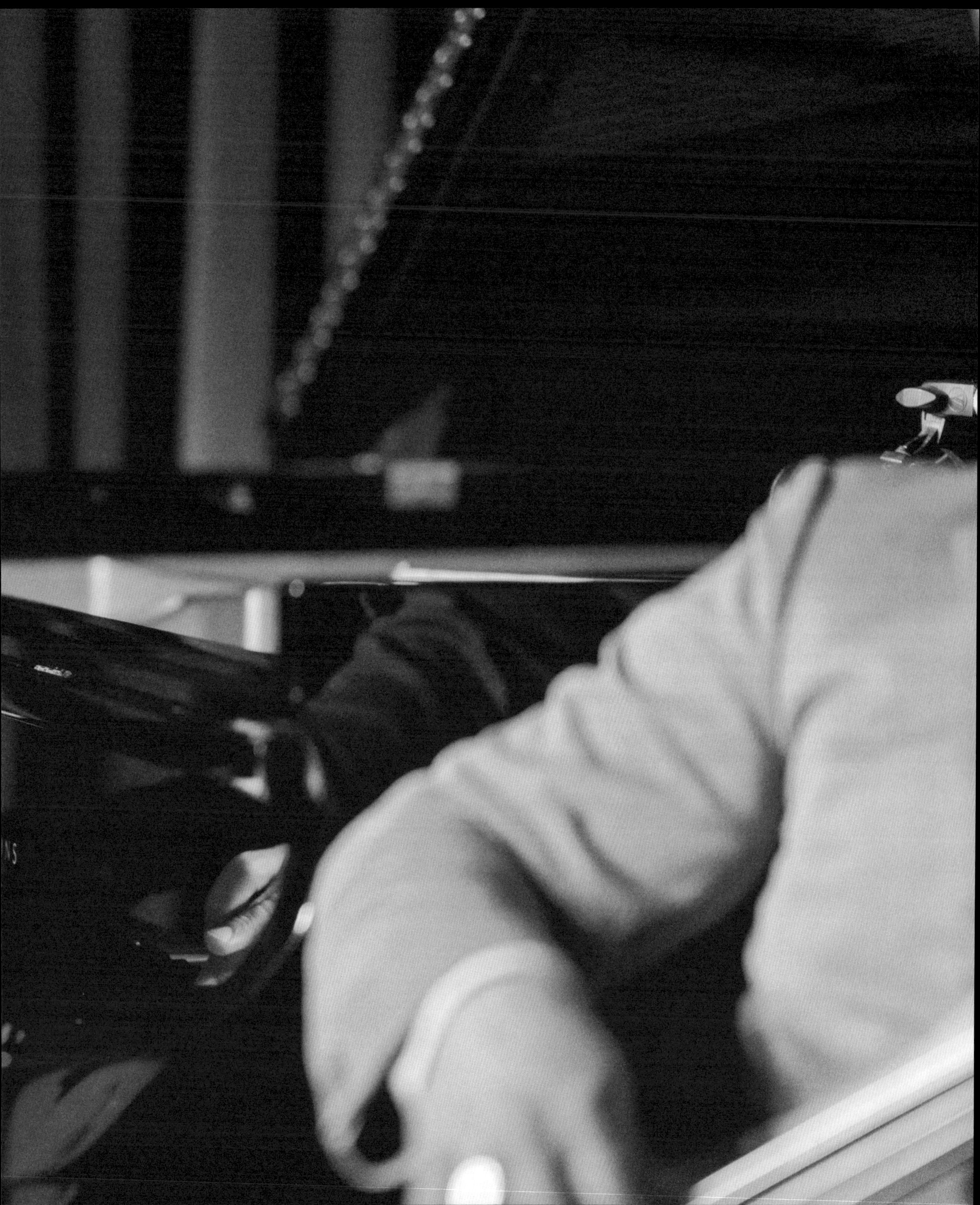

SPACE IS THE PLACE.

"You descend into this basement, and there's John Coltrane," Jason said, regarding the history of the Vanguard. "He's talking about interstellar space, but you have to go down there to get it."[2] As musicians such as Coltrane, Sun Ra, and others have demonstrated, sound is a vehicle for transportation; it takes you from one place to another. But, as Cecil Taylor suggests, music also changes space itself, turns a basement into a citadel, puts the bottom on the top. Poet and cultural theorist Fred Moten once defined blackness as a "disruptive surprise moving in the rich nonfullness of every term it modifies,"[3] and I want to think more about Jason's recent installation works, which re-create stages on which jazz musicians performed, as a meditation on blackness, transportation, and transformation.

In *All the World's Futures*, the central exhibition, curated by Okwui Enwezor, of the 2015 Venice Biennale, Jason presented *STAGED: Savoy Ballroom 1* and *STAGED: Three Deuces*. Both installations were based on celebrated clubs: the Savoy Ballroom, a massive dance hall in Harlem where big bands played during the 1920s, '30s, and '40s; and the Three Deuces, a jazz club in Midtown Manhattan where Charlie Parker, Miles Davis, Max Roach, and Charles Mingus played during the height of the bebop era in the 1940s. Jason re-created sections of these no longer extant spaces from archival photographs, written accounts, and interviews he conducted, capturing the high-arched, patterned glamour of the Savoy Ballroom bandstand and the low-ceiling, padded-wall claustrophobia of the Three Deuces stage. He activated these spaces with work songs, spirituals, prison field recordings, jazz, and live performances, creating a call-and-response between various musical traditions. Jason once said in an interview that he can attribute every note he plays to a lesson learned from a specific musician. Likewise, the Savoy Ballroom and the Three Deuces—spaces transformed by black musicians—also taught him lessons and are a crucial part of his musical roots. To highlight their importance, he has re-created them out of memory, fantasy, and desire, making them platforms to express a kind of gratitude and to transport a musical legacy into the present. To play on those fragmented stages is to acknowledge loss but also to acknowledge the survival and continued vitality of the tradition. It is to know where one comes from. Gertrude Stein once said, "Our roots can be anywhere and we can survive, because if you think about it, we take our roots with us."[4] *STAGED: Savoy Ballroom 1* and *STAGED: Three Deuces* are roots that survive because Jason has taken them with him.

Previous pages:
Jason Moran performing at the Village Vanguard, New York, 2017

Following pages:
View of the Village Vanguard stage, New York, 2015

GLENN LIGON

NOTES

The title of the essay was derived from a passage on the work of Paul Gilroy in Kobena Mercer's introduction to the book *The Fateful Triangle: Race, Ethnicity, Nation*, which was drawn from lectures given by Stuart Hall at Harvard University in 1994.

1. Hank Shteamer, "Jason Moran discusses the legacy and lore of the Village Vanguard," *Time Out New York*, February 27, 2015, https://www.timeout.com/newyork/music/jason-moran-discusses-the-legacy-and-lore-of-the-village-vanguard.
2. Jason Moran, "STAGED," lecture presented at the American Academy in Rome, June 21, 2017.
3. Fred Moten, *In the Break: The Aesthetics of the Black Radical Tradition* (Minneapolis: University of Minnesota Press, 2003), 255.
4. Linda Simon, ed., *Gertrude Stein Remembered* (Lincoln: University of Nebraska Press, 1997), 157.

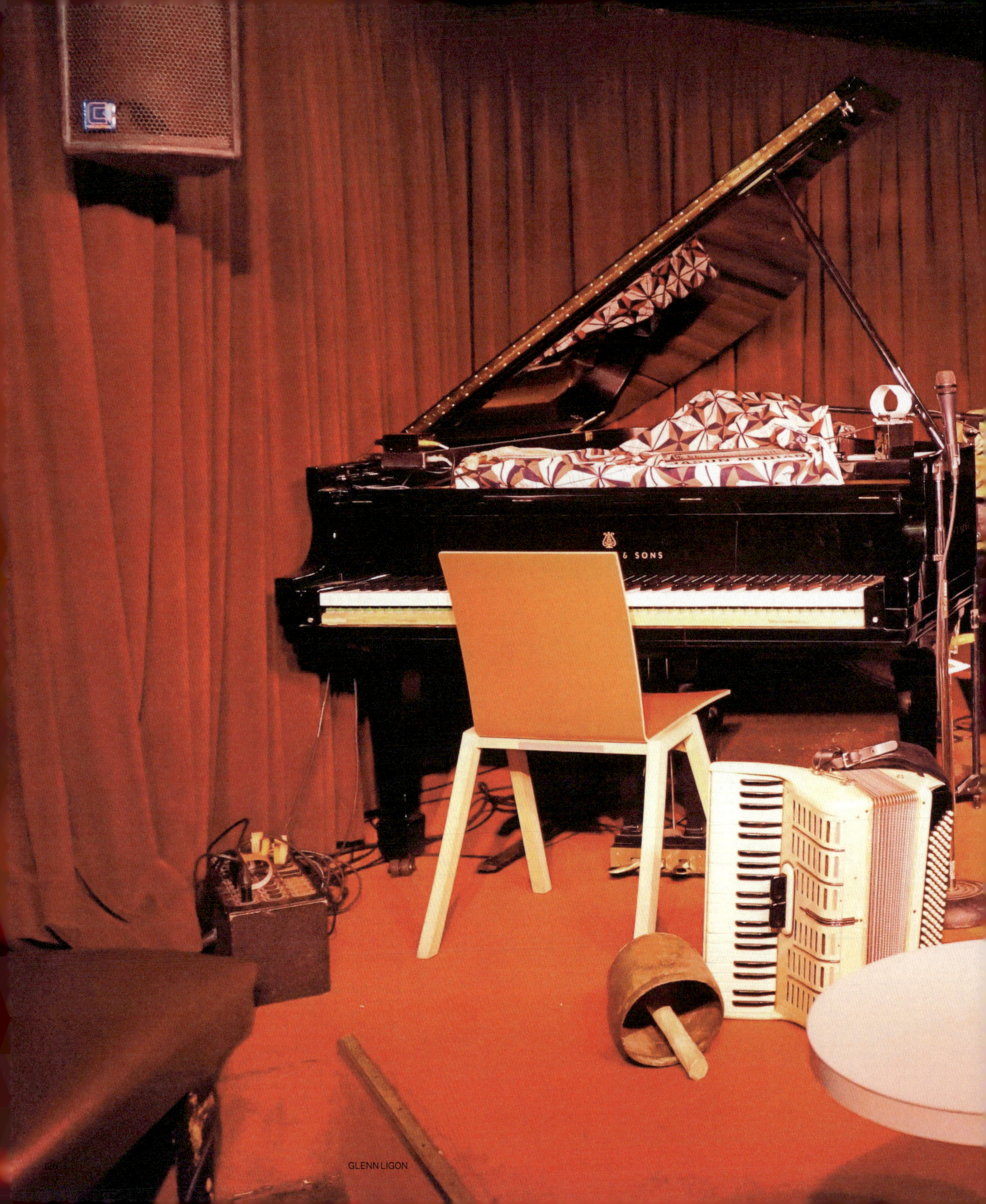

GLENN LIGON

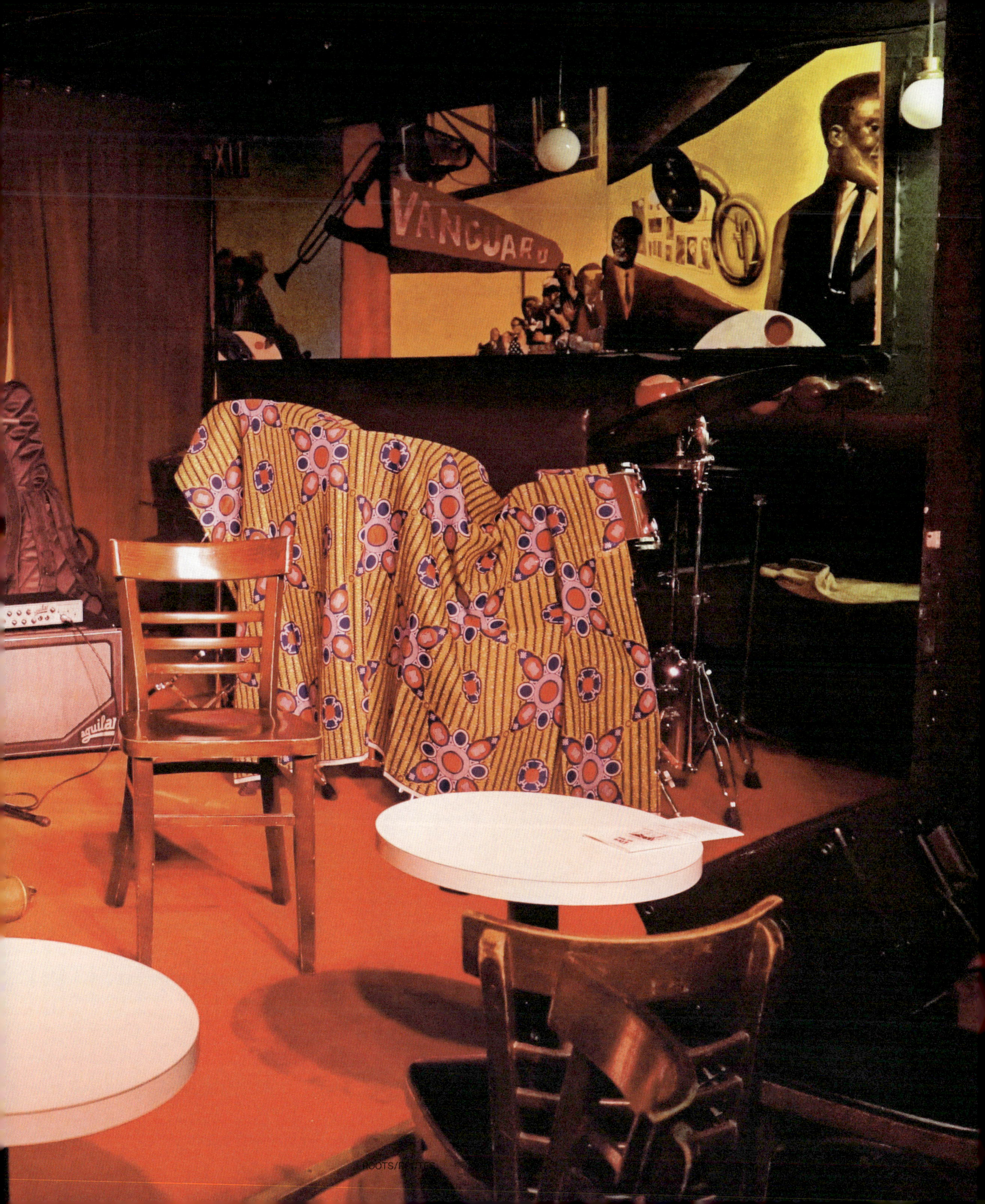

ROOTS/ROUTES

ASSEMBLY

Alicia Hall Moran performing *Run the World* with the Kaoru
Watanabe Taiko Ensemble during *BLEED,* a five-day residency
as part of the Whitney Biennial, New York, 2012

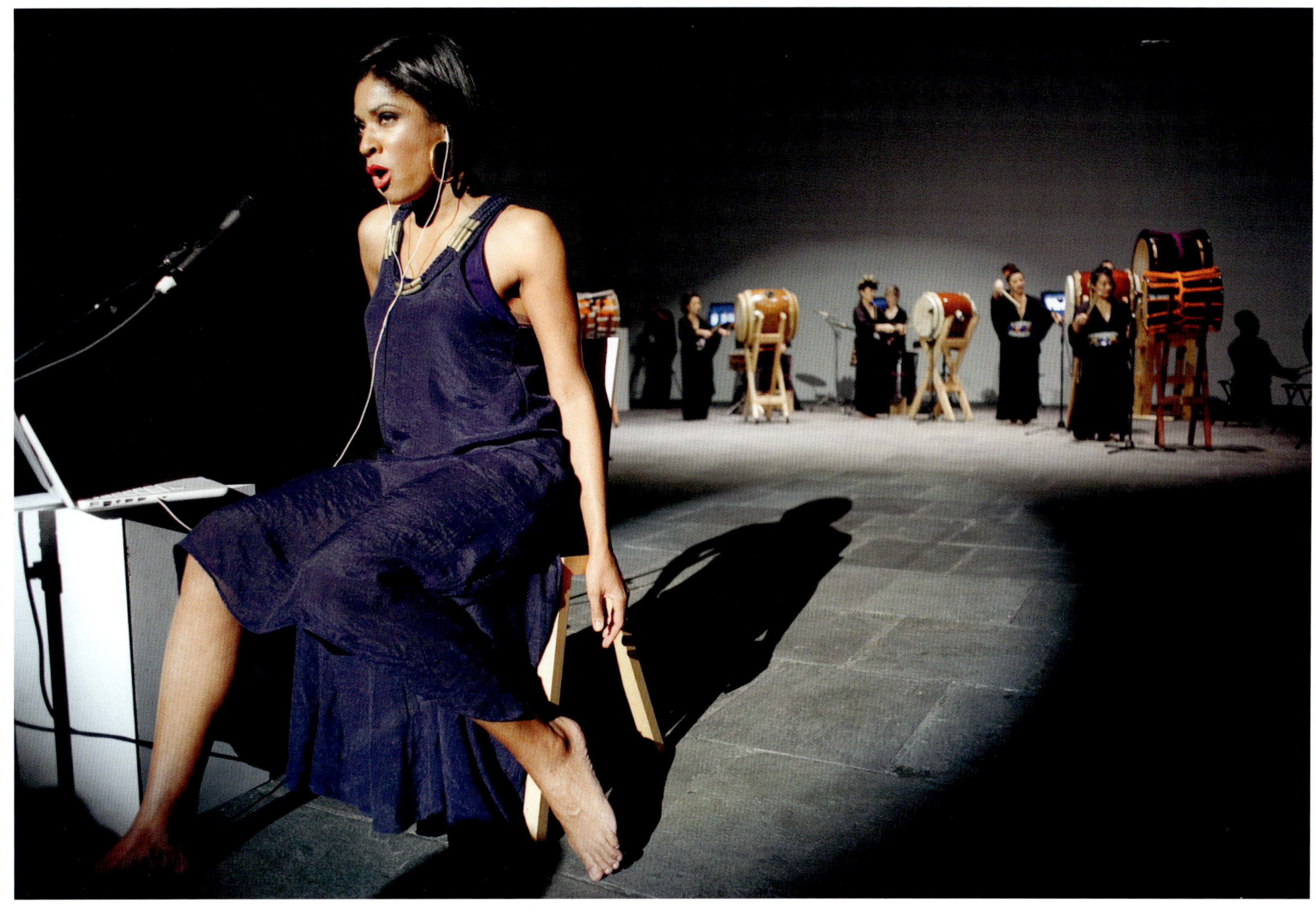

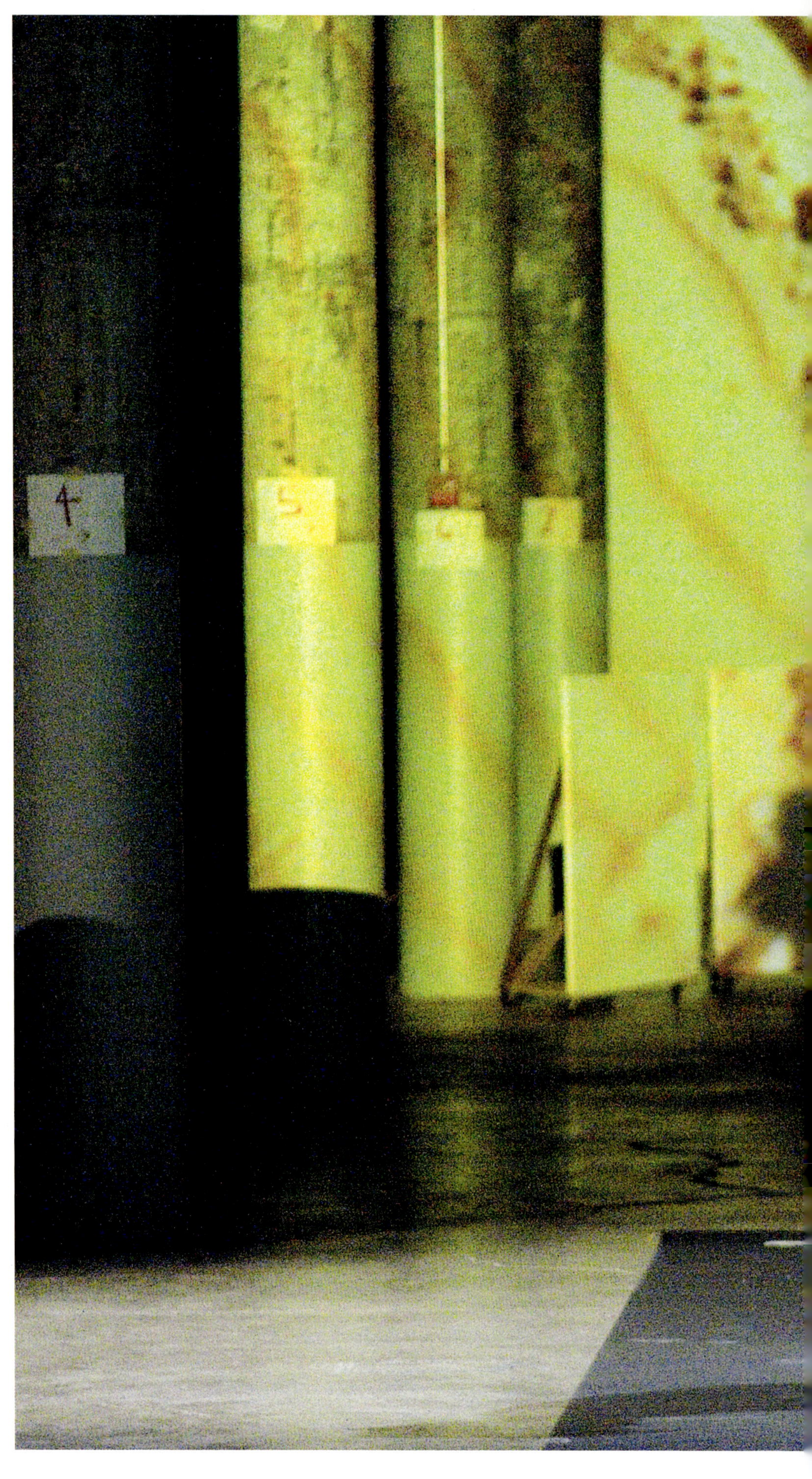

Joan Jonas performing *The Shape, the Scent, the Feel of Things*
(2005) at Dia: Beacon, New York, 2005

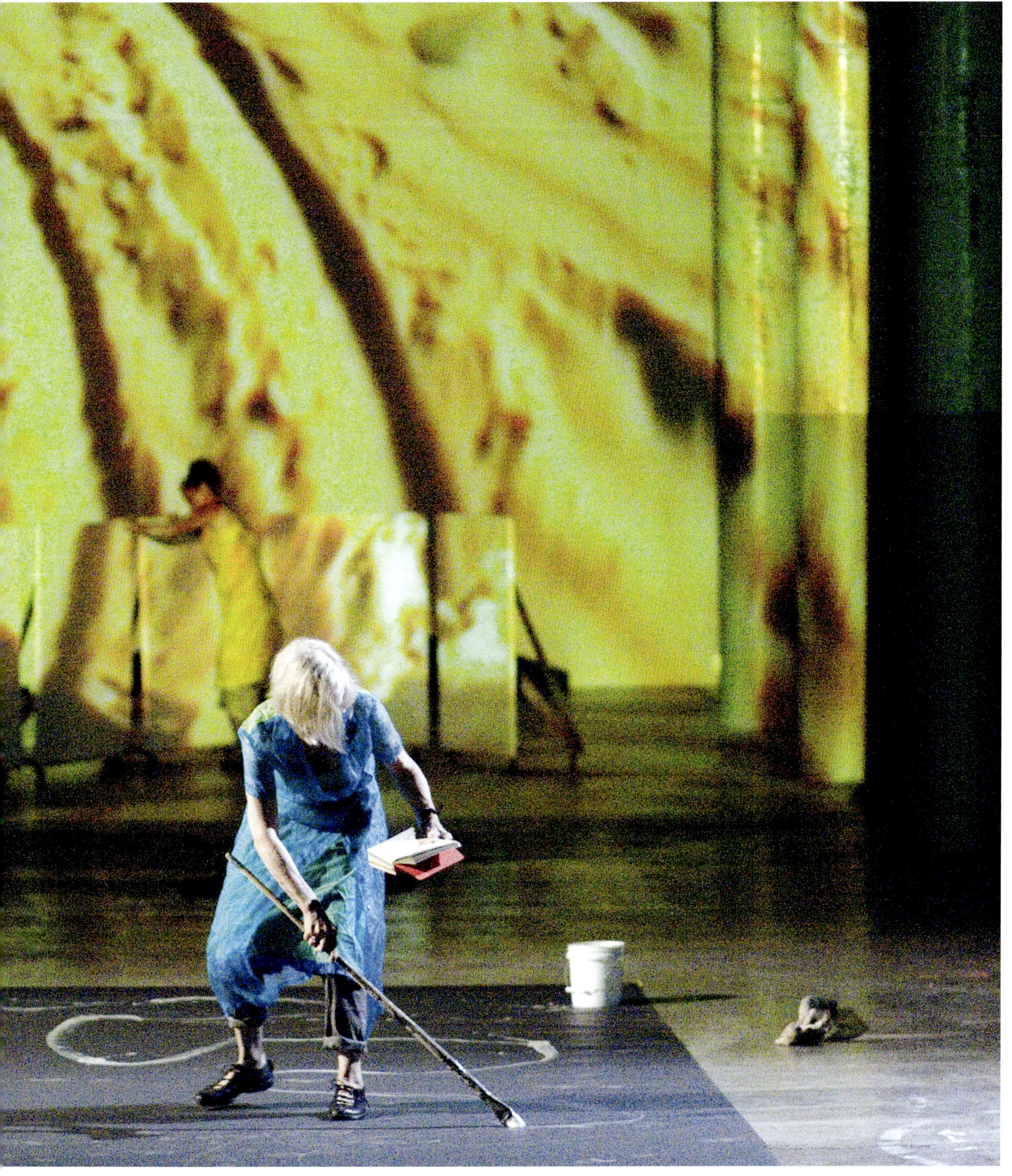

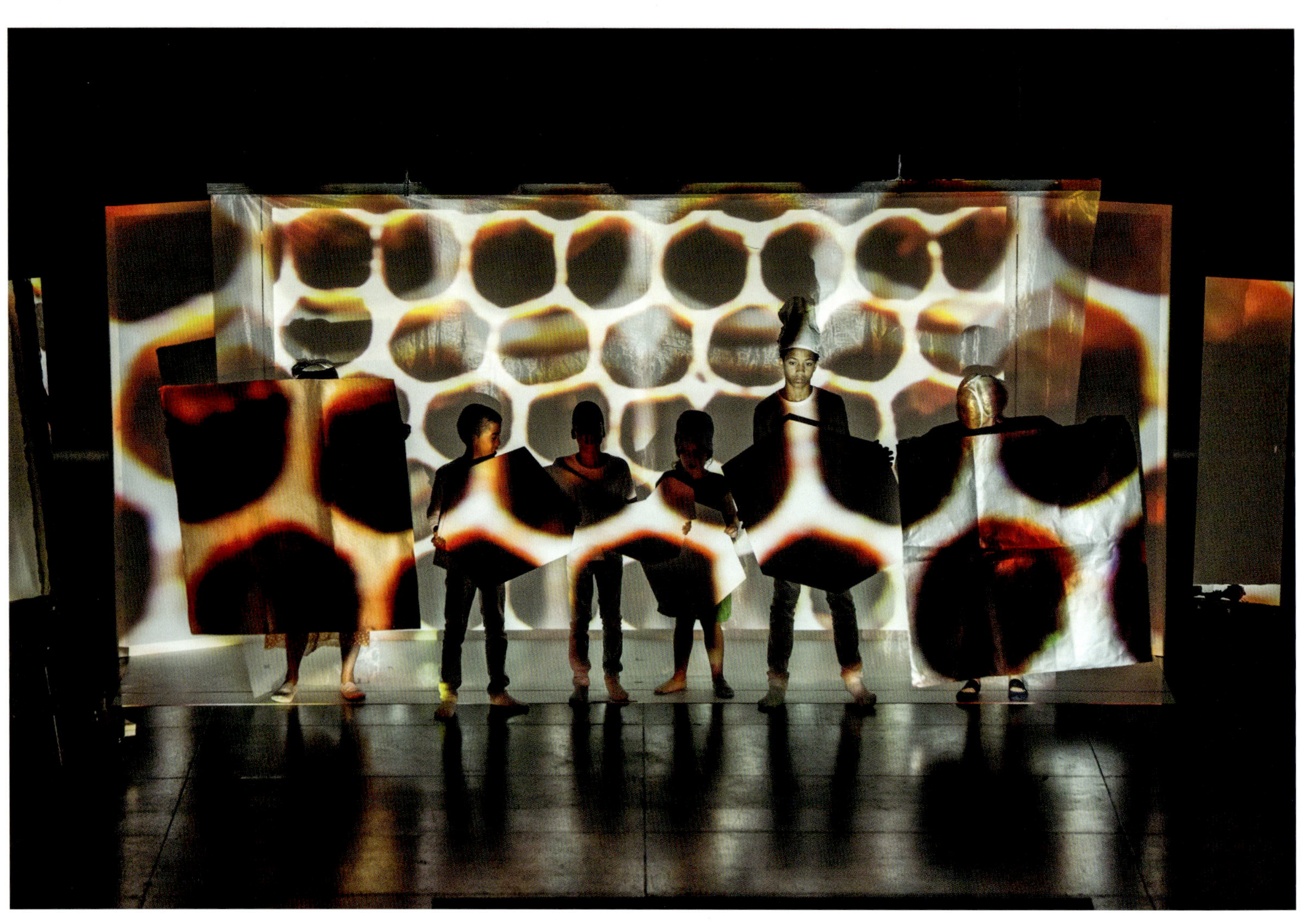

(left to right): Jin Jung, Jonas and Malcolm Moran, Lila Gavagan, Noah Delorme, and Joan Jonas performing *They Come to Us Without a Word II* at Teatro Piccolo Arsenale, Venice, 2015

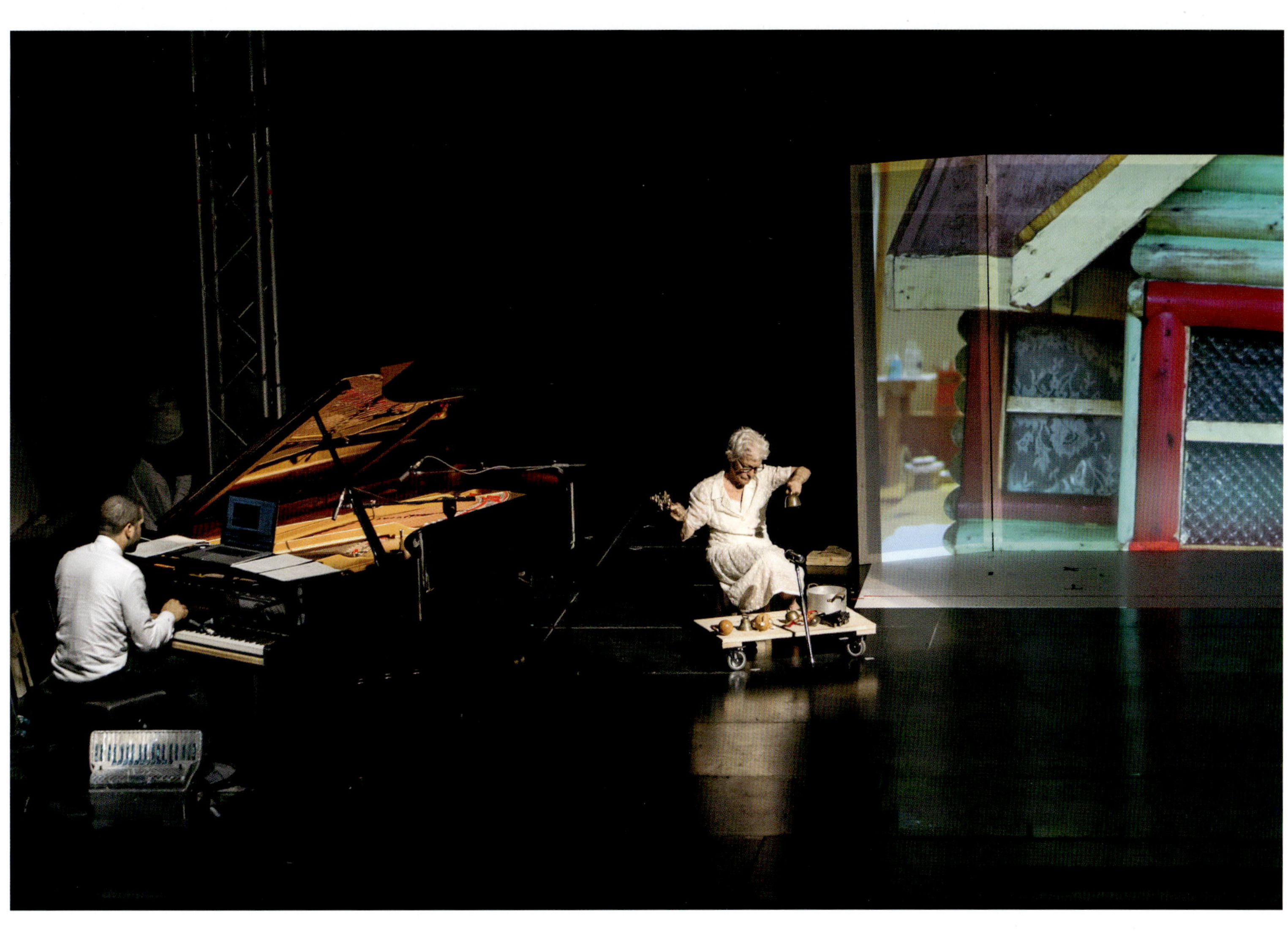

Jason Moran and Joan Jonas performing *They Come to Us Without a Word II* at Teatro Piccolo Arsenale, Venice, 2015

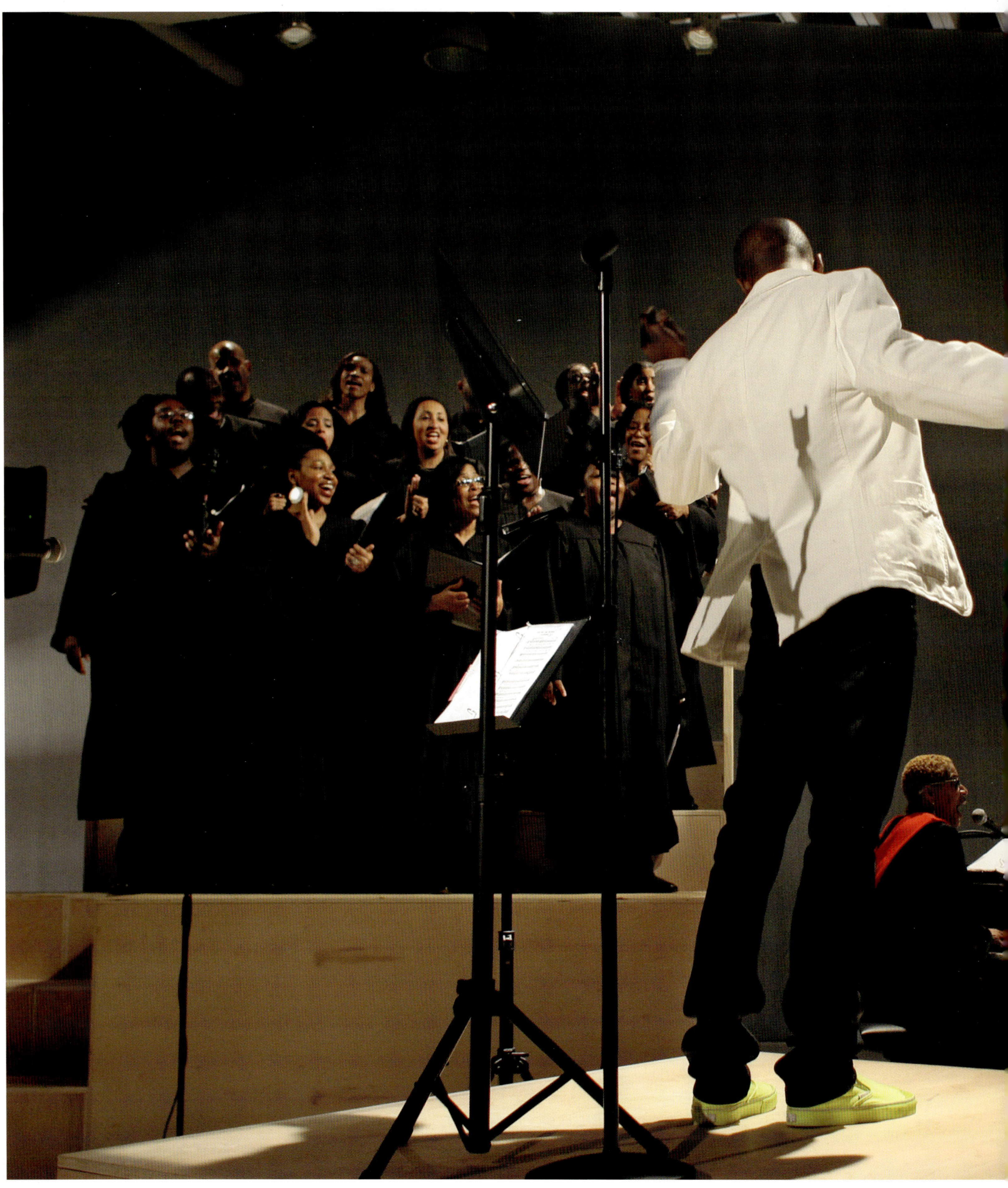

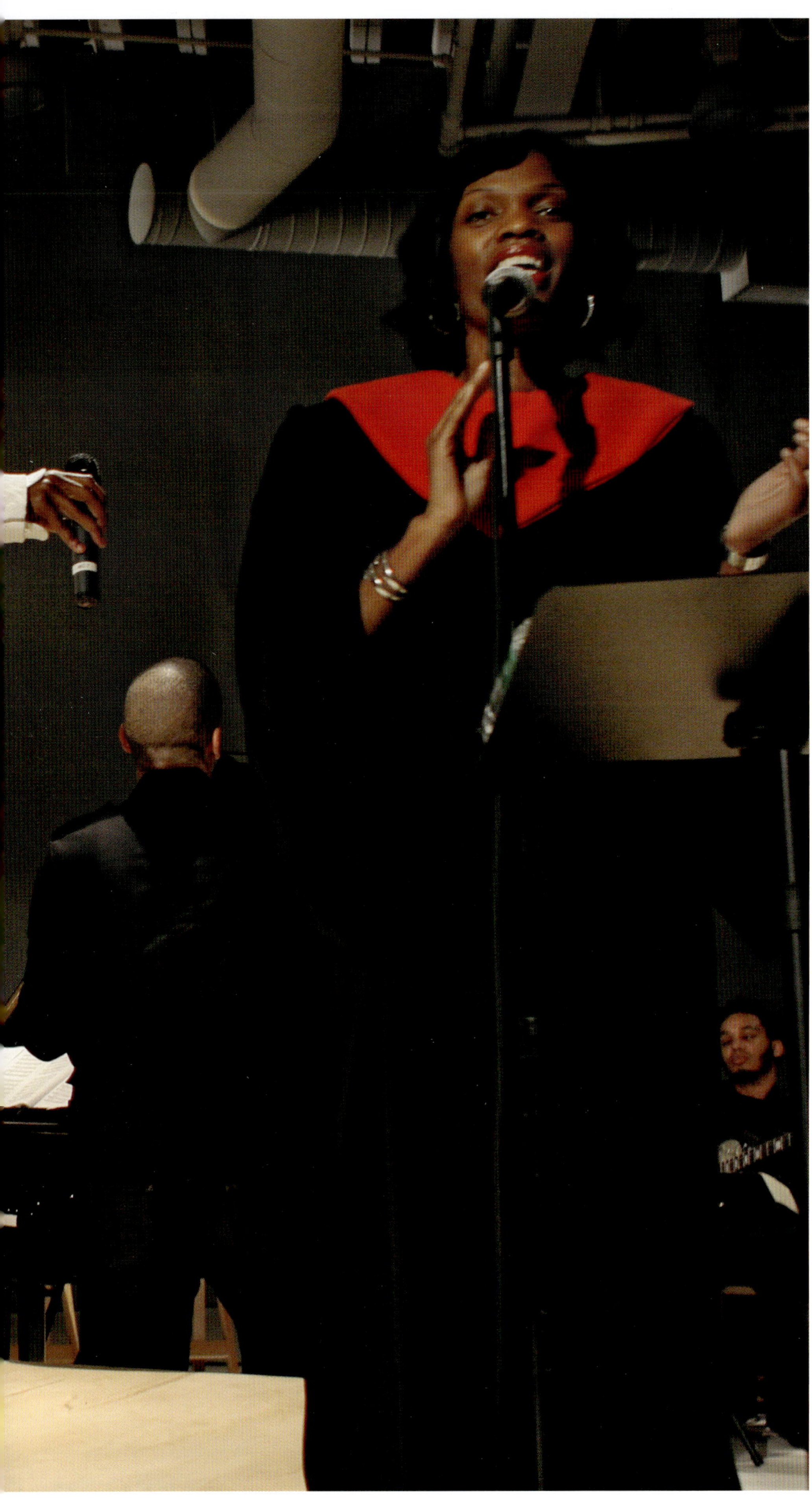

Adam Pendleton and Jason Moran, with soloists Vaneese Thomas and Renee Neufville and gospel choir, performing in *The Revival* at Stephen Weiss Studio, New York, as part of Performa 07, 2007

Glenn Ligon, *The Death of Tom*, 2008, 16mm film (black and white, sound) transferred to video; installation view at Regen Projects, Los Angeles

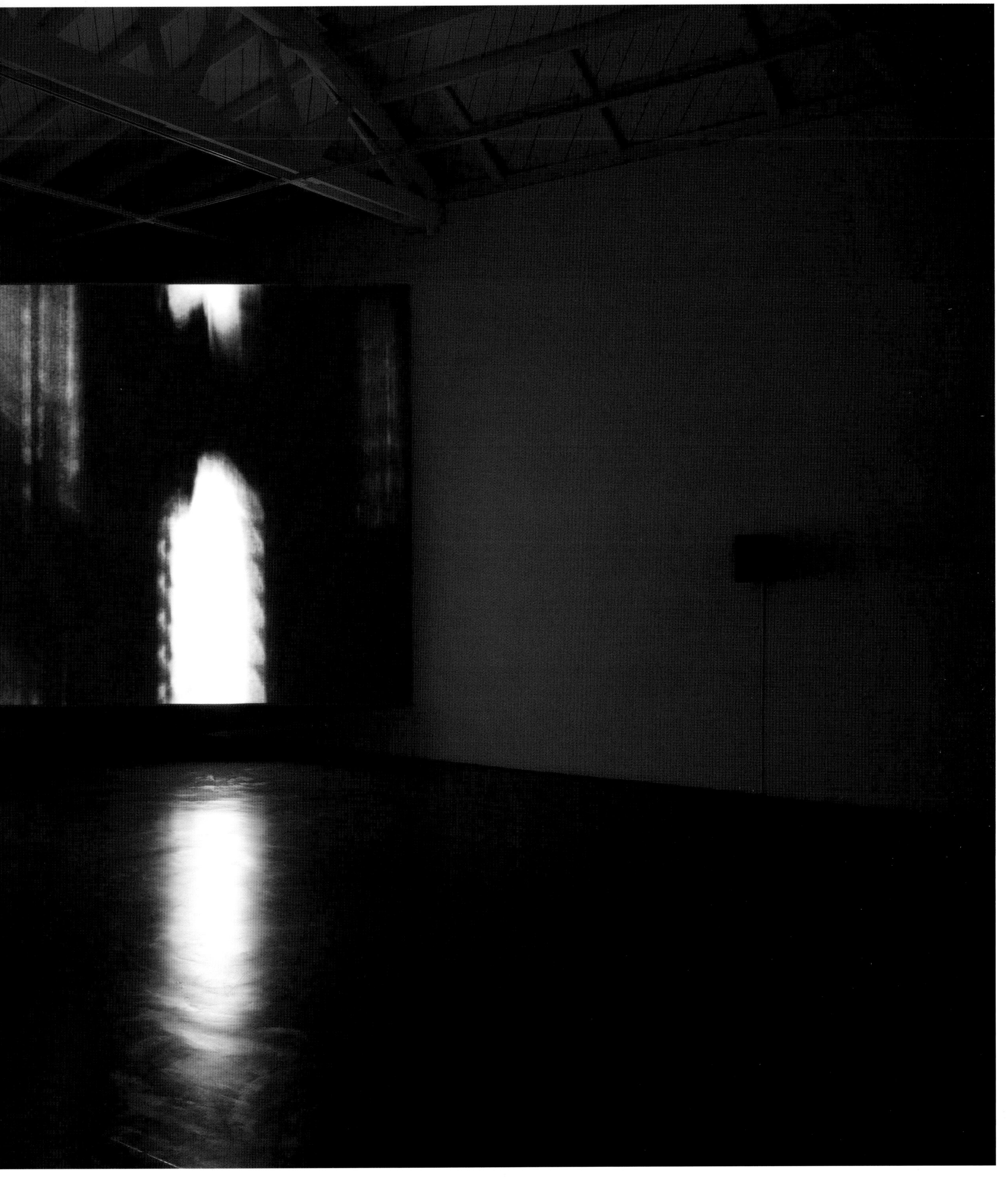

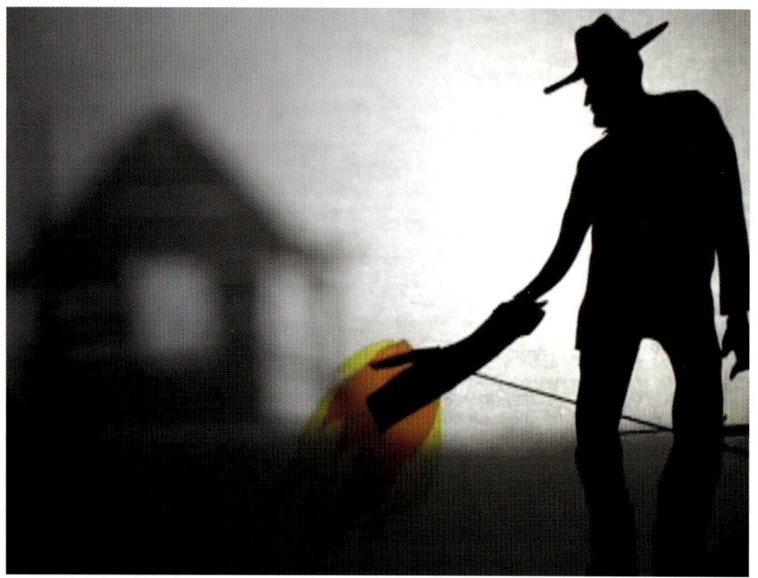

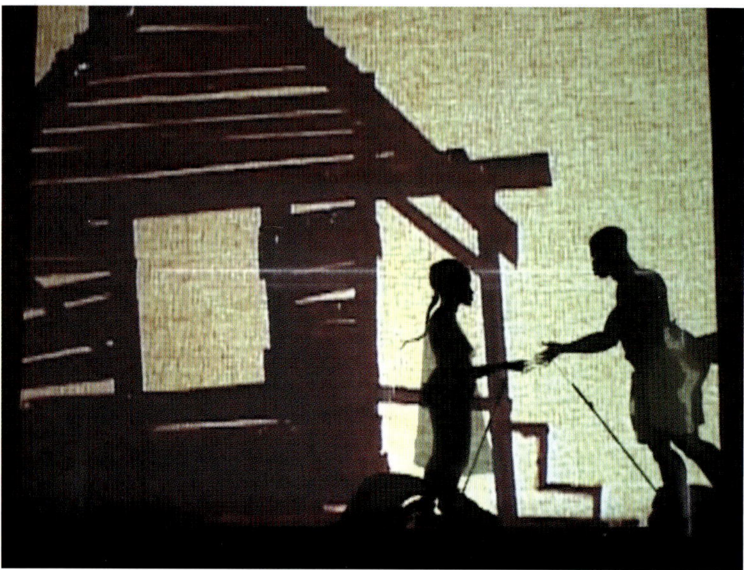

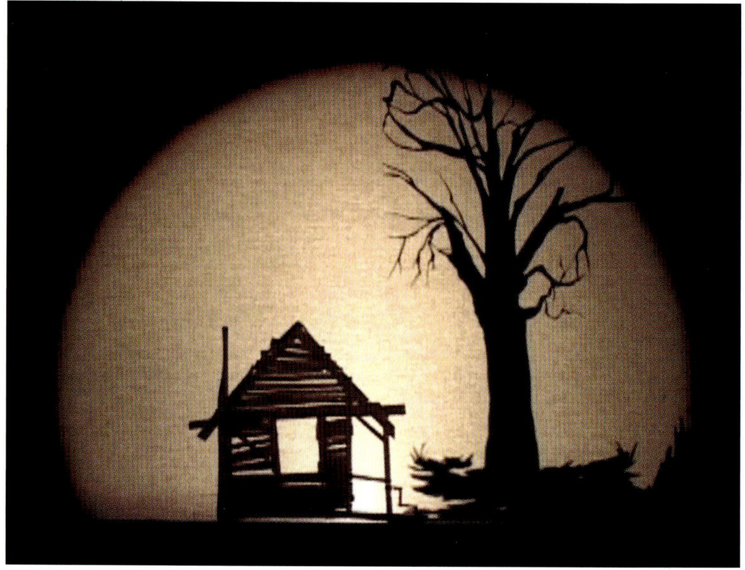

Kara Walker, Stills from *National Archives Microfilm M999 Roll 34: Bureau of Refugees, Freedmen and Abandoned Lands: Six Miles from Springfield on the Franklin Road*, 2009, digital video with original score by Alicia Hall Moran and Jason Moran

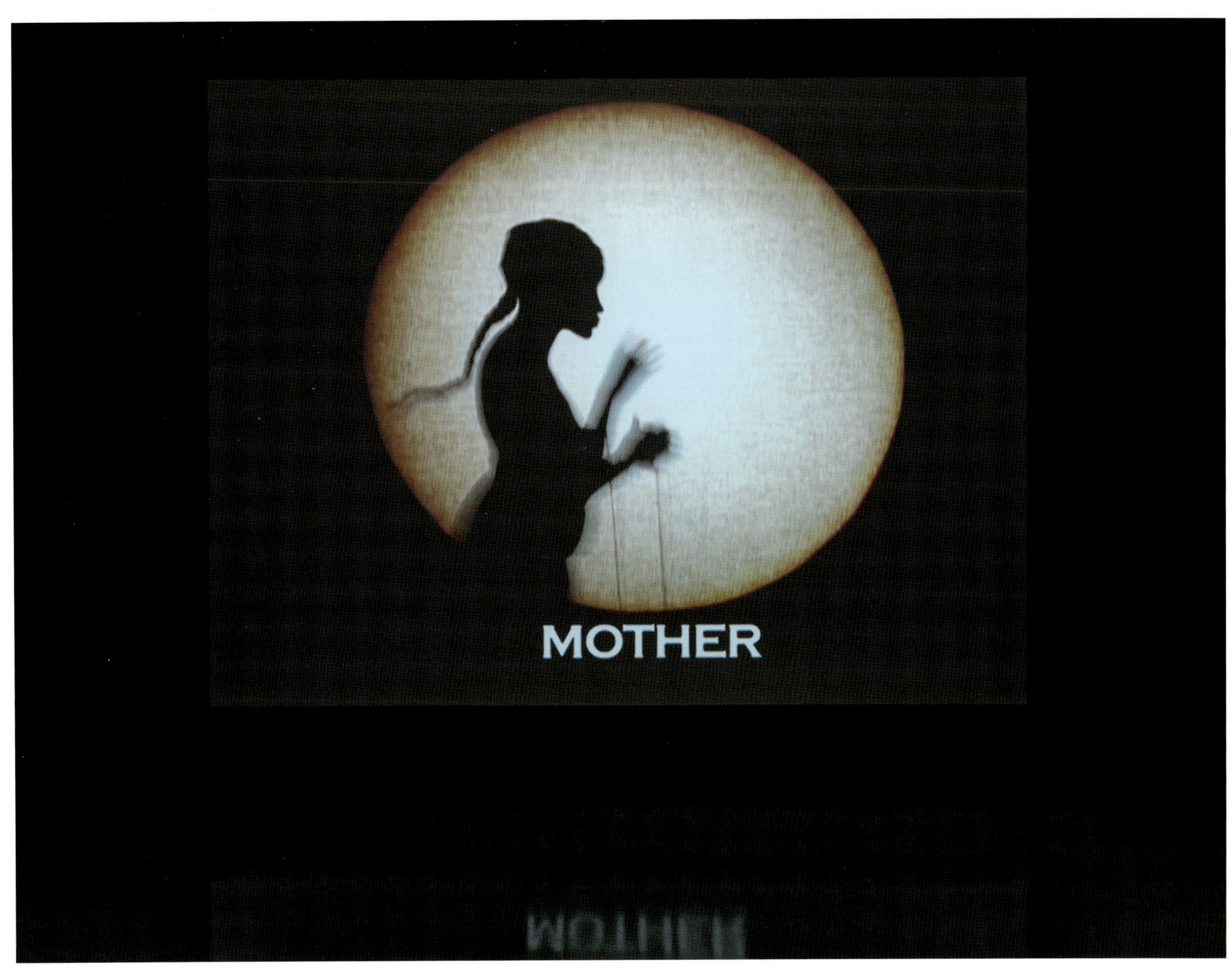

Kara Walker, *National Archives Microfilm M999 Roll 34: Bureau of Refugees, Freedmen and Abandoned Lands: Six Miles from Springfield on the Franklin Road*, 2009; installation view in the exhibition *POWER: Work by African American Women from the Nineteenth Century to Now*, Sprüth Magers, Los Angeles, 2017

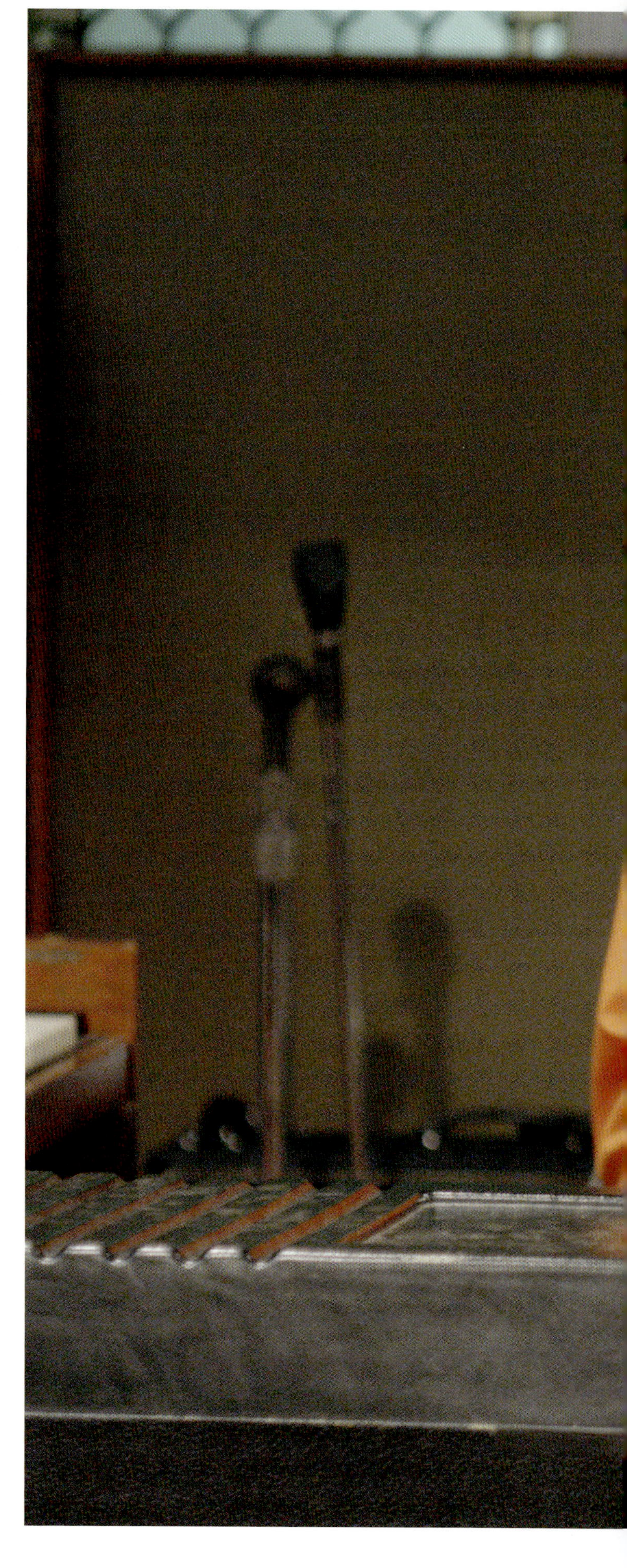

Right and following pages:
Stan Douglas, Stills from *Luanda-Kinshasa*,
2013, video projection (color, sound)

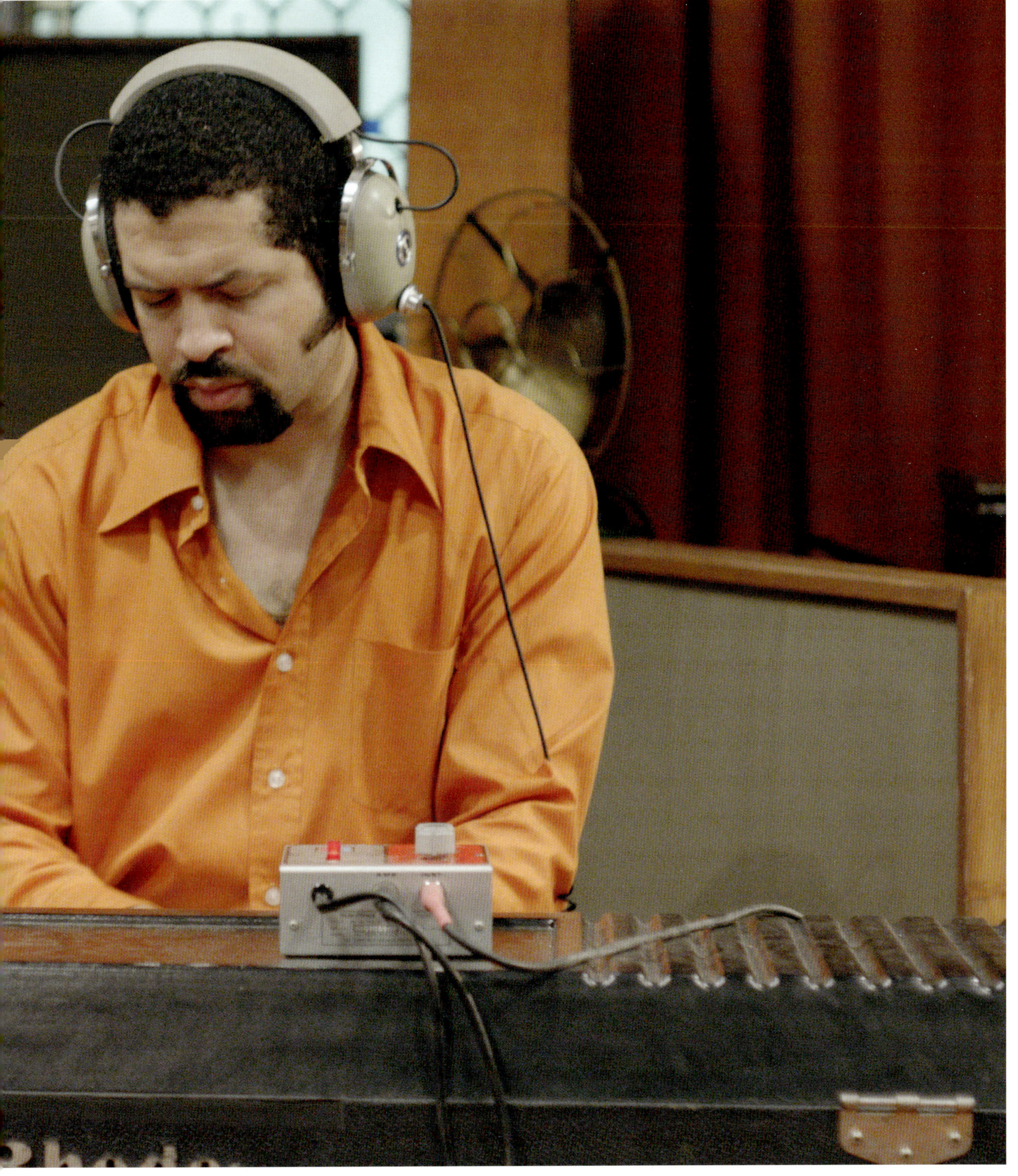
Rhod

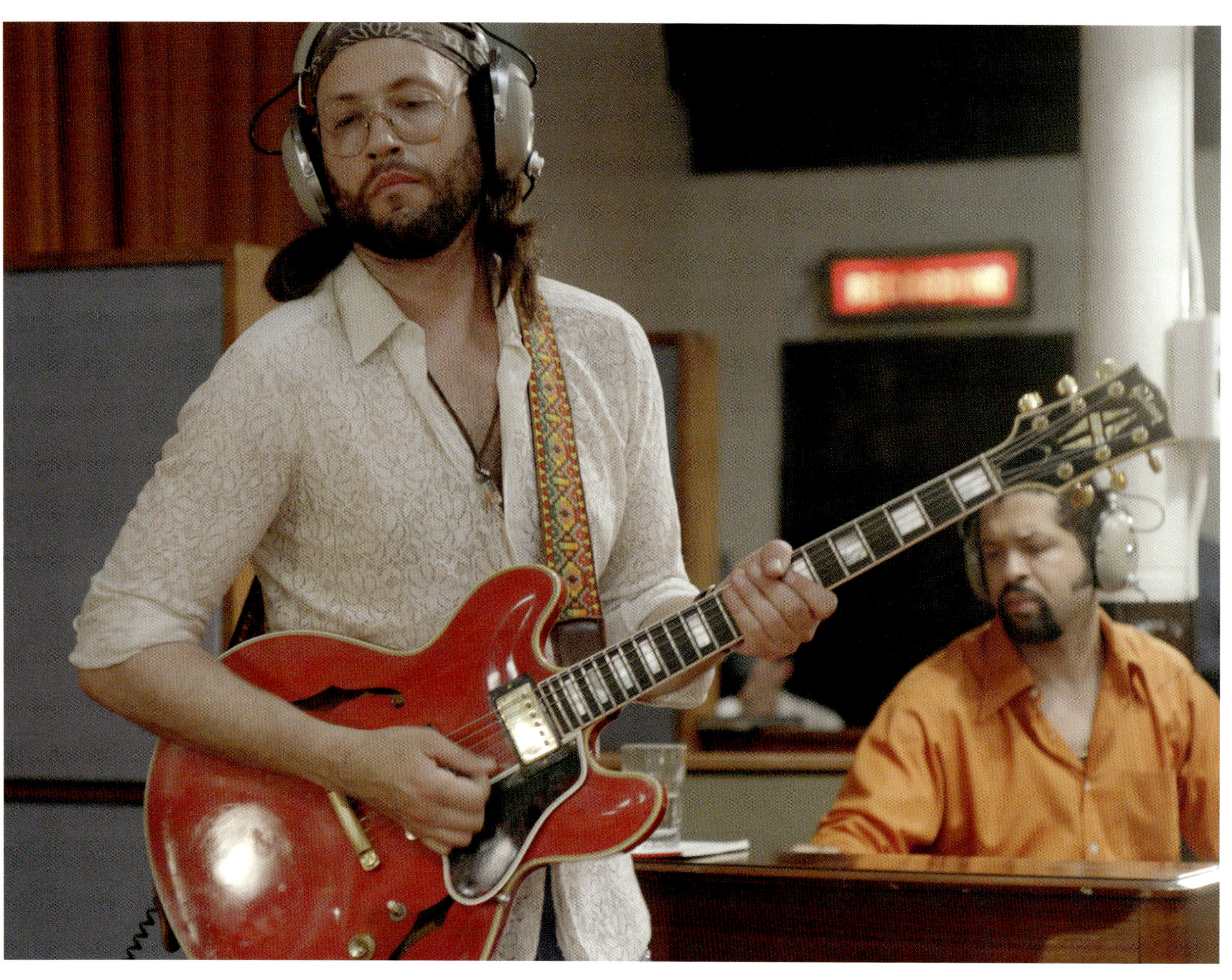

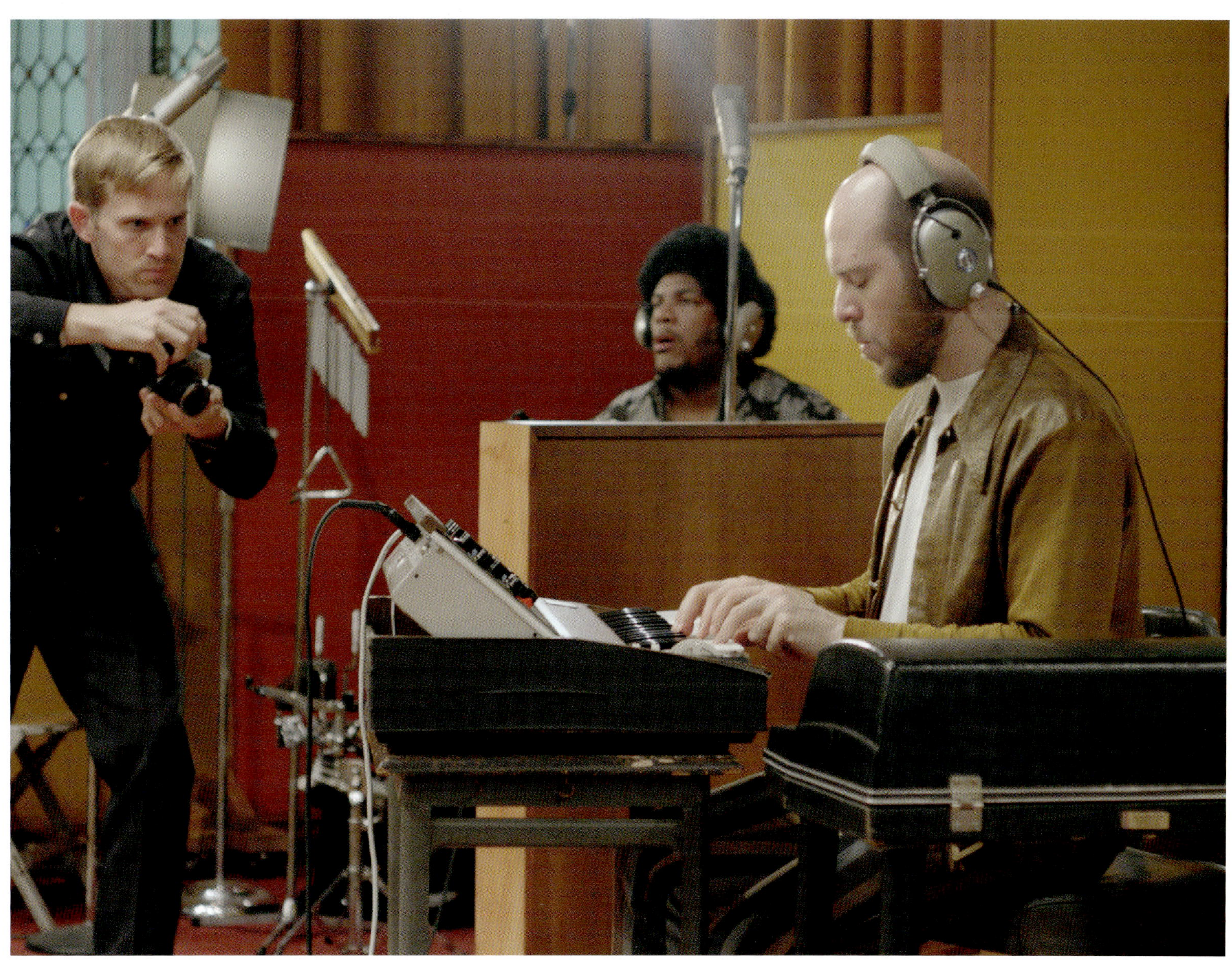

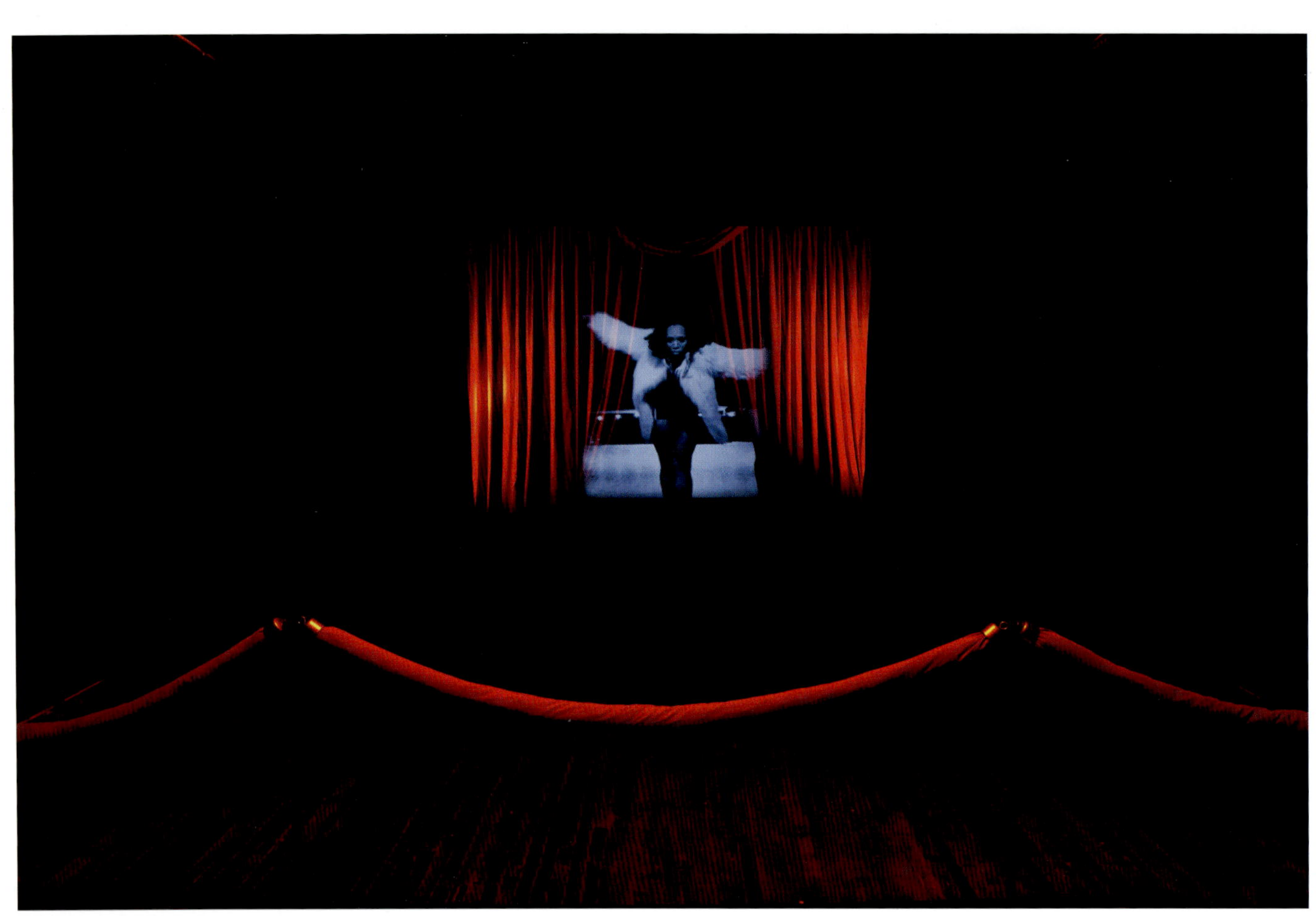

Carrie Mae Weems, *Lincoln, Lonnie, and Me—A Story in 5 Parts*, 2012, video installation and mixed media, dimensions variable

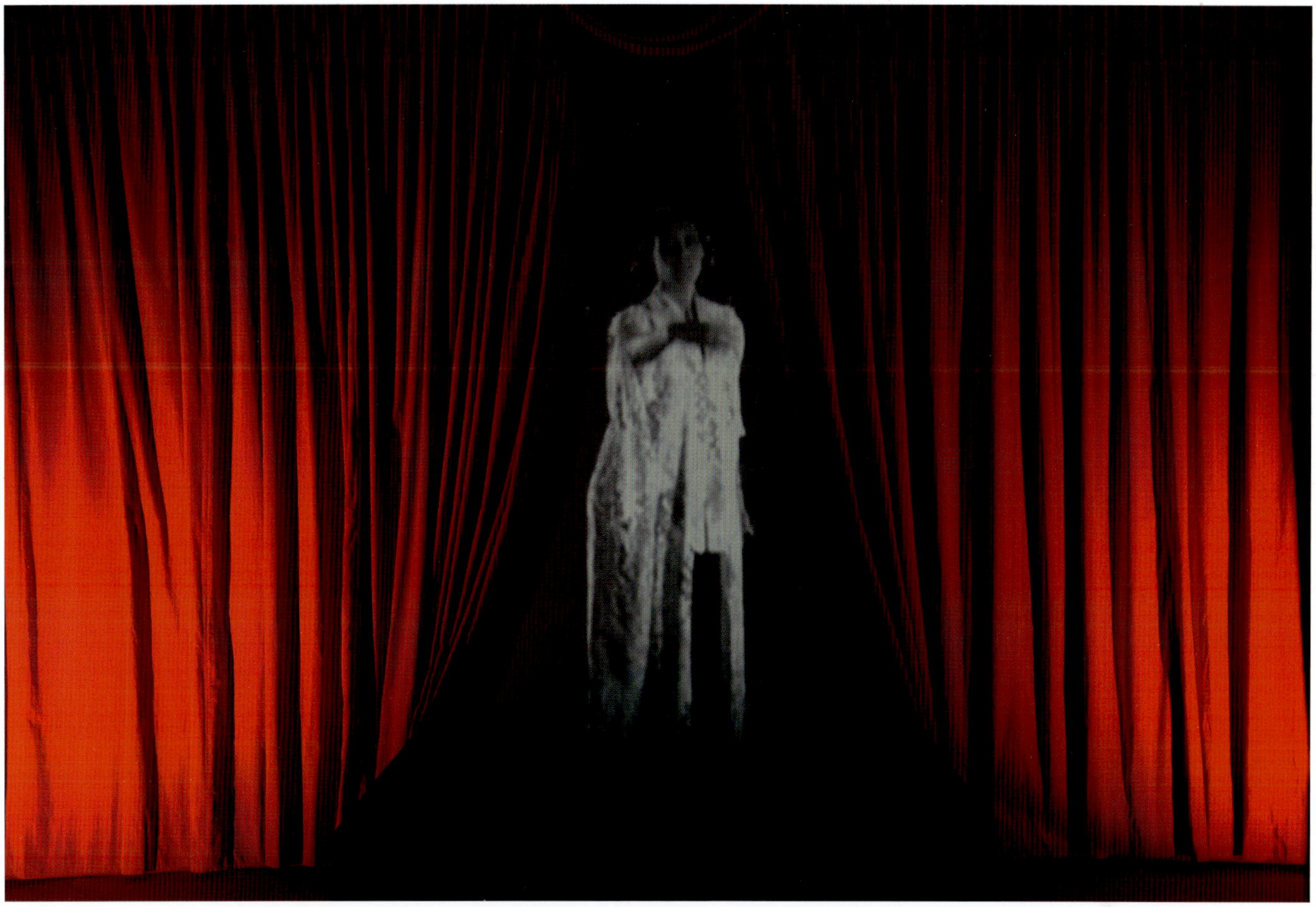

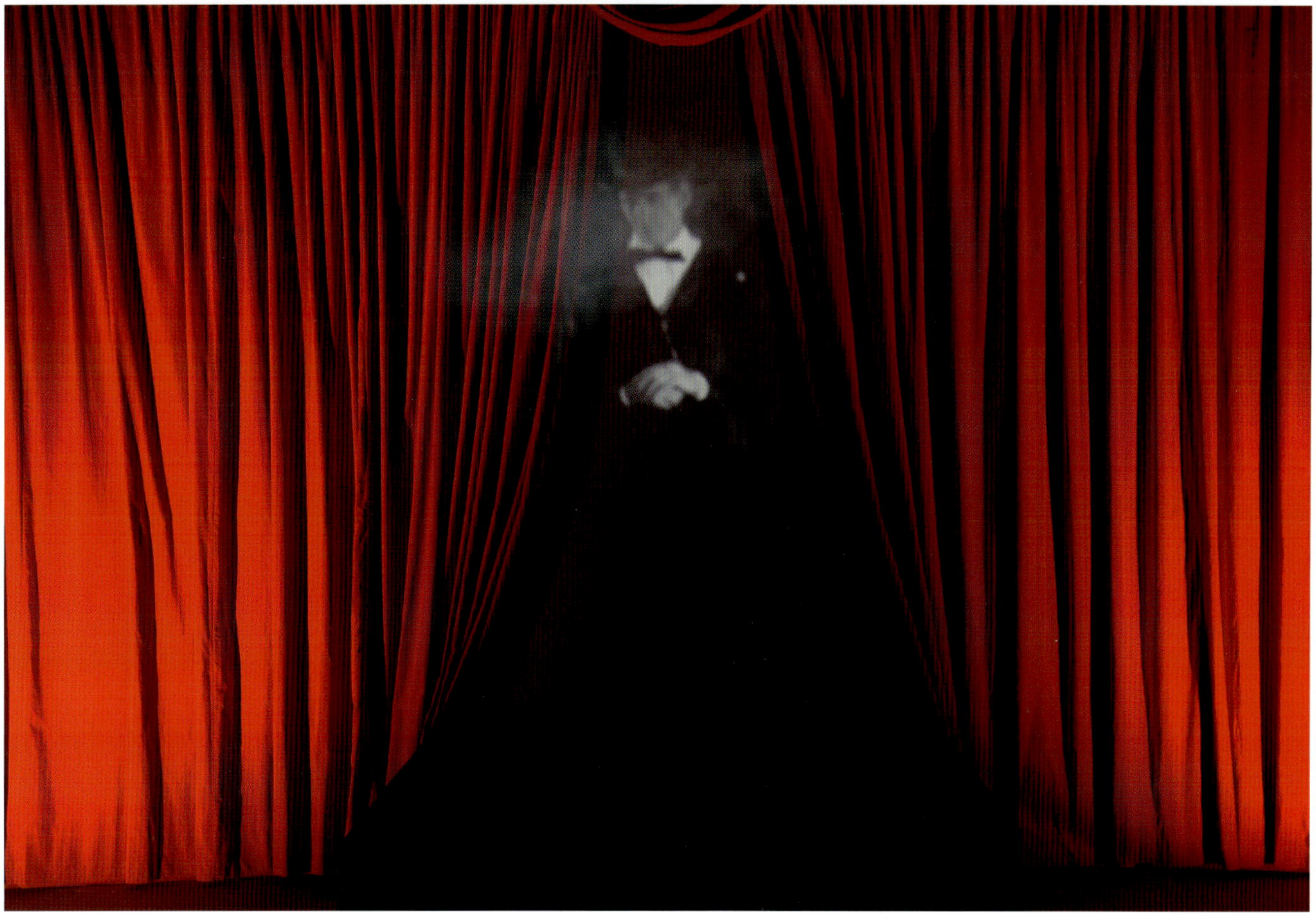

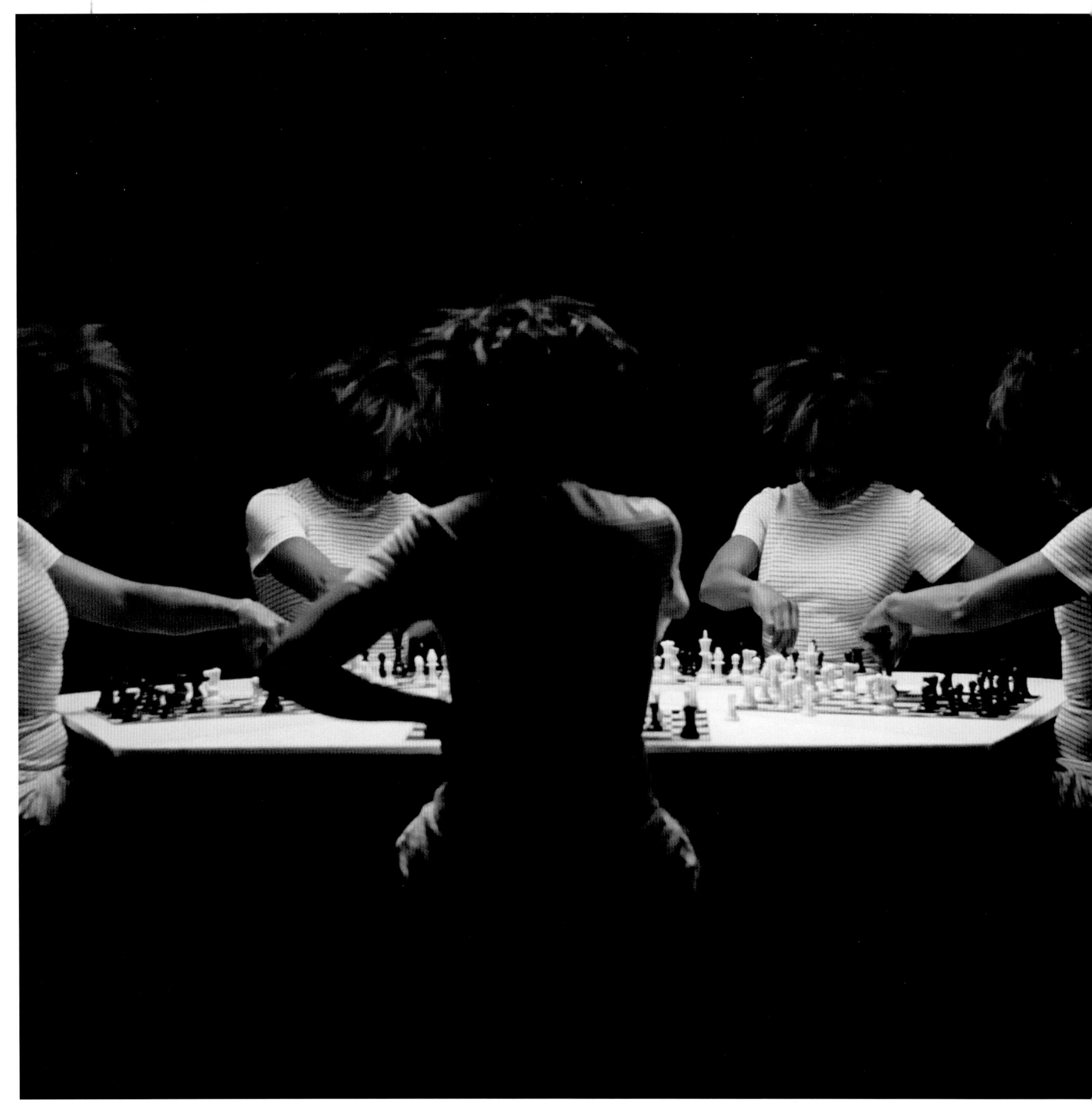

Above and following pages:
Lorna Simpson, *Chess*, 2013, three-channel HD video
(black and white, sound); installation views

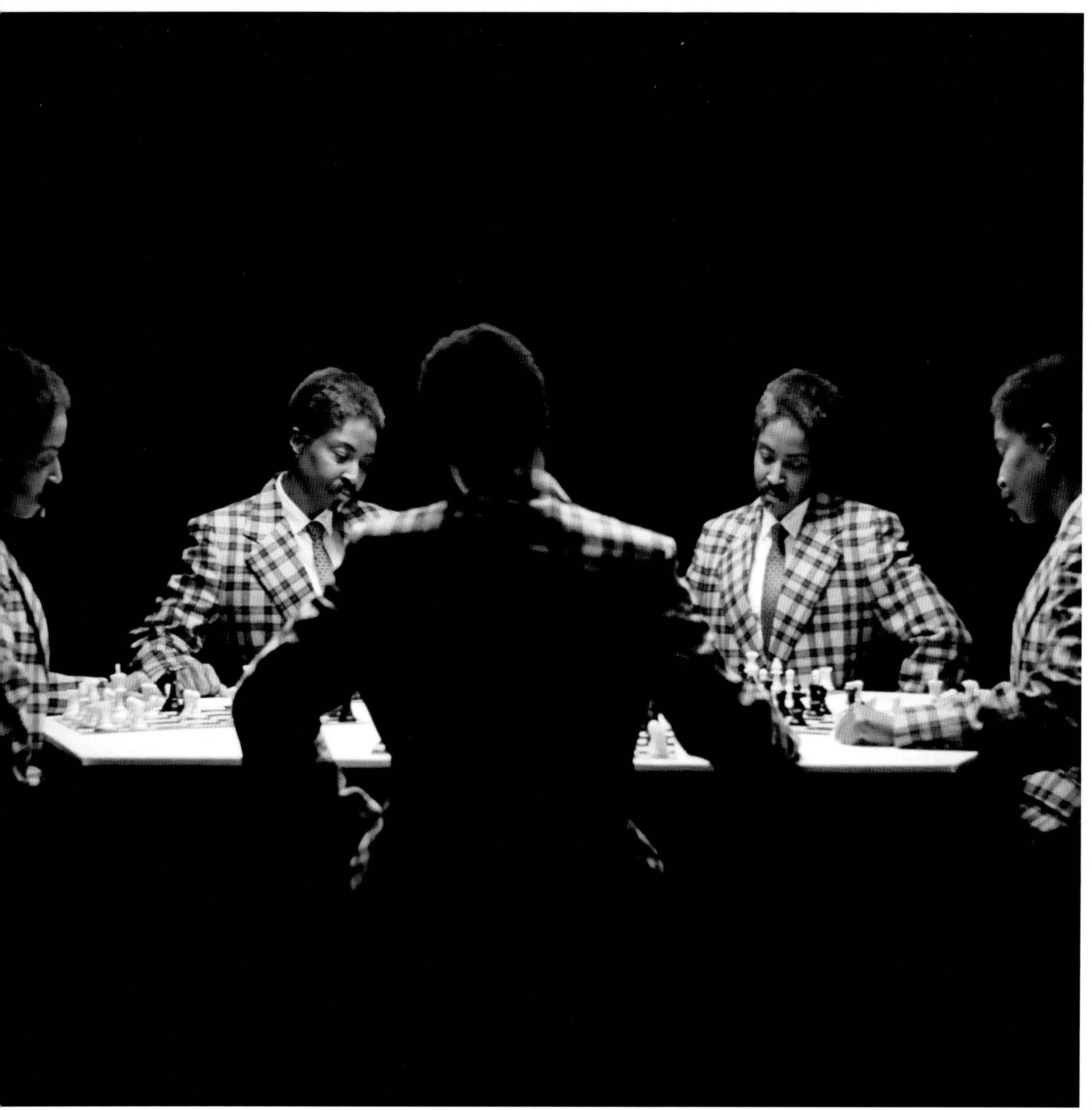

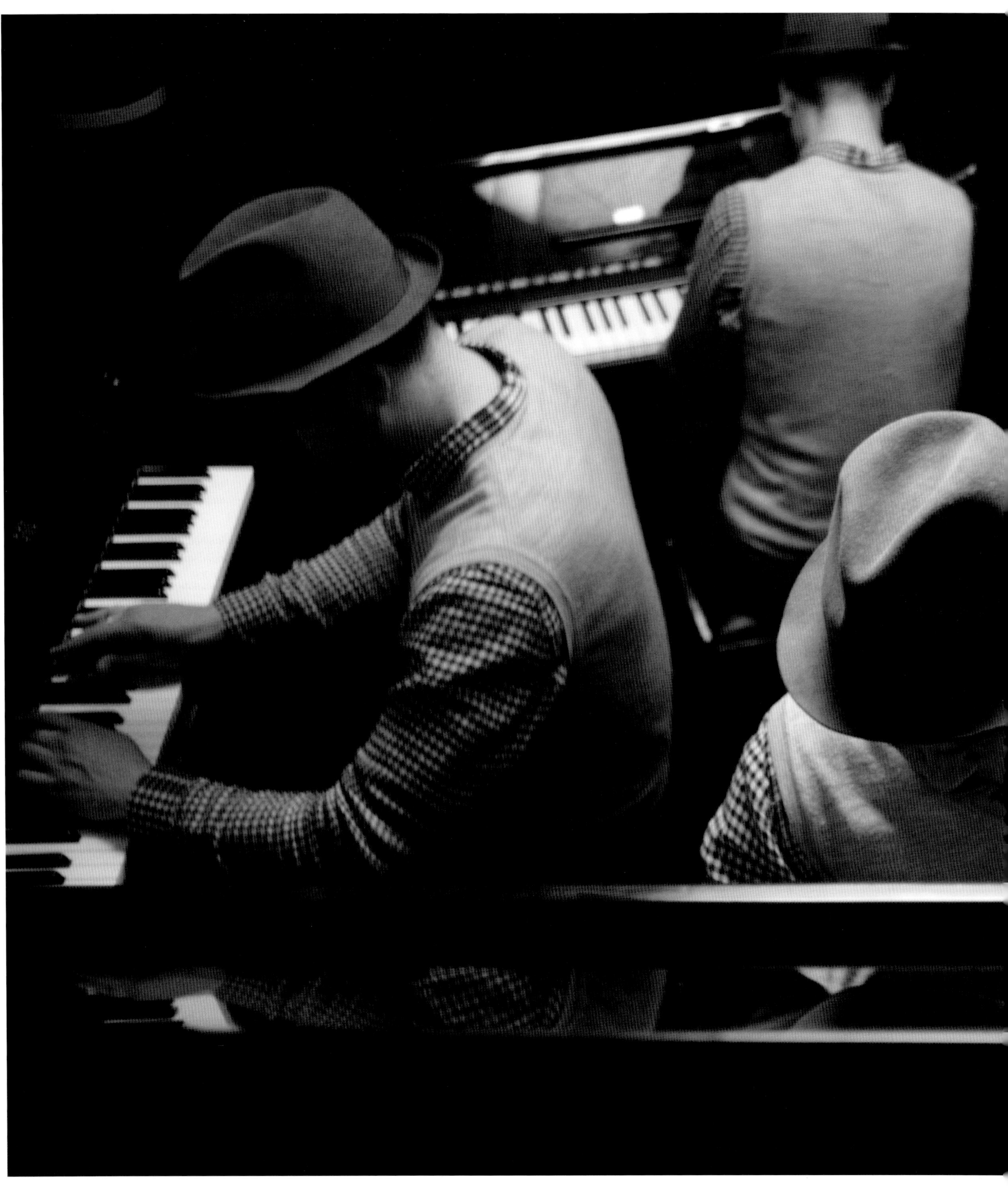

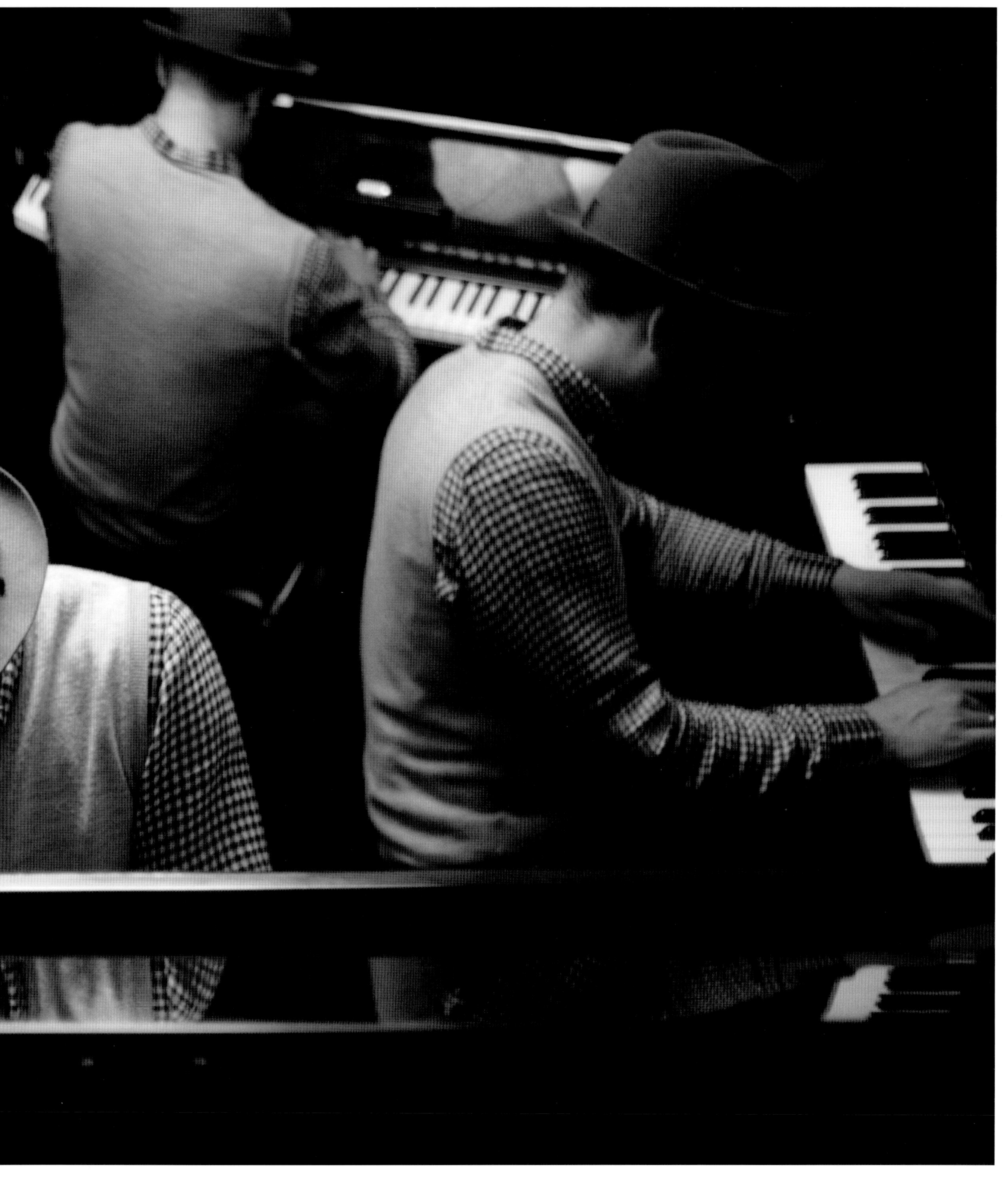

Jason Moran performing in *Looks of a Lot* at the Symphony Center,
Chicago, May 30, 2014

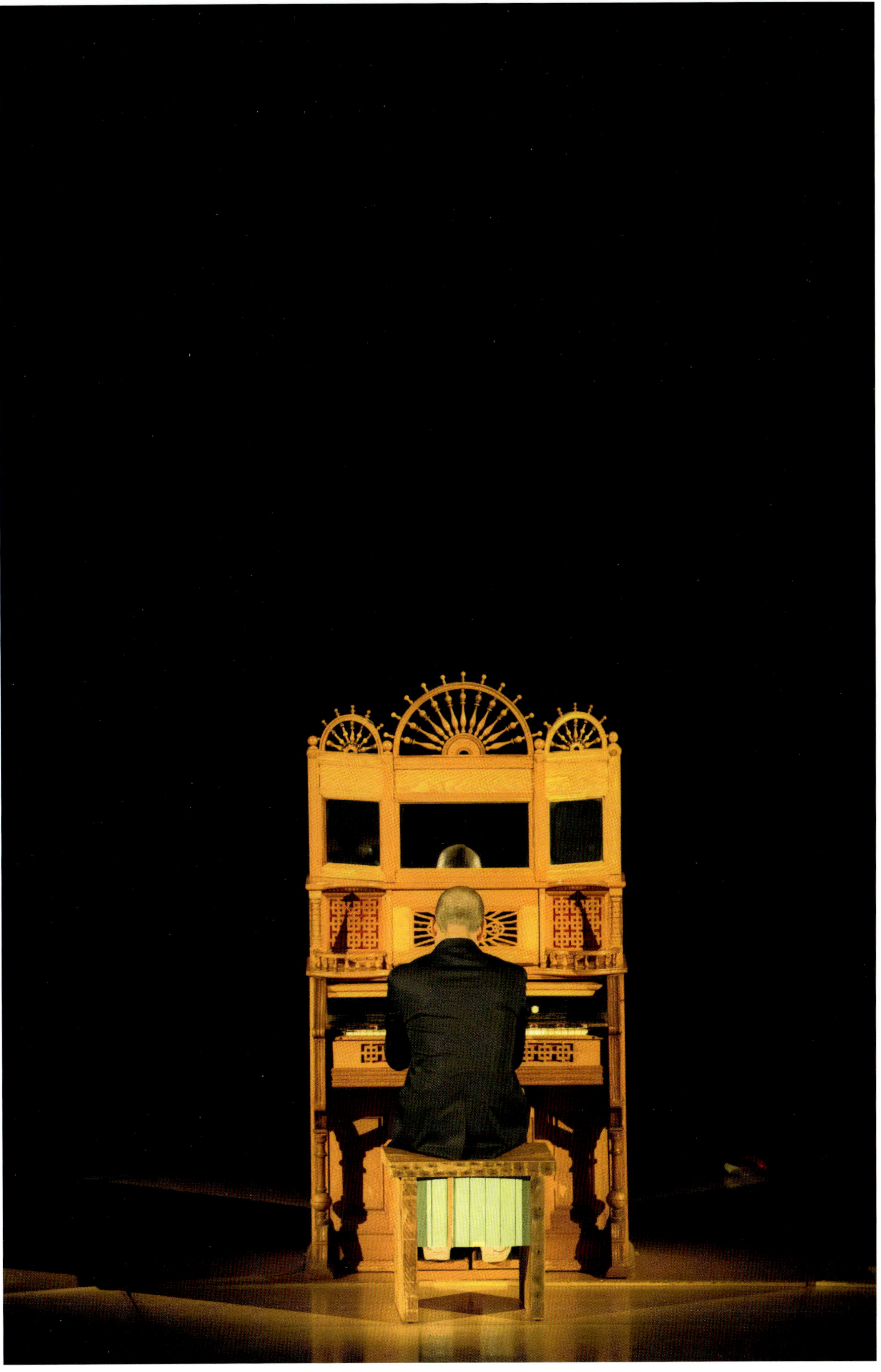

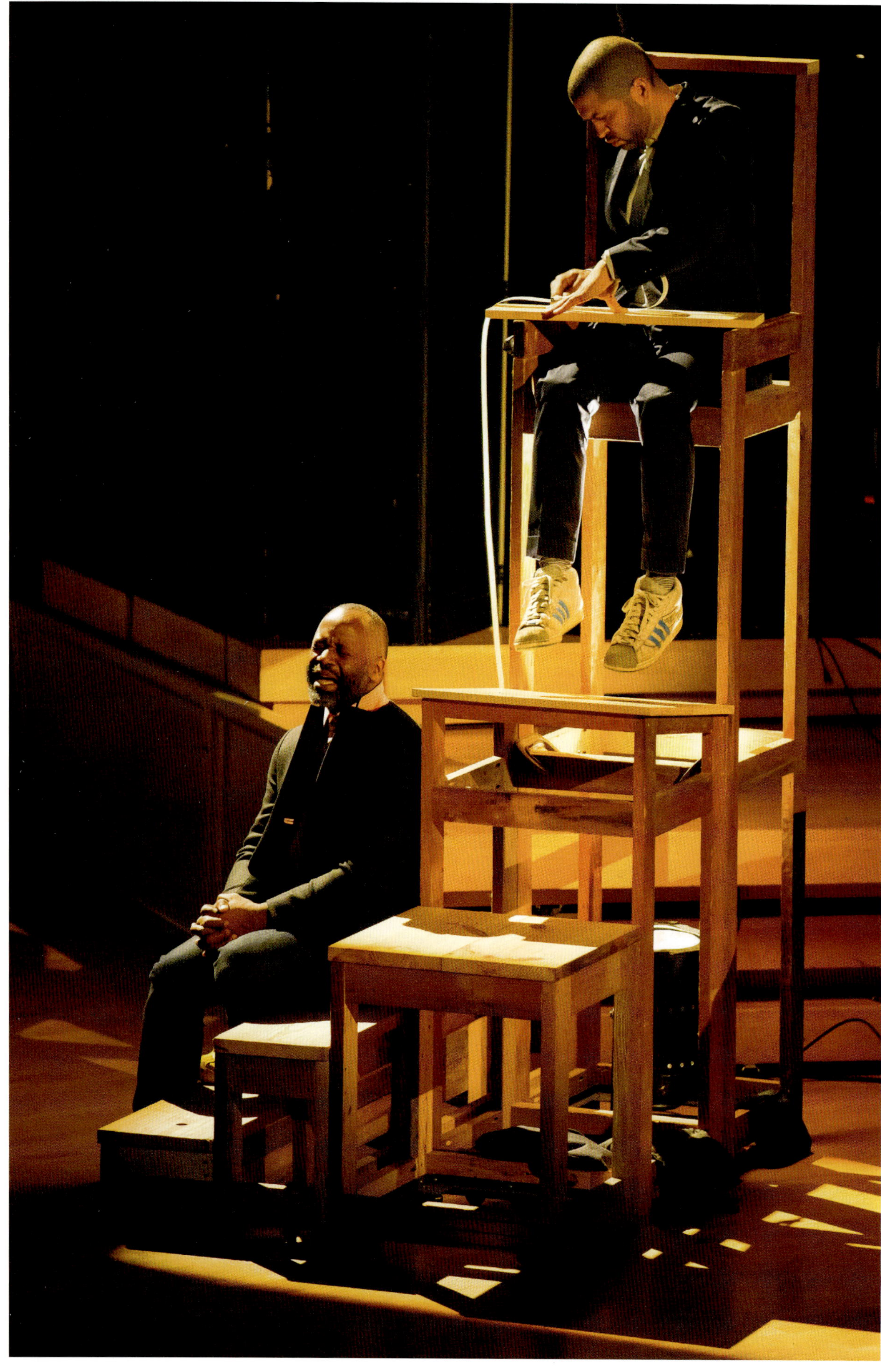

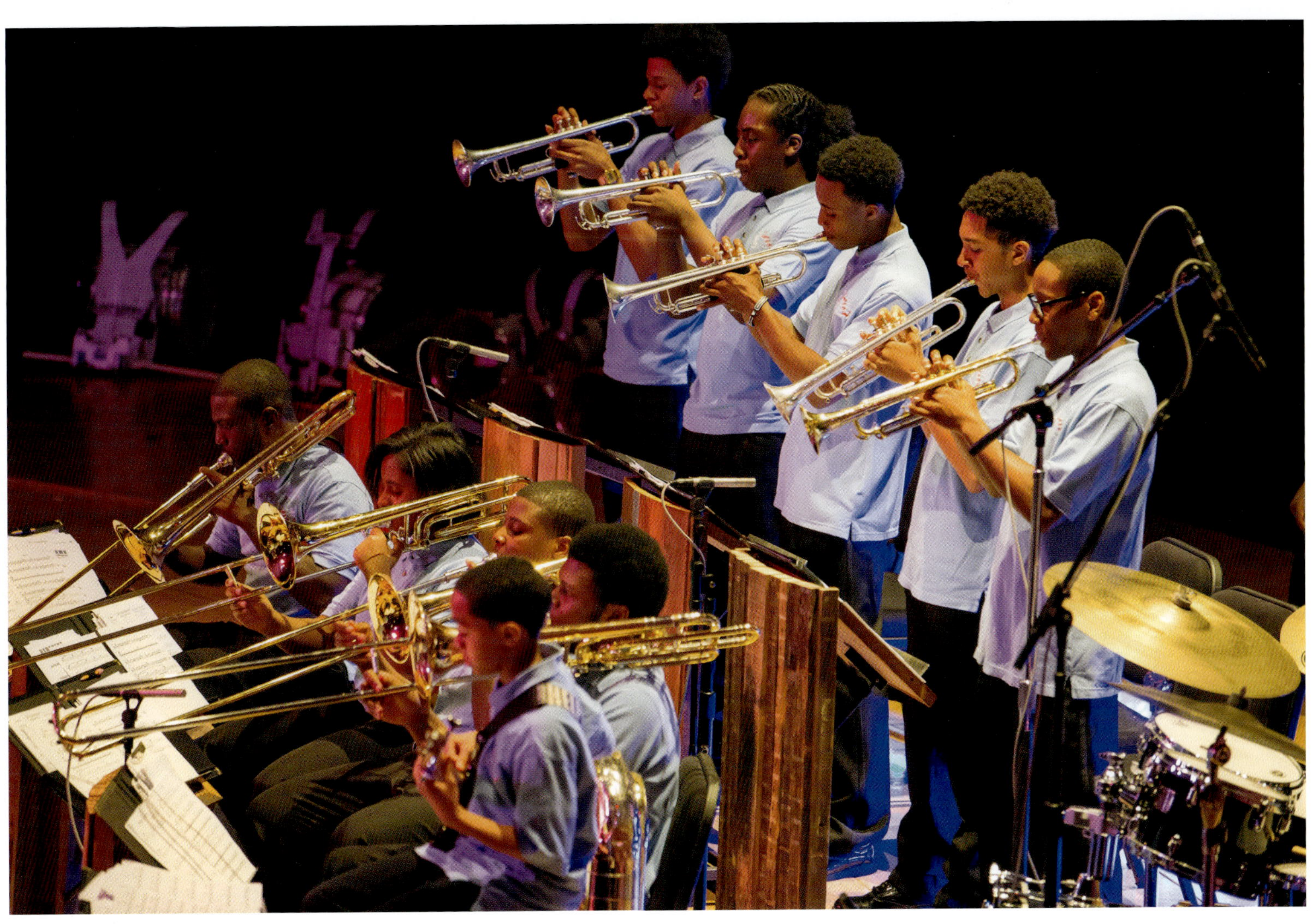

Left to right:
Theaster Gates and Jason Moran performing in *Looks of a Lot* at the Symphony Center, Chicago, May 30, 2014

The Kenwood Academy Jazz Band performing in *Looks of a Lot* at the Symphony Center, Chicago, May 30, 2014

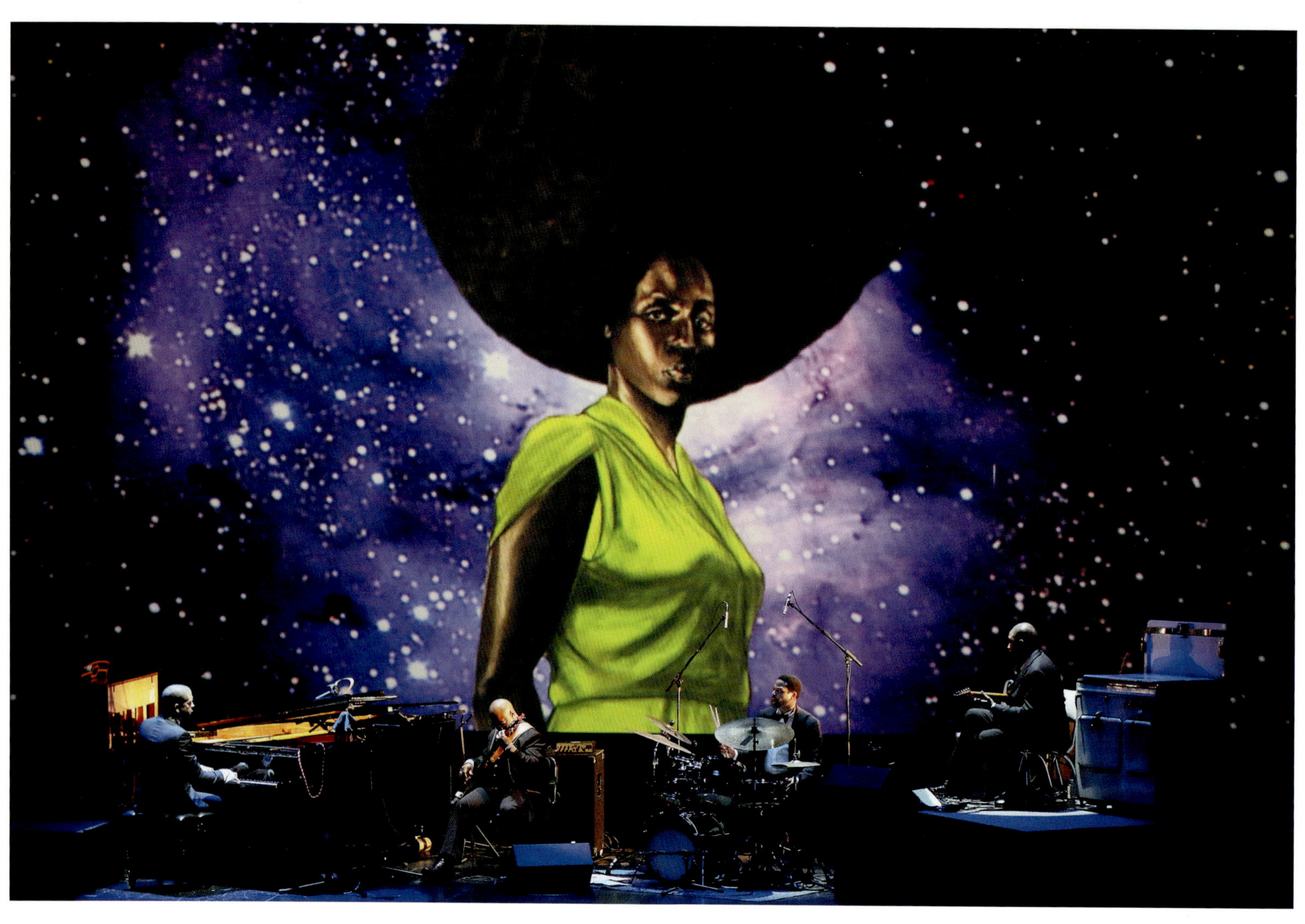

Above and following pages:
Jason Moran, Tarus Mateen, Nasheet Waits, and Marvin Sewell performing in *The Rauschenberg Project: Holed Up*, with video design by Robert Pruitt, at the Wortham Center, Houston, February 7, 2015

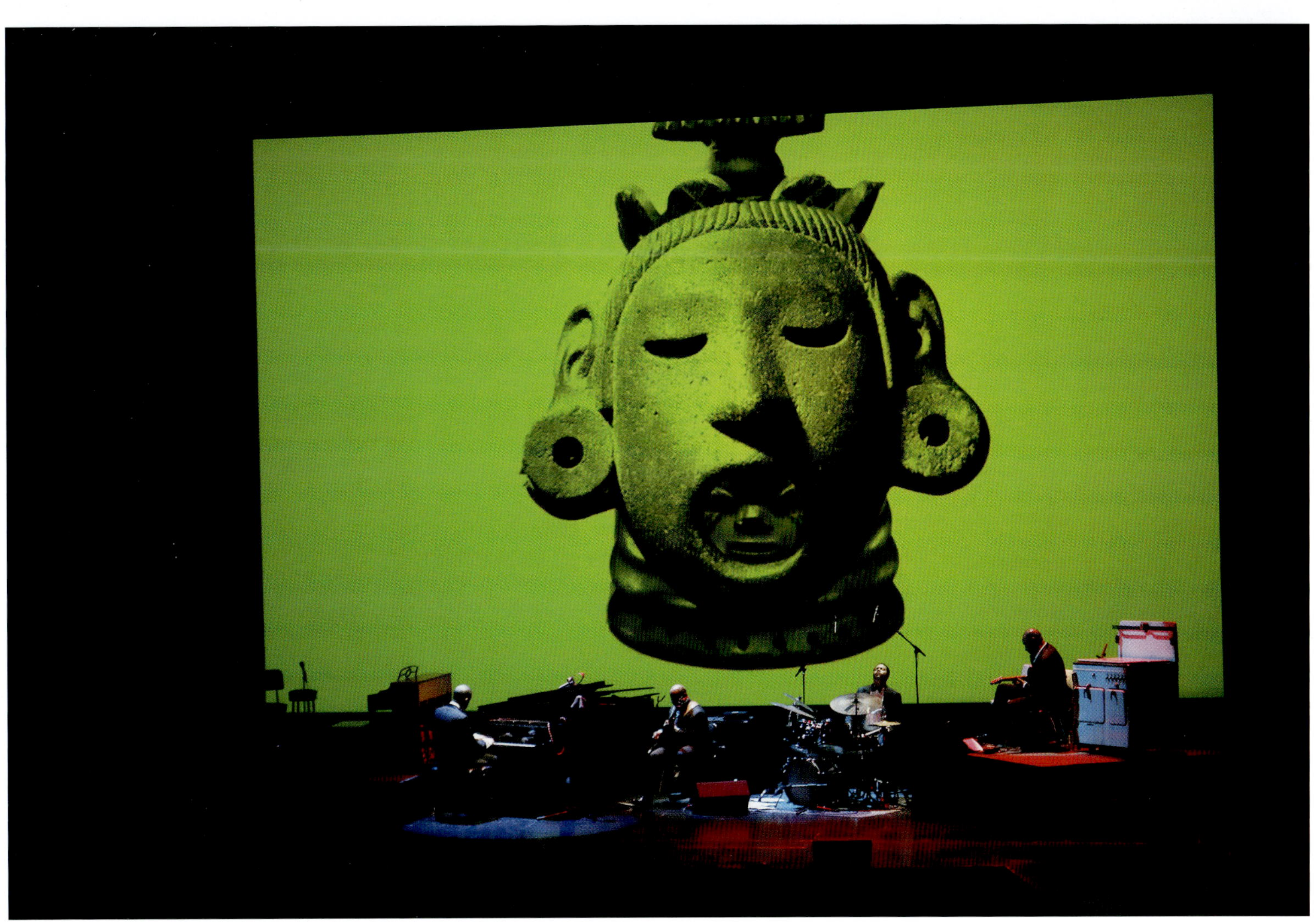

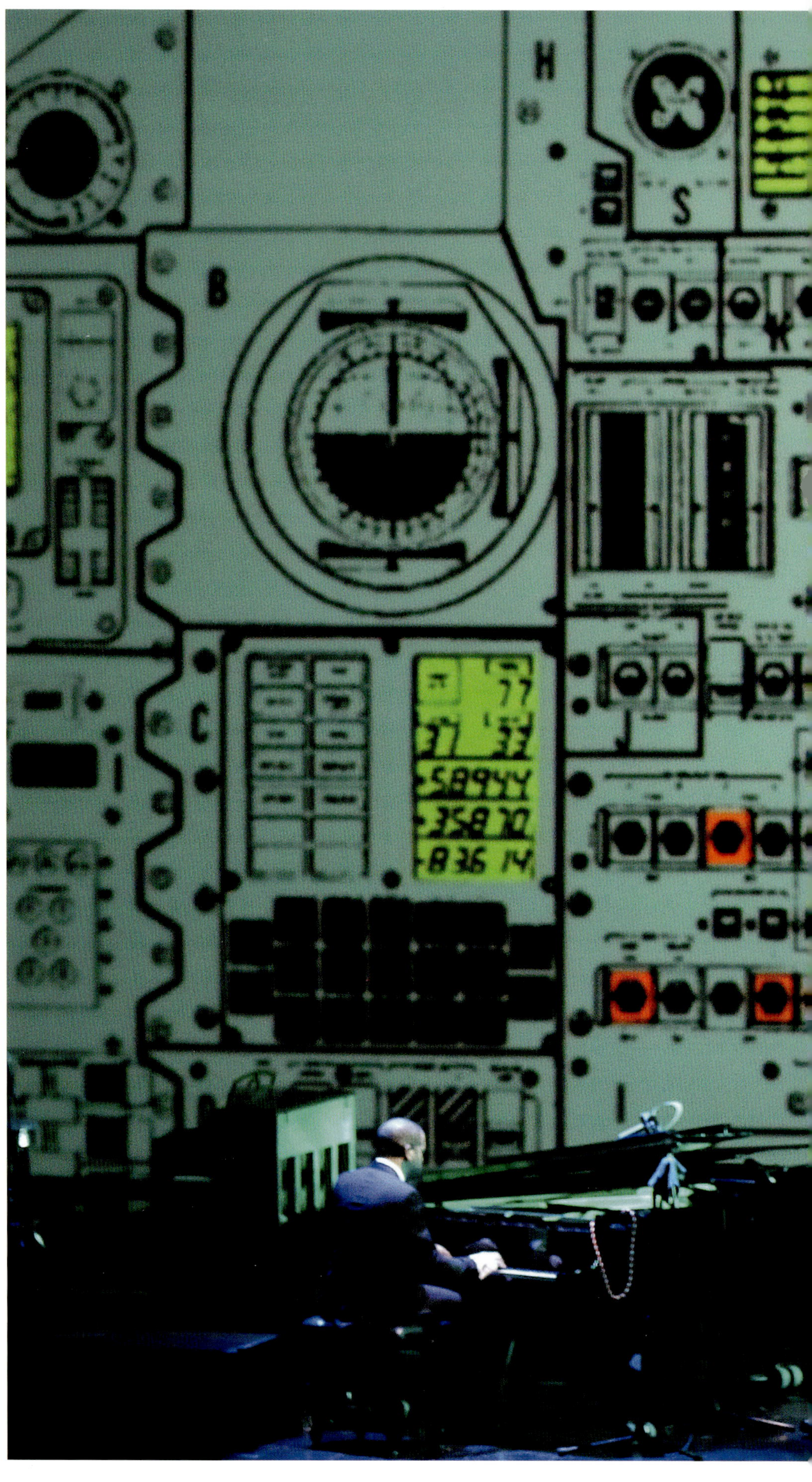

77
37 37
-5.8944
-358 70
-8 26 14

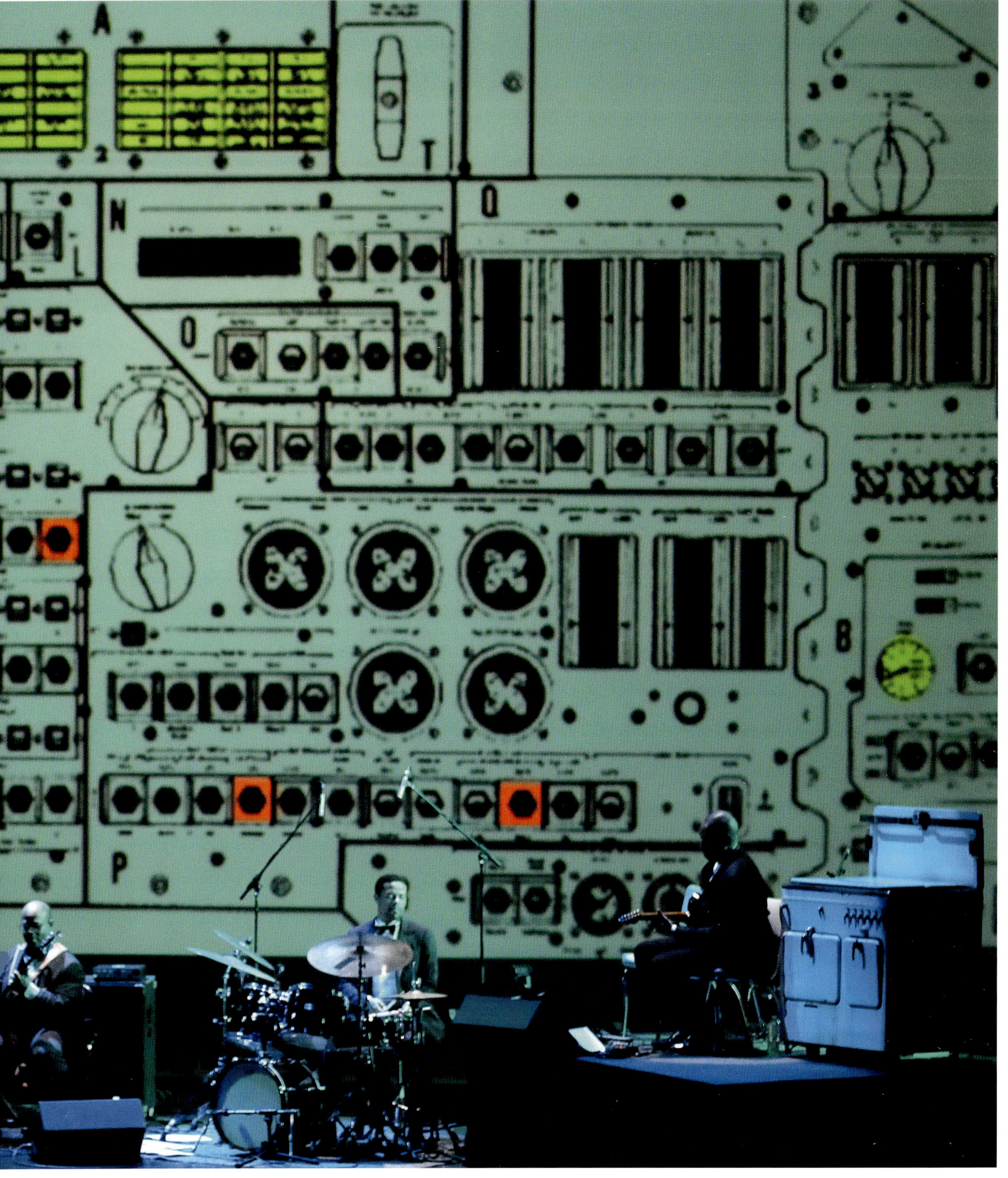

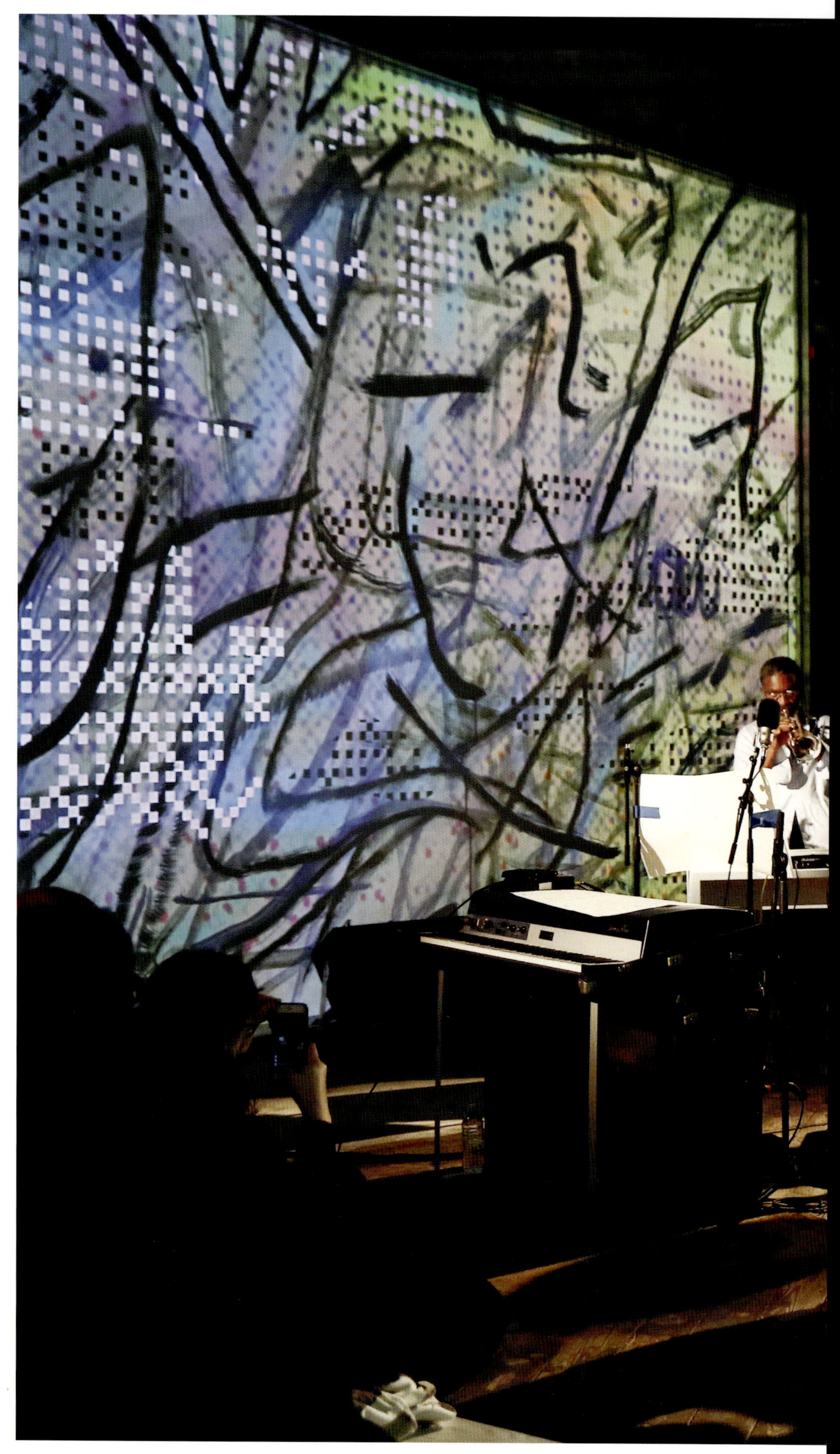

Right and following pages:
Graham Haynes, Jason Moran, and Jamire Williams performing
in *MASS (HOWL, eon)*, with a video installation of paintings
by Julie Mehretu, at the Harlem Parish, New York, as part of
Performa 17, 2017

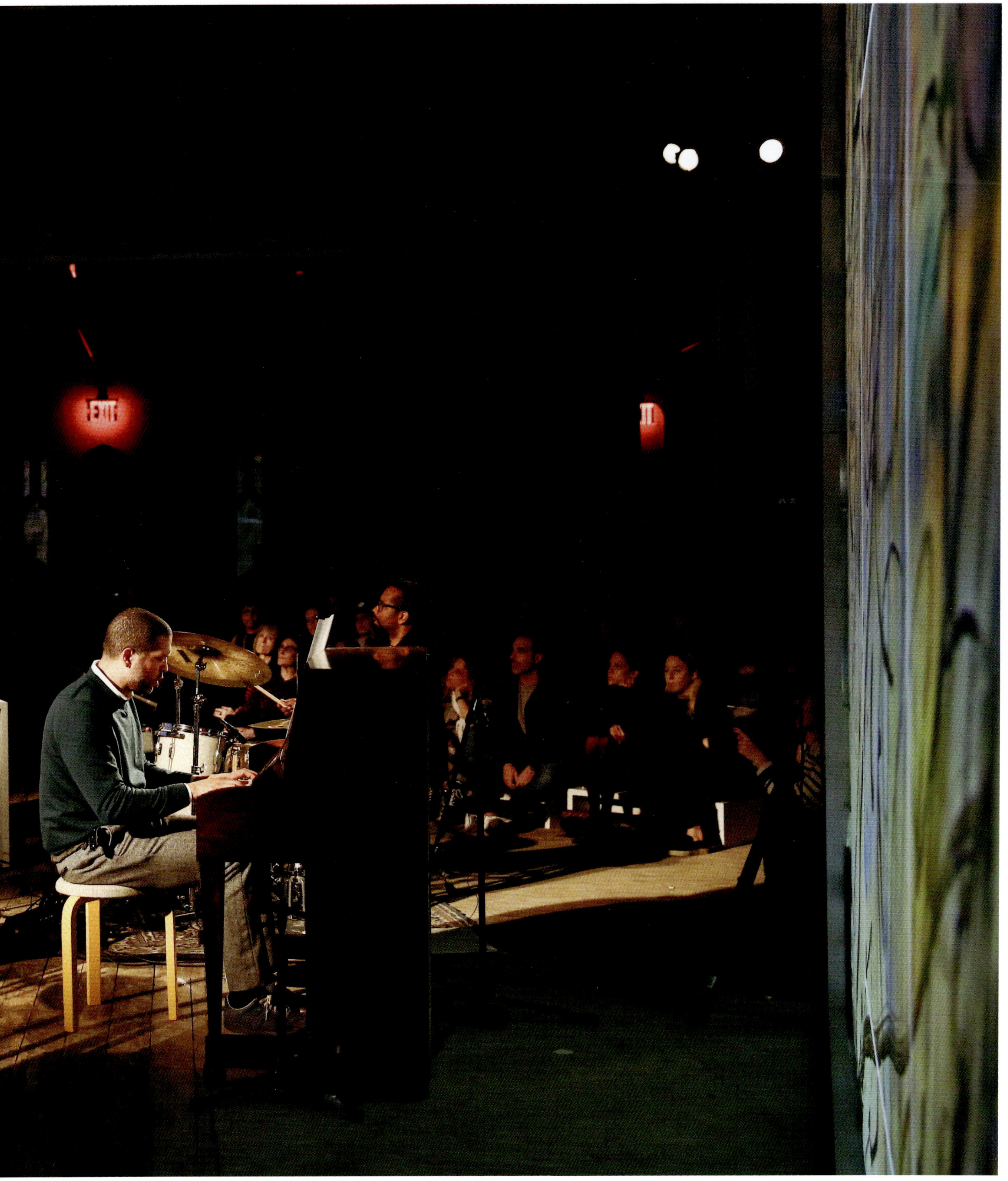

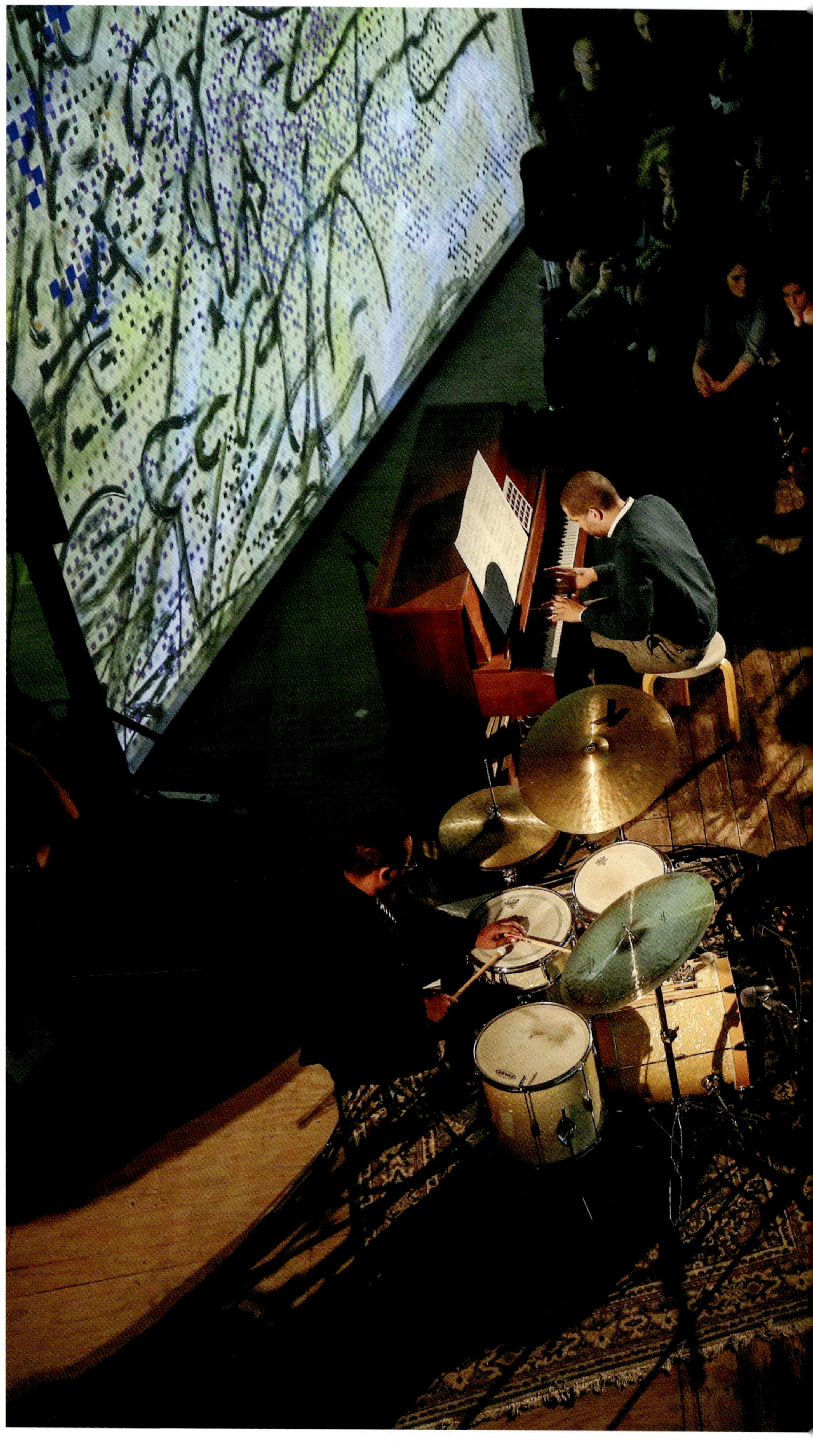

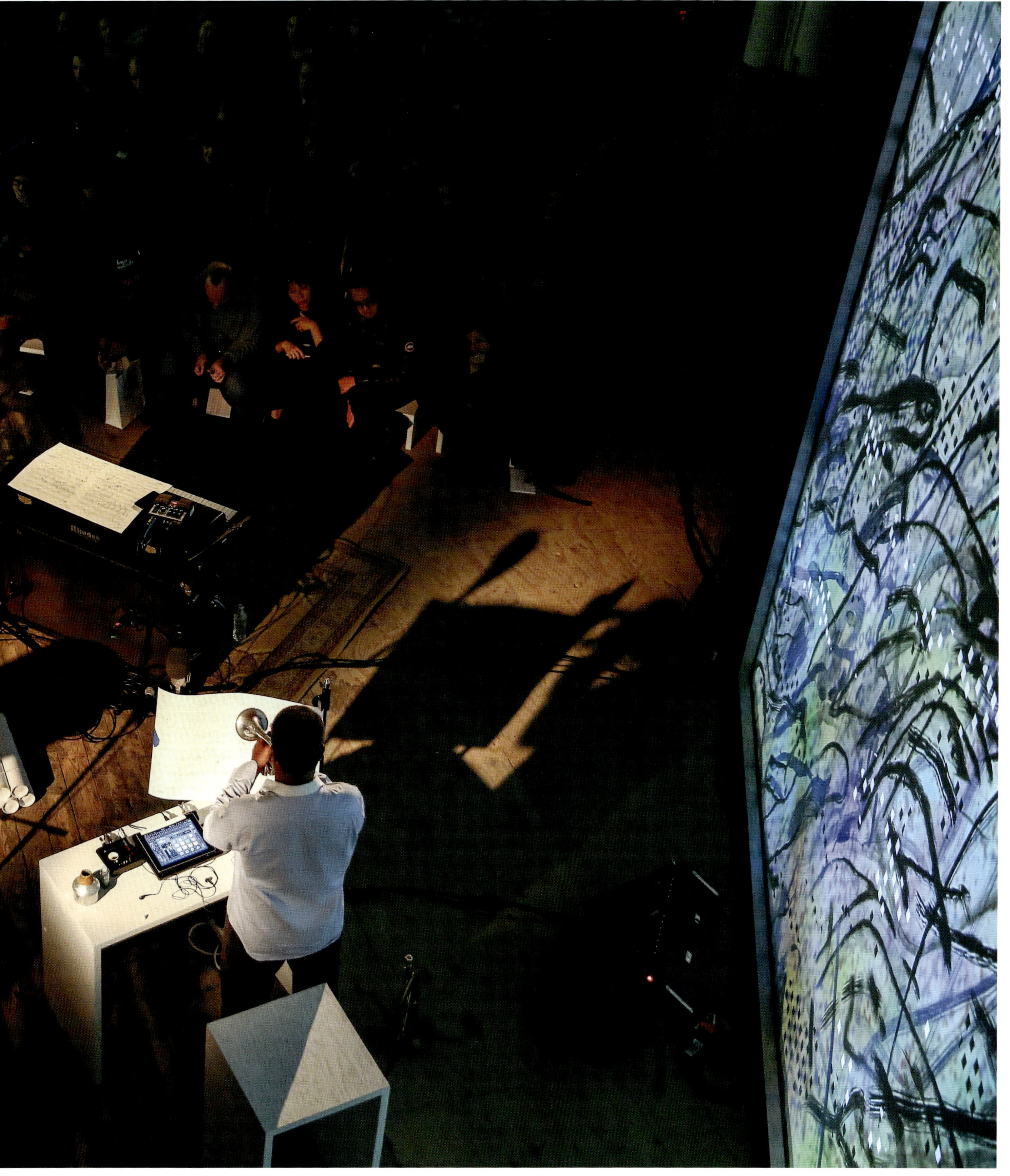

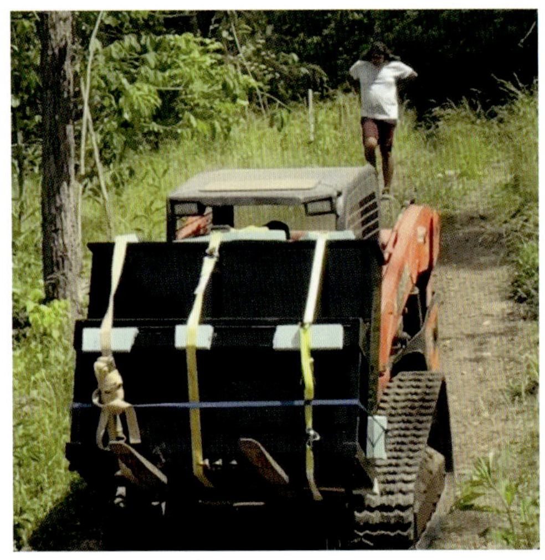
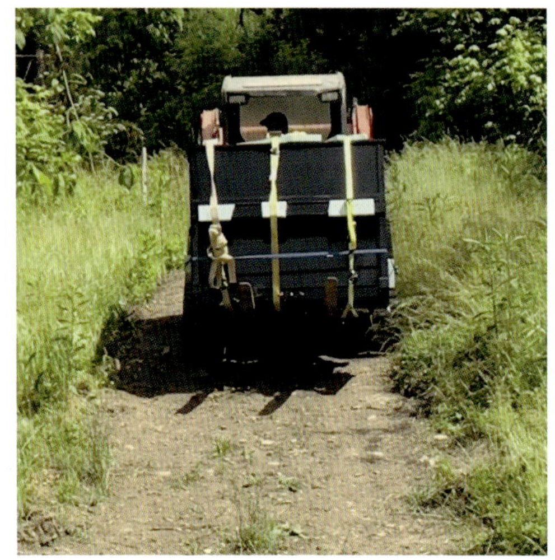
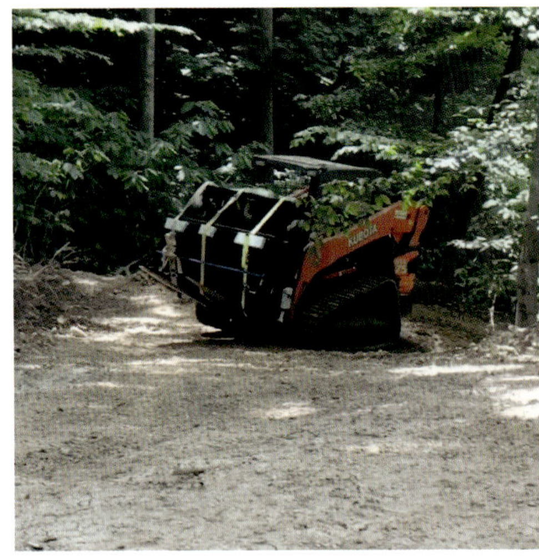
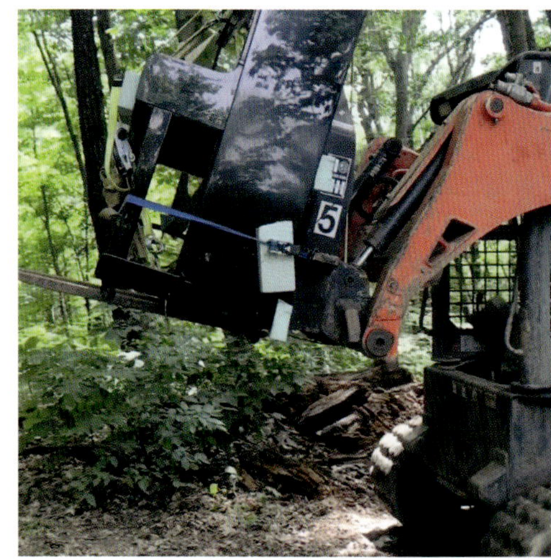
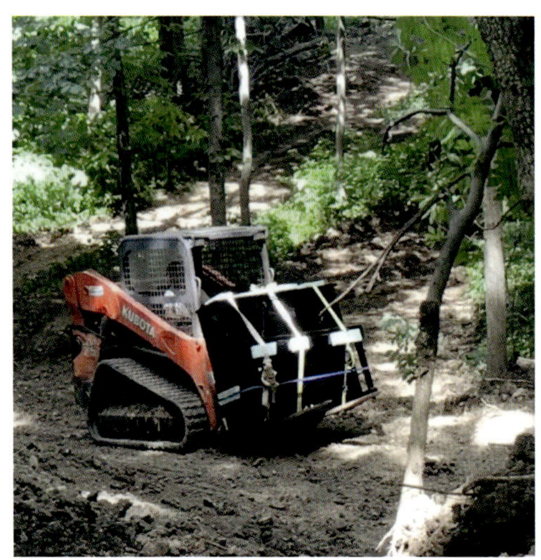
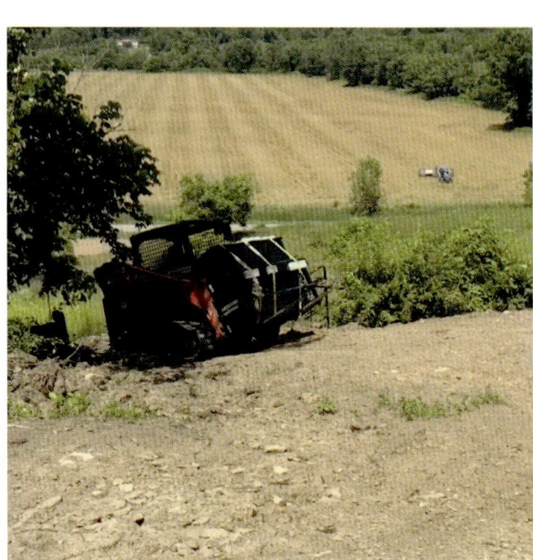

Ryan Trecartin and Lizzie Fitch, Stills from *Tree Bath Jazz*, 2017, video (color, sound); presented as part of *The Last Jazz Fest* performance at the Walker Art Center, Minneapolis, 2018

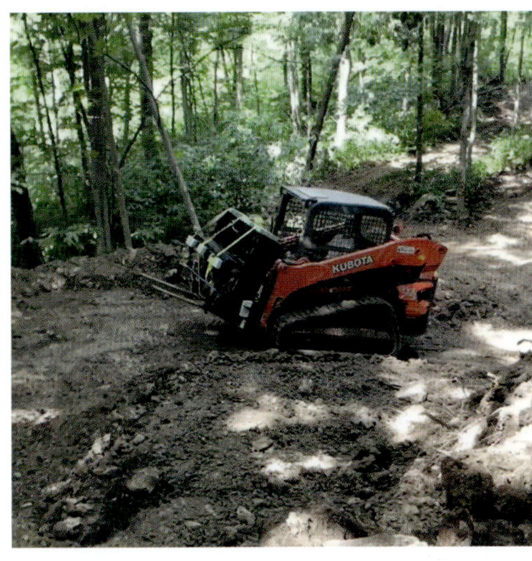

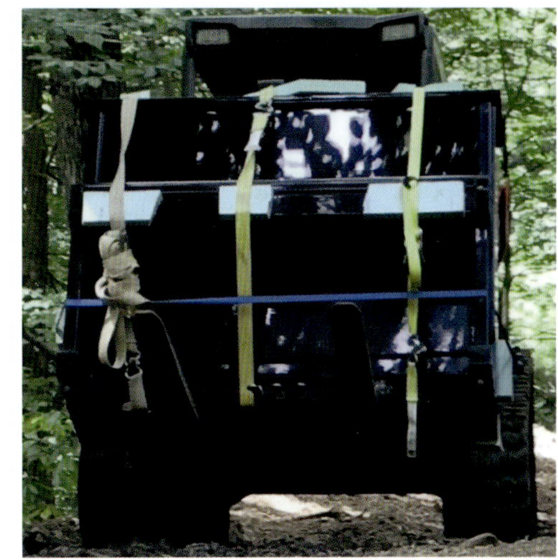

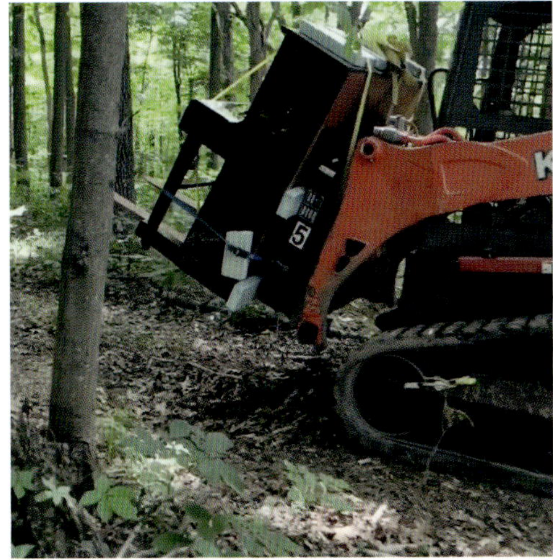

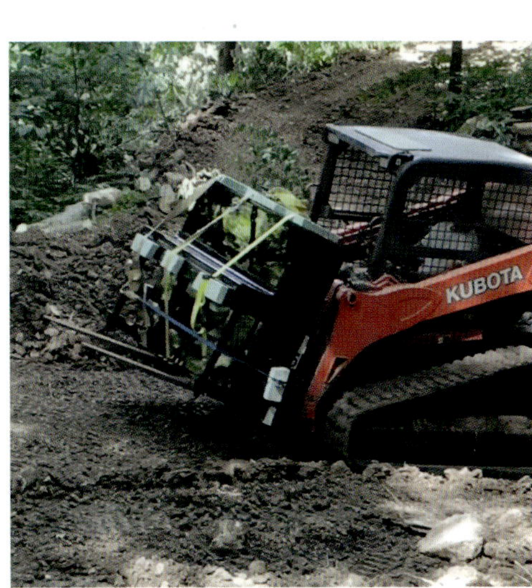

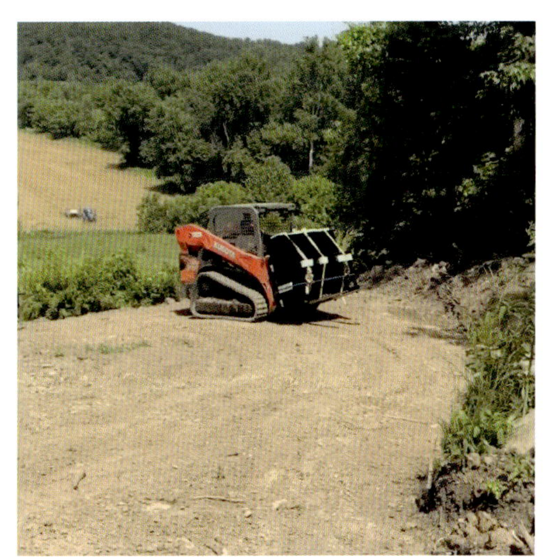

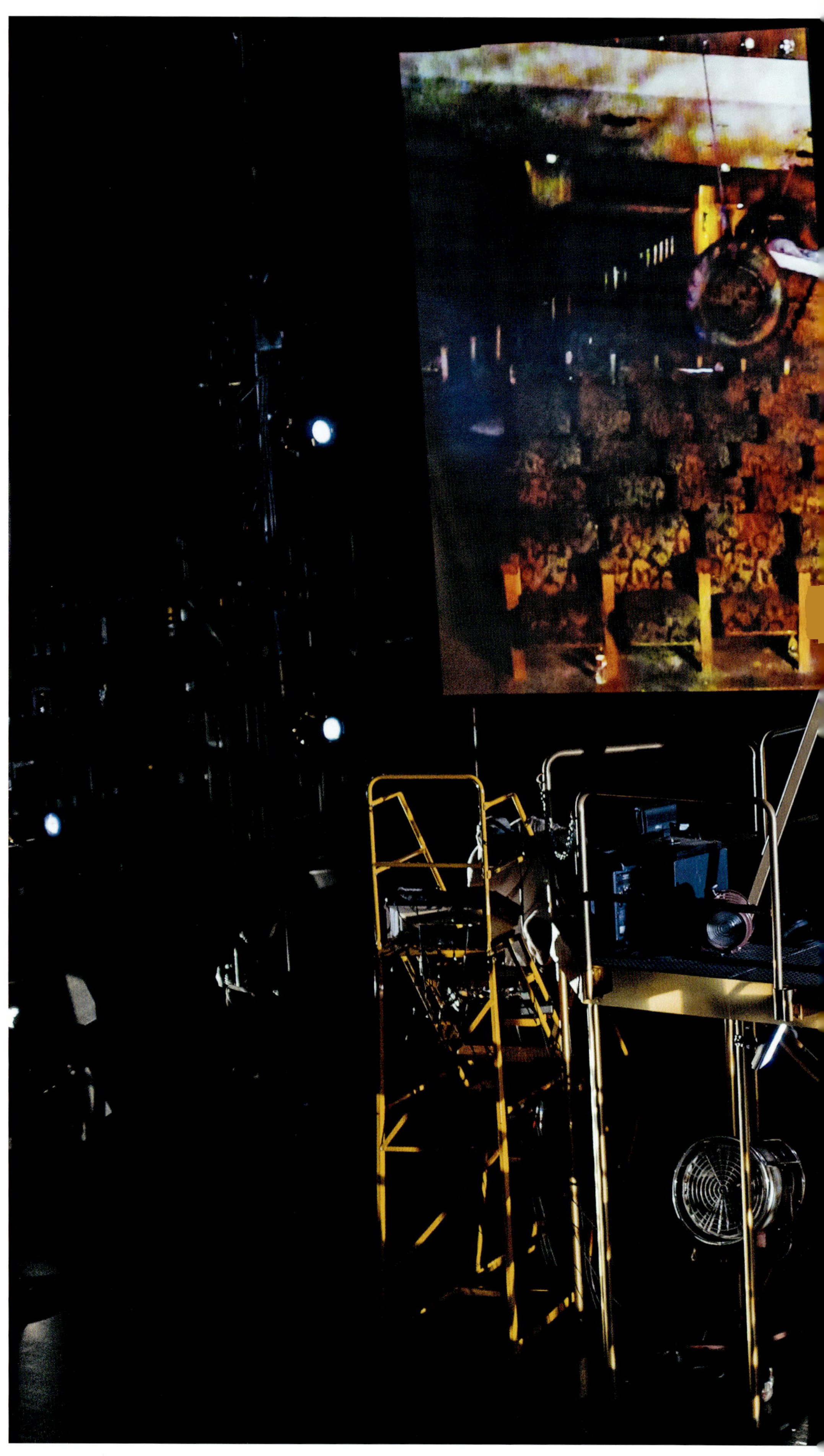

Jason Moran and the Bandwagon, Ryan Trecartin, Lizzie Fitch, and DJ Ashland Mines (Total Freedom) performing at the premiere of *The Last Jazz Fest* in the McGuire Theater, Walker Art Center, Minneapolis, May 18, 2018

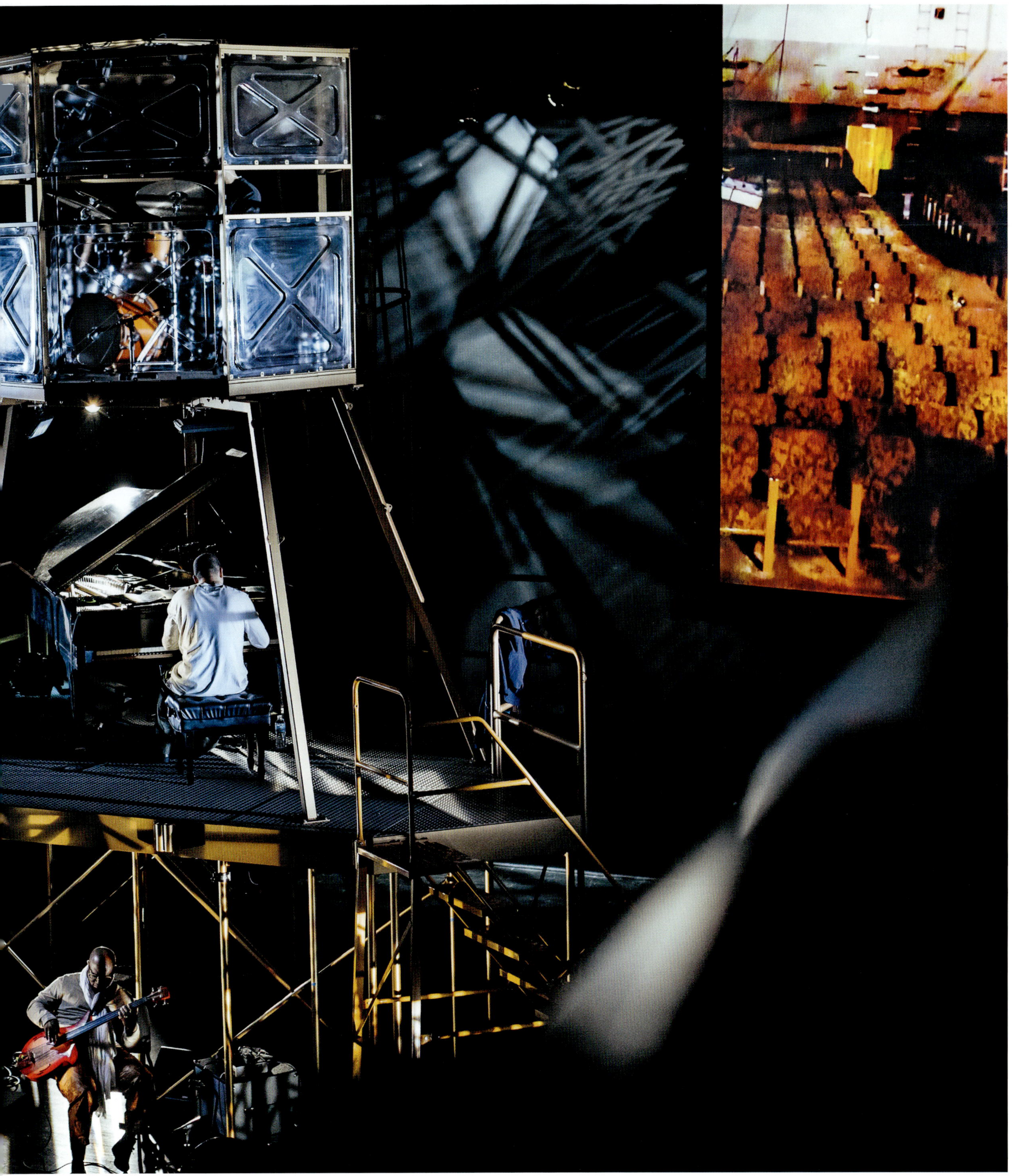

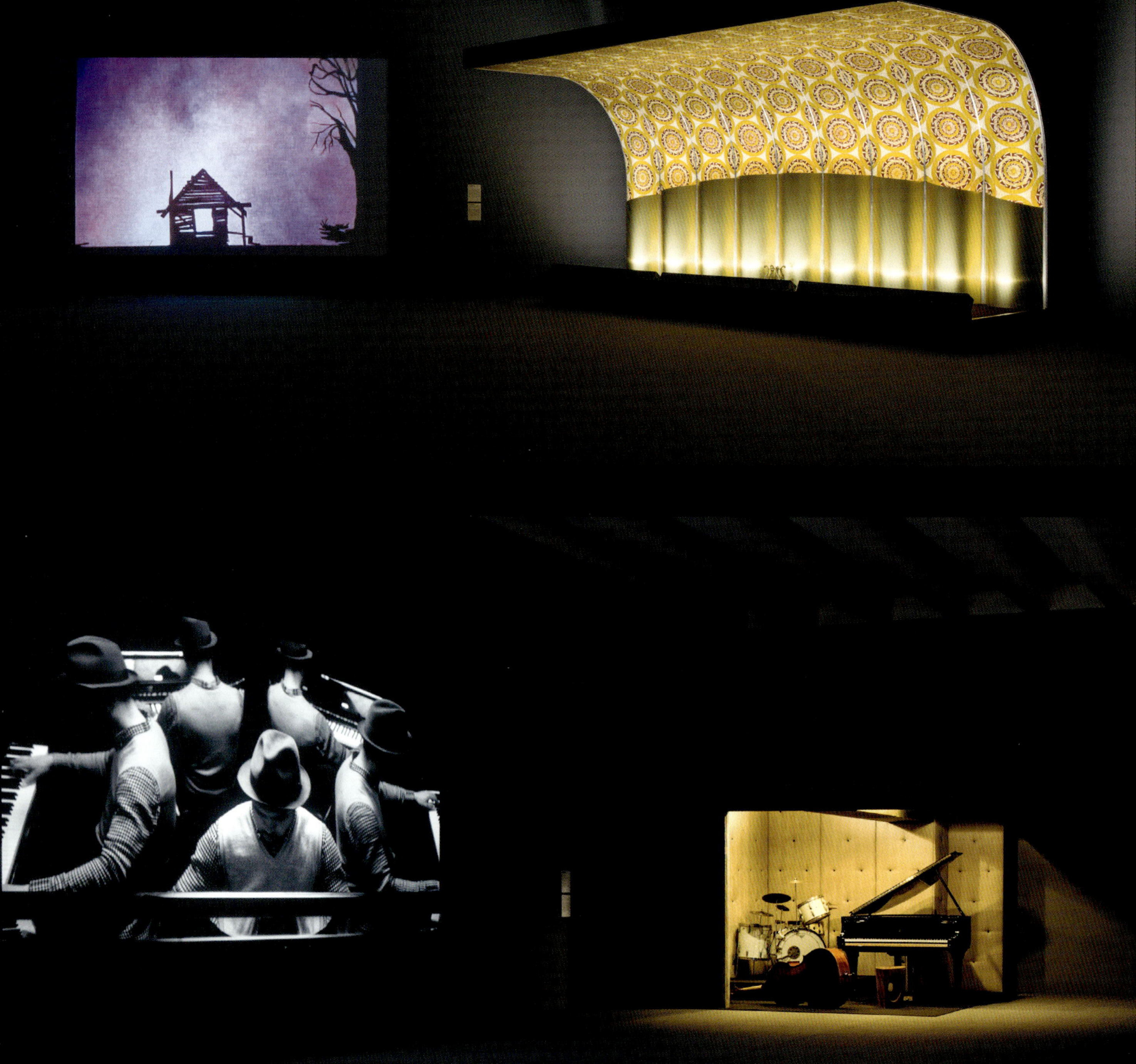

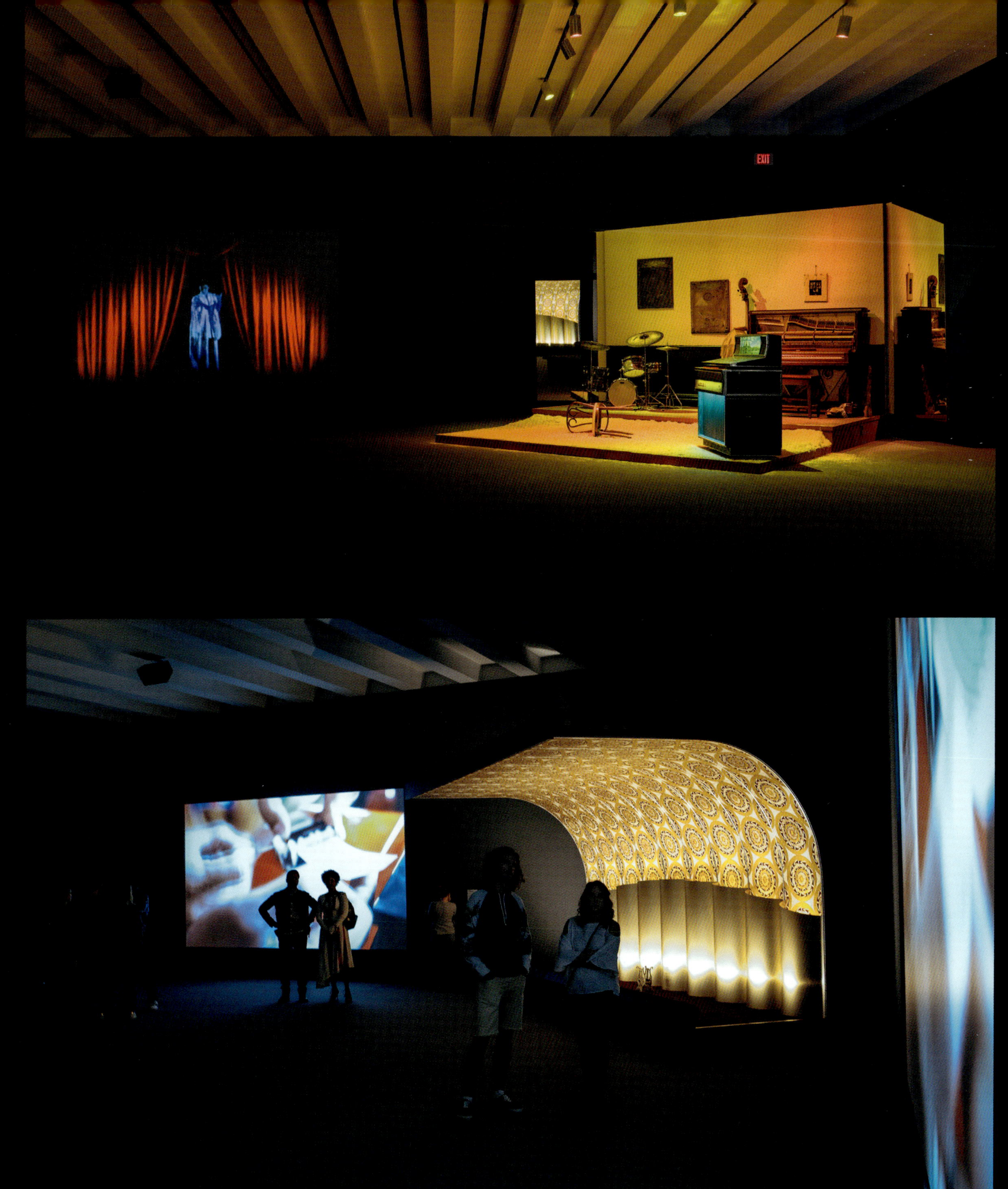

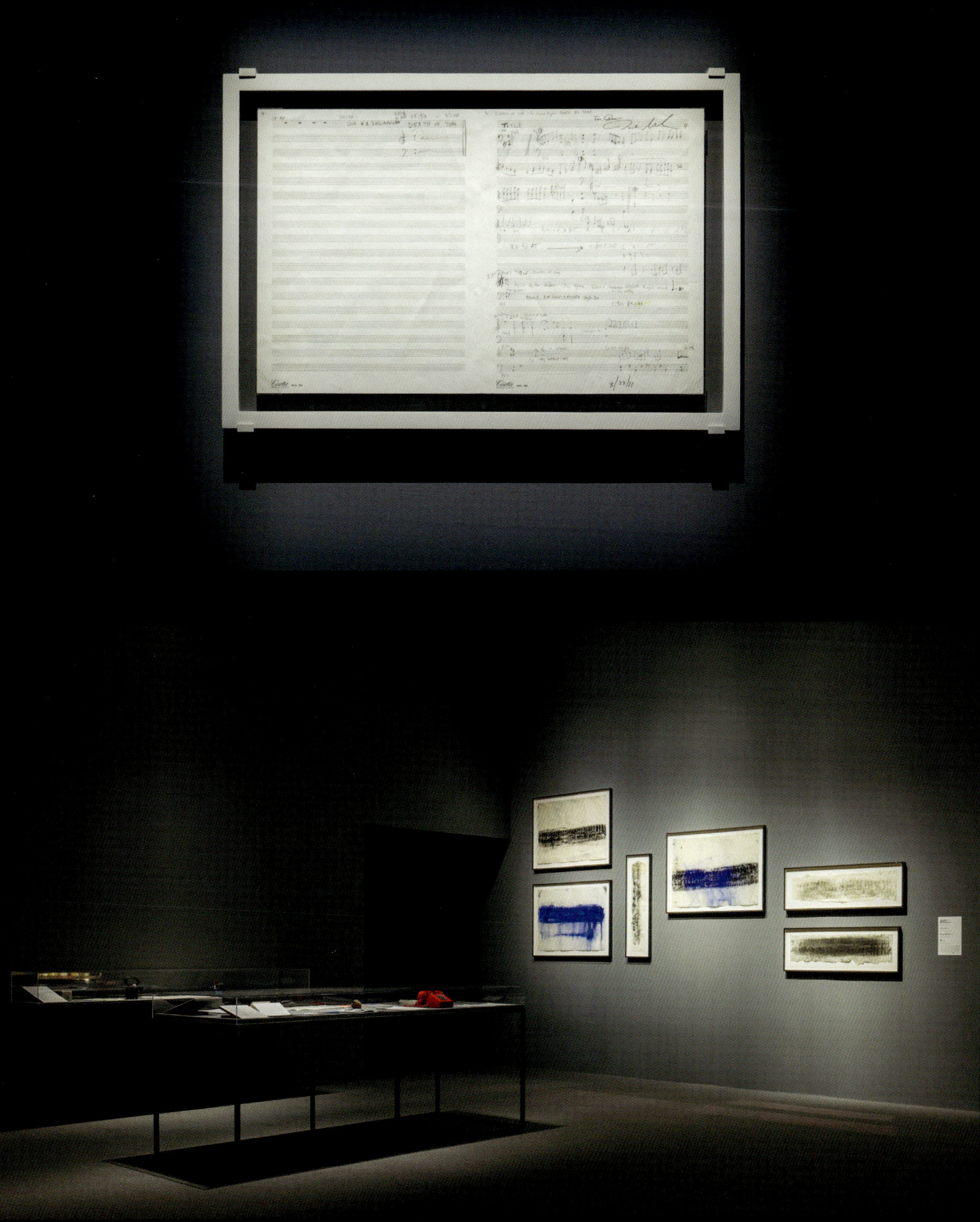

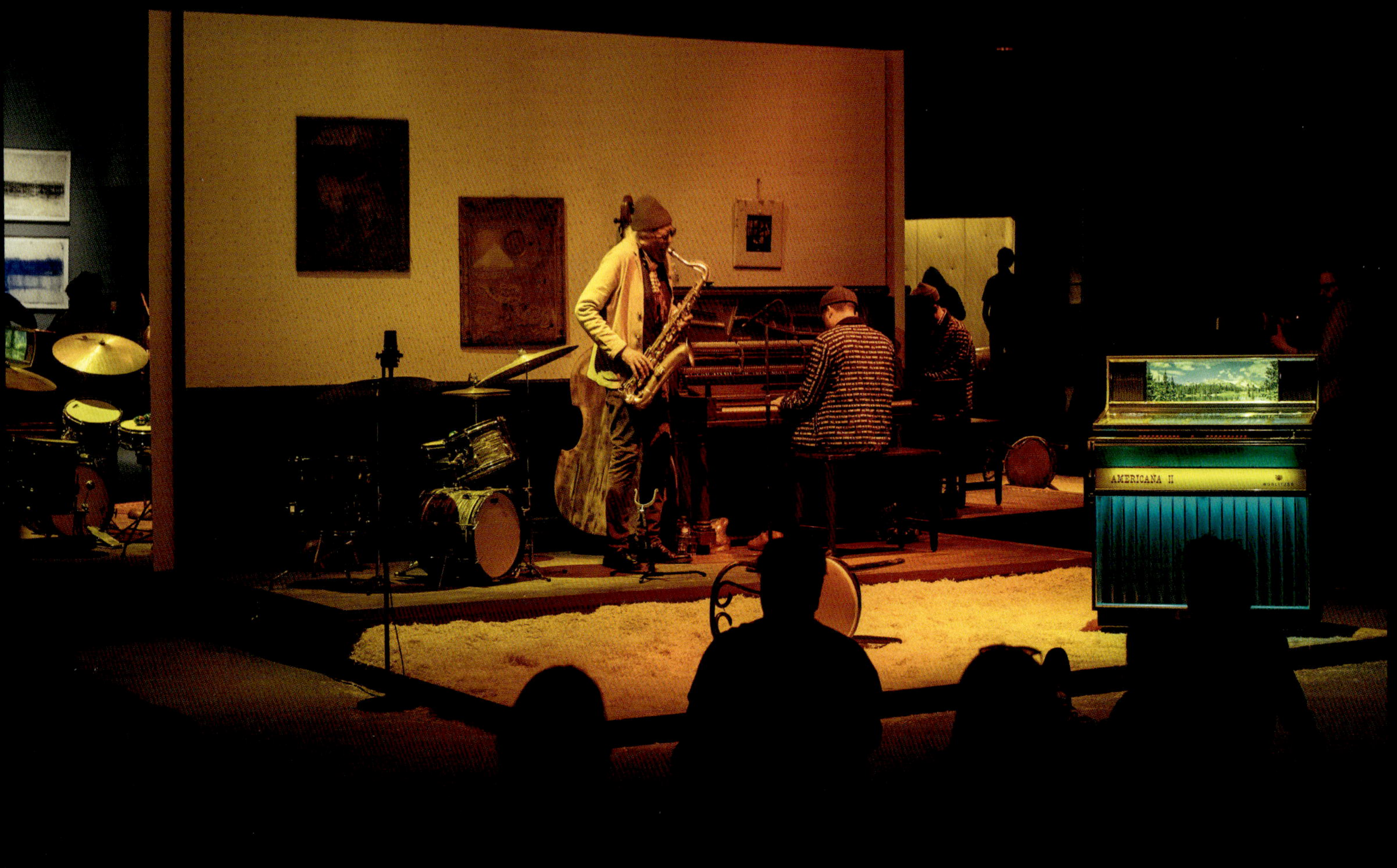

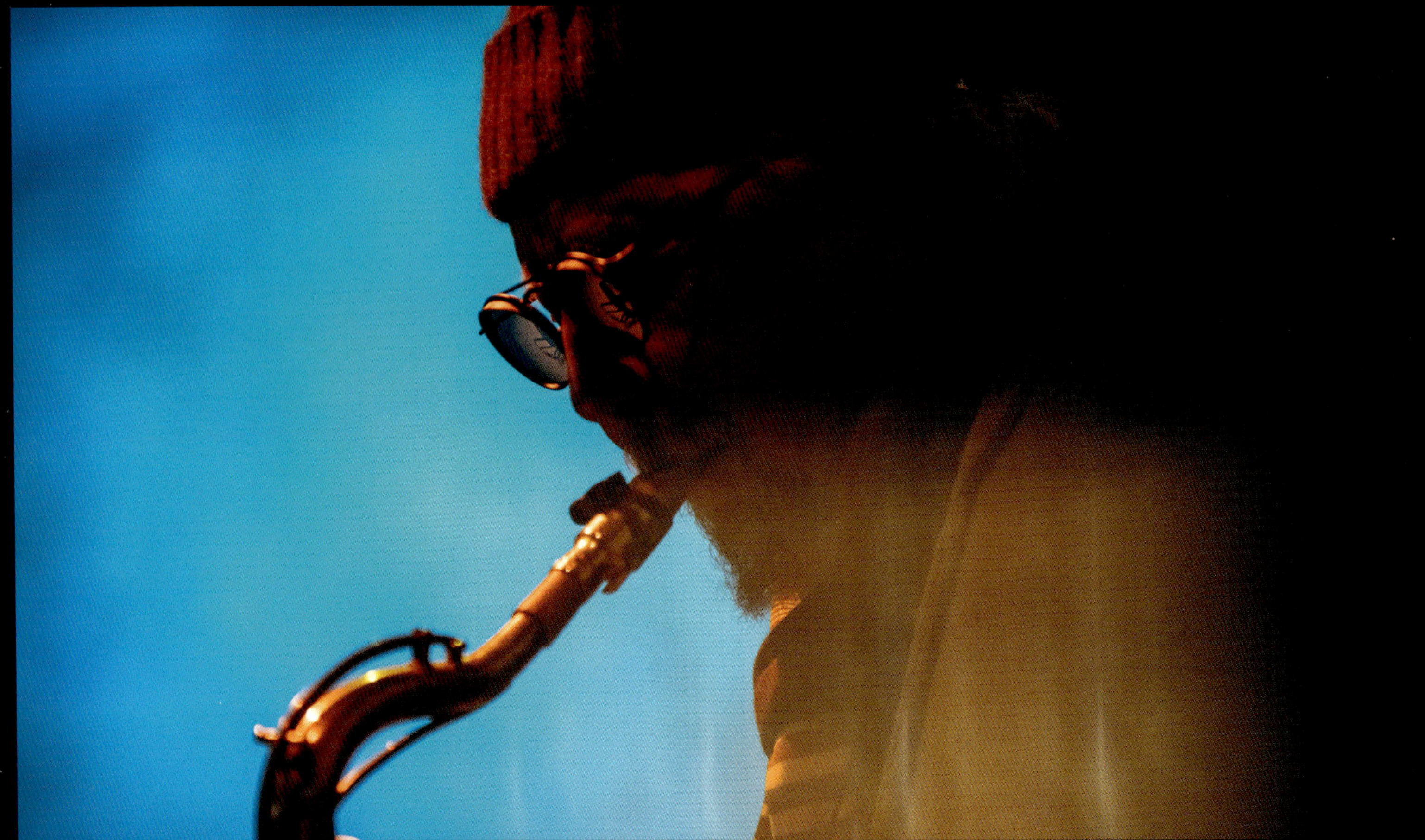

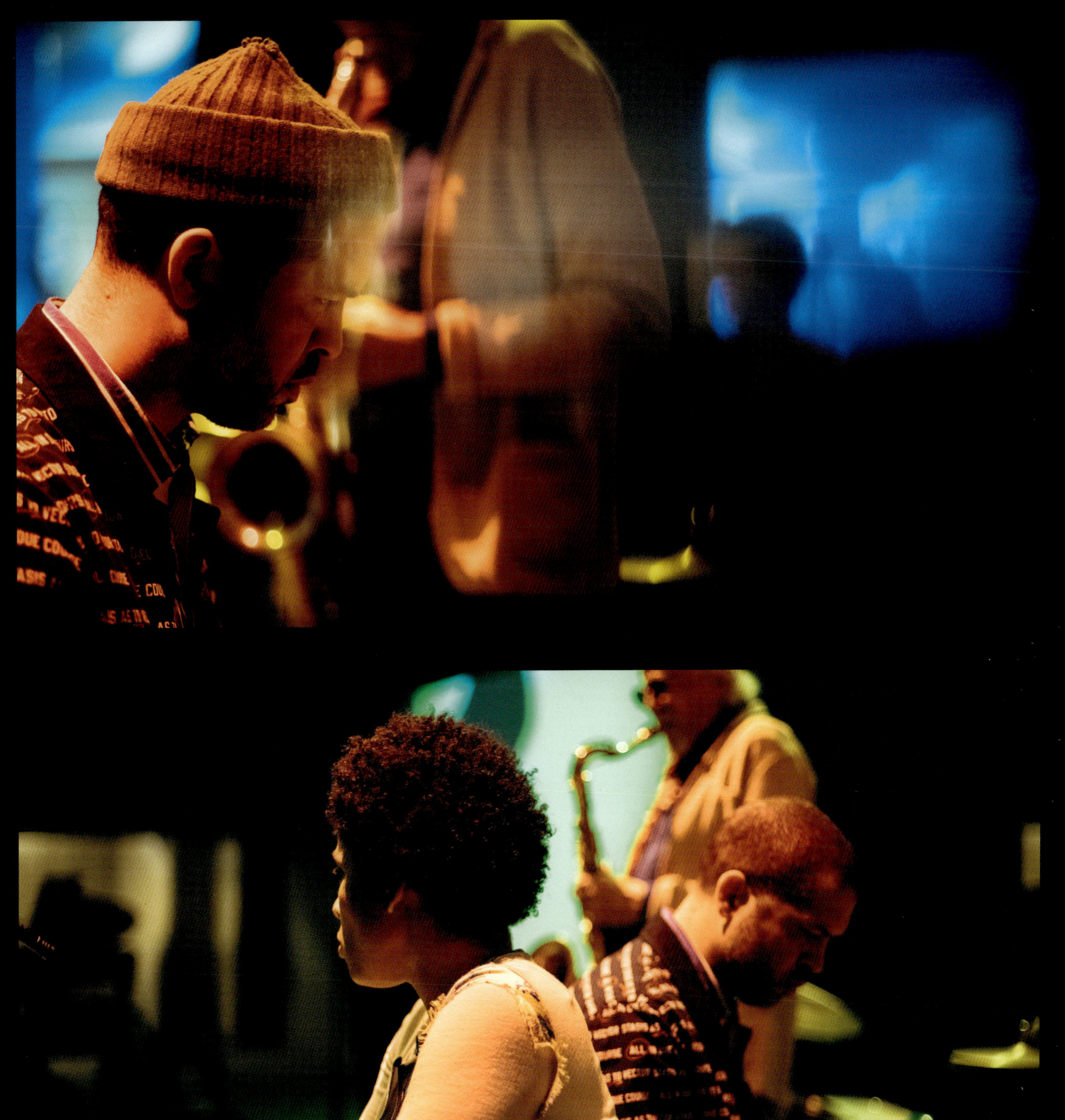

Previous pages:
Installation views of the exhibition *Jason Moran* and
opening-night performance by Alicia Hall Moran,
Charles Lloyd, and Jason Moran at the Walker Art
Center, Minneapolis, April 26, 2018

SPACE, TRACE, AND TRANSFORMATION IN THE ART OF JASON MORAN

The improviser's hand becomes the artist's hand.

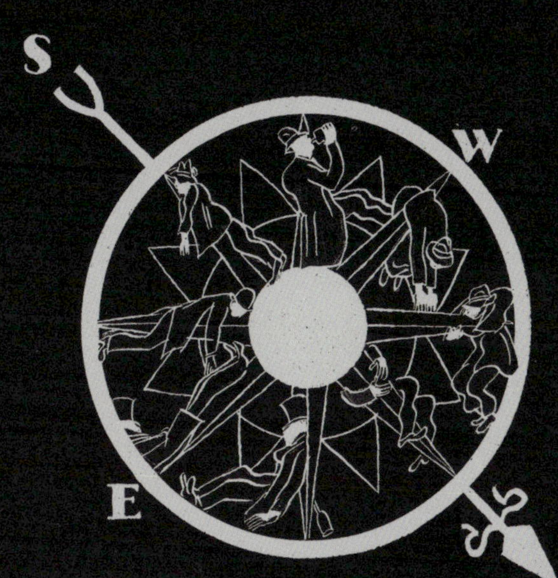

GEORGE E. LEWIS

GEORGE E. LEWIS

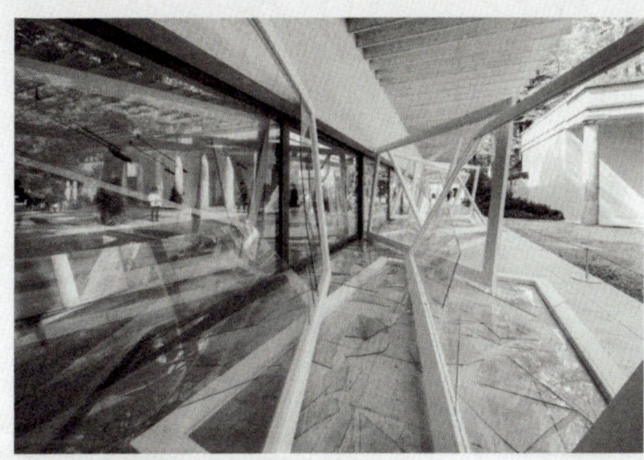

Installation view of Camille Norment's *Rapture* (2015) in the Nordic Pavilion at the 56th Venice Biennale, 2015

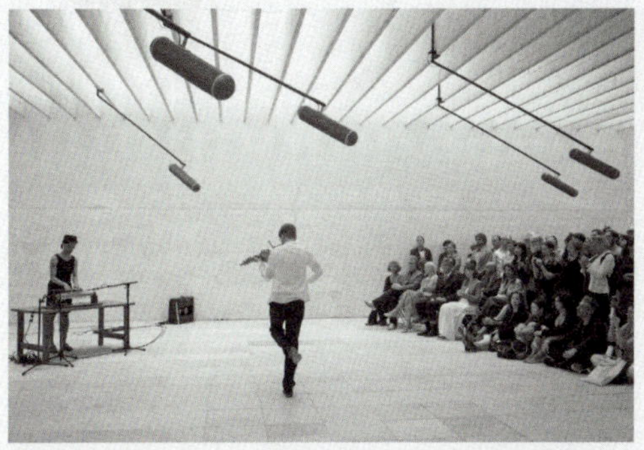

Camille Norment Trio during the inaugural performance of *Rapture* in the Nordic Pavilion at the Venice Biennale, May 6, 2015

Jason Moran came to international prominence at the turn of the twenty-first century as a pianist of rare gifts, and almost immediately branched out into the contemporary visual art world. Moran's musicality was strongly influenced by pianist Jaki Byard as well as by the experimental ethos of pianist-composer Muhal Richard Abrams, a cofounder of the Association for the Advancement of Creative Musicians.[1] Like Moran, AACM composer-performers such as Abrams, Roscoe Mitchell, and Douglas R. Ewart work in visual forms such as painting, sculpture, and installation with alacrity. Wadada Leo Smith's musical scores, bringing together sound and image in the course of their realization as music by performers, have been exhibited as artworks in their own right. Closer to Moran's visual work are the graphic scores of Matana Roberts (a saxophonist, composer, and collagist of a later AACM generation), whose work makes common cause with Moran's in foregrounding the recovery of history.[2]

Moran's early collaborations with visual, performance, and media artists, including Glenn Ligon, Adrian Piper, Lorna Simpson, and Joan Jonas, decisively framed jazz as a site for the most thoroughgoing interdisciplinarity, while establishing Moran himself as a multifaceted creative artist for whom disciplinary boundaries posed no obstacles.[3] In the recent series of works presented in this catalogue, Moran establishes his independent voice, using improvisation as a metaphor to explore the merging of the visual and the sonic, even if the resulting work does not invariably deploy improvisation as a medium.

Moran's single-authored work in this catalogue straddles the ever-widening divide between music and sound art, while at the same time troubling standard histories and codings of both. Sound art's framing as Euro American in terms of cultural provenance, artistic production, and conceptual and historical engagement[4] is contradicted not only by Moran, but also by a host of African American sound artists, including Kabir Carter, Jennie C. Jones, Keith Obadike, Mendi Obadike, Tracie Morris, Pamela Z, Camille Norment, Beth Coleman, Kevin Beasley, Terry Adkins, Jace Clayton, DJ Spooky, and Douglas R. Ewart. Some of these artists, such as Jones and Adkins, assert strong links with jazz[5]; others draw from practices of assemblage that have a distinctly trans-African hue, working in the wake of Noah Purifoy, David Hammons, Betye Saar, and John Outterbridge.[6] Still others, like Morris, foreground performance and writing, while Z, DJ Spooky, and Coleman incorporate digital technologies.[7]

Moran's work in the visual arts crosscuts these diverse directions to establish a practice that treats sound and music as embodied—either directly or virtually, but in every case, historically. In particular, I want to examine how his work animates space and leaves trace. Two installations from Moran's *STAGED* series, *Savoy Ballroom 1* and *Three Deuces* (both 2015), reconfigure space historically, while the "sudden pianisms" of the *Run* series explore the trace as expressive medium.

E. Simms Campbell's 1932 *A Night-Club Map of Harlem* portrays the 24/7 world of "Negro revues" that, among others, the young Malcolm Little got to know so well when he came to New York in the 1940s to take up life as a hustler. Venues such as the Savoy Ballroom, the Cotton Club, the Lafayette Theatre, the Theatrical Grill, Club Hot-Cha, Small's Paradise, and seemingly innumerable others are found on Campbell's whimsical map, along with references to performers including Cab Calloway, Don Redman, Earl "Snakehips" Tucker, Bill "Bojangles" Robinson, and Dickie Wells.[8]

Moran's *Savoy Ballroom 1* stands nearly ten feet high and eighteen feet across, representing in half-size the stage of the venerable theater, which closed in 1958 and was later torn down to make way for a housing project.[9] As Moran remarks in my 2017 interview with him, "It was a regal space."[10] Thus, it comes as no accident that Moran's stage, with its golden mien, looks like a crown. At the same time, the colorful, repetitive design of the kente cloth on the stage wall—a pointed revision of the original floral design—recalls the wide range of Africoid epidermises that performed on that stage during the Savoy's glory years.

Moran's intermedia strategy for *Savoy Ballroom 1* involves reconstruction, reimagining, and recovery. Of the three, Moran sees recovery as the most vital:

> I'm totally getting tired of watching those histories kind of go into the mist. … I'm starting to get nervous about what can be ours—I mean black people. The Lenox Lounge, they just knocked the whole thing down. They didn't consider that it was a place where a lot of things happened. Maybe someone would want to take care of some of the things that are inside. They just tore the whole thing down, without any kind of respect. And we have dealt with that long line of disrespect for so long.[11]

Like E. Simms Campbell's map, Moran's *Savoy Ballroom 1* not only celebrates Harlem and New York as the capital of Black America, but also pays homage to black creativity itself. Moran's invocation of gold leads the viewer to consider the jazz stage as a shrine, a site of veneration, a place of homage and heroism. In fact, Moran says that the people this shrine celebrates are more than heroes:

> They are superheroes—like Chick Webb and so many people who performed in these places—the dancers who invented entirely new moves. It was a space that allowed that kind of creativity. … People who came up with that early stuff like the big band. That is quite possibly the most mind-boggling, genius thing to ever happen. Folks of color in the 1920s, making something so dense. How do they come up with that? People come in there to hear that, and they *dance* to that.

"I'm romantic enough to say that nostalgia plays a huge part. Nostalgia for an era," Moran affirms. At the same time, two factors about Moran's use of space in *Savoy Ballroom 1* contradict any simple longing for a bygone age. The first of these is the sonic content of the piece. The embedded speakers project not the music typically heard at the Savoy but rather a mash-up from field recordings of prison workers at the Louisiana State Penitentiary (known as "Angola"), whose friends and relatives might well have been performing at the Savoy. The club, like most of these Harlem performance arenas, was not black-owned and did not often welcome African Americans as customers.[12]

The effect compels an experiencer to consider the thornier side of the jazz life: the fact that for many African Americans, the good life came ironically amid the hardest times. In the installation, the voices of the Angola workers are largely edited out, leaving ghostly traces of voice and the attacks of the chains, hammers, and other tools that accompanied their forced labor, strongly evoking the distance between the silencing of slavery and the creation by the formerly enslaved of a music that encouraged all to speak their piece. As Moran sees it, this new freedom is hardly untrammeled:

> The thing that we love about the freedom we have on the stage also means that the place that we get to do it is on the stage. So it's never really quite as free as we think it is. And it's never free of the history that led up to that point. Chick Webb behind those drums is partially about those dances, but it's partially about that struggle to be free. That solo is a revolutionary act, because it allows the person to say something that they were not really allowed to say with their mouth.

"That's partially why the *Savoy* doesn't have Sarah Vaughan blasting out of the speakers," Moran observes. "Because it's not as free as that." He says that the pointed irony of this history of freedom, served up in juxtaposition with a "glamorous glitzy beautiful place that not all black folks were allowed to go to," tells us "why the sound in the *Savoy* is not pretty. It's a kind of haunting, ghostly sound." Here we can invoke the second way in which *Savoy Ballroom 1* utilizes space. Like the original, Moran's *Savoy* is conceived as an active performance space, in which musicians improvise music live, albeit via saxophone duos and other

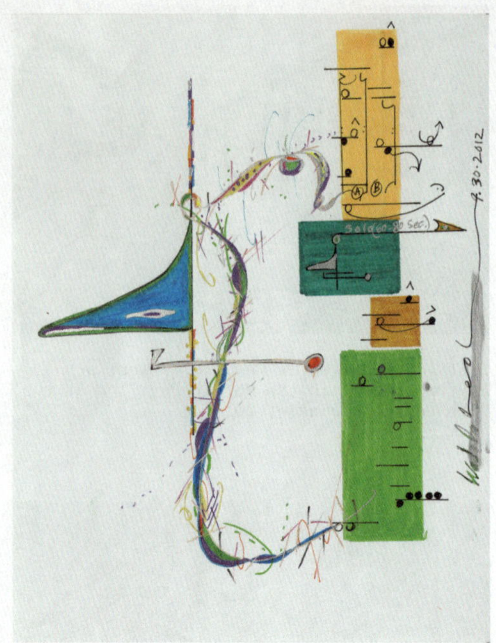

Wadada Leo Smith, *Koral Reef*, n.d., mixed media, 8½ x 11 in. (21.4 x 28 cm)

GEORGE E. LEWIS

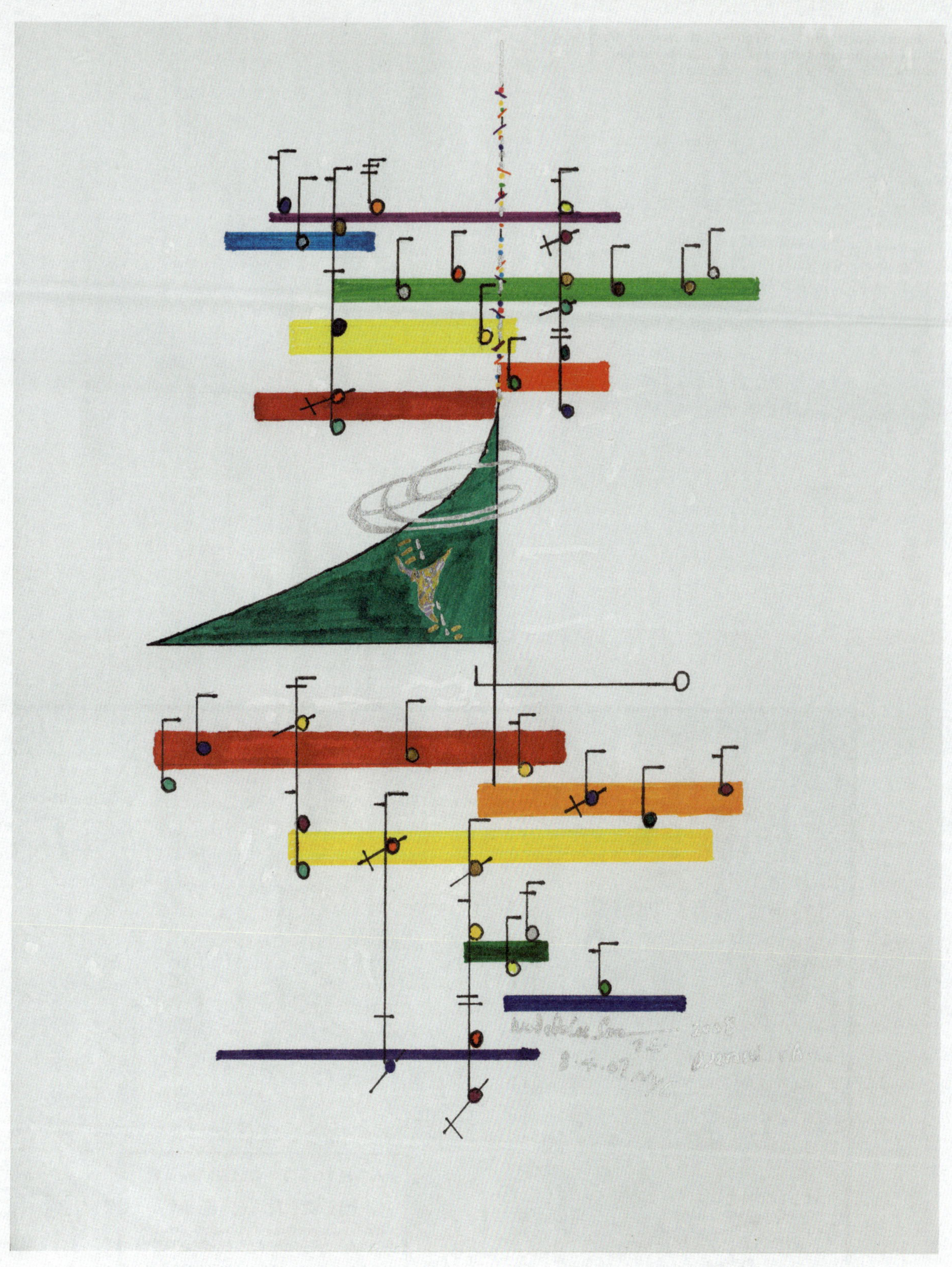

Wadada Leo Smith, *Koral Reef*, n.d., mixed
media, 8½ x 11 in. (21.4 x 28 cm)

E. Simms Campbell, *A Night-Club Map of Harlem*,
1932, ink and watercolor on illustration
boards, 25 x 35 in. (63 x 89 cm)

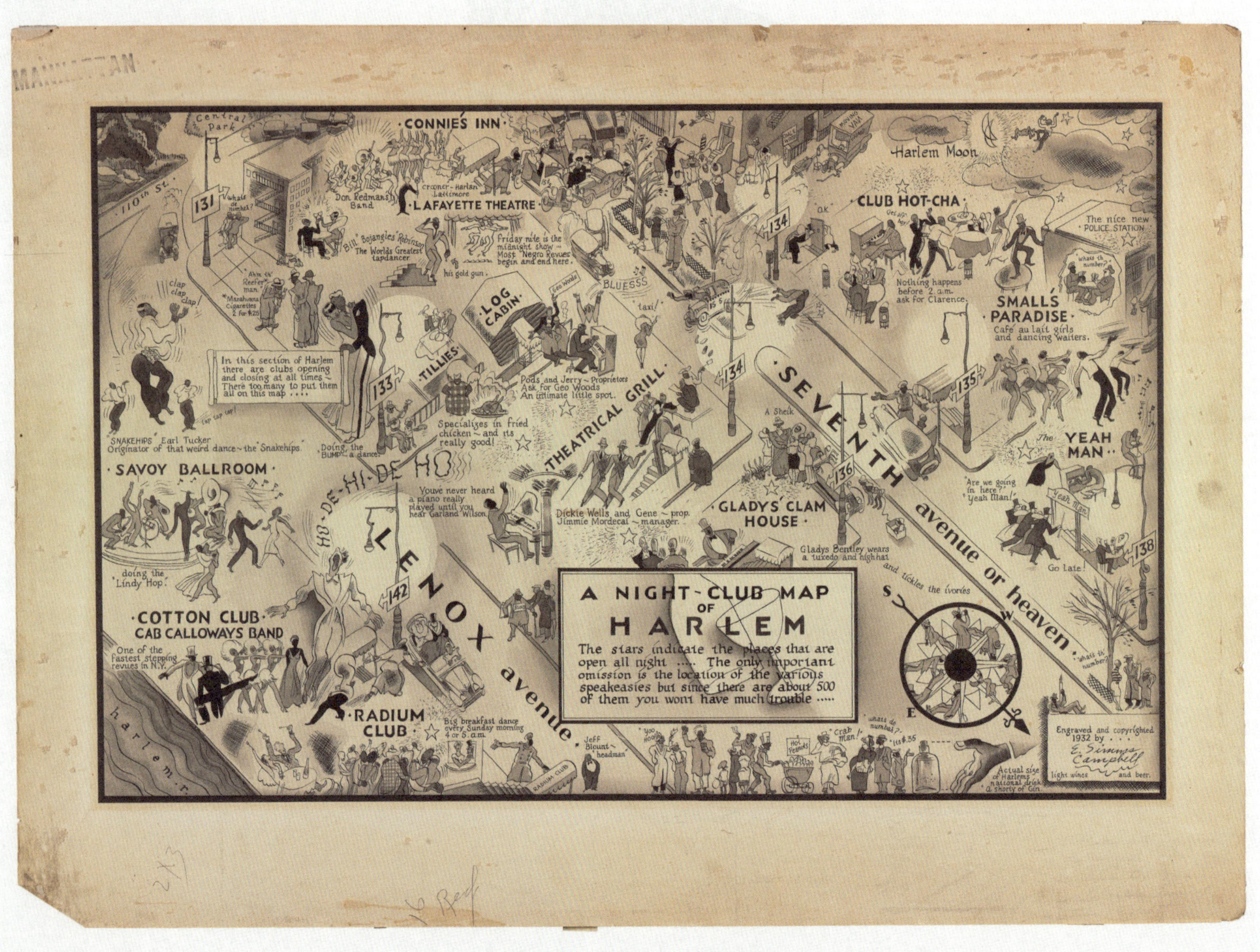

modes of musical expression that were not necessarily situated in the vein of the performance styles that animated the original venue.

In an exhibition at Luhring Augustine gallery in the Brooklyn neighborhood of Bushwick, *Savoy* stood nearby *Three Deuces*, an installation portraying the stage of a small bebop-era club that consists of a simple padded box, constructed to near-scale and complete with piano, bass, and forties-era Slingerland drum set. Moran's re-presentation of the Three Deuces takes experiencers to the next stage in the music's development. As he describes:

> I couldn't get over the fact that the Savoy was this massive place with all these people dancing, and then when the music moves fifty blocks down, from 125th Street to 52nd, all of a sudden it goes into this tiny corner. And then to see Max Roach, who's about to become this *dude*, in this corner with a total padded wall around him, *containing* the sound, *containing* the drums, shoving them in a corner, literally. And so they come out, Bird and Miles and Dizzy, playing themselves out of the corner.

The *Three Deuces* installation recalls the move toward freedom that Roach and his partner Abbey Lincoln asserted with their 1960 recording, *We Insist! Max Roach's Freedom Now Suite*.[13] Unlike the *Savoy*, which seems to stand as an untouchable monument to eternity, the *Three Deuces* is all about now, and the setup seems to invite performance, even by nonmusicians. "There's something that an open piano does to a human being, sitting there waiting," Moran observes. "People just wanted to go inside the space, even in a museum, where those 'don't cross this line' kind of signs are at play." The summons to perform is reminiscent of Brenda Hutchinson's radio artwork *How Do You Get to Carnegie Hall?,* from 1996, in which she loaded her childhood piano onto a truck and went on the road, stopping from time to time to invite people to play her piano and tell piano stories, which were later broadcast.[14] At the Bushwick gallery, while Moran and his friends were performing in the *Three Deuces* space, saxophonists Darius Jones and Ingrid Laubrock were playing in the *Savoy*. At some point, Moran says, the two just walked over and joined them in the *Three Deuces*.

The desire evoked by the *Three Deuces* emerges in part from Moran's own background as a pianist:

> I always think as a player, because I play all these rooms all around the world, and they all sound different. But what does this room feel like? What's the approximate scale of the room? The Village Vanguard is a certain kind of room—very original. Or take Constellation in Chicago—a very original space. The rooms feel a certain way. And I was just curious as a player: What if you play in there? Does that room make you want to play some bebop? Does it make you want to play what you think you should play right now?

Even so, the *Three Deuces* is not necessarily all about freedom:

> When we go inside and play in the space I cannot say that I am free. I don't feel like I do in the Vanguard, the way we play in the Vanguard. So I wanted to experience that as a player, to make the space to try to experience what it's like inside—even though it's not a replication. You can't go back to 1948 or 1945.

The ecology of people and space explored in the *Three Deuces* becomes more complex when no one is onstage and the piano, activated by computer, plays Moran's compositions seemingly without intervention.[15] The ethereal traces of the improvisations suggest recovered memories and the occult as well as the player pianos of old, whose punched rolls stored music by everyone from Ignacy Jan Paderewski to James P. Johnson, and later, the complex jazz-tinged "studies" of Conlon Nancarrow.

When the humans and the machines go home, the *Three Deuces* experiences an uneasy period of rest. Moran says:

> The space is in recovery. I can't help but think about the people who play there, or played in a space like that—what they drop on the stage. Those stages are therapeutic spaces, not just for the audience but mostly for the musicians.

In eighteenth-century German musical culture, the notion of *Begeisterung*, routinely translated as "enthusiasm" but in this context more directly as "inspiration," indicated a dynamic paroxysm of creative ecstasy. Theorists seeking an understanding of human creativity prized Beethoven's sketchbooks as a primary artifact of the immediacy central to *Begeisterung*. Musicologist Richard Kramer draws upon a quote from Johann Georg Sulzer's *Allgemeine Theorie der Schönen Künste* (*General Theory of the Fine Arts*) that was meant to offer insight into the creative soul of *Begeisterung*: "Sketches, when they are by the great masters, are often more highly prized than works more completely realized, for all the fire of imagination, often dissipated in the execution of the work, is to be met in them. The *Entwurf* [sketch] is the product of genius. The working out, on the other hand, is primarily the doing of Art and of Taste."[16]

In contrast to this view, Kramer notes the tendency of later generations of musicologists "to describe the earliest sketches as if they were the products of some primitive being, a naif not quite competent to compose the works that we all know will issue from these ungainly, inchoate efforts."[17] This attitude recalls the view of improvisation that dominated aesthetic theory, performance practice, and compositional methodology in European classical music until the early 1950s, when composers began to experiment with open forms and more personally expressive systems of notation. Designating salient aspects of a composition as performer-supplied rather than composer-specified, these composers renewed an interest in the generation of musical structure in real time.[18]

Jason Moran's *Run* series of charcoal drawings crystallizes what philosopher-clarinetist David Rothenberg calls "sudden music" in a set of pianistic "runs," quick, rising or falling complexes of notes.[19] The manner of Moran's mark-making is embedded in the marks themselves. First, pieces of paper are affixed to the keyboard of a piano. Then, Moran says, "I grab all this charcoal dust and coat my hands with it, and start playing on the piano. Now you flub all your notes, and also, depending on the attack, you break the paper too. You also destroy your piano in the process with all this coal dust. It's really just a process of improvising that I do on those pieces, when it's just on the white paper."

The *Run* series is much in the spirit of Charles Bernstein's poem "Last Words," in which Bernstein creates a new poem from the last word of every line in his earlier poem, "Sentences My Father Used."[20] Also related is the work of Czech sound artist Eliška Cílková, who in the detritus of Pripyat, the Northern Ukraine ghost town destroyed by the Chernobyl reactor explosion, performed on ruined pianos in a real-time, real-world process that featured her anxiously watching a Geiger counter.[21]

According to Kramer, it was the Romantics who "sought to cultivate that quality in their works that suggests the improvisatory. Work as sketch. The sketchlike as work."[22] With Moran, each improvised *Run* articulates a spontaneity that, as with the *Savoy* and the *Three Deuces*, is firmly based in history and memory. What the viewer sees are the traces of an improvisation, a short fantasy full of the *Begeisterung* of that moment. Indeed, as Kramer writes,

> Sulzer's ideal *Entwurf* is a graphic artifact. The artist's vision is recorded directly through the drawing hand. For the composer, the vision is expressed less directly. … The writing hand serves the composer not quite so truly as the drawing hand the artist. If the composer's sketch does not speak as eloquently as the draftsman's, that is because sketches only stand for an imagined performance, at another remove from the inspired thought.[23]

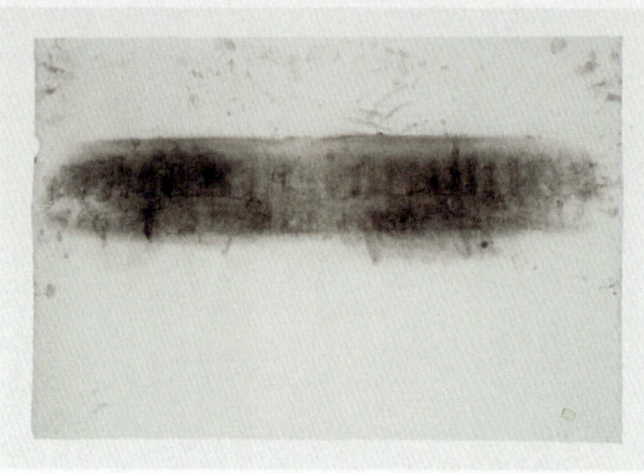

Jason Moran, *Run 4*, 2016, charcoal on paper, 25 x 37 ½ (63.5 x 95.3 cm)

 GEORGE E. LEWIS

Brenda Hutchinson's performance of *How Do You Get to Carnegie Hall?* at the Corn Palace in Mitchell, South Dakota, August 1996

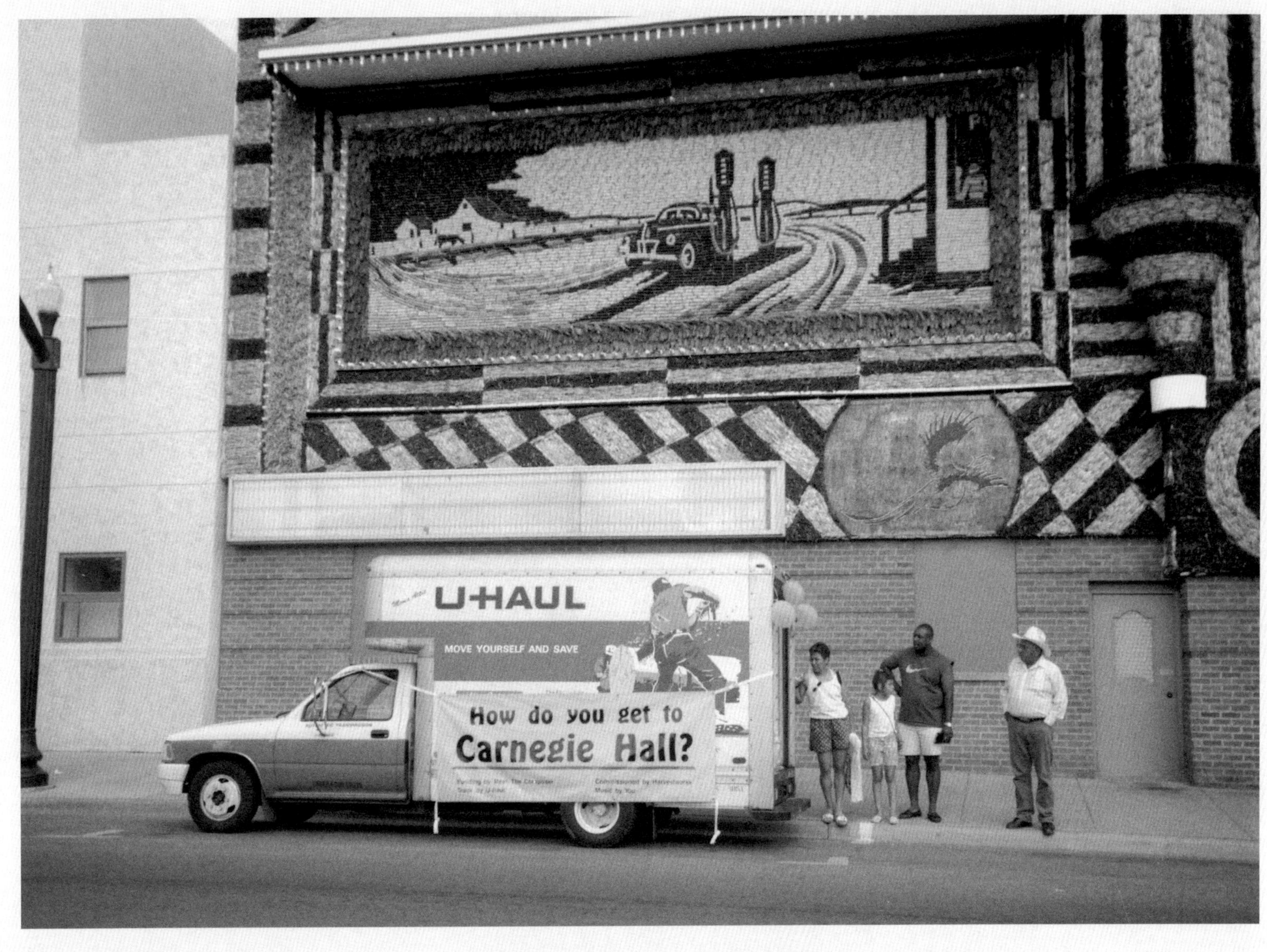

But Moran's *Run*s are not sketches for an eventual work. The drawings have a dual ontology: they are visual traces of a musical action that resulted not in a finished musical work but in a finished work of visual art. Here, beyond the cherished Euro-Classical binary between composition and improvisation, the improviser's hand becomes the artist's hand, and the distinction between imagined and actual performance is superseded. What we are left with is not a score that specifies an eventual performance, but a trace that, in the instant of performance, became transformed from the virtually sonic to the visual domain.

Jazz has been a source of inspiration, depiction, and translation for visual artists since its birth. A short list of artists who have drawn from, depicted, or been otherwise inspired by jazz and/or the culture surrounding it includes Arthur Dove, Henri Matisse, Jackson Pollock, Stuart Davis, Romare Bearden, Larry Rivers, Norman Lewis, Wadsworth Jarrell, Jeff Donaldson, A.R. Penck, Jean-Michel Basquiat, Faith Ringgold, William T. Williams, Terry Adkins, Stan Douglas, and Jennie C. Jones.[24] Much visual work, particularly after 1960, treats the music as a site of contestation and discovery, pointing up its inherent instability in the midst of search and experimentation. Artists such as Jones and Douglas show that listening as well as performing are improvisative acts that engage agency and power.[25]

Such matters may be more routinely explored in the improvisative performance that is the lifeblood of jazz, but Moran's work takes us further in this new criticality. Like his music, Moran's installations and drawings make us acutely aware of our own quotidian improvisations in the worlds around us, improvisations that mark out the broadest outlines of our human experience.

NOTES

1. Jim Santella, "Jason Moran: Facing Left," *All About Jazz*, August 1, 2000, https://www.allaboutjazz.com/facing-left-jason-moran-blue-note-records-review-by-jim-santella.php.

2. For examples of this visual work, see Naomi Beckwith and Dieter Roelstraete, eds., *The Freedom Principle: Experiments in Art and Music, 1965 to Now* (Chicago: Museum of Contemporary Art Chicago, in association with the University of Chicago Press, 2015).

3. See Joan Simon, "In the Studio: Joan Jonas and Jason Moran," *Art in America*, May 1, 2015, http://www.artinamerica magazine.com/news-features/magazine/in-the-studio-joan-jonas-and-jason-moran/.

4. An early and influential example is Douglas Kahn and Gregory Whitehead, "Introduction: Histories of Sound Once Removed," in *Wireless Imagination: Sound, Radio, and the Avant-Garde*, ed. Douglas Kahn and Gregory Whitehead (Cambridge, MA: MIT Press, 1992).

5. George E. Lewis, "The Sound of Terry Adkins," in *Terry Adkins: Recital*, ed. Ian Berry (Munich: DelMonico Books-Prestel, 2017); "Jennie C. Jones: 'Amazing Parallels'," in *Jennie C. Jones: Compilation*, ed. Valerie Cassel Oliver (Houston: Gregory R. Miller/Contemporary Arts Museum Houston, 2015).

6. Kellie Jones, "Black West: Thoughts on Art in Los Angeles," in *New Thoughts on the Black Arts Movement*, ed. Lisa Gail Collins and Margo Natalie Crawford (New Brunswick, NJ: Rutgers University Press, 2006).

7. George E. Lewis, "The Virtual Discourses of Pamela Z," in *Diaspora, Memory, Place: David Hammons, Maria Magdalena Campos-Pons, Pamela Z*, ed. Salah M. Hassan and Cheryl Finley (Munich: Prestel, 2008); Christine Hume, "Improvisational Insurrection: The Sound Poetry of Tracie Morris," *Contemporary Literature* 47, no. 3 (Autumn 2006). See also references to Coleman in Paul D. Miller, aka DJ Spooky that Subliminal Kid, *Sound Unbound: Sampling Digital Music and Culture* (Cambridge, MA: MIT Press, 2008).

8. E. Simms Campbell, *A Night-Club Map of Harlem*, 1932, housed in Beinecke Rare Book and Manuscript Library, Yale University. Image accessed at https://www.cooperhewitt.org /event/a-jazz-age-night-in-harlem-walking-tour-05-18-2017/.

9. Manny Fernandez, "Where Feet Flew and the Lindy Hopped," *New York Times*, March 12, 2006, http://www.nytimes.com/2006/03/12 /nyregion/where-feet-flew-and-the-lindy-hopped.html.

10. Quotes from Jason Moran throughout this essay come from George E. Lewis, "Interview with Jason Moran," via Skype, May 16, 2017.

11. For a compact account of the peripatetic history of Harlem's Lenox Lounge, see Kia Gregory, "In Harlem, a Nightspot So Iconic They'll Reopen It. Twice," *New York Times*, January 9, 2013, http://www.nytimes.com/2013/01/10 /nyregion/the-lenox-lounge-a-harlem-nightspot-so-iconic-theyll-reopen-it-twice.html?mcubz=1.

12. Information on the creative process for this work comes from Lewis, "Interview with Jason Moran."

13. Max Roach, *We Insist! Max Roach's Freedom Now Suite* (Candid CCD 79002, compact disc, 1997).

14. Alexandra Gardner, "Brenda Hutchinson: Expanding the Ordinary Moment," *New Music Box*, June 20, 2012, http://www.newmusicbox.org/articles/brenda-hutchinson-expanding-the-ordinary-moment/.

15. Lewis, "Interview with Jason Moran."

16. Johann Georg Sulzer, quoted in Richard Kramer, "The Sketch Itself," in *Beethoven's Compositional Process*, ed. William Kinderman (Lincoln: University of Nebraska Press, [1986] 1991), 3.

17. Kramer, 4.

18. See George E. Lewis, "Improvised Music after 1950: Afrological and Eurological Perspectives," *Black Music Research Journal* 16, no. 1 (Spring 1996).

19. David Rothenberg, *Sudden Music: Improvisation, Sound, Nature* (Athens: University of Georgia Press, 2002).

20. Charles Bernstein, *Recalculating* (Chicago: University of Chicago Press, 2013), 57–64.

21. Eliška Cílková, "Pripyat Piano: Sound Documentary of Chernobyl Zone," http://www.pripyatpiano.com.

22. Kramer, 4.

23. Kramer, 4.

24. See, for example, Graham Lock and David Murray, eds., *The Hearing Eye: Jazz and Blues Influences in African American Visual Art* (New York: Oxford University Press, 2008); Pierre Sauvanet, "Jackson Pollock et Ornette Coleman: Vraie ou Fausse Rencontre?," *Filigrane*, http://revues .mshparisnord.org/filigrane/index.php?id=583 (September 2013); Chad Mandeles, "Jackson Pollock and Jazz: Structural Parallels," *Arts Magazine*, no. 57 (1981).

25. George E. Lewis, "Stan Douglas's Suspiria: Genealogies of Recombinant Narrativity," in Stan Douglas, *Past Imperfect: Works 1986–2007*, ed. Hans D. Christ and Iris Dressler (Ostfildern, Germany: Hatje Cantz, 2008); Lewis, "Jennie C. Jones: 'Amazing Parallels.'"

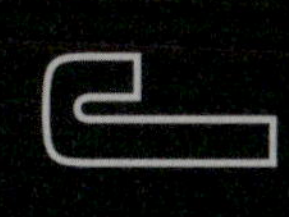

TRANSFORMING

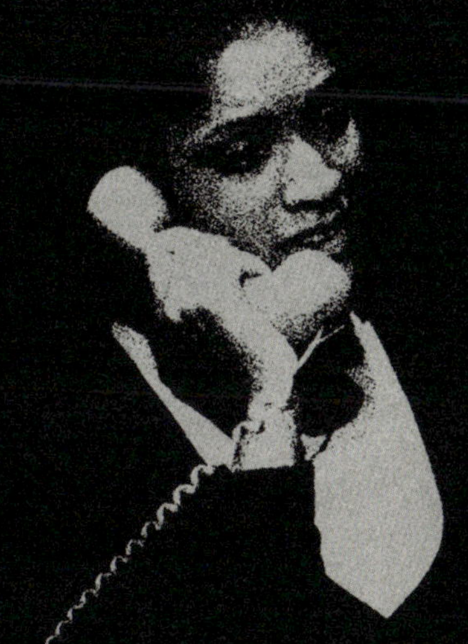

PHILIP BITHER

Artists ought to be writing.

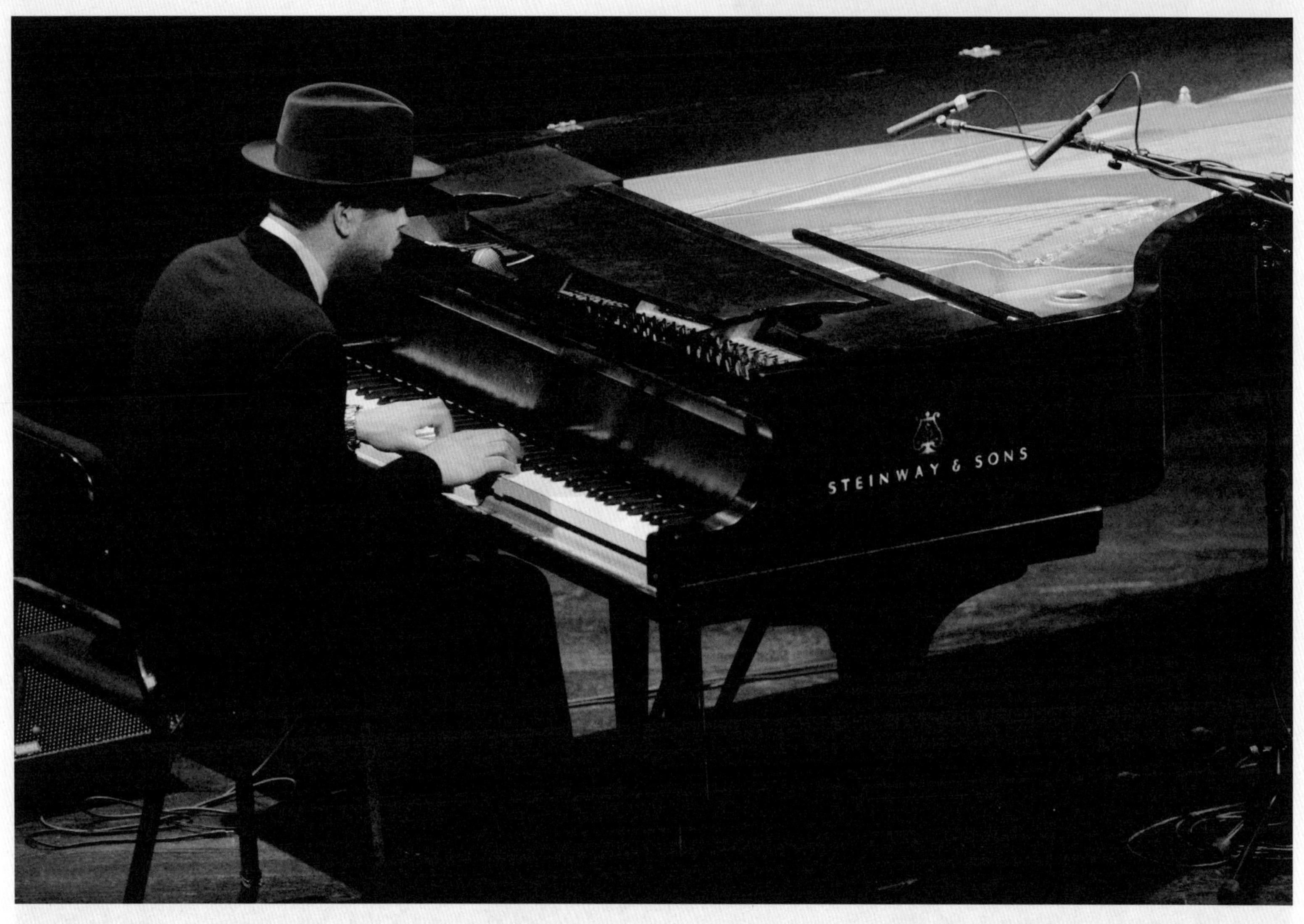

Jason Moran performing during the premiere of *Milestone* in the McGuire Theater, Walker Art Center, May 20, 2005

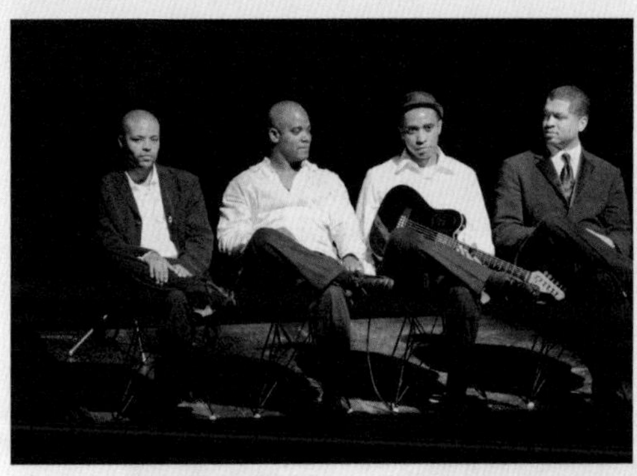

(left to right): Nasheet Waits, Tarus Mateen, Marvin Sewell, and Jason Moran performing during the premiere of *Milestone*, 2005

"The possibilities are limitless" was Jason Moran's concluding thought in the letter he sent to me in March 2003. He was outlining his hopes for the new commission that the Walker Art Center had just awarded him to create an interdisciplinary evening-length jazz performance inspired by the institution's permanent collection. Looking back, his sentiment could have applied equally to the relationship that would develop over the next fifteen years between the artist and the Walker. The resulting theatrical suite, *Milestone,* which premiered in May 2005, is the type of boundary-crossing achievement that shapes the future of both artist and institution.

Although the Walker had long been a multidisciplinary center committed to art forms that overlap and influence one another, the "new Walker," which opened in 2005 with an expansion by Herzog & de Meuron, called for greater intentionality in its blurring of disciplines. The updated catalogue of the collection, *Bits & Pieces Put Together to Present a Semblance of a Whole*, featured for the first time essays on film and performing artists supported by the Walker (such as Moran's work). Alcoves for music and moving image were built into new public spaces. Dance, music, and performance artists were given increased license to animate the museum galleries and common areas, and the Walker's first dedicated stage, the McGuire Theater, offered a new platform for contemporary performing arts, often in the form of interdisciplinary collaboration.

Moran had already made a mark at the Walker in 2001, having appeared with his trio the Bandwagon (Tarus Mateen, bass, and Nasheet Waits, drums) and guest artist free jazz saxophone legend Sam Rivers for the first live performances of *Black Stars* (Blue Note, 2001), an album melding experimental sensibilities across generational lines. On the day of the concert, during an afternoon rehearsal break, I found Moran enmeshed in Sol LeWitt's wall painting *Four Geometric Figures in a Room* (1984), originally commissioned by former Walker director Martin Friedman. Discussions of jazz, art, hip-hop, performance, and the audience-artist relationship ensued, revealing the depth of Moran's curiosity and the breadth of his art and design enthusiasms. These passions were already evident in his subtle nods to painters Egon Schiele, Jean-Michel Basquiat, and Robert Rauschenberg on his first recordings and in the modernist-designed piano stool/chair he often toured with.[1] When Moran returned to the Walker in April 2002 to play in composer and saxophonist Greg Osby's chamber jazz octet *Symbols of Light,* he and I continued to discuss the museum's history, its collection, and the ideas embedded in artworks.

Not long after, two years before the new theater opened, I invited Moran to make a work for the premiere. He accepted immediately, and within months he and his collaborator and partner (now wife), mezzo-soprano Alicia Hall Moran, traveled to the museum to scour our storage vaults under the guidance of Walker visual arts curators Joan Rothfuss and Elizabeth Carpenter and registrar Joe King. Over the next year, Moran and Hall Moran returned several times for multiday visits, their commitment to research far exceeding my expectations. Initially attracted to works by influential artists including Robert Motherwell, Ellsworth Kelly, Alice Neel, Mark Rothko, and Rauschenberg, Moran ultimately decided, at Hall Moran's urging, to look inward, at his own life, and to "go some place where the light is not so bright" for inspiration.[2] While on tour a year later, Moran came upon a retrospective of Adrian Piper's work at the Museu d'Art Contemporani de Barcelona. He called this encounter with the conceptual artist, writer, and educator "one of the most powerful experiences I had felt in a museum in my life."[3] He was drawn to both the heat and the light of her work—bold, subversive, clever, and penetrating examinations of race, bigotry, and personal identity—and to her advocacy around the artist's role in society. Piper's use of her own life as material for her work, her attention to black identity, and her incorporation of text ran parallel to his inclinations to open up abstractions of contemporary jazz.

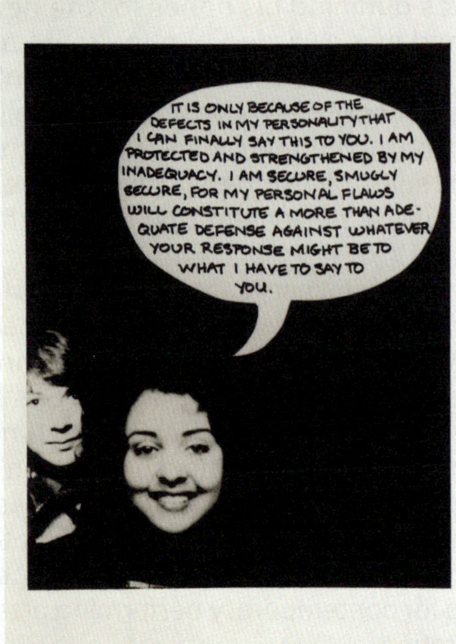

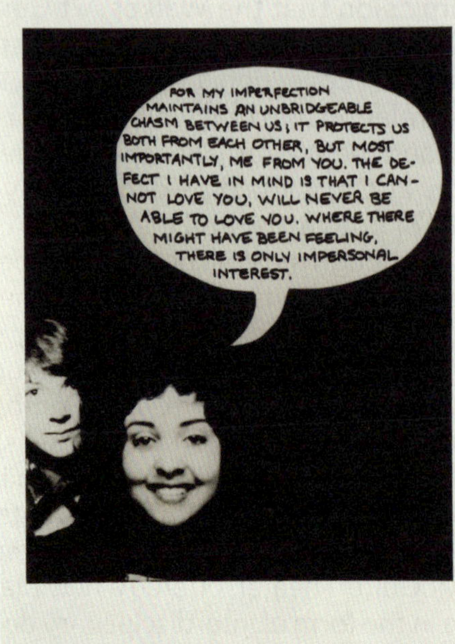

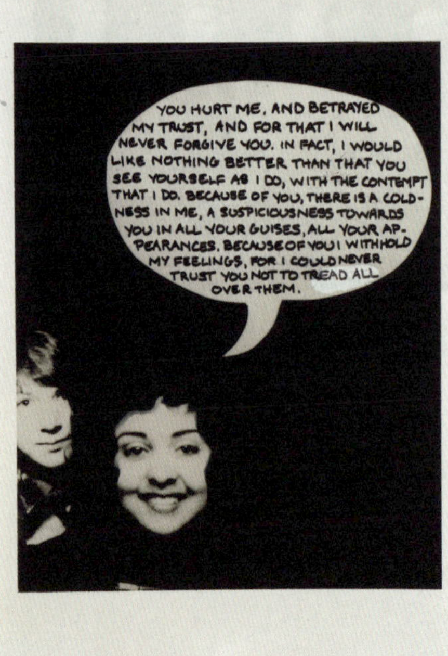

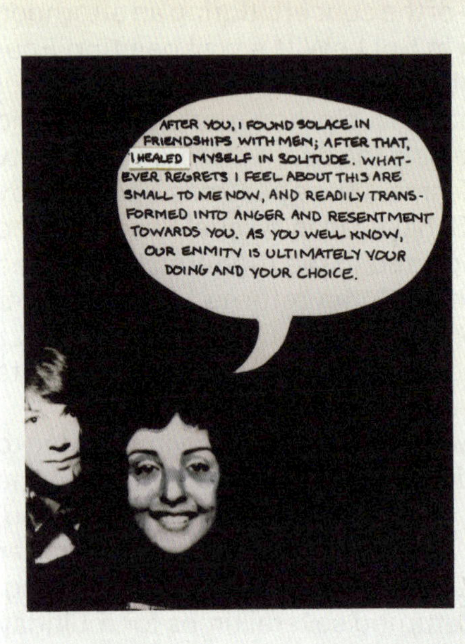

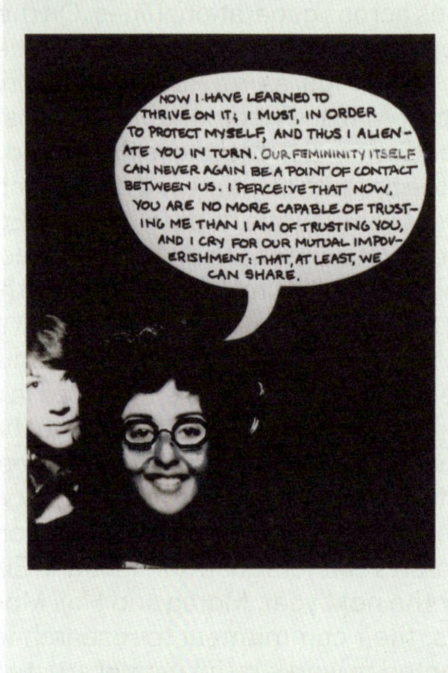

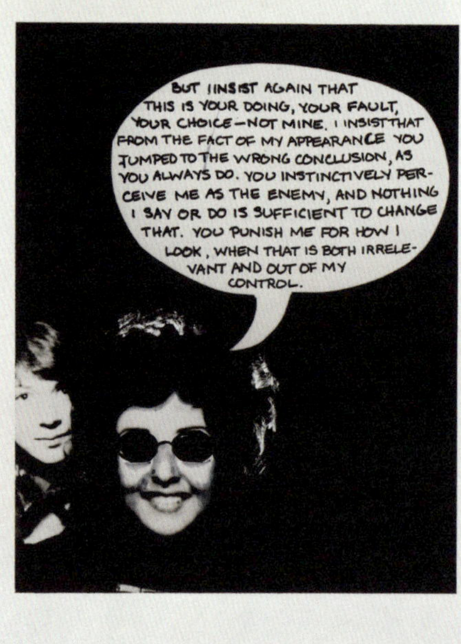

Adrian Piper, *The Mythic Being; I/You (Her)*, 1974, ten black-and-white enlargements of machine-made portrait photographs, overdrawn with gouache and tempera pasted up with paper label, 8 x 5 in. (20.3 x 12.7 cm) each

     PHILIP BITHER

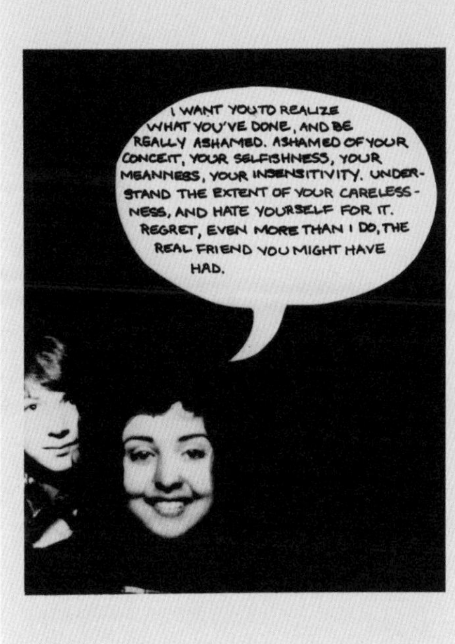

I WANT YOU TO REALIZE WHAT YOU'VE DONE, AND BE REALLY ASHAMED. ASHAMED OF YOUR CONCEIT, YOUR SELFISHNESS, YOUR MEANNESS, YOUR INSENSITIVITY. UNDERSTAND THE EXTENT OF YOUR CARELESSNESS, AND HATE YOURSELF FOR IT. REGRET, EVEN MORE THAN I DO, THE REAL FRIEND YOU MIGHT HAVE HAD.
The Mythic Being: I/You (Her), 4.

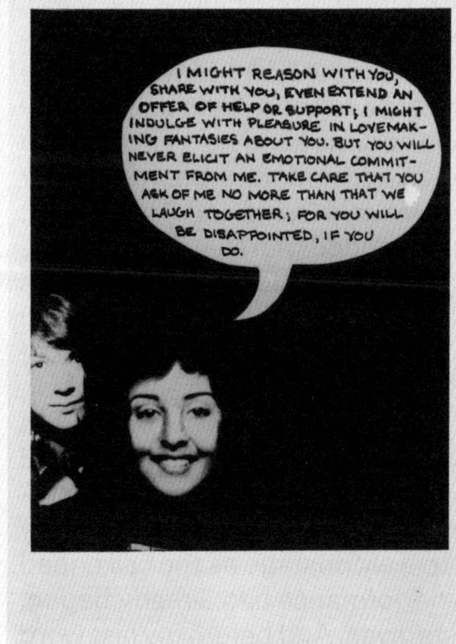

I MIGHT REASON WITH YOU, SHARE WITH YOU, EVEN EXTEND AN OFFER OF HELP OR SUPPORT; I MIGHT INDULGE WITH PLEASURE IN LOVEMAKING FANTASIES ABOUT YOU. BUT YOU WILL NEVER ELICIT AN EMOTIONAL COMMITMENT FROM ME. TAKE CARE THAT YOU ASK OF ME NO MORE THAN THAT WE LAUGH TOGETHER; FOR YOU WILL BE DISAPPOINTED, IF YOU DO.
The Mythic Being: I/You (Her), 5.

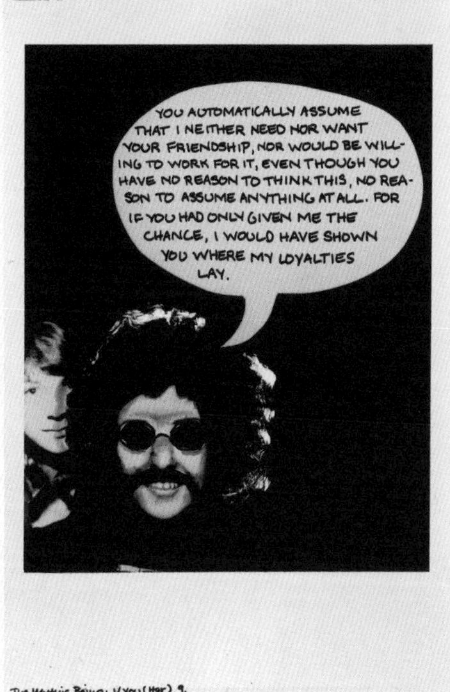

YOU AUTOMATICALLY ASSUME THAT I NEITHER NEED NOR WANT YOUR FRIENDSHIP, NOR WOULD BE WILLING TO WORK FOR IT, EVEN THOUGH YOU HAVE NO REASON TO THINK THIS, NO REASON TO ASSUME ANYTHING AT ALL. FOR IF YOU HAD ONLY GIVEN ME THE CHANCE, I WOULD HAVE SHOWN YOU WHERE MY LOYALTIES LAY.
The Mythic Being: I/You (Her), 9.

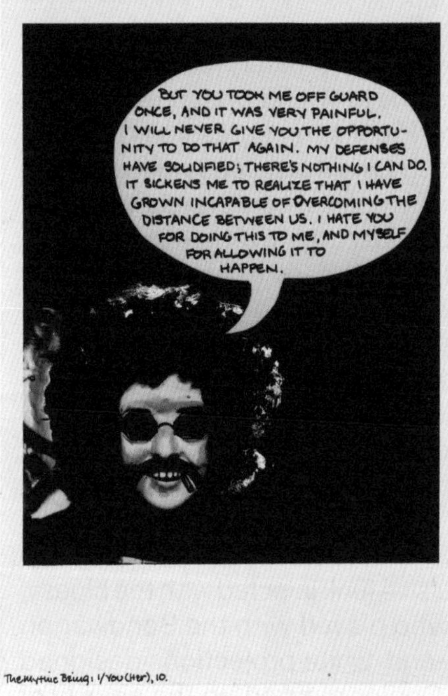

BUT YOU TOOK ME OFF GUARD ONCE, AND IT WAS VERY PAINFUL. I WILL NEVER GIVE YOU THE OPPORTUNITY TO DO THAT AGAIN. MY DEFENSES HAVE SOLIDIFIED; THERE'S NOTHING I CAN DO. IT SICKENS ME TO REALIZE THAT I HAVE GROWN INCAPABLE OF OVERCOMING THE DISTANCE BETWEEN US. I HATE YOU FOR DOING THIS TO ME, AND MYSELF FOR ALLOWING IT TO HAPPEN.
The Mythic Being: I/You (Her), 10.

He was drawn to her fierceness, to the "persistent jabbing" her work evoked.[4] "It felt like she was saying … 'wake up,'" he said. He knew then that he wanted to focus exclusively on Piper, in particular her work *The Mythic Being; I/You (Her)*, (1974) in the Walker's collection, for his commission.

Moran contacted Piper, and she warmly welcomed him to her home in Massachusetts. They seemed to forge an immediate rapport, talking for nearly five hours. In the end, Piper allowed Moran to use her voice and her words for the basis of several of *Milestone*'s signature compositions. Moran regarded Piper as a kind of mentor, much as he had piano pioneers Jaki Byard and Andrew Hill.

Piper's interrogations of personal identity provided Moran with a creative road map. Puncturing the cliché of the cool male jazz musician who keeps his private life well hidden away, Moran decided to use his relationship with Hall Moran as a theatrical frame. When the lights dimmed on the opening night of *Milestone*, Moran's ambitions were clear. Hall Moran stepped out from the dark, singing something of a lament, reflecting on what her spouse far away might be doing at that moment. Further mixing autobiography, real-time reality, and fiction, a red dial telephone on the stage rang, followed by a recorded conversation between the couple about how the Walker gig was going, a quiet poignancy filling spaces between their words. I was cued to walk onstage as the call ended to give my standard welcome speech, as if no performance had already begun, as if no window had been opened onto the artists' lives. And before my last word was spoken, the Bandwagon's prerecorded musical theme—propulsive piano, harmonica, electronics, hip-hop beats, and sampled radio voices—blasted out in the auditorium, and the four musicians walked out in choreographed unison. They stood in a line under harsh overhead lighting, silently staring at the audience. It was a destabilizing image, suggesting a police lineup or a group of community protectors, and signaled that this was not going to be a typical jazz evening.

Moran was, in fact, determined to use *Milestone* to upend what he saw as the tired formula of the concert-hall jazz event. Using Piper's transgressions of visual art protocols as inspiration, he realized that "each time musicians walk onstage it is theater."[5] Anything was possible. *Milestone*'s musical centerpiece, "Artists Ought to Be Writing," was drawn from a speech by Piper urging artists to articulate their process and the intent of their work. Moran had already experimented with joining the spoken word to melody and improvisation, having sampled Chinese and Turkish voices in earlier recordings. But he had not done so with the English language or with the ideas of a fellow artist communicating something of a manifesto. Moran accompanied Piper's words in multiple ways. He backed them with parallel chord changes, followed the cadence and tune of each spoken syllable, note by note, and launched into a piano solo based on Piper's spoken melody with the words stripped away.

"Breakdown" focused on just a few words from the same Piper speech. The sampled parts were repeated over a bed of propulsive funk injected with the bluesy, harmolodic[6] edge of guitarist Marvin Sewell, who played with the Bandwagon as a guest artist for this work. Arresting black-and-white projections designed by the Walker's in-house videographer Brian Dehler ramped up the energy of "Breakdown" further, as words in different typefaces and at varying sizes and angles shot across the large screen in synch with the piece's spiky rhythms.

Forty minutes into the concert, Moran announced an intermission and the band left the stage. As audience members started moving up the aisles, the Bandwagon reappeared behind a scrim on a raised platform outfitted to look like a backstage green room, with a table, chairs, and an upright piano. The musicians sat facing forward—the confrontation between artists and audience recalling Piper's insistence on hanging her frontal portrait photos of people at eye level—as a recording played the layered, intimate flows and cross melodies of casual laughter, storytelling, and eating, further paralleling Piper's use of

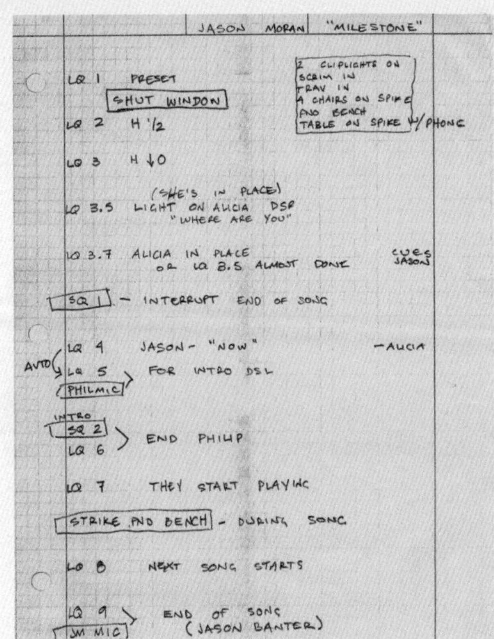

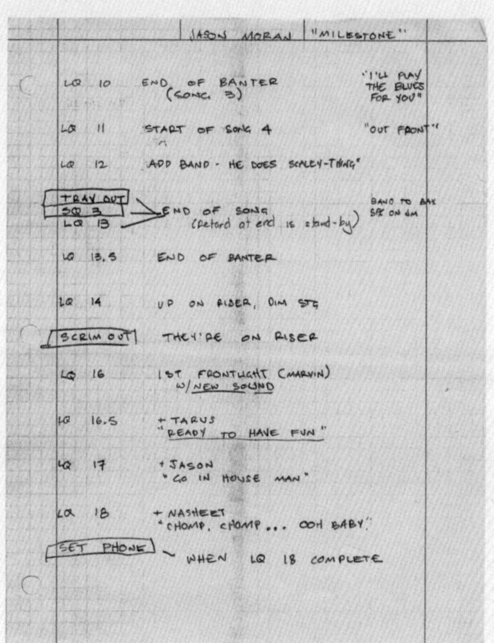

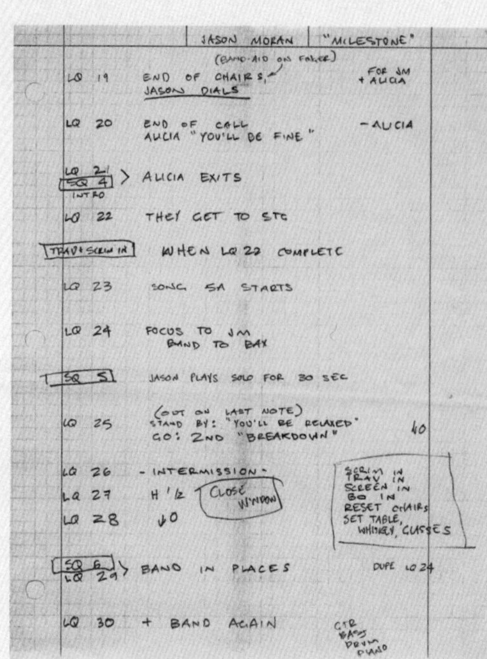

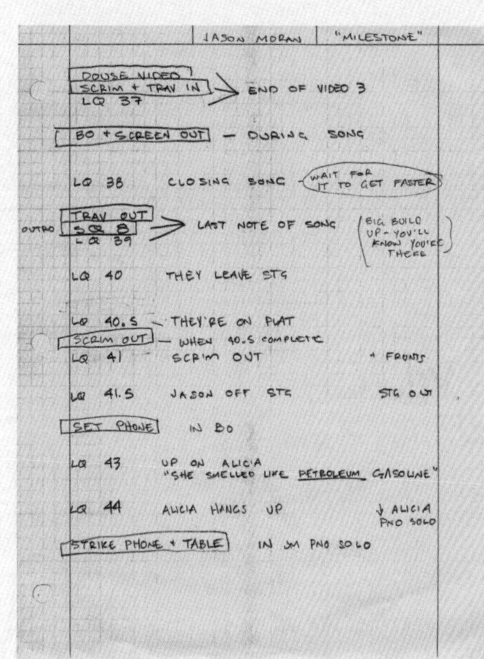

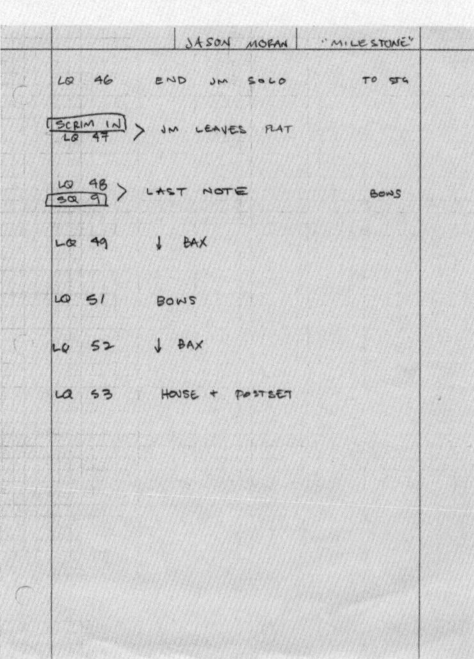

Jason Moran's cue sheets for the commission *Milestone*, 2005, 8½ x 11 in. (21.6 x 27.9 cm) each

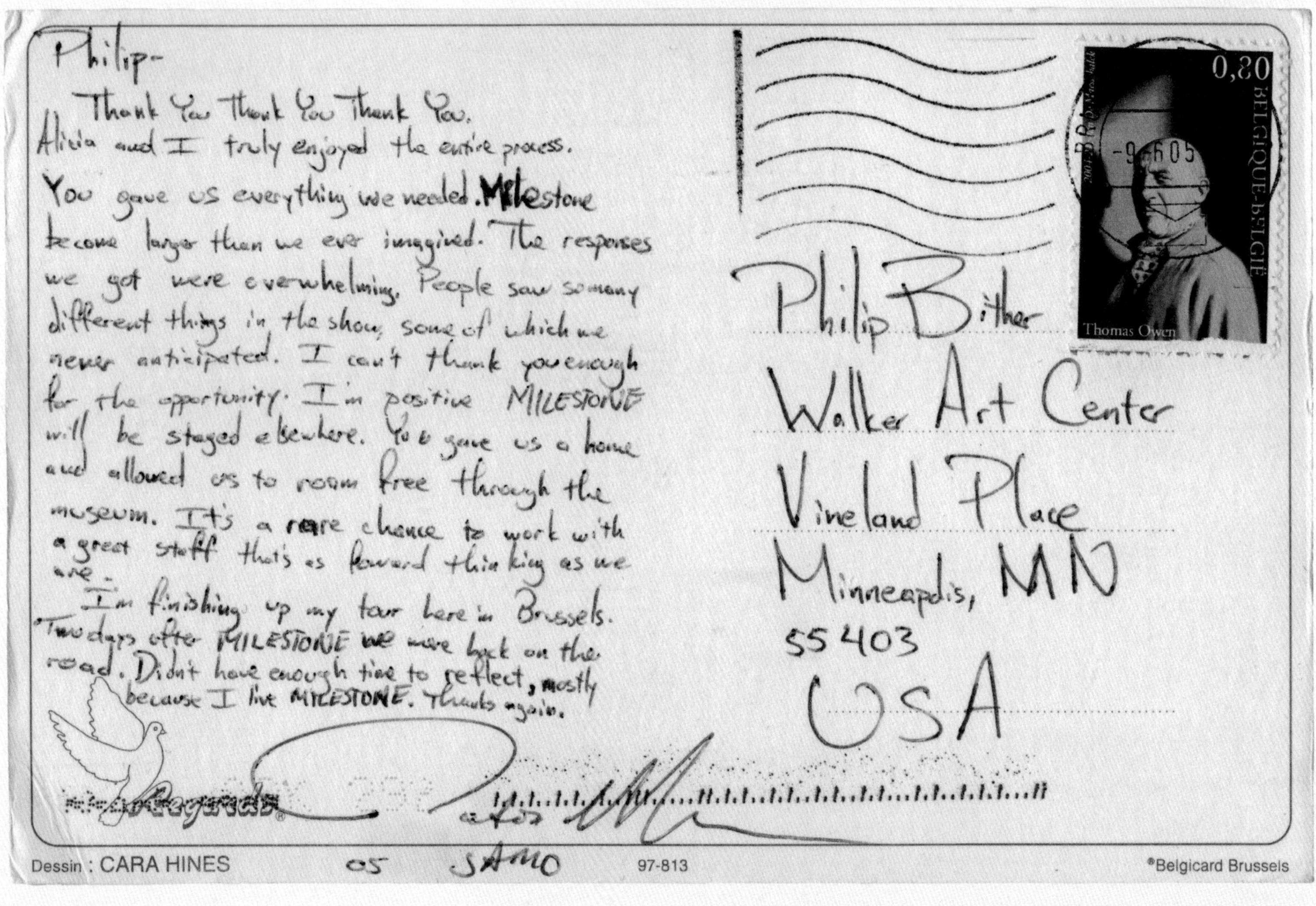
Philip—
Thank You Thank You Thank You.
Alicia and I truly enjoyed the entire process.
You gave us everything we needed. Milestone
became larger than we ever imagined. The responses
we got were overwhelming. People saw so many
different things in the show, some of which we
never anticipated. I can't thank you enough
for the opportunity. I'm positive MILESTONE
will be staged elsewhere. You gave us a home
and allowed us to roam free through the
museum. It's a rare chance to work with
a great staff that's as forward thinking as we
are. I'm finishing up my tour here in Brussels.
Two days after MILESTONE we were back on the
road. Didn't have enough time to reflect, mostly
because I live MILESTONE. Thanks again.
Regards,
Jason
Philip Bither
Walker Art Center
Vineland Place
Minneapolis, MN
55403
USA
0,20 BELGIQUE-bELGIE
Thomas Owen
Dessin : CARA HINES   05   SAMO   97-813   ®Belgicard Brussels

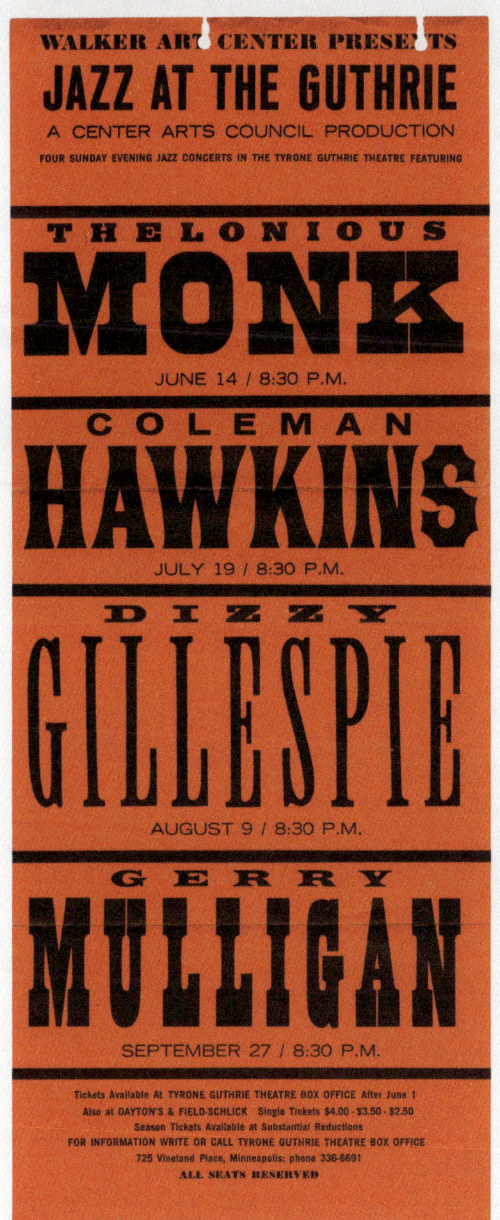
Poster promoting the Walker Art Center's
Jazz at the Guthrie series, 1964

autobiographical elements. As the nuanced live-concert aspects of *Milestone* continued, elements of electronic and sampled sounds integrated with the power of the quartet. After Moran's solo, "On Cradle Song" (an homage to Carl Maria von Weber's *Cradle Song*), the ten images from Piper's *The Mythic Being; I/You (Her)* were projected at a large scale above the musicians' heads, while an audio recording of Piper's voice was heard.

Jazz concerts that incorporate other art forms have been generally overlooked by historians and shunned by conservative fans. Ornette Coleman's historic spectacle at the 1994 San Francisco Jazz festival brought together video art, contortionists, and body piercers; Sun Ra and his Arkestra held home-spun Afro-Futurist tribal pageants; the Art Ensemble of Chicago performed in face paint and Nigerian dashikis; Thelonious Monk and Cecil Taylor danced in their performances, and Taylor included poetry readings. Even with these precedents, *Milestone* felt very new. Something of a leap for the artist and the institution, we all agreed early on to a full-fledged theatrical production mixing Moran and Hall Moran's dramaturgical and directorial abilities with the creative contributions (projections, lighting, and scene design) of the Walker's curatorial and technical staff. Piper herself, gracious and generous, flew to Minneapolis for the opening. At the same time that *Milestone* was a success with audiences and critics, it was an essential turning point for the artist. "Since working here and since studying Adrian Piper's work … Alicia and I began to actively seek out other artists."[7] New collaborative relationships and friendships emerged with Joan Jonas, Glenn Ligon, Stan Douglas, Kara Walker, Theaster Gates, and others.

The following year, Moran's 2006 Blue Note release (with collaged images of the Walker's building on the cover), appropriately titled *Artist in Residence,* included four compositions from *Milestone*. Even jazz critics, typically suspect of the art world, were won over.[8] Moran found himself applying his recently attained skills again, three years later, for a tribute to Thelonious Monk (a central influence on Moran) and his 1959 "large band" concert at New York's Town Hall. Moran's homage *In My Mind: Monk at Town Hall 1959* (2007, initially commissioned by Duke University, SFJazz, Chicago Symphony Center, and the Washington Performing Arts Society) balanced the rich heritage of jazz with forward-looking musical and media elements. At Moran's invitation, Ligon produced an untitled text painting that stressed through repetition the phrase "in my mind," which was often used by Monk. Video artist David Dempewolf paired images of Ligon's painting with video and audio excerpts of Monk and his arranger Hall Overton, acquired from the archive of noted photographer W. Eugene Smith.[9] The Monk tribute, held in the McGuire Theater in May 2007, had a special resonance. Not only had the Walker presented *Milestone* four years earlier, but the institution had hosted Monk himself in 1964.

Moran also appeared at the Walker for an emotional piano solo and spoken-word farewell for departing Walker director Kathy Halbreich in 2007, and a public talk turned lecture-demonstration that same year on the opening weekend of the exhibition *Kara Walker: My Complement, My Enemy, My Oppressor, My Love*. In May 2015, Moran performed a concert of piano duos with fellow Houstonian Robert Glasper. While Moran and Glasper have both been widely noted for complicating the boundaries between jazz and hip-hop, the sold-out concert also explored earlier eras of jazz piano—stride, swing, bebop—and reinvented some pop and soul classics.

The relationship between Moran and the Walker Art Center moved to a new level with this exhibition, the artist's first solo museum show, which also featured the commissioned, large-scale performance titled *The Last Jazz Fest,* in collaboration with video artists Ryan Trecartin and Lizzie Fitch and electronic musician DJ Ashland Mines (Total Freedom). A massive, metal set housed the Bandwagon on three separate stories, serving as something of a sculptural jazz shrine of the future—one that complemented the other three Moran *STAGED* creations that lived in the exhibition galleries. Both a bold critique and refutation of the nostalgic or overly commercial cultural corners that jazz has been relegated to in our times, *The Last Jazz Fest*'s sonic, textual, visual, and theatrical elements coalesced into the kind of commanding statement that *Milestone* hinted at thirteen years earlier. It had become abundantly clear that Moran's leadership and vision were helping jazz reclaim a key place in the firmament of contemporary music, performance, and art.

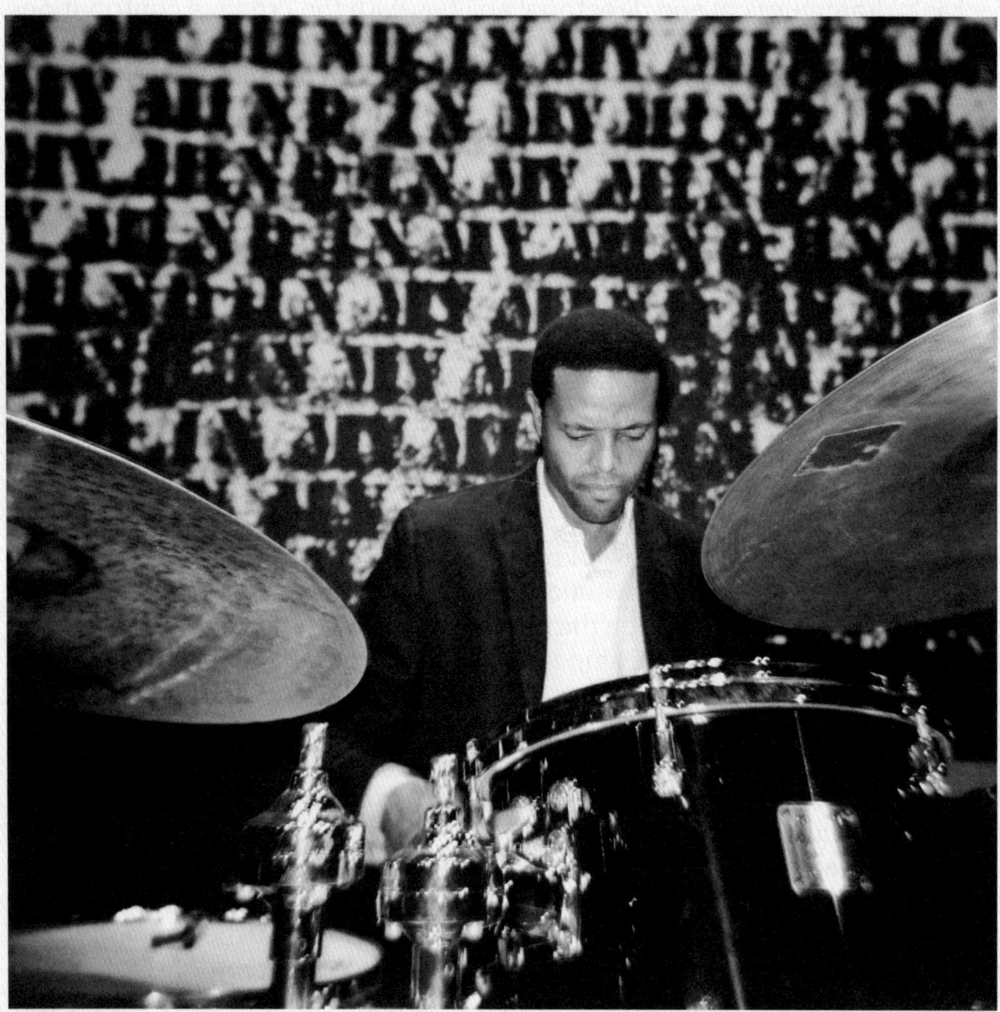

The Bandwagon's Nasheet Waits performing
during *In My Mind: Monk at Town Hall 1959*
at Flagey, Brussels, 2017; Glenn Ligon's
untitled painting (2007) in the background

   PHILIP BITHER

NOTES

1. For Moran's first recordings inspired by the works of Egon Schiele, Jean-Michel Basquiat, and Robert Rauschenberg, see *Soundtrack to Human Motion* (Blue Note, 1998), particularly the track "Jamo meets Samo," *Facing Left* (Blue Note, 2000) and *Black Stars* (Blue Note, 2001).
2. Jason Moran, public interview by the author at the Walker Art Center, Minneapolis, February 16, 2007, video recording, 1:24, https://walkerart.org/magazine/jason-moran-and-performing-arts-curator-phili.
3. Jason Moran, interview by Willard Jenkins, "A Conversation with Jason Moran," DC Jazz Festival Meet the Artist Conversation, NYU Washington, DC, December 1, 2016, video recording, 1:01, https://www.youtube.com/watch?v=tronyWcXXtk&t=2084s.
4. Jason Moran, interview by the author, 2007.
5. Jenkins, "A Conversation with Jason Moran."
6. "Harmolodic" is a term coined by composer/saxophonist Ornette Coleman that, among more expansive philosophical/musical meanings, can refer to style of electrified free-jazz funk that Coleman constructed in the 1970s and 1980s.
7. Jason Moran, interview by the author, 2007.
8. See for example, Will Lyman, "Jason Moran: Artist in Residence," *Pop Matters*, September 25, 2006: "I f major US Arts Institutions are ready, willing, and able to fund this kind of thing, then all the better. It's the kind of thing that could give music in academia a good name. And it's definitely the kind of thing that will give jazz a very good name."
9. Martin Johnson, "The Jazz Standard," *New York Magazine*, February 22, 2009, http://nymag.com/arts/popmusic/features/54627/.

DANIELLE A. JACKSON

SAVOY

The Savoy

the showplace of Harlem, has acquired an international reputation for its unique styles of dancing. Such dances as the Lindy-Hop, Big Apple, and the latest of all sensations, the Mutiny Swing, had their origin at the SAVOY.

"AS THEIR BODIES DIGESTED AND RESPONDED TO THE BAND IN A RIFF OF SORTS, CALL AND RESPONSE"

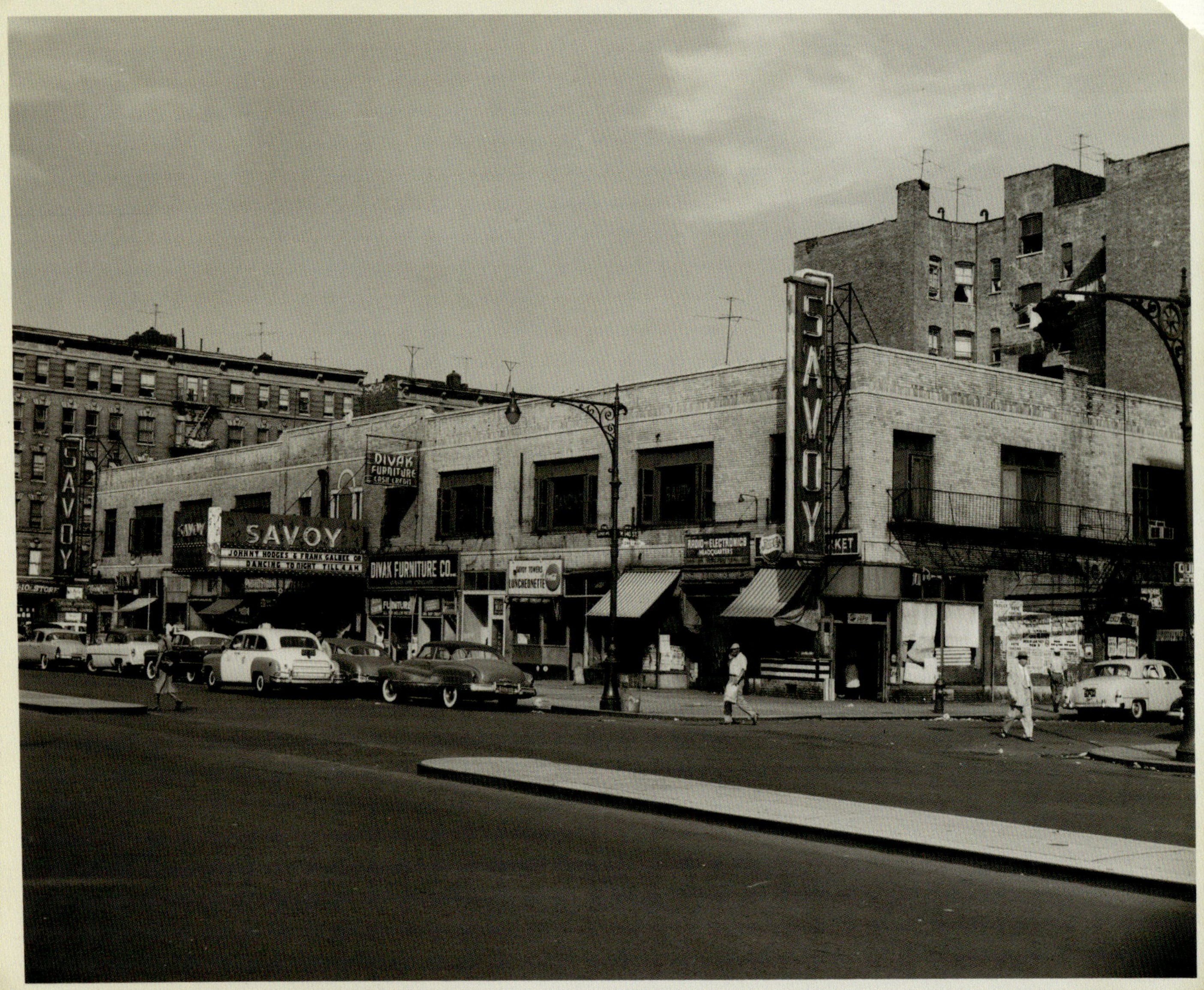

SAVOY
SAVOY
SAVOY
DIVAK FURNITURE CO.
DIVAK FURNITURE CASH OR CREDIT
JOHNNY HODGES & FRANK GALBEE OR
DANCING TONIGHT TILL 4 A.M.
LUNCHEONETTE
RADIO and ELECTRONICS HEADQUARTERS
MARKET

 showtime. *I knew and Laura knew that she couldn't match the veteran showtime girls, but she told me that she wanted to compete. And the next thing I knew she was among those girls over on the sidelines changing into sneakers. I shook my head when a couple of free-lancing girls ran up to me. As always the crowd clapped and shouted in time with the blasting band: "Go Red, go!" Partly it was my reputation, and partly Laura's ballet style of dancing that helped turn the spotlight—and the crowd's attention—to us. They never had seen the feather-lightness that she gave to lindying, a completely fresh style—and they were connoisseurs of styles. I turned up the steam, Laura's feet were flying; I had her in the air, down, sideways, around; backwards, up again, down, whirling. … Little Laura inspired me to drive to new heights. Her hair was all over her face, it was running sweat, and I couldn't believe her strength. The crowd was shouting and stomping.*

In *The Autobiography of Malcolm X* (1965), Muslim minister and activist Malcolm X (then Malcolm Little, and referred to by his friends as Red) recounts an evening at Harlem's Savoy Ballroom. His narration describes the Lindy Hop, a seminal social dance of African American origins whose loosely improvised choreography of fast, syncopated footwork, acrobatic partnering, and aerial maneuvers was perfected on the floors of the Savoy, famously known as "The Home of the Happy Feet." The event outlined above occurred at a point in the evening reserved for only the greatest Lindy Hoppers, who would one-up each other in elimination rounds as their bodies digested and responded to the band in a riff of sorts, a call and response. In particular they would flock to an area of the block-long dance floor on the northeast side, dubbed Cats' Corner.

The Savoy opened in 1926. It was a racially diverse venue (the first in the United States to have an integrated dance floor) located on Lenox Avenue between 140th and 141st streets, in a neighborhood that was a mecca for black musicians, writers, poets, and playwrights. It was one of the most important ballrooms in the country, where black musicians and dancers converged, and swing ruled. And like the dancers, the musicians battled one another. Imagine Count Basie's band in 1941 firing off "Swingin' the Blues" in response to Chick Webb's rhythmic up-tempo "God Bless." Despite occupying a relatively small section of the club (considering the dimensions of the dance floor), the bandstand emanated sounds, often described as "hot," and imagery that resonated through the ages. However, in the moment, these sensations raised the room's "temperature," that is, its palpable energy and passion.

Considered a community proposition by owners Charles Buchanan and Mole Gale, the Savoy gave Harlem residents during the Depression years both a club that was of the caliber of the Roseland Ballroom (which catered exclusively

to white audiences) at an affordable admission price, and the opportunity to encounter the most prominent bandleaders and jazz singers of the day: Cab Calloway, Ella Fitzgerald, Fess Williams, Chick Webb, Count Basie, and Duke Ellington, to name only a few. The raised, double bandstand accommodated two orchestras, instruments gleaming, and visitors had to climb two flights of mirrored marble steps before they found themselves in front of it. The structure was backed by a scalloped curved wall and ceiling that produced a kind of menacing overhang. It was once lined with velvet, and later with paisley, but Jason Moran alters this element in *STAGED: Savoy Ballroom 1* with the inclusion of an intricately patterned Dutch wax print (today a material made cheaply in China) that is everywhere in Africa and closely associated with West and Central African fashion.

The Savoy was, in a word, magnificent. The club was redecorated at least five times during its thirty-year existence to keep up with the very latest styles in décor, a characteristic echoed in the pristine quality of Moran's monument. It survived the Depression, World War II, and the postwar baby boom. Much to the dismay of its community, the venue was demolished in 1958 to make way for a middle-income housing project, and its contents were auctioned off, including the Steinway piano that had served as a vessel for so many legendary players.

NOTES

1. Malcolm X and Alex Haley, *The Autobiography of Malcolm X* (New York: Ballantine Books, 1973), 82–83.
2. The nickname originated with the actress Lana Turner, who, while watching dancers at the Savoy, observed, "What happy feet these people have."
3. See Barbara Engelbrecht, "Swing at the Savoy," *Dance Research Journal* 15, no. 2 (Spring 1983): 4.
4. Wax print fabric is a concretization of privilege and wealth with ties to a complex colonial history. Commonly identified as "African," its motifs are customarily machine-spun in Indonesia, and it is patented and heavily targeted to foreign markets, in particular regions of Africa, by firms in England and the Netherlands. The result is the rapid dissemination of these fabrics and the appropriation of Indonesian textile techniques for capitalistic profit.
5. "Savoy, 'The Home of the Happy Feet,' Falls under Auctioneer's Gavel," *Jet*, October 16, 1958, 61.

A.

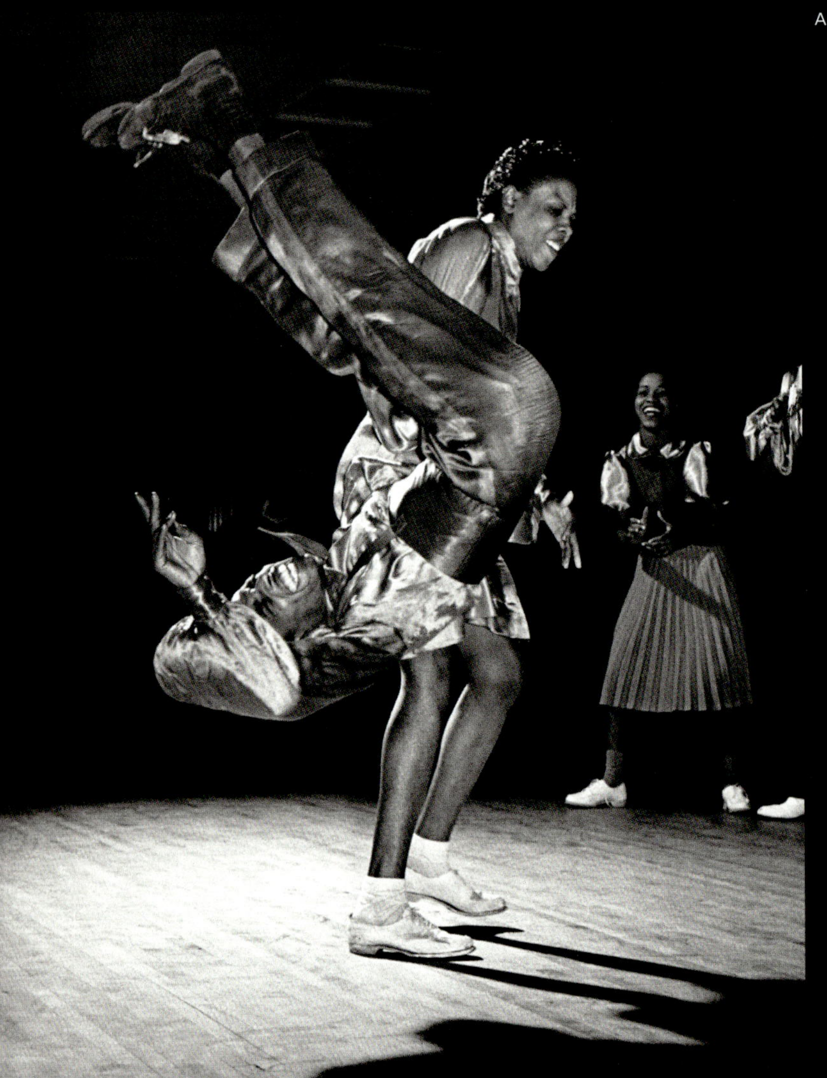

C.

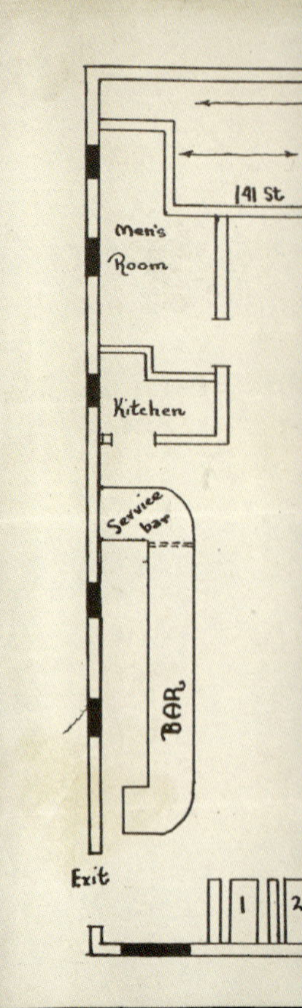

B.

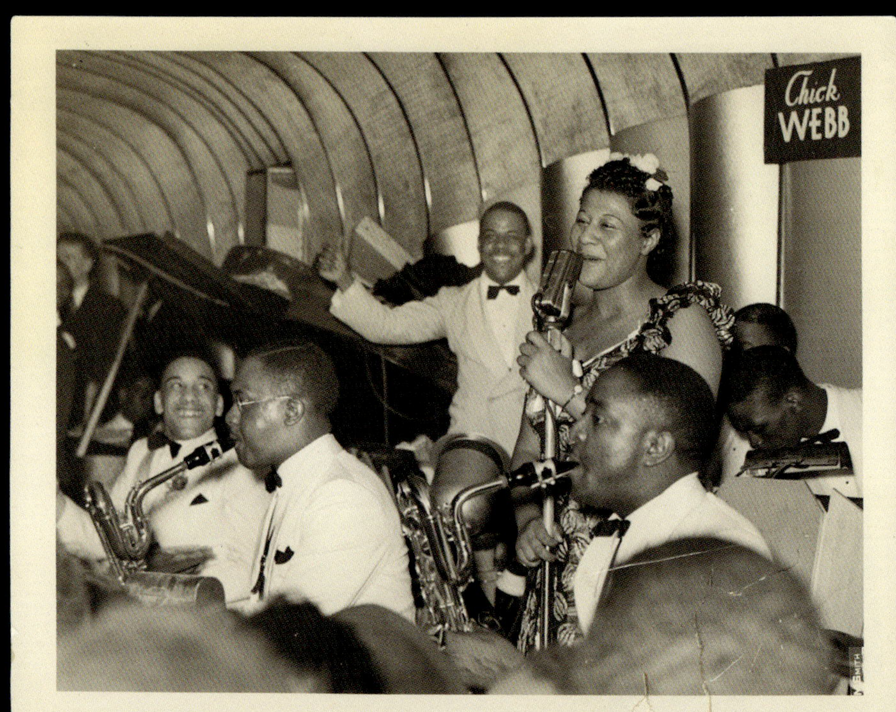

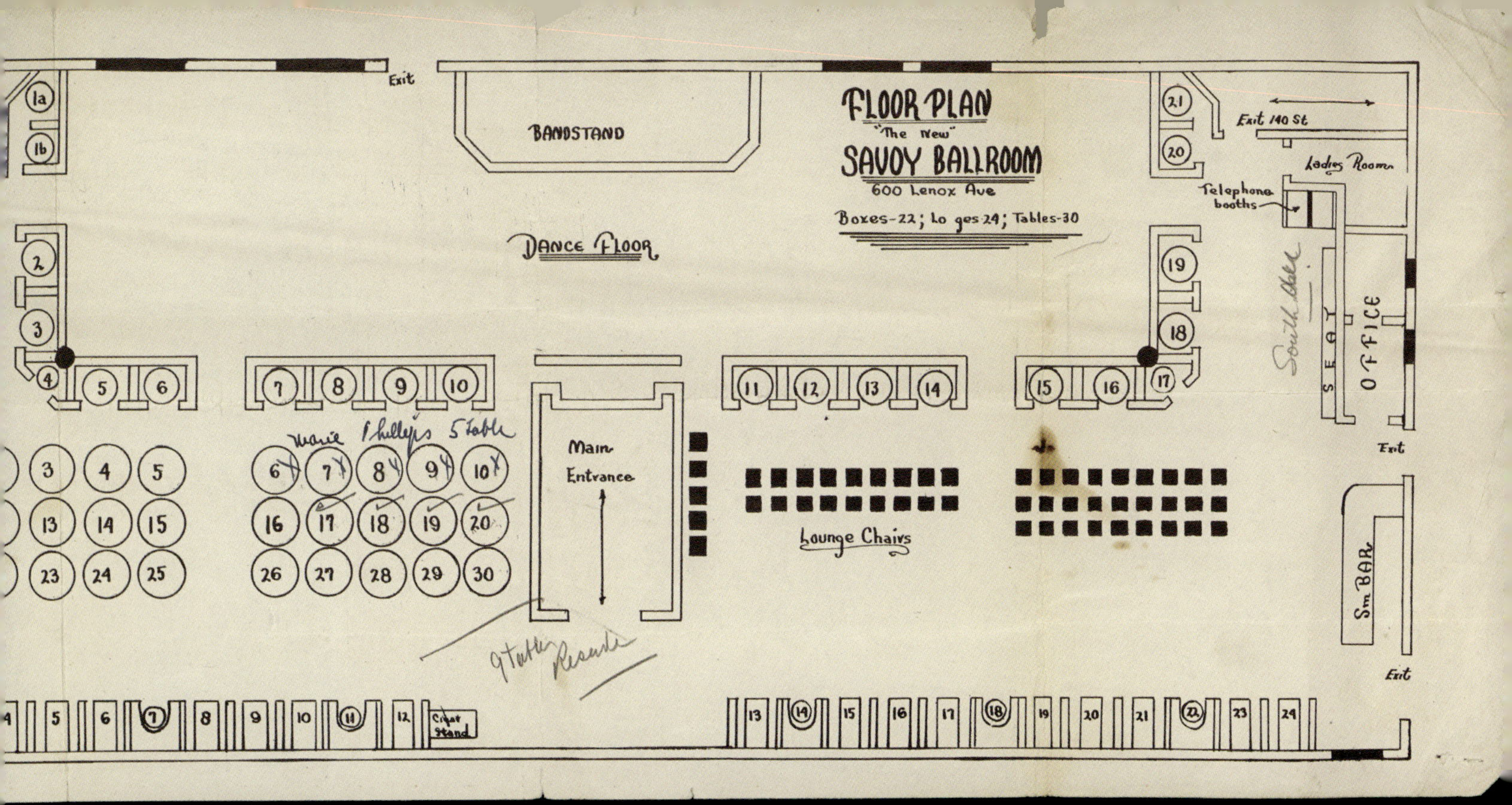

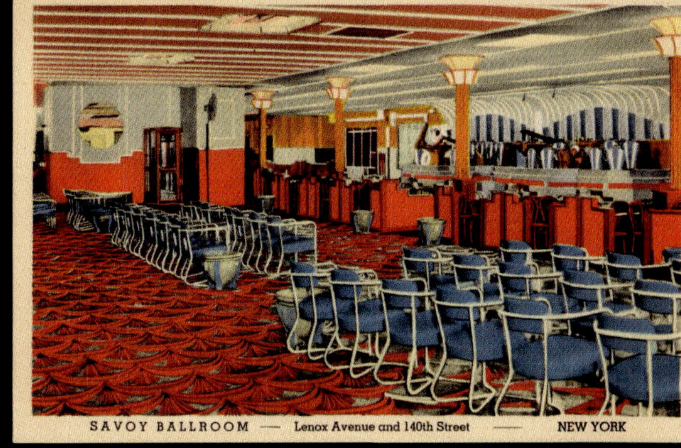

D.

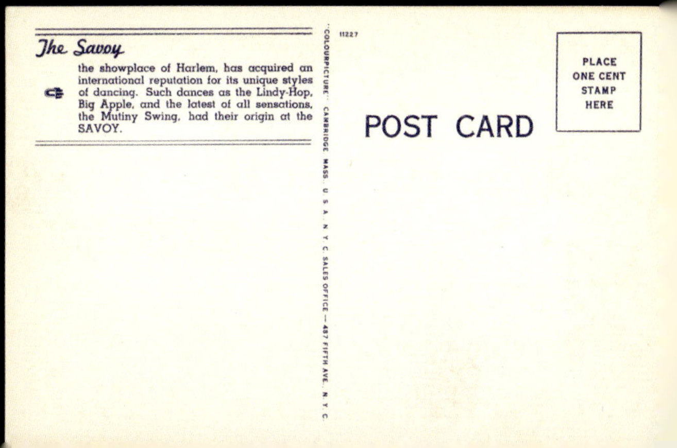

A. Lindy hoppers Gladys Crowder and Eddie "Shorty" Davis performing at the Savoy Ballroom, New York. Mickey Jones stands in the background, 1939

B. Morgan and Marvin Smith, *Ella Fitzgerald and Chick Webb's Orchestra at the Savoy Ballroom*, 1938, digital image, dimensions variable

C. Floor plan of the Savoy Ballroom, New York, n.d.

D. Postcard from the Savoy Ballroom, New York, circa 1930

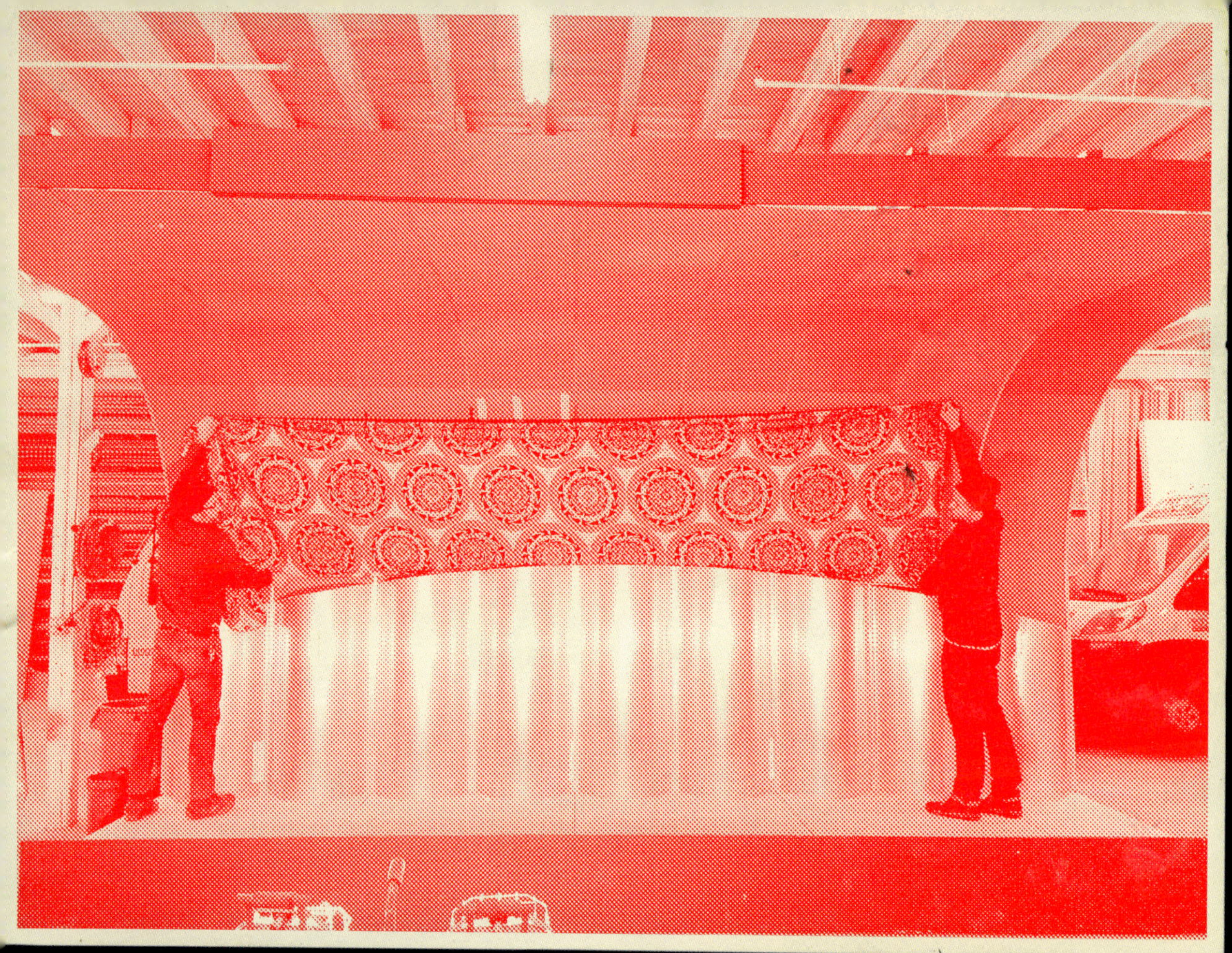

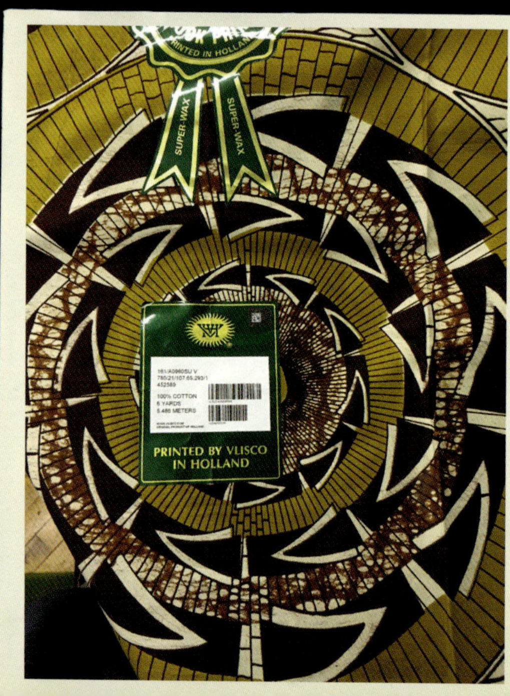

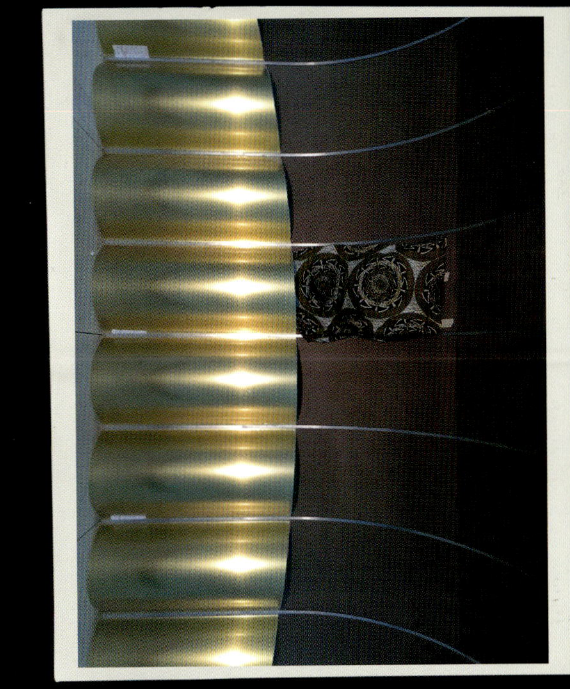

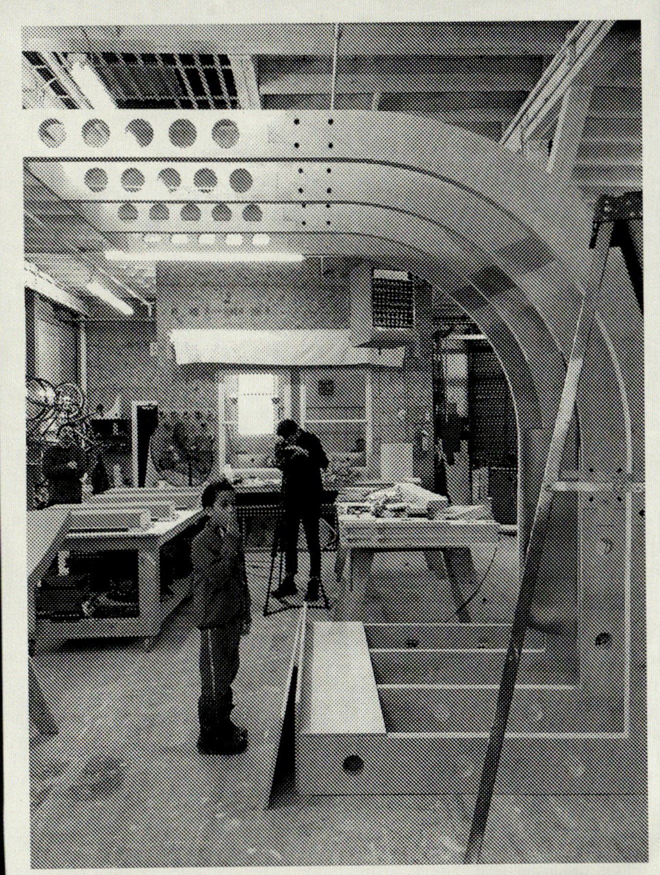

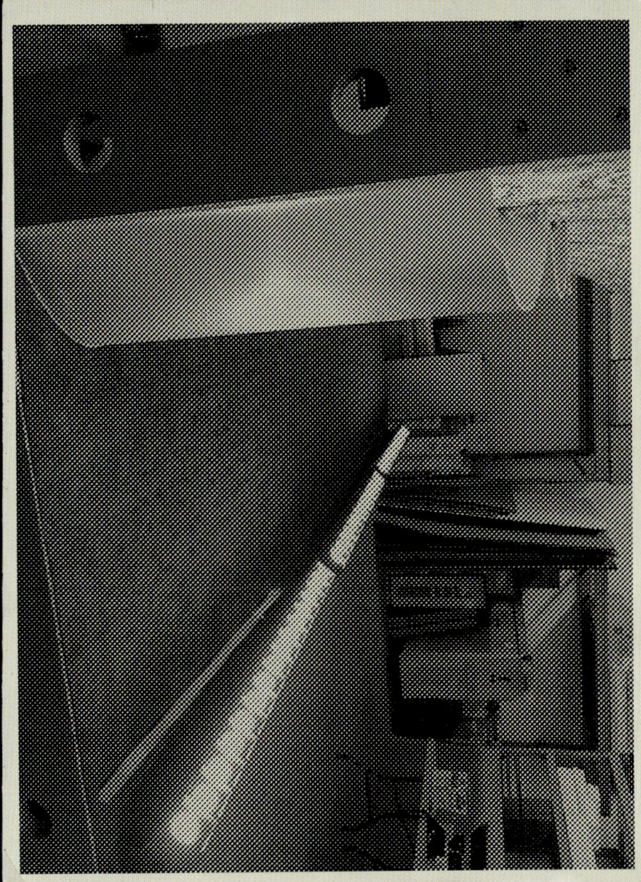

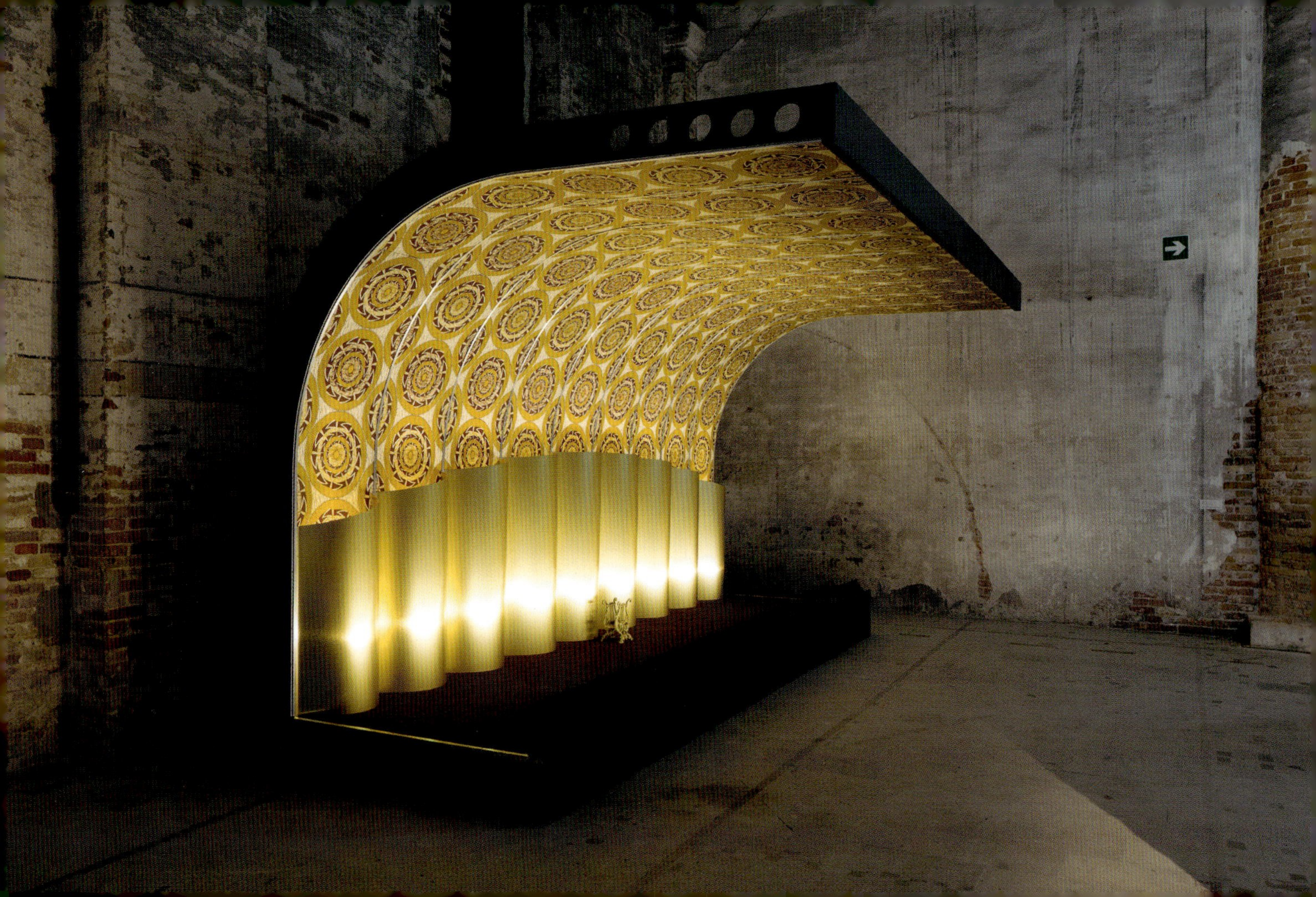

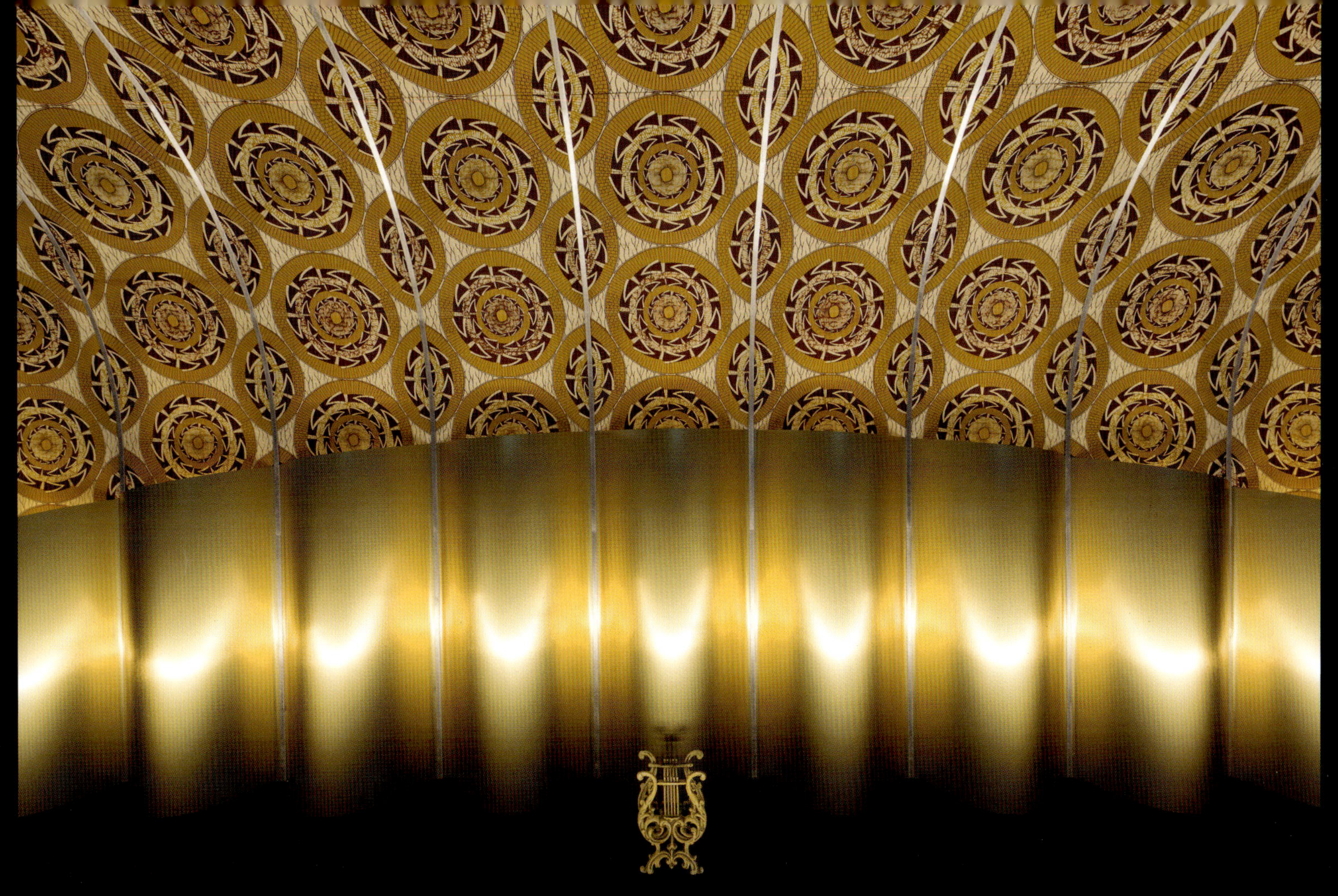

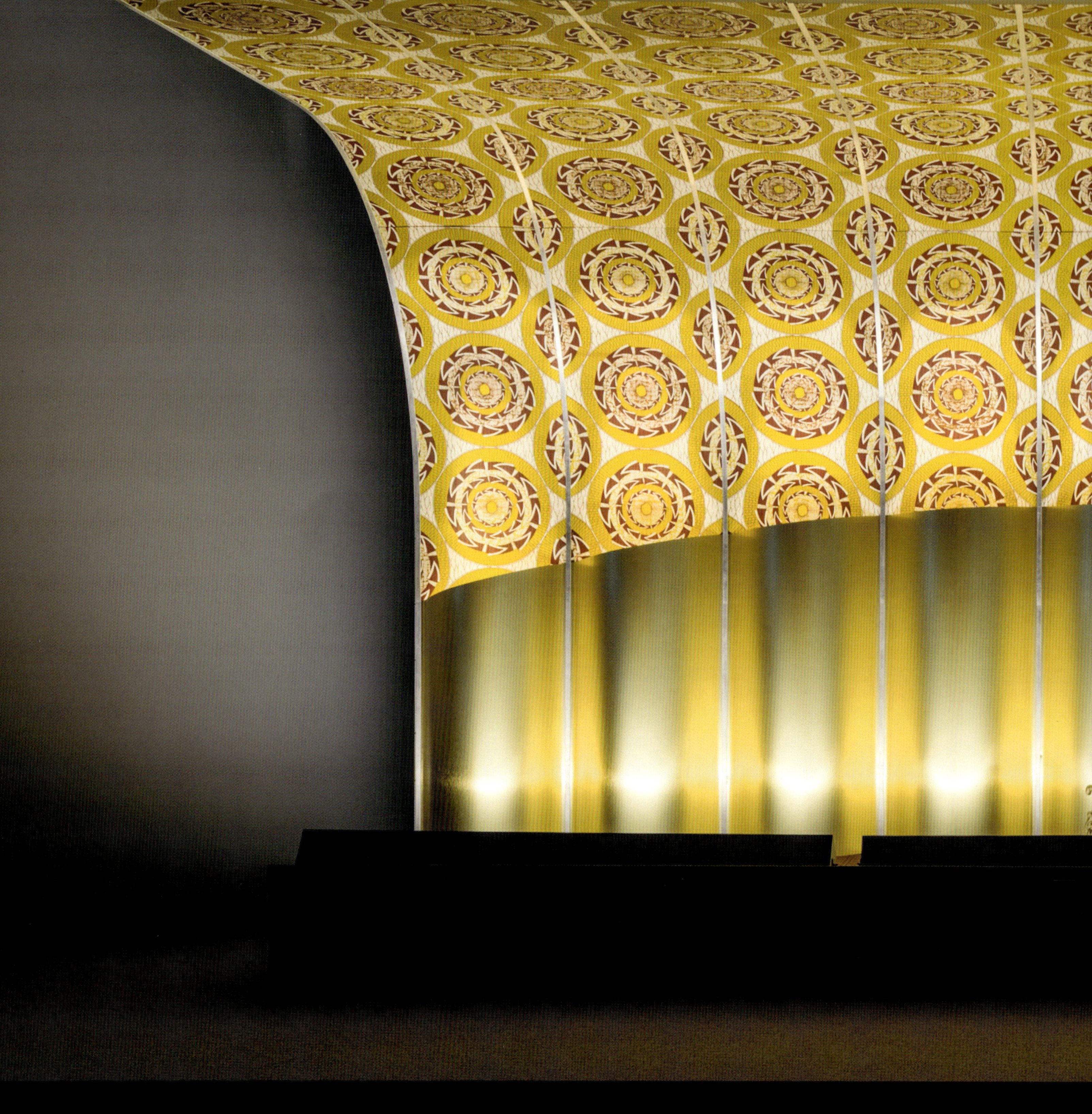

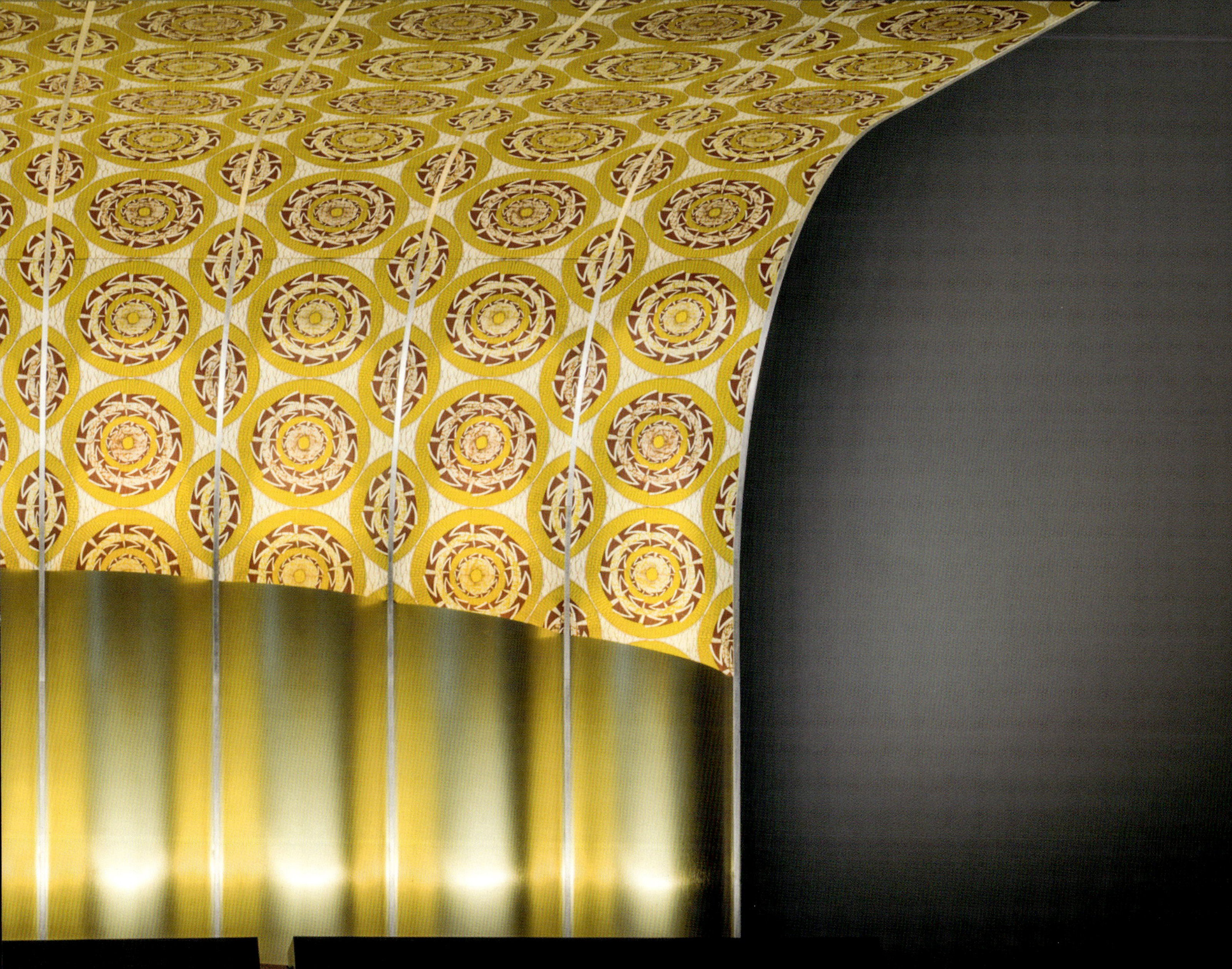

THREE DEUCES

DANIELLE A. JACKSON

215 —— 226

"THE JAZZ MUSICIAN WAS A POWERFUL, MESMERIZING FIGURE WHOSE ARTISTRY DEMANDED ATTENTION"

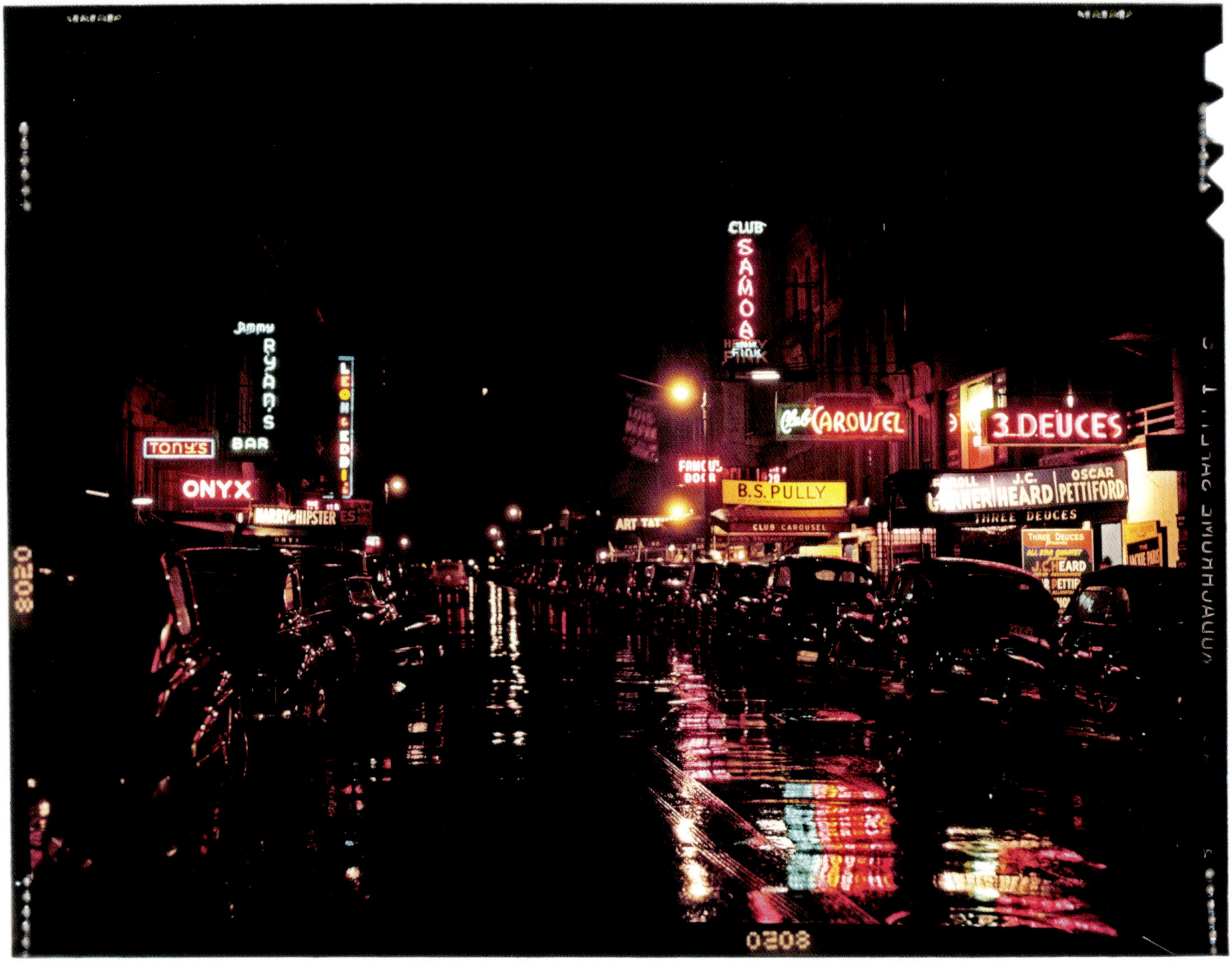

CLUB
SAMOA
HARRY FINK
JIMMY RYAN'S BAR
LEON & EDDIE'S
TONY'S
ONYX
HARRY THE HIPSTER
Club CAROUSEL
3 DEUCES
FAMOUS DOOR
B.S. PULLY
ART TATUM
CLUB CAROUSEL
ERROLL GARNER
J.C. HEARD
OSCAR PETTIFORD
THREE DEUCES
THREE DEUCES
ALL STAR CONCERT
J.C. HEARD
PETTIFORD
JACKIE PARIS

Charlie Parker and Dizzy Gillespie came in with their instruments and came up to the bandstand. Up until that time I was very secure and hiding behind bars and people and listening and watching, but, Jesus! This was at the Spotlite. So both of them hurled themselves up on the bandstand and started playing something like "Shaw 'Nuff," which was just incredible. This was my first experience with Charlie Parker, too. It was just shocking. I was there with our group—Eddie Nicholson and myself and Gene Ramey. But what that was in fact was an audition because when I got through—when they got through, they said, "We're forming a quintet. We'd like to know if you're interested in joining the group." It was very upsetting. But I said "Sure." They said they'd be in touch, packed up their instruments and went out. I felt sure that I'd never hear from them, but indeed I did in a month or six weeks. That was the beginning of that quintet that went into Three Deuces. I think we did the records a month later.

Here, pianist Al Haig describes unknowingly auditioning for a quintet assembled by saxophonist Charlie Parker and trumpet player Dizzy Gillespie. Drummer Stan Levey and bass player Curly Russell were the other original band members. Known by many as the "first great group in bebop," they opened at the Three Deuces on April 26, 1945, and quickly became the hottest act in New York. Their small group embodied and set the standard for an emerging style of spontaneous music, its sound characterized by critic Ross Russell as a "music of revolt; revolt against big bands, arrangers, and vertical harmonies." At the invitation of Three Deuces owners Sammy Kay and Irving Alexander, the quintet was in residence for three months. As a result of tensions between Parker and Gillespie, a young Miles Davis replaced the trumpet player after that, and the band returned to the venue in October 1945 for a two-week run. Later Max Roach, Tommy Potter, and Duke Jordan joined. Tap dancer Baby Laurence was the floor show during that time and sometimes performed at the same time as the music. His feet sounded like the polyrhythmic riffs of a jazz drummer, according to Davis—an element that complemented the sounds firing from the musicians' platform.

The club's reputation may have been larger than life, but its bandstand was a tiny square that could barely hold a piano, and its padded walls were reminiscent of a soundproofed recording studio—or an asylum. The venue was a long basement with a row of tables on either side of a center aisle, and the musicians set up at the far end in a corner. The Three Deuces was located on Fifty-Second Street between Fifth and Sixth Avenues, a block known as "The Street," consisting of three- and four-story brownstone buildings that had once been homes for New York's elite. By the time of Prohibition, the original owners had departed and the basements had been converted to speakeasies. The Three Deuces was one of many clubs on "The Street"; others included

the Downbeat Club, the Spotlite, Jimmy Ryan's, Kelly's Stable, the Onyx, and more. Colorful, blinking neon lights lined the block, an illuminating backdrop recalling a theatrical stage. Musicians would often have multiple gigs in one night and walk from club to club. For example, pianist and composer Billy Taylor would play with Gillespie's band at the Onyx, and then head over to the Three Deuces for a set with a different lineup.

Swing culture, epitomized by the Savoy, began to wane in popularity with the debut of Parker and Gillespie's quintet, and the subsequent ascendance of bebop. And "The Street" became the epicenter of this new form of jazz. Structurally complex, bebop signaled the rise of the individual creative musician rather than the big band, and the club's architecture mirrored that. The stages were smaller, the acoustics were dampened, and the massive dance floors like the Savoy's were replaced with smaller rooms filled with tables and chairs. The jazz musician was a powerful, mesmerizing figure whose artistry demanded close listening. Bebop featured rapid tempos, alternating chord progressions, improvised solos, and rhythm sections that did more than just keep the beat. "The Street" was a stage to the most innovative musicians of the time, from Davis, Roach, Gillespie, Parker, Potter, and Jordan to Thelonious Monk, whose composition "52nd Street Theme" was adopted as a bebop anthem.

By the end of the 1940s, "The Street" as a phenomenon had ended, the result of converging forces, principally an economic recession that hit the music industry hard, and encroaching drugs, which in turn attracted the attention of the narcotics squad. New York police raids would frequently close down the Three Deuces, the Spotlite, the Downbeat, the Onyx, and others. After a few days of darkness, they would reopen with a new line of acts (a kind of rebranding) but this couldn't last.

NOTES

1. Al Haig, quoted in Ira Gitler, *Swing to Bop: An Oral History of the Transition in Jazz in the 1940s* (New York: Oxford University Pres, 1987), 144.
2. Ross Russell, "Bebop," in *The Art of Jazz*, ed. Martin Williams (New York: Oxford University Press, 1959), 202. Other scholars, like Frank Kofsy, have proclaimed that the rebellious nature of the music was about a refusal to submit to economic exploitation.
3. Gillespie and Parker came together out of a shared pursuit of a musical breakthrough, but had different personalities and lifestyles. Parker was a brilliant artist, but he had a tumultuous personal life due to capricious behavior and drug use. According to Miles Davis, one reason for the split between these two musicians was that Parker began to miss rehearsals and Gillespie was strict about such things. See Miles Davis and Quincy Trope, *Miles: The Autobiography* (New York: Simon and Schuster, 1989), 71.
4. Ibid., 68.
5. Billy Taylor and Teresa L. Reed, *The Jazz Life of Dr. Billy Taylor* (Bloomington: Indiana University Press, 2013), 9.

A. Souvenir card from Three Deuces,
New York, n.d.

B. Tommy Potter and Charlie Parker
performing at Three Deuces, New York,
August 1947

C. (left to right): Charlie Ventura, Curley
Russell, Bill Harris, Ralph Burns, and Dave
Tough performing at Three Deuces, New
York, April 1947

D. (left to right): Tommy Potter, Max
Roach, Charlie Parker, Miles Davis, and
Duke Jordan performing at Three Deuces,
New York, July 1947

E. Photograph inside souvenir card from
Three Deuces, New York, n.d.

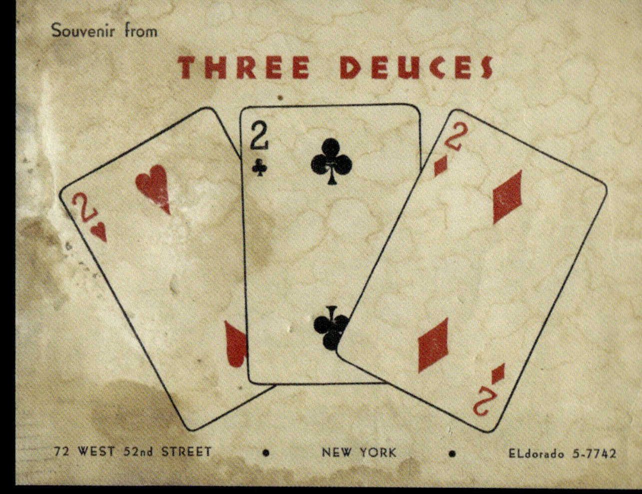

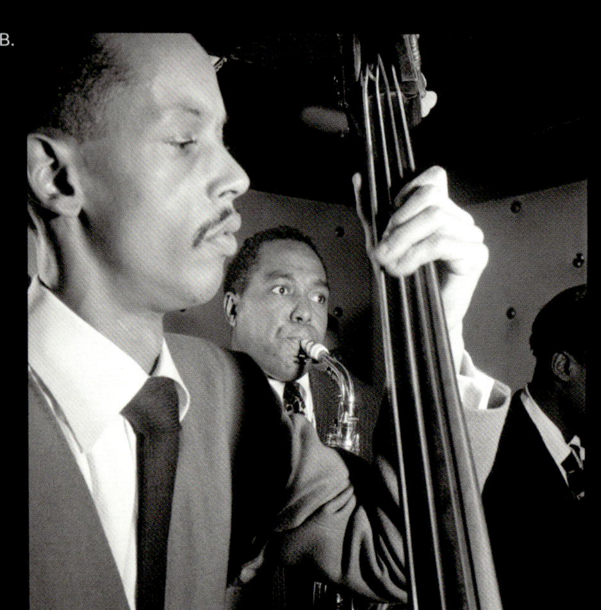

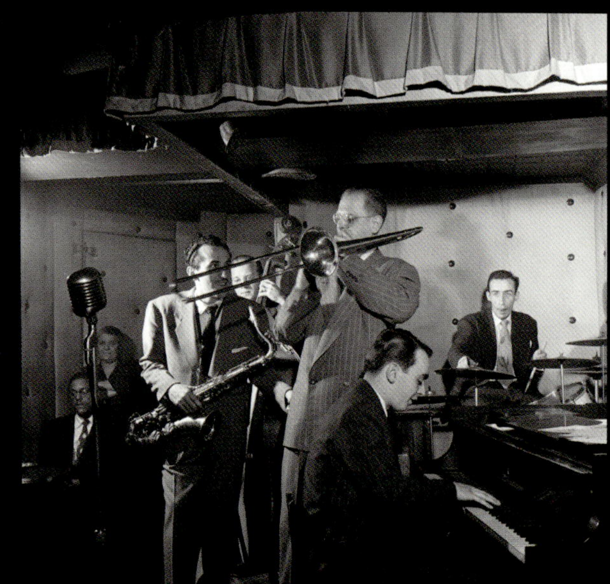

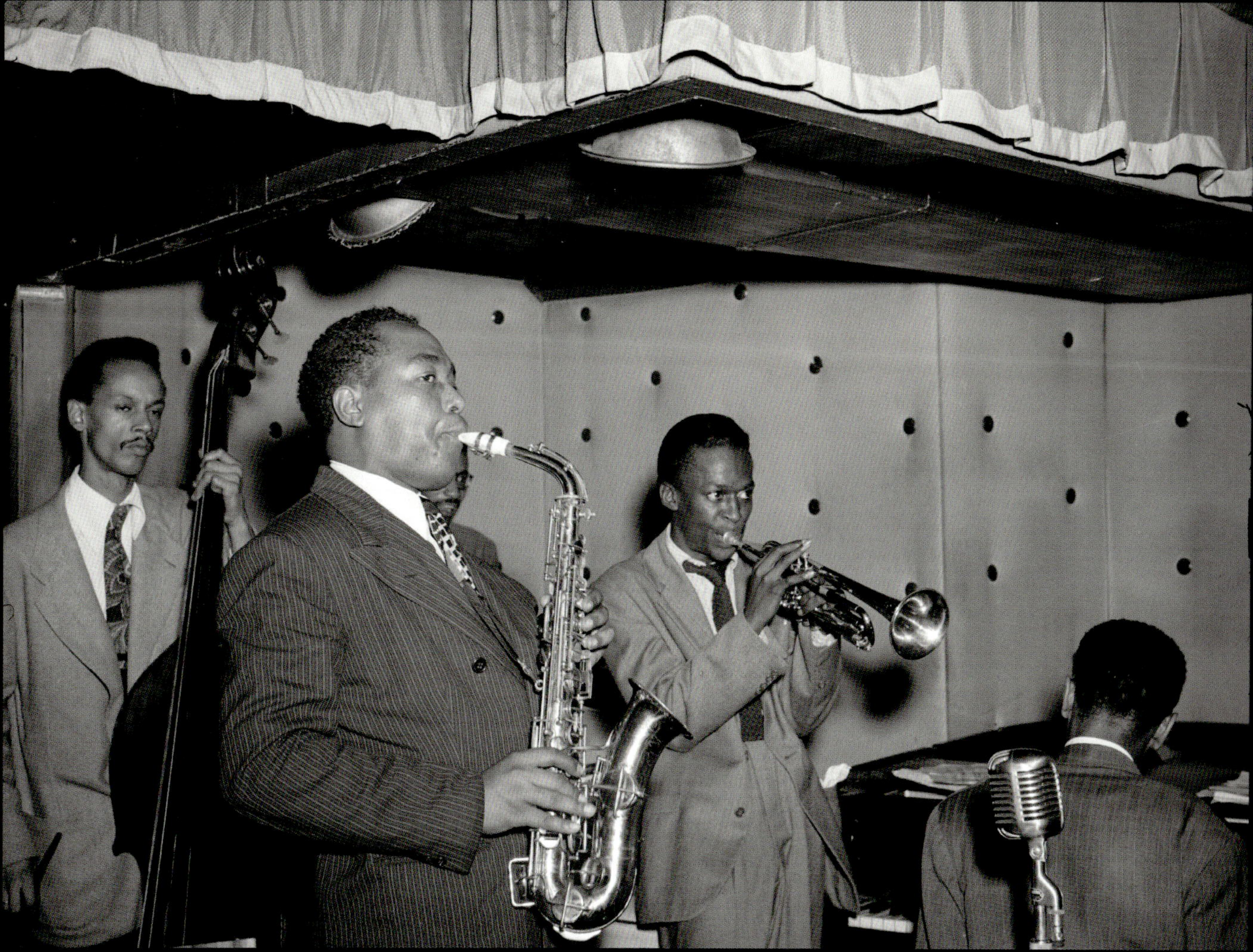

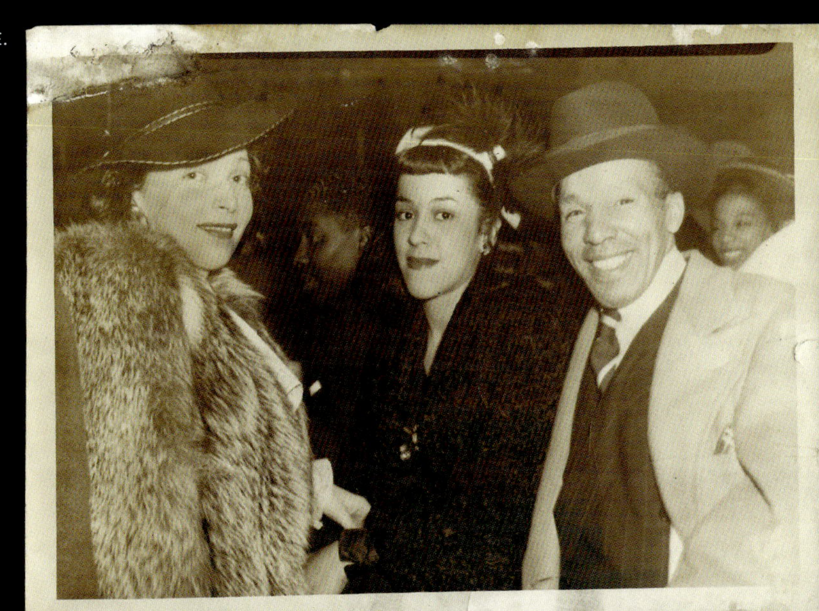

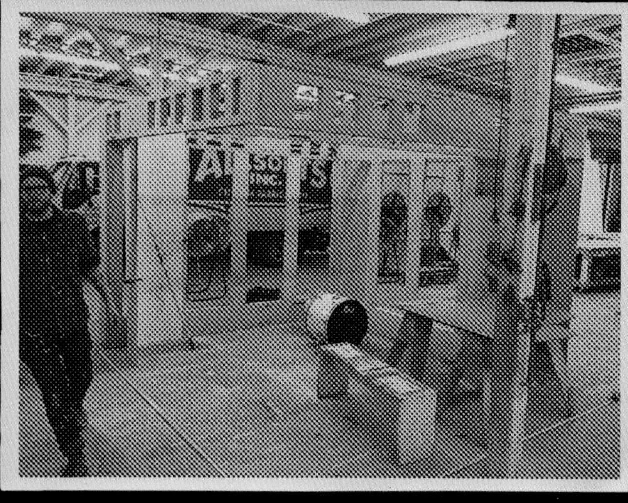
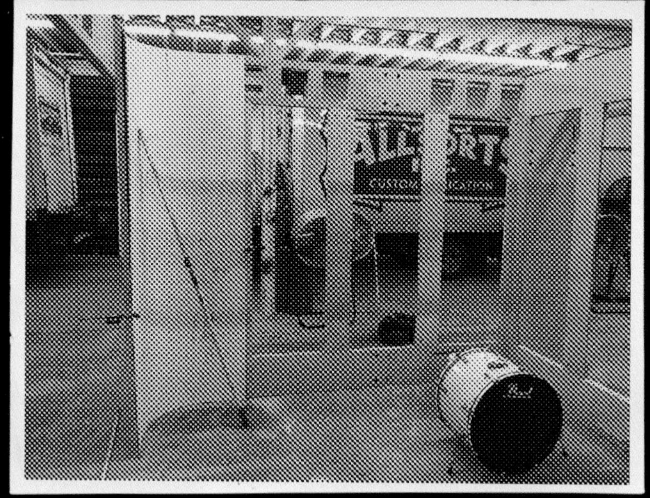
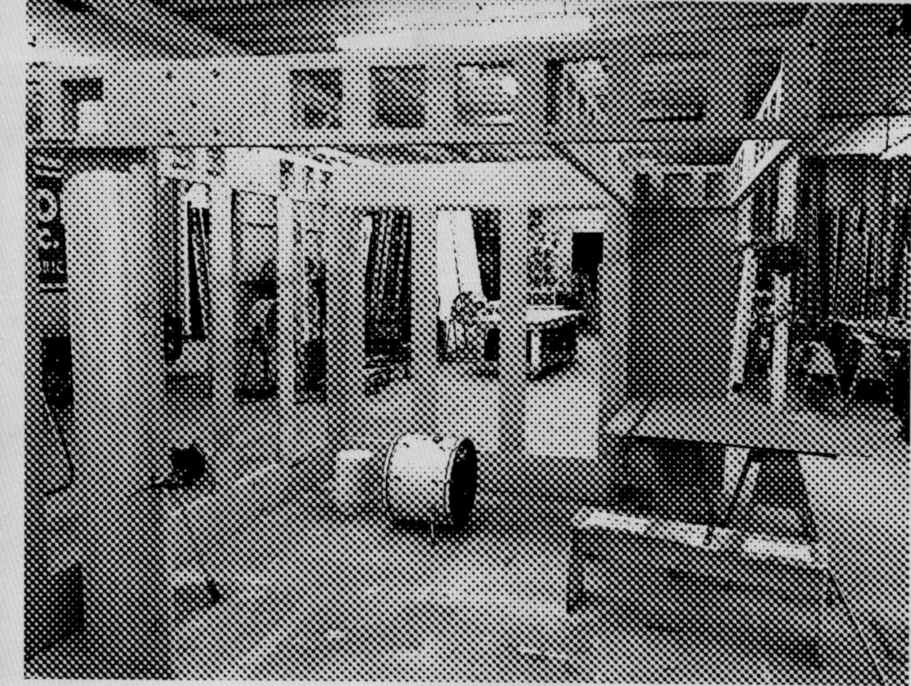

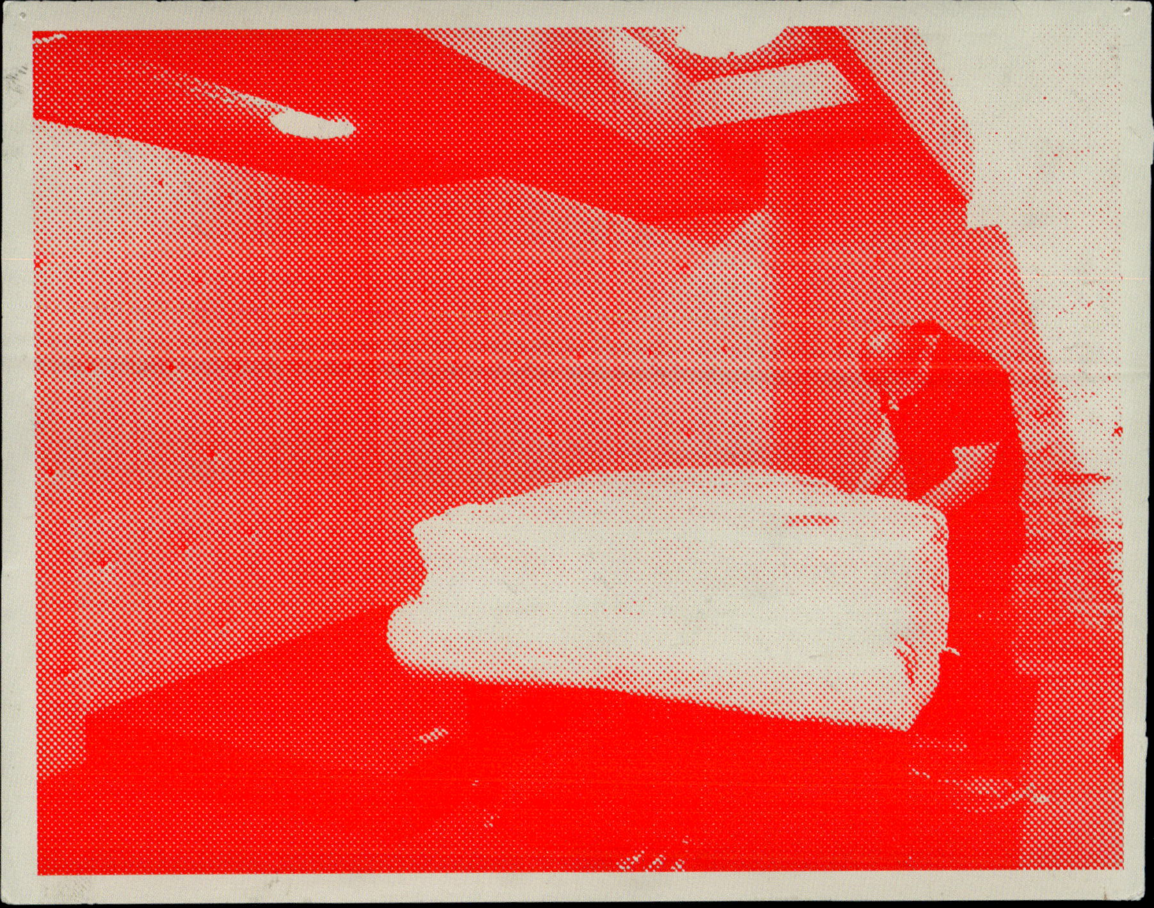

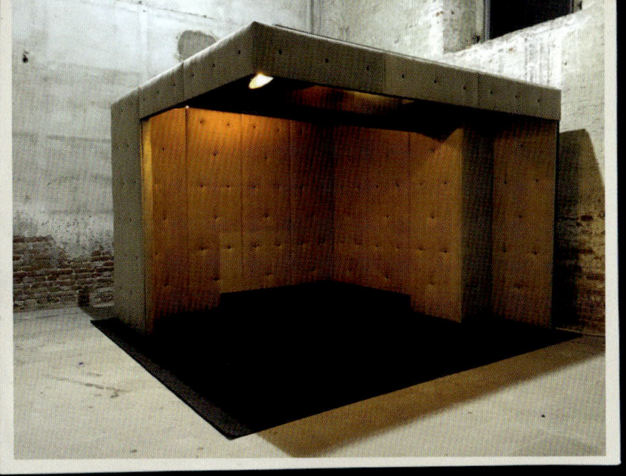

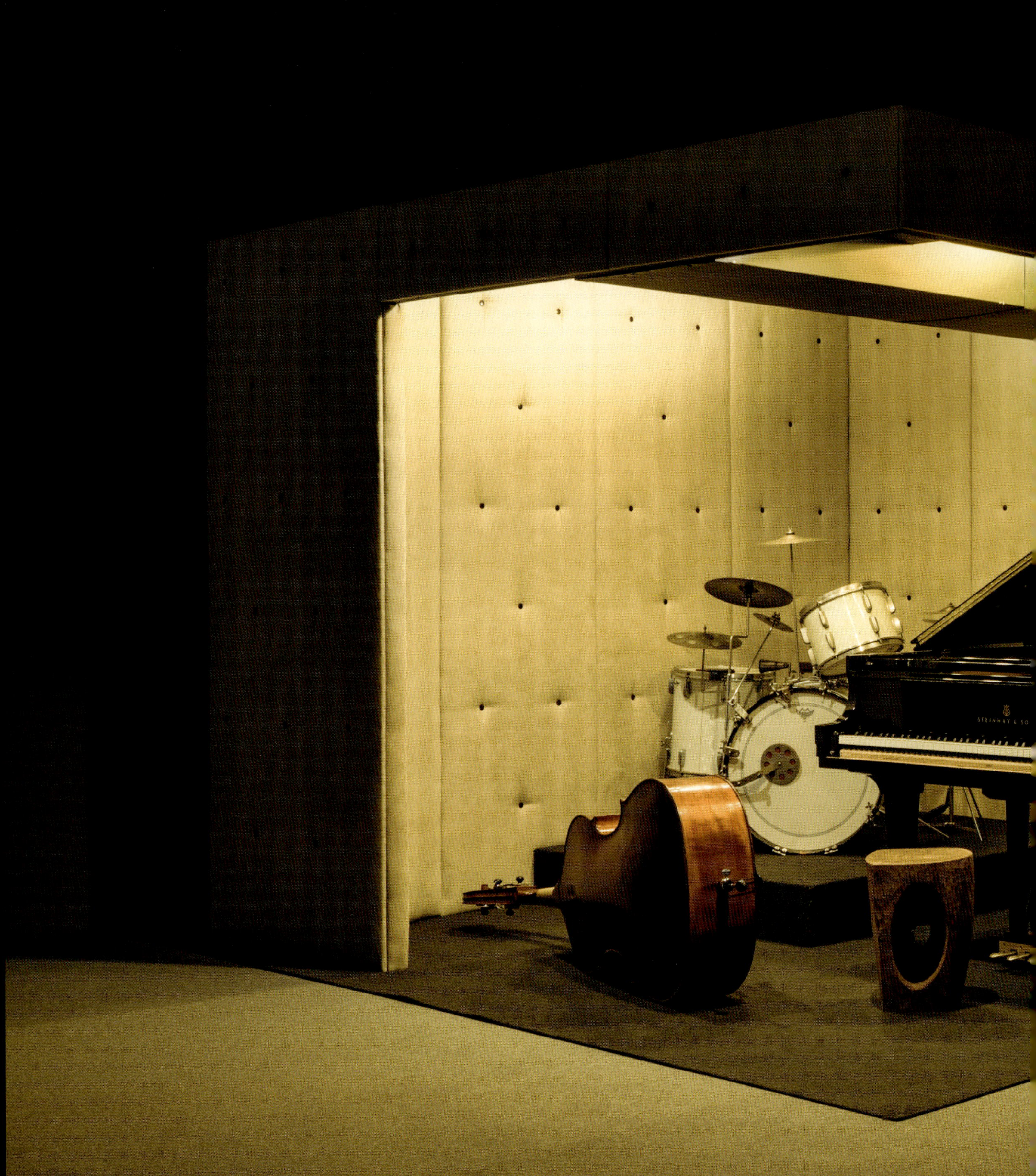

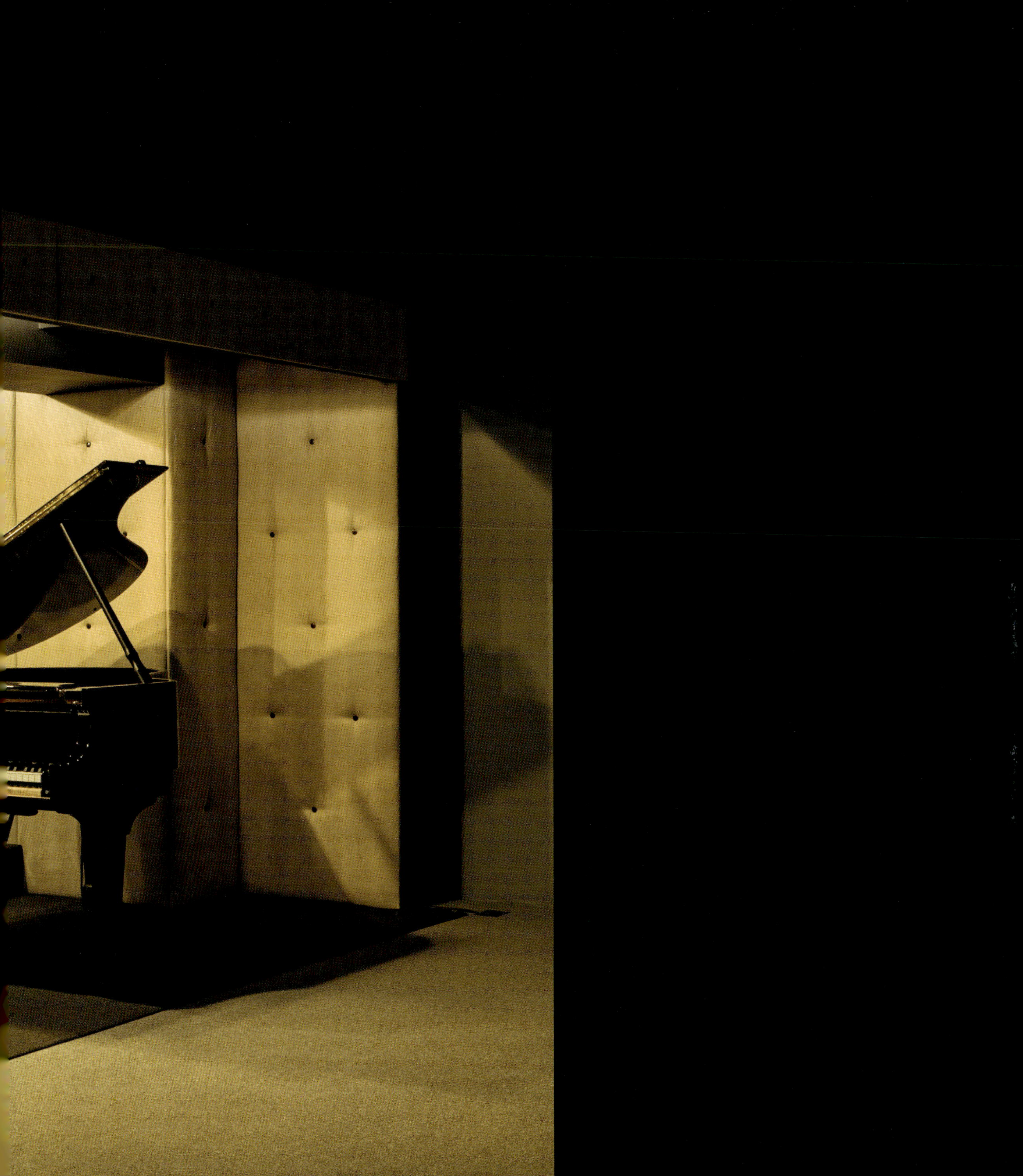

Right and previous pages:
Jason Moran, *STAGED: Three Deuces,* 2015, mixed media, sound,
96 x 120 x 156 in. (243.8 x 304.8 x 396.2 cm); installation views at the
56th Venice Biennale, May 9 – November 22, 2015

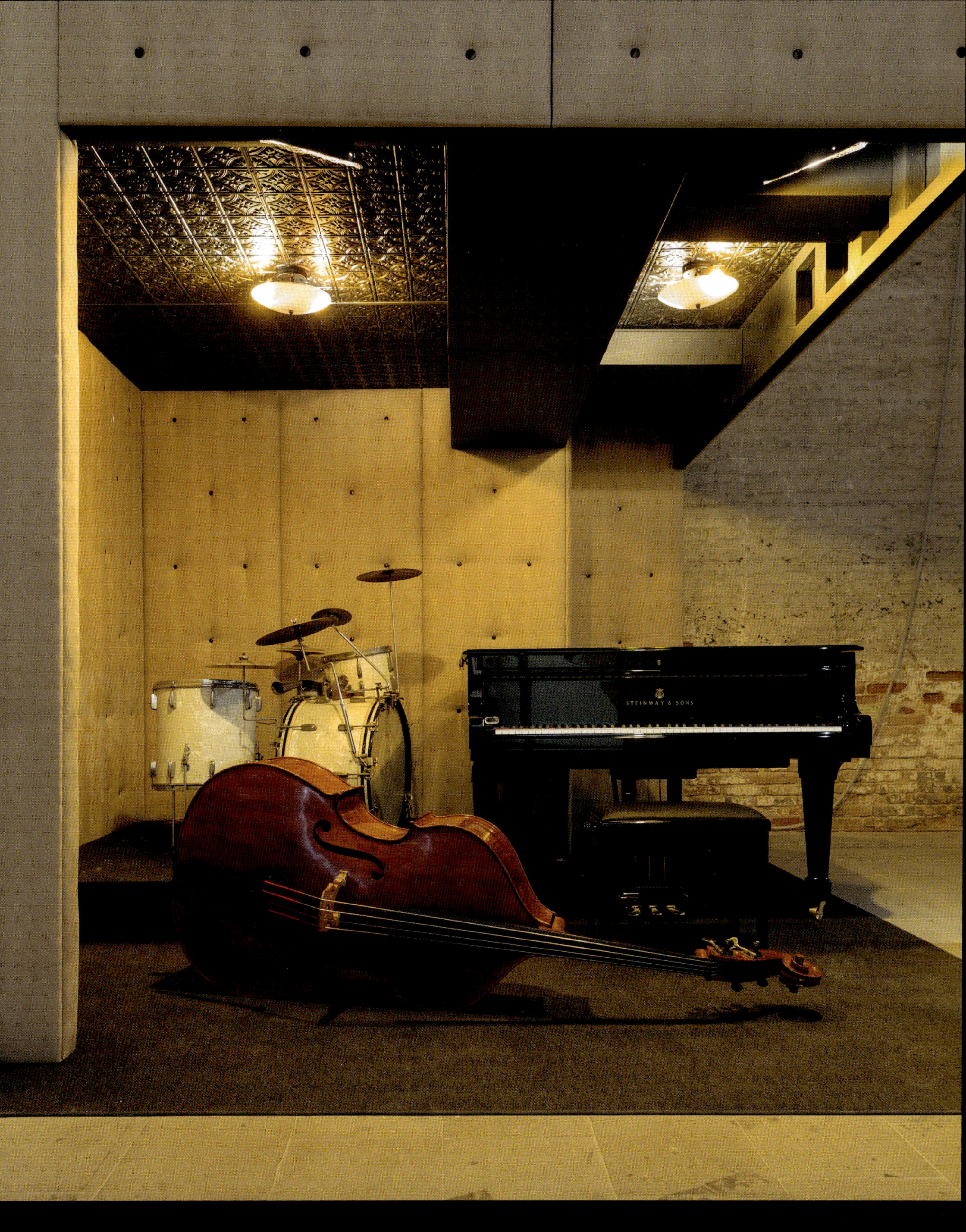
STEINWAY & SONS

SLUGS'

DANIELLE A. JACKSON

"SOMETHING SO FAR AWAY THAT IT SEEMS NONEXISTENT"

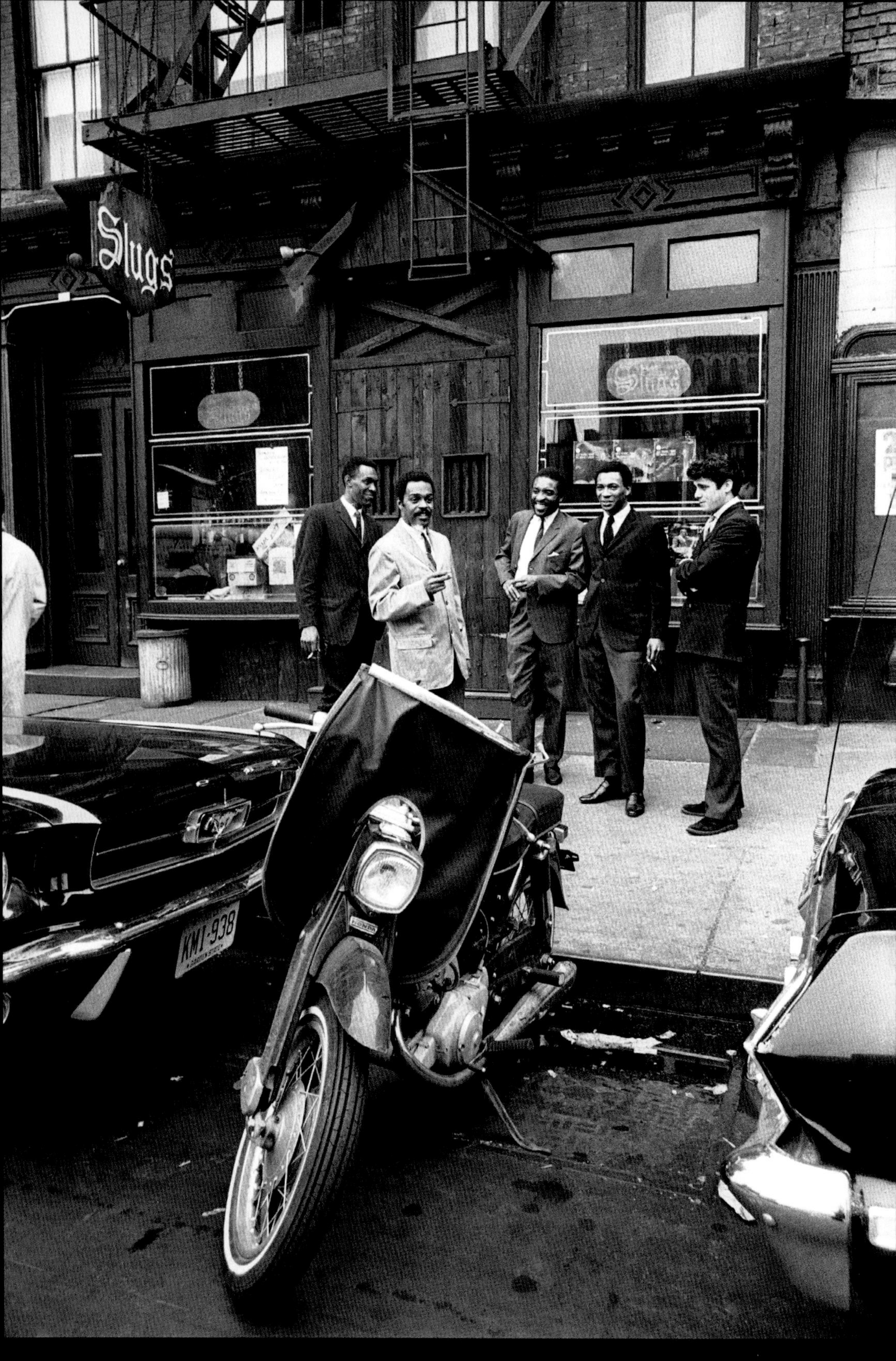

Albert Ayler Quintet outside of Slugs', New York, 1966
(left to right): Donald Ayler, Albert Ayler, Lewis Worrell,
Ronald Shannon Jackson, and Michael Sampson

The above conversation comes from *The Ark and the Ankh*, a 1966 recording of a discussion between writer and poet Henry Dumas and avant-garde musician and cosmic philosopher Sun Ra. The recording—discovered and released in 2002 on Ikef records—was made at Slugs' (also known as Slugs' Saloon and Slugs' in the Far East). The jazz dive between Avenue B and Avenue C in New York's East Village, a notoriously squalid area at the time, had rustic brick walls, colored spherical light fixtures hanging from the ceiling on delicate wires, and sawdust and peanut shells on the floor. The small stage was covered in aging linoleum tiles. Dumas and Sun Ra converse amid the unwieldy, dissonant sounds of Sun Ra's Arkestra, making their words at times barely audible. Dumas probed the musician for his thoughts on a range of topics, from the Black Arts Movement to theological speculations on new forms of jazz then emerging.

At the time, Sun Ra was performing at Slugs' regularly on Monday nights. The venue attracted a range of people—music enthusiasts, neighborhood drug dealers, and influential visual artists, writers, poets, and avant-garde jazz musicians, including Amiri Baraka, A.B. Spellman, Allen Ginsberg, Bob Thompson, Jackie McLean, Art Blakey, Pharoah Sanders, and Herman Grimes, to name a few. The owners, Jerry Schultz (now known as Gopal Krishna) and Robert Schoenholt (now deceased), were part of an esoteric group following the philosophies of spiritual mystic and composer George Ivanovitch Gurdjieff, who identified the "Fourth Way" method. They opened Slugs' in 1964 as a kind of existential investigation into human interaction in response to the group leader's call to involve themselves with people.

The club's name came from Gurdjieff's first publication, *All and Everything: Beelzebub's Tales to His Grandson* (1950), the first in a trilogy intended as a repository of all the mystic's teachings. The narrative hinges on the legend of Beelzebub, an extraterrestrial astronaut whose banishment from his homeland of Ors brings him into contact with strange three-brained beings of planet Earth, whom Beelzebub's grandson Hassien nicknames Slugs. While traveling to a conference aboard the spaceship *Karnak*, Beelzebub recounts the story of his exile and his encounters with these beings. By the story's end, Beelzebub is pardoned and welcomed as an Elder—a kind of once wrongfully persecuted, now revered Yahweh in an extraterrestrial universe.

There are connections between the origins of Slugs' and the teachings of Sun Ra relating to alternative cosmologies and consciousness, but Slugs' relationship to jazz experimentalism is arguably happenstance. The musicians Jackie McLean, Rashid Ali, and Ritchie Havens lived in the neighborhood, and McLean's suggestion to the owners that he play a New Year's Eve concert in 1964 laid the groundwork for a steady roster of experimental jazz happenings throughout the 1960s and into the 1970s. As noted in a 1965 *Sounds & Fury* article, something about performing at Slugs' made musicians "play harder and listeners pay attention."

Slugs' accumulated a rich body of lore peppered with colorful anecdotes and its share of ghosts. Saxophonist Charles McPherson recalls the audience's emotional connection to a teary-eyed Charles Mingus one night, as he bemoaned being hassled by cops on his way to the club. Pianist Cecil Taylor would sneak past the doorman and strategically wait for a musician's set to end so that he could play an impromptu, unauthorized set. Salvador Dalí visited Slugs', circling the room with a dimly lit candle and inspecting each painting on its walls. I imagine him stepping onto the stage between sets to gaze at the Bob Thompson painting that served as the backdrop for the nightly performances; surely he enjoyed its surrealistic seagull-like figure, whose prominent eye looks upward as a single tear falls upon its cheek. Albert Ayler recorded an EP there shortly before his body was found in the East River. A drunken patron who could whistle every song in the club's jukebox and Miles Davis auditioning prospective band members are frequent recollections. Slugs' continued until 1972, closing shortly after famed trumpeter Lee Morgan (known for the tune "The Sidewinder") was shot to death there, at the age of thirty-three, by his longtime companion and manager Helen Moore. Slugs' existed on another plane; its door was a portal to a musical, mystical realm where the logic of the outside world didn't seem to apply.

A. *Sounds & Fury* magazine cover featuring interior of Slugs' and Charles Lloyd band, December 1965

B. Slugs' in *Sounds & Fury* magazine, December 1965

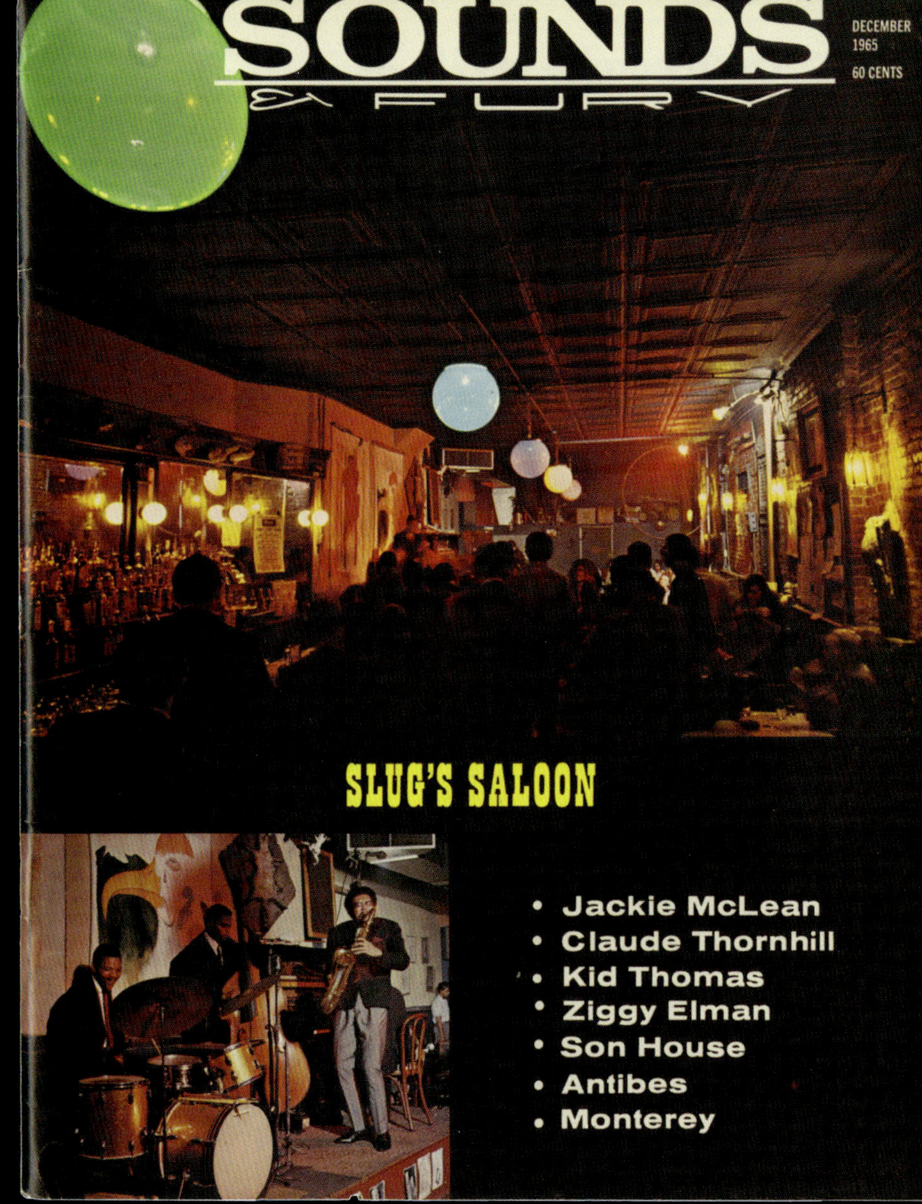

NOTES

1. This was a part of a series of ongoing conversations between Sun Ra and Dumas dating back to the early 1960s. Dumas also wrote the liner notes for the Sun Ra Arkestra album *Cosmic Tones for Mental Therapy*, recorded in 1963 and released in 1967. See Nathan Ragain, "A 'Reconstituted Am': Language, Nature, and Collectivity in Sun Ra and Henry Dumas," *Criticism* 24, no. 4 (Fall 2012): 539–565.

2. Gurdjieff's esoteric system, although varied, included a series of physical and mental exercises. The mystic believed human functioning occurred on three levels: cognition, emotion, and movement. The "Fourth Way" was seen, by its followers, as a response to dismembering forces in the world. It was a method of self-transformation that could propel an awareness of one's relationship to everyone and everything, forcing a kind of harmonious connection to the cosmos. Later in Gurdjieff's teachings music became a key component. In collaboration with his pupil Russian composer Thomas de Hartmann, the mystic created hymns inspired by various folk and Russian Orthodox traditions. Pianist Keith Jarett, a Gurdjieff devotee, recorded and performed the hymns as part of his album *G.I. Gurdjieff Sacred Hymns* (1980) released on ECM records. See Jacob Needleman et al., *Gurdjieff: Essays and Reflections on the Man and His Teachings* (New York: Bloomsbury, 1998).

3. Recorded interview with Jerry Schultz and Daniel Beban, August 9, 2014, http://www.radionz.co.nz/national/programmes/nat-music/audio/20145088/slugs-saloon.

4. Ahmad Basheer, "The Audience," *Sounds & Fury*, December 1965, 9.

5. Frank Mastropolo, "It Was a Joint: Jazz Musicians Remember Slugs' in the Far East," *Bedford and Bowery*, September 10, 2014, http://bedfordandbowery.com/2014/09/it-was-a-joint-jazz-musicians-remember-slugs-in-the-far-east/.

8. See James Gavin, "Inside Slugs' Saloon, Jazz's Most Notorious Nightclub," *Jazz Times*, September 10, 2015, https://jazztimes.com/features/inside-slugs-saloon-jazzs-most-notorious-nightclub/.

9. Aspects of the Thompson painting recall *The Eye*, one of five paintings Dalí made as studies for the dream sequence in Alfred Hitchcock's *Spellbound* (1945), and *Un Chien Andalou*, the 1929 film by Dalí and Luis Buñuel.

10. Recorded interview with Jerry Schultz and Daniel Beban, August 9, 2014, http://www.radionz.co.nz/national/programmes/nat-music/audio/20145088/slugs-saloon.

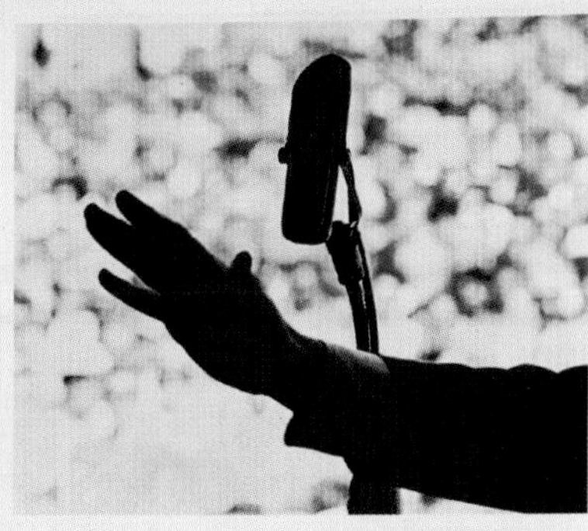

The Audience

by Ahmad Basheer

One evening a very down-to-earth brown lady rose from her seat and started dancing, moving about the entire Village Vanguard to Sonny Rollin's group. Some of the patrons smiled at each other when the uninhibited customer danced past; some were visibly embarrassed for her — and probably at their inability to let *themselves* go; others were surprised and even shocked at a display of this sort in that club. The realization was absent of how different audiences are in other neighborhoods, cities and countries.

Singer Earl Tenneyson—a close friend of Sonny who's been "sittin in" with him a lot recently — said, "This is hilarious, you know! To see something like that in this club . . . she's not going to sit there all sophisticated and proper: she feels the spirit of the music and wants to show it. I'm used to that where I hung around years back . . . Harlem."

Rollins was delighted with what he saw and remarked, "I think most of the people who came in tonight were here to see Memphis Slim (he shared the bill) but they liked us also! I guess if you can do that, you're doing something. A crowd like this is usually interested in folk music from an intellectual standpoint so they sit and study the performers. He continued, laughing, "Seeing that chick dancing in the Vanguard sure was funny!"

Any visitor to New York's Apollo Theatre will tell you what "hard-to-please" means. The up-towners prefer a good beat with soulful renditions. Even a proven professional will occasionally run into trouble and get booed if there are too many awkward moments. A winner on Amateur Night is *very good* and those who hear of this—familiar with the Apollo's reputation—have no doubt *that* performer is "on the climb." When a contestant is on and the audience begins to "act up," an employee of the theatre walks on, dressed in long underwear, harshly blowing a trombone following the unsuccessful one off the stage.

Sometimes a professional has trouble with one, a few, or even many members of the crowd and it takes additional skill to deal with the situation. Ernestine Anderson was singing at the Apollo one afternoon and a woman was "talking away" in the balcony, loud enough for everyone to hear. Miss Anderson waited patiently for her to stop; but she persisted. The singer finally became exasperated; stopped herself and signalled the band to stop. "This must really be important! Let's all hear it!", she said. A strange silence came over the place . . . then she started the orchestra and began again.

Comedian Redd Foxx gets rid of hecklers fast. Musicians admire this and may on occasion use his methods. One foil Redd has for a loud talker is, "Who left the cage open? It's time to feed the animals!"

Ahmad Jamal has been severely criticized because of his approach to a disrespectful group, "Some people are just rude although it's a pleasure to play for some," he says. "If they talk too much you might as well stop. . . . However, I find colleges are very nice to work! I like them!"

Roy Haynes, the drummer, has a very wholesome attitude toward listeners. . . . "Most audiences are good. But some are very good, like in Baltimore. Slugs is great! They're mostly painters and writers—fellow artists and appreciators of same — over there: it really makes you feel like playing!"

Chastisement came from Haynes at the old Five Spot when it seemed the whole club was deeply steeped in conversation. "Ladies and gentlemen," he spoke in the mike, "we're stopping . . . and will not continue until we have your attention. We're performing for you and do not intend to compete. You're disrespecting us!" The excessive noise was stopped and the evening turned into a pleasant one.

Pianist McCoy Tyner tells us, "As far as crowds are concerned, I find them all different; some listen and some talk constantly, of course all artists prefer attentive ones."

The reception that musicians have been getting in Europe has been bragged about for years. Bassist Art Davis reports, "We're kings over there! The people are so appreciative it's hard to leave, which compensates for the 'just average' financial arrangements made."

Africa, Tokyo, Hong Kong and South America are new areas that have welcomed jazz, and Max Roach, Thelonious Monk and Tony Scott are praising the conditions that are almost tantamount to worship.

Monk feels very good about the people in Hong Kong, "They sure are some swell cats in Hong Kong: they really like us! And those Hilton Hotels — like the one we played in — are crazy!"

Over the states there is the same atmosphere in places similar to that in others. You can walk into a Chicago club almost like one in New York; one in San Francisco similar to one in Philadelphia. To the fans the experience of facing audiences are absent and it's not generally thought of that this is a constant part of the artist's life: communicating from the stage to us.

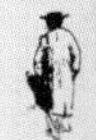

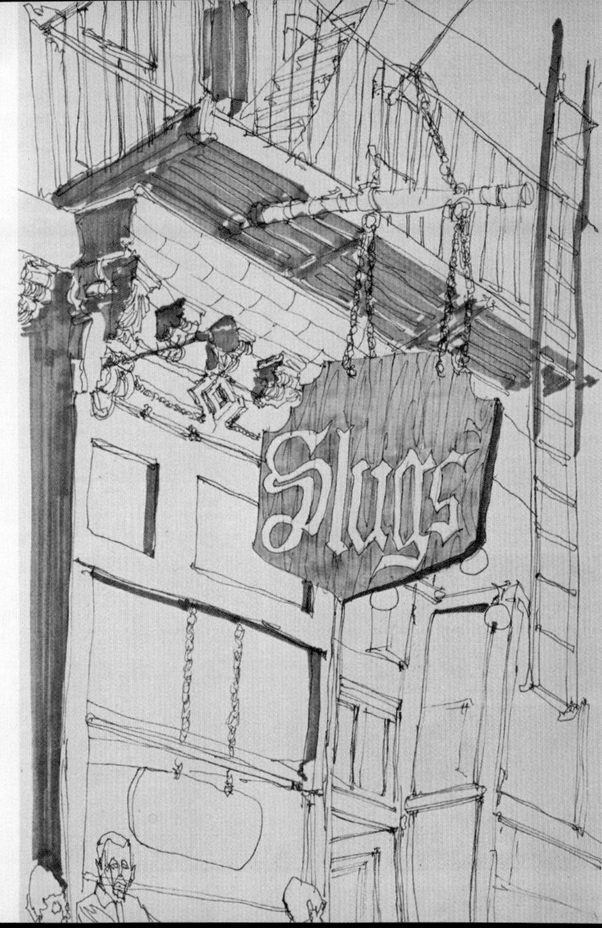

8

SLUG'S SALOON IS DOWN . . . on the lower east side of New York City. The neighborhood is shabby. The streets are dirty and the buildings dirtier. It's hard to get to Slug's. It's on a one-way street (3rd Street) between Avenue B and Avenue C (which, unless you are very familiar with the city, sounds like you're in Brooklyn, already). The place itself looks grimy from the outside. The windows are usually dirty and the front door is hard to open. Yet, with all this against it and with other clubowners screaming "Jazz is dead," Slug's is always busy, and always booking jazz. It certainly can't be the location, since Birdland had one of the best locations in the city and Birdland is out of business. It can't be because the bartenders are so friendly; because they're not. Neither Jerry nor Robert (co-owners Schultz and Schoenholt) enjoy tending bar and it shows. Besides, the friendliest group around is the Canterino gang (which includes affable Al the waiter) at the Half Note. The sad truth is that you can have the Half Note to yourself (just you, Clark and Bob) many weeknights. And the famous Five Spot looks like the Hall of the Mountain King when mid-week emptiness hits. What's left? Booze is pretty much the same wherever you go. Slug's secret is that it is a neighborhood bar. Jerry explains that the east Village is what the Village was years ago. The intense affectation of McDougal and Bleecker is not found on East Third Street or in Slug's. Artist types are in evidence but their manner is relaxed and not at all the "let me show you just how creative I am" attitude of the Village proper.

Photos by Roy Ross

Innkeeper; Schultz

Gary Bartz

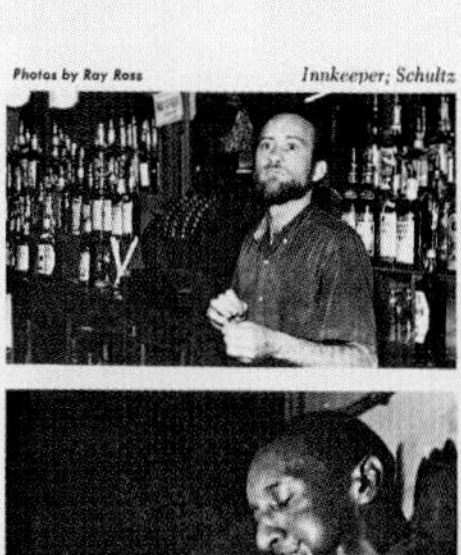

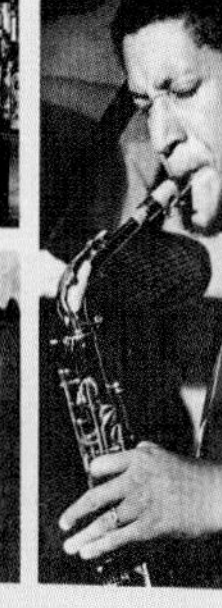

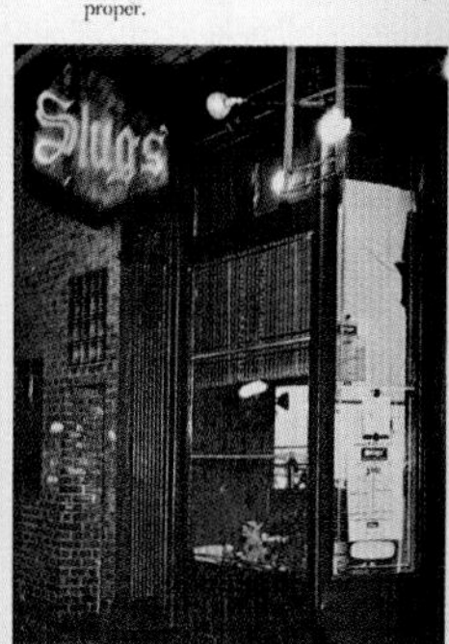

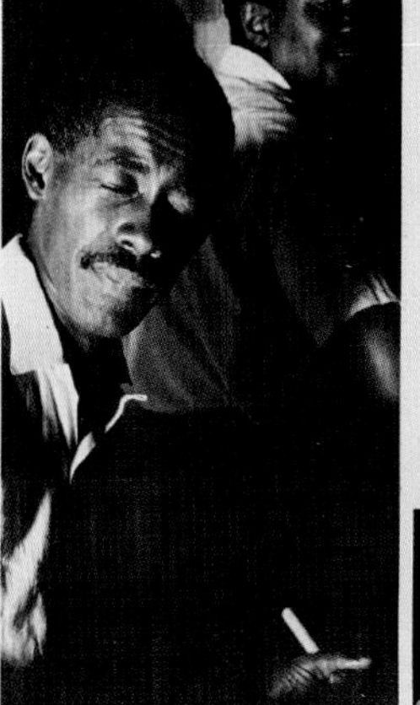

9

Lenny McBrown

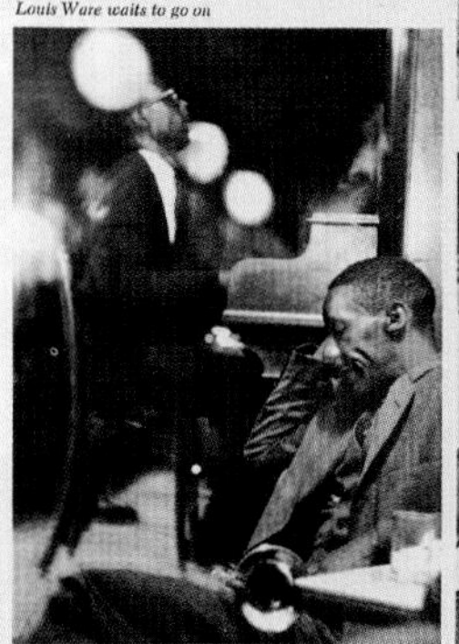

Louis Ware waits to go on

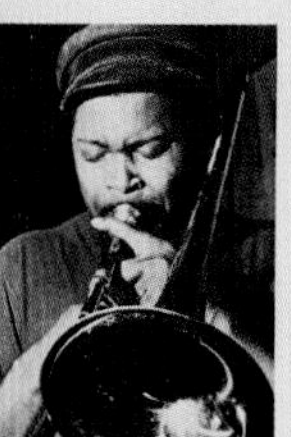

Musicians dig Slug's. It is the place to both play and listen. It began less than a year ago during New Year's week. Jackie McLean (who doesn't work often in N.Y.C. due to his lack of the gestapo required cabaret card) suggested an afternoon concert charging a buck at the door and splitting the take with the club. Jackie was late and the concert ran into evening. Over two hundred people paid a dollar each to listen. Prior to this, Slug's evening crowd was strictly the juke box and fifty cent beer variety. Jerry and Robert got a glimpse of that dollar at the door and it's been there ever since.

As well as using top names (Wayne Shorter, Roy Haynes, Charles Lloyd, Curtis Fuller, Charles Davis, Thad Jones, Pepper Adams, etc., etc.) the stand at Slug's supports new names. Some of the young unknown players are exceptionally good and will become tomorrow's front line. Others, equally as good, will never be heard. This is the kind of club that jazz needs more of. No acts or routines are being presented here; just good old creative, hard-working, blowing. Unfortunately, no one can plan a club to have what this one has. There is a fresh feeling about Slug's that makes players work harder and listeners pay attention. It is a feeling that cannot be fabricated or contrived. No amount of special lighting or "show biz" atmosphere can produce the stretch out feeling that exists here. Everything has to be just right; the time, the place, the people, the communication. There may just never ever be another Slug's Saloon.

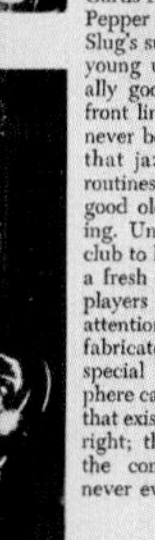

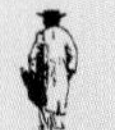

A.

Slugs'
in the far east
GR 7-9737
242 EAST 3rd ST (Bet. Aves. B & C) NEW YORK CITY

OCTOBER 11 THRU OCTOBER 16
BENNY POWELL
QUARTET

SPECIAL ATTRACTION ! - 3 DAYS ONLY !
OCTOBER 14 - 15 AND 16
ORNETTE
COLEMAN
TRIO

OCTOBER 18 THRU OCTOBER 23
GRANT GREEN - JOHN PATTON
QUARTET

OCTOBER 25 THRU OCTOBER 30
CURTIS FULLER
QUINTET
featuring JIMMY HEATH

NOVEMBER 1 THRU NOVEMBER 6
LOU DONALDSON
QUARTET

NOVEMBER 8 THRU NOVEMBER 13
STANLEY TURRENTINE
SHIRLEY SCOTT
TRIO

Slugs'
in the far east

Guest Stars Every Sun. aft & Mon. nites
Promotion:
Jim Harrison

SUN. to FRI. 9:30 PM - 4 AM - SAT. 8:30 PM - 3 AM

B.

MARCH 7-12 THE WAYNE SHORTER QUARTET
MARCH 14-19 THE JOE HENDERSON SEXTET
MARCH 21-26 THE YUSEF LATEEF QUARTET
MARCH 28 ~ APRIL 2 THE JACKIE McLEAN QUARTET
SUN RA
Slugs'
IN THE FAR EAST
242 EAST 3RD ST.
BETWEEN AVE. B & C WA 1-9900

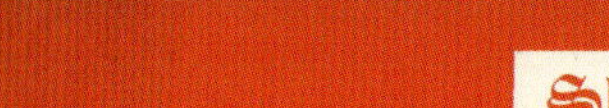

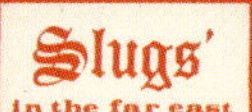

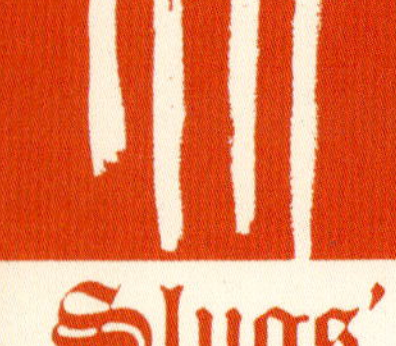

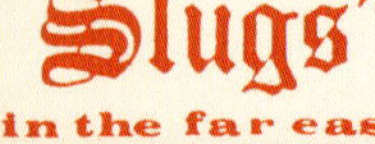

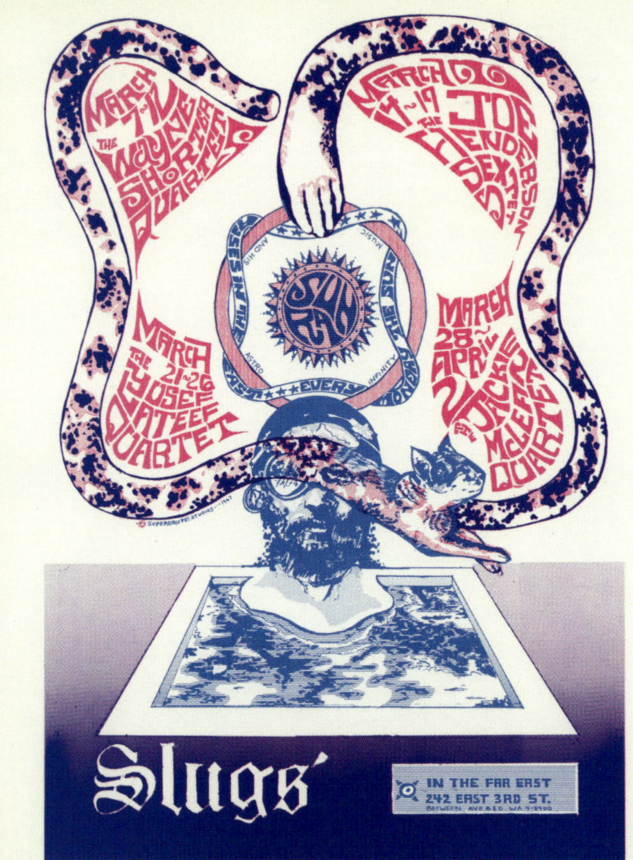

A. Slugs' October/November handbill, featuring Benny Powell, Ornette Coleman, Grant Green/John Patton, Curtis Fuller, Lou Donaldson, Stanley Turrentine/Shirley Scott, and Jim Harrison, 1966

B. Slugs' poster featuring Sun Ra, Wayne Shorter Quartet, Joe Henderson Sextet, Jackie McLean Quartet, and Yusef Lateef Quartet, 1967

C. Audience at Slugs', 1965

D. Jazz at Slugs', New York, 1964 (left to right): Bob Thompson, Nancy Dannenberg, unknown, A. B. Spellman, Danielle Spellman, and unknown

C.

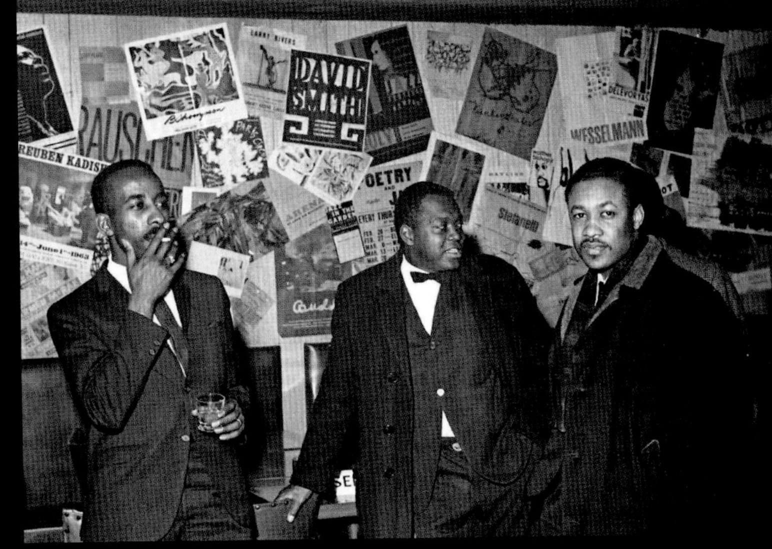

D.

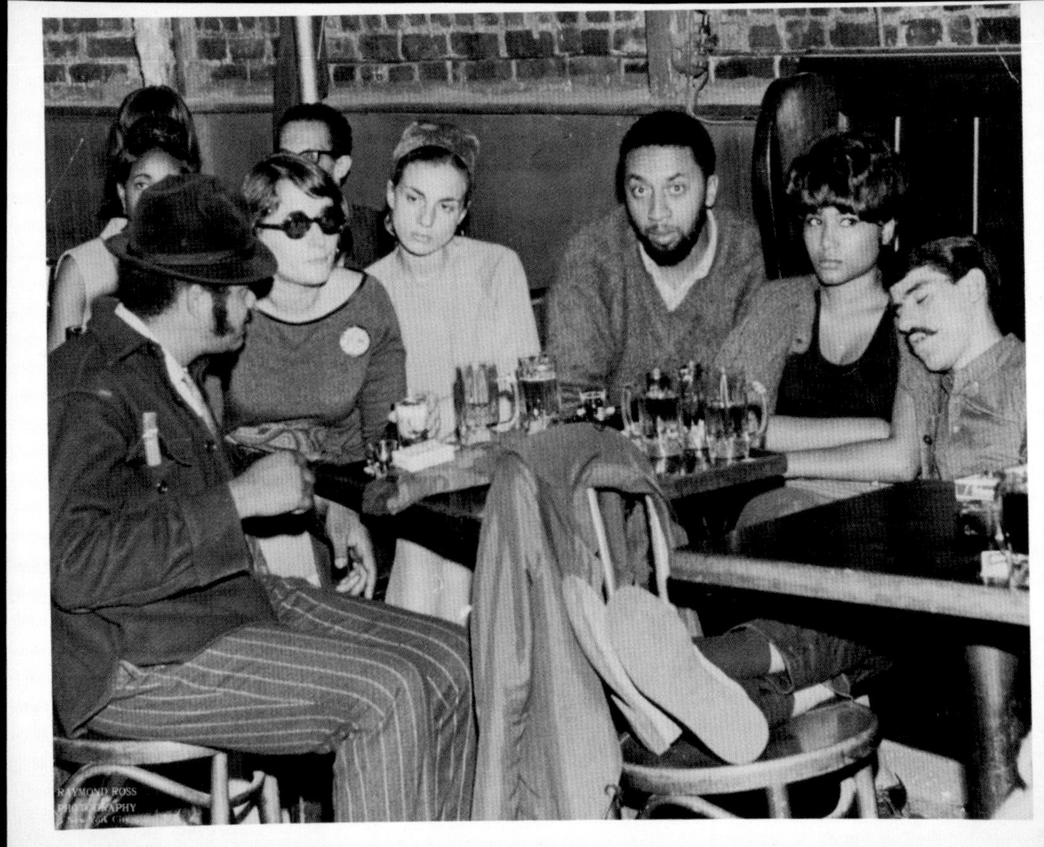

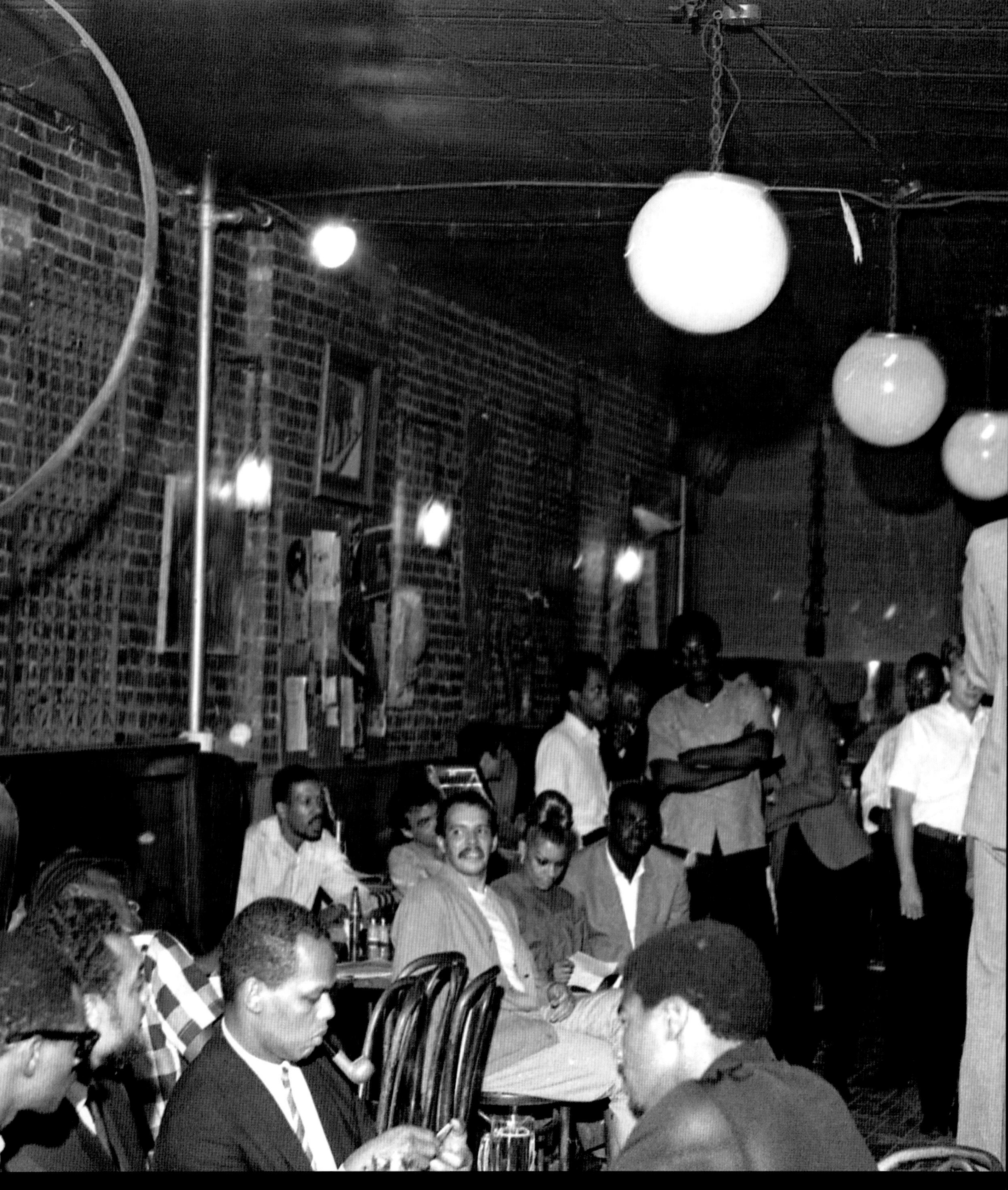

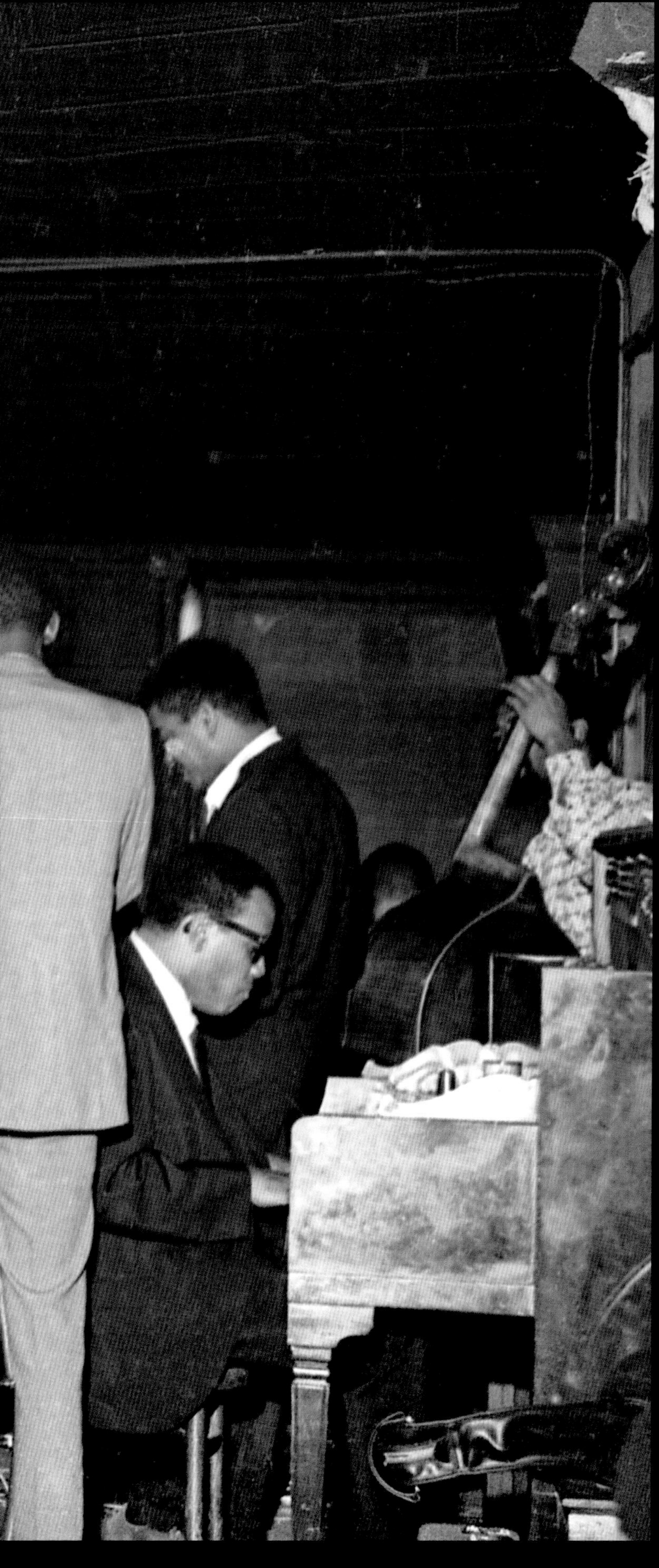

Band performing at Slugs' with Jackie
McLean in audience (front row), 1965

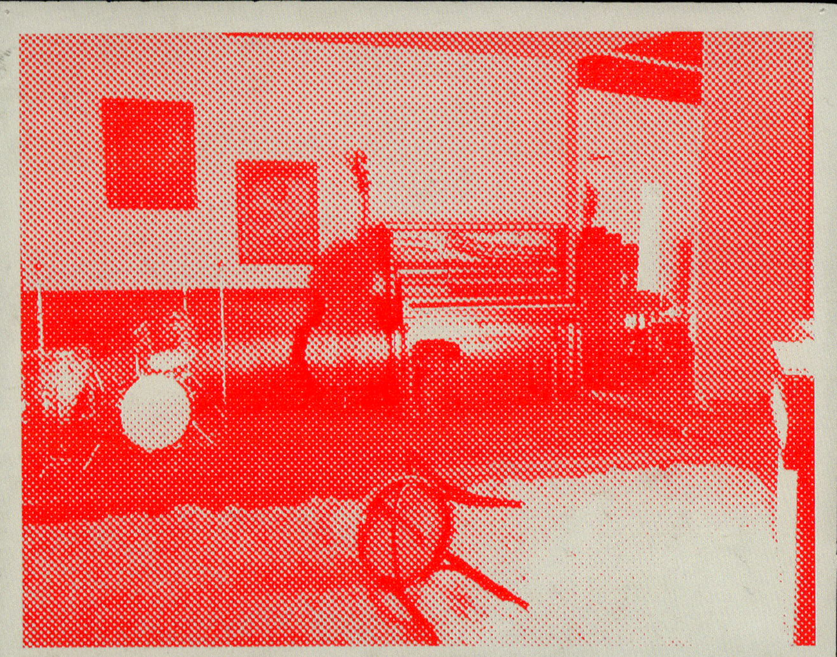

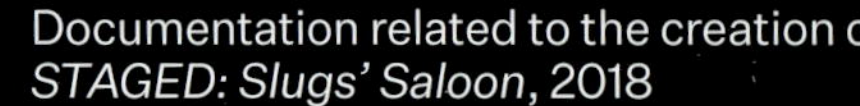

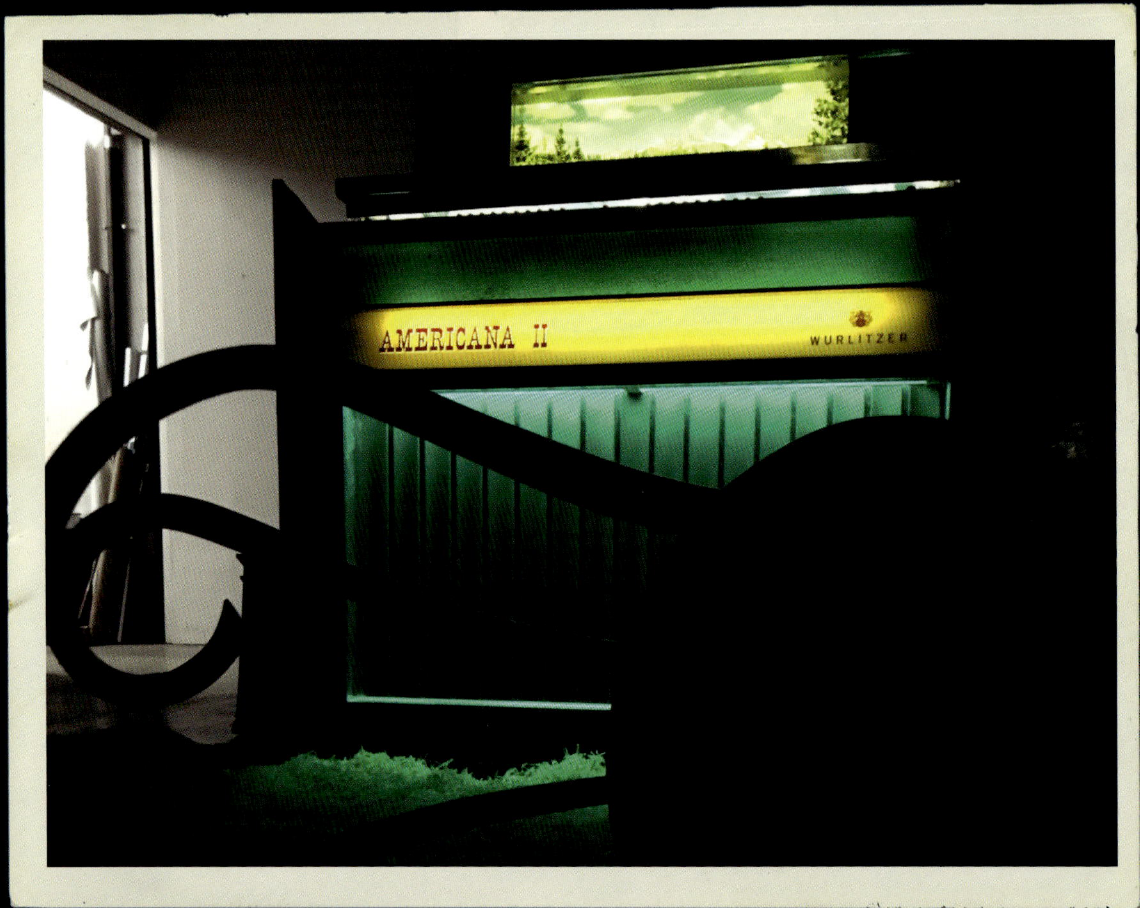

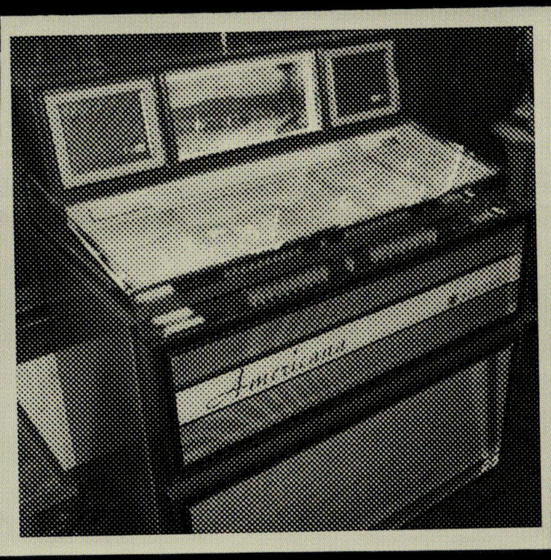
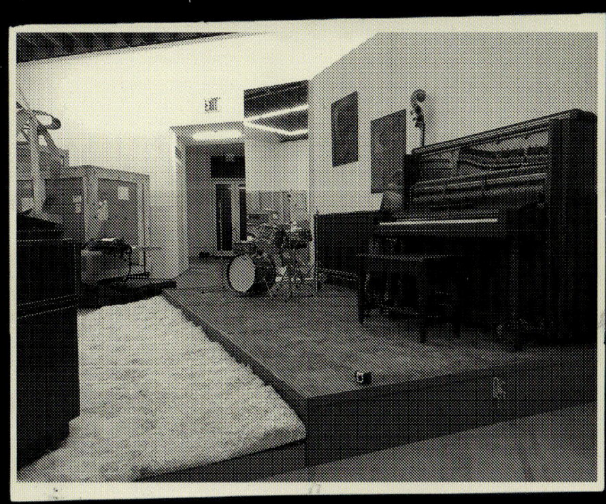

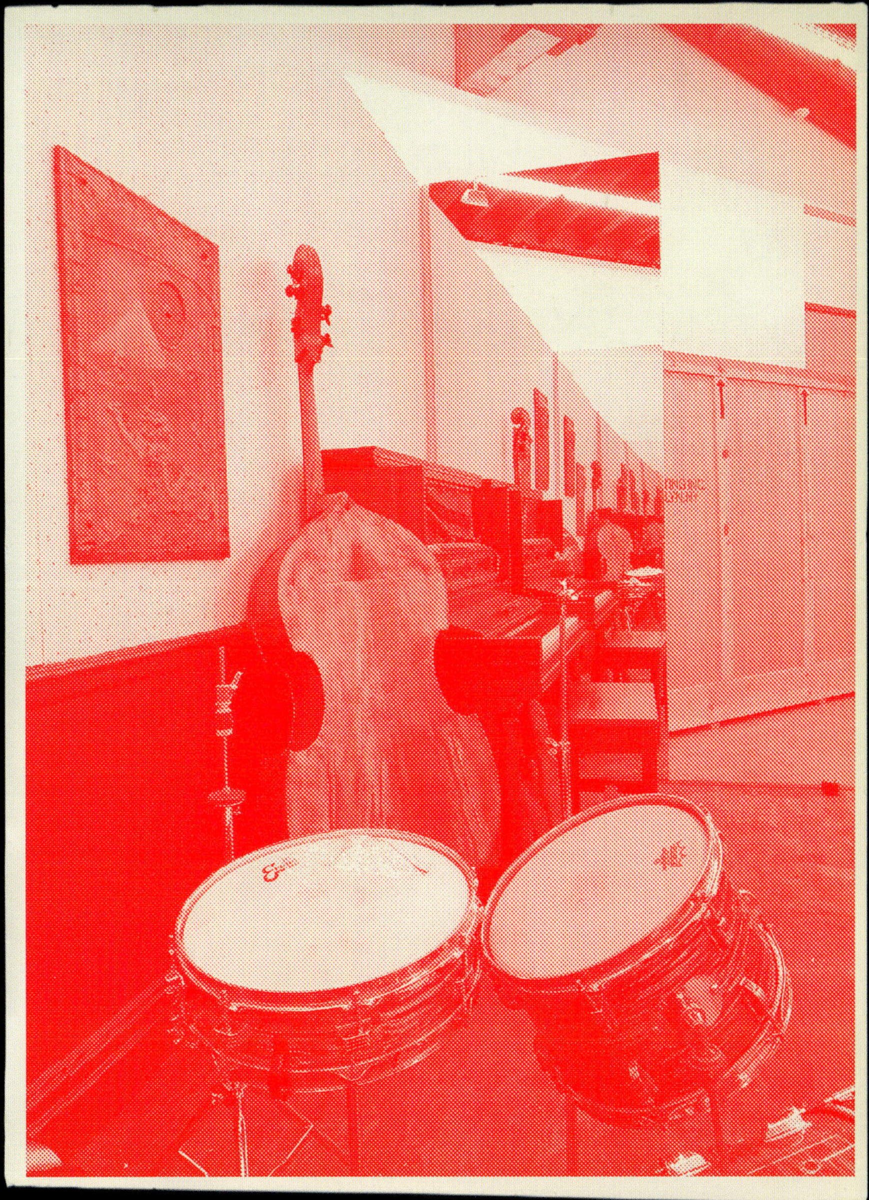

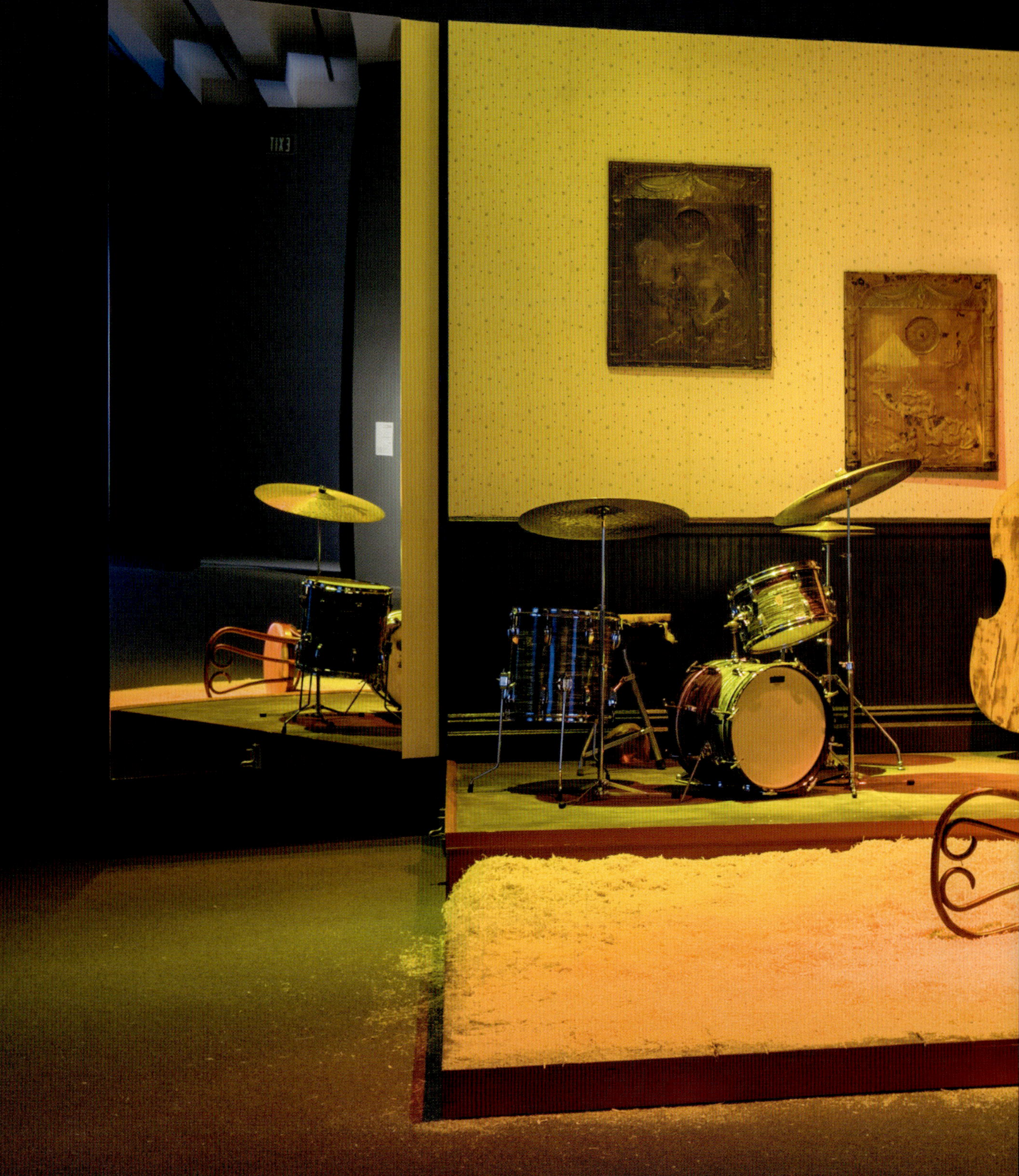
EXIT

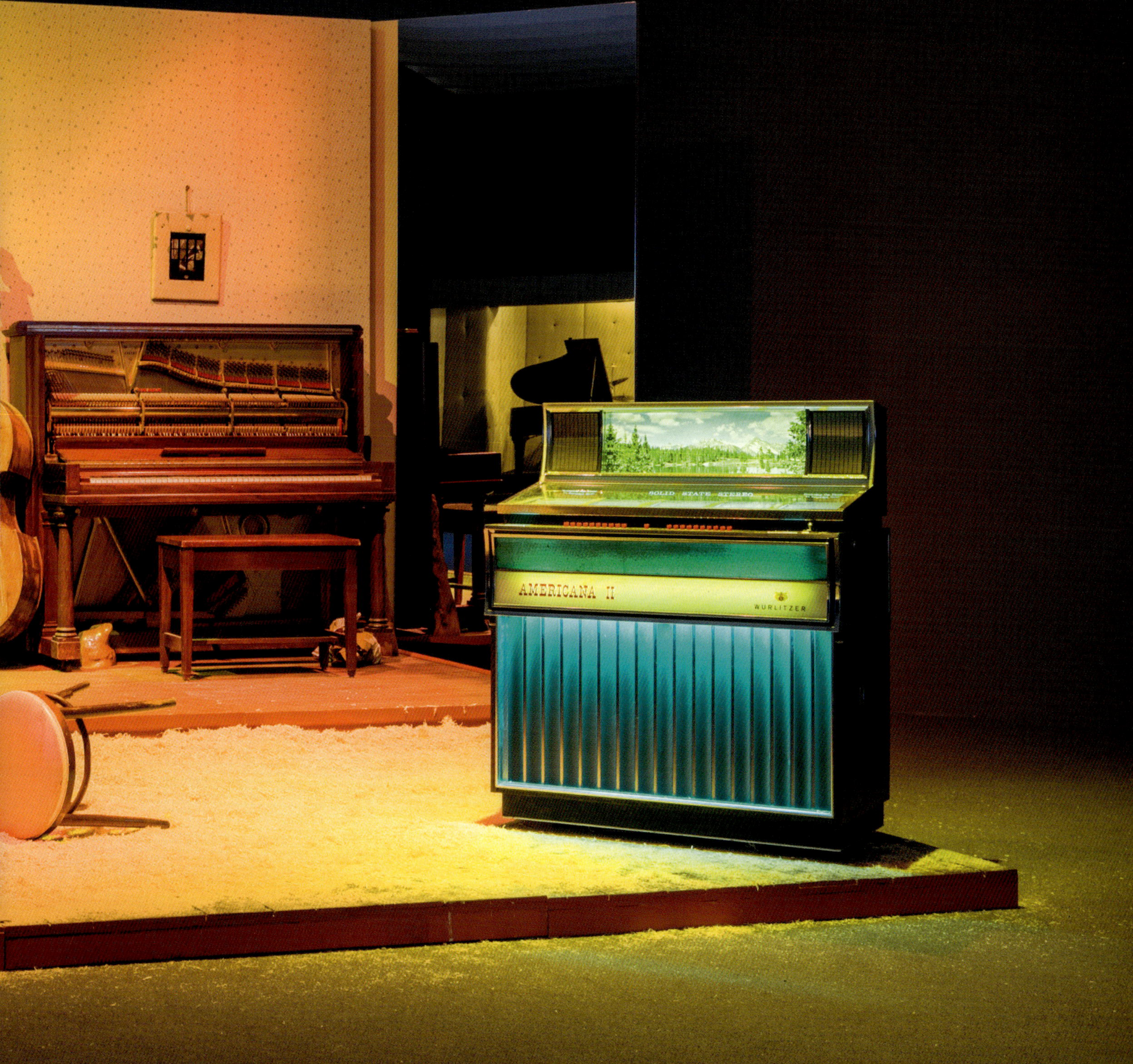

SOLID STATE STEREO
AMERICANA II
WURLITZER

Previous pages:
Jason Moran, *STAGED: Slugs' Saloon*, 2018, mixed media, sound,
120 x 168 x 171 in. (304.8 x 426.7 x 434.3 cm); installation view in the
exhibition *Jason Moran* at the Walker Art Center, Minneapolis, 2018

WORKS ON PAPER

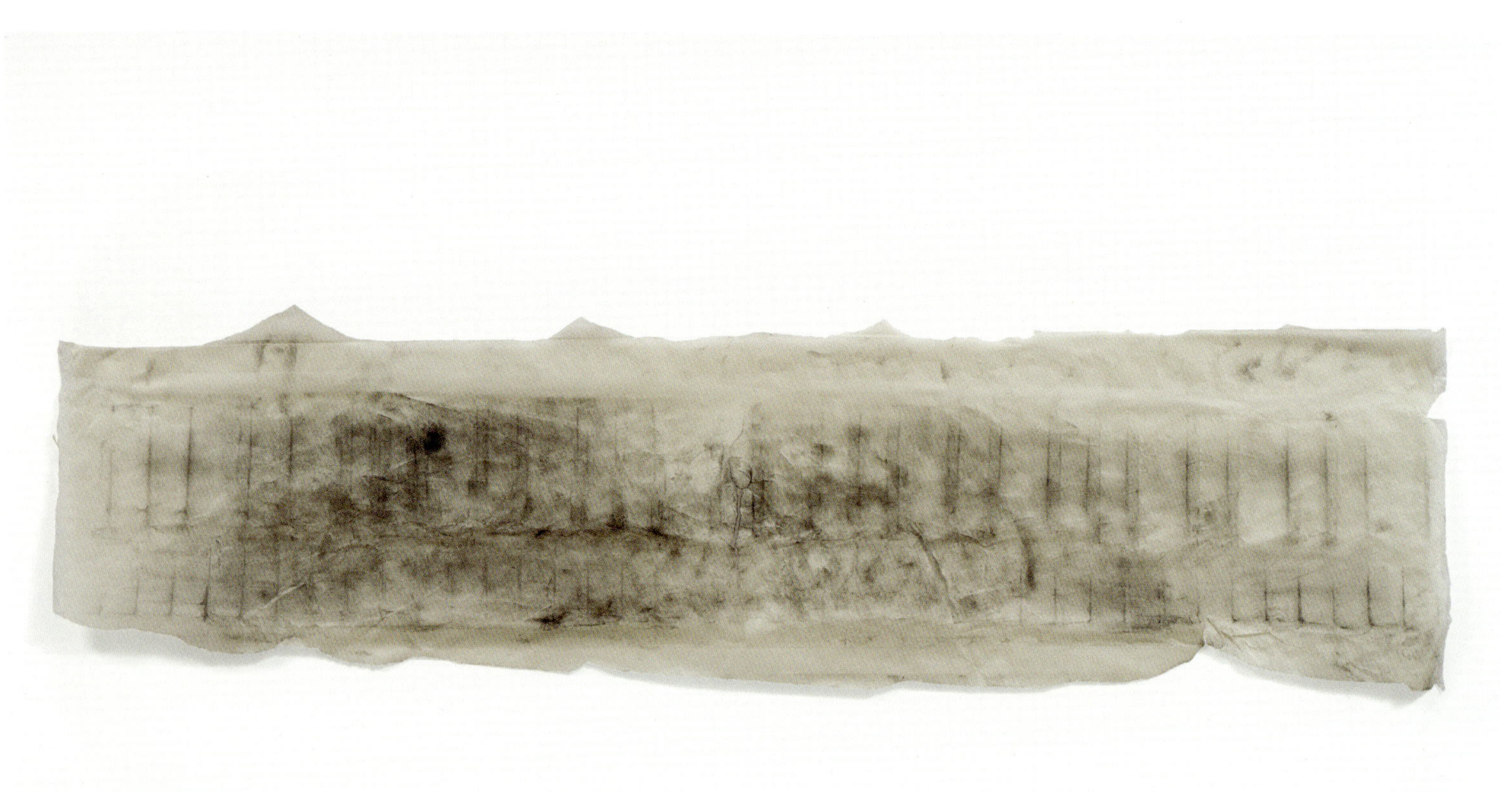

Jason Moran, *Run 2*, 2016, charcoal on paper, 9 ½ x 37 ¾ in.
(24.1 x 95.9 cm)

Jason Moran, *Run 4*, 2016, charcoal on paper,
25 x 37 ½ in. (63.5 x 95.3 cm)

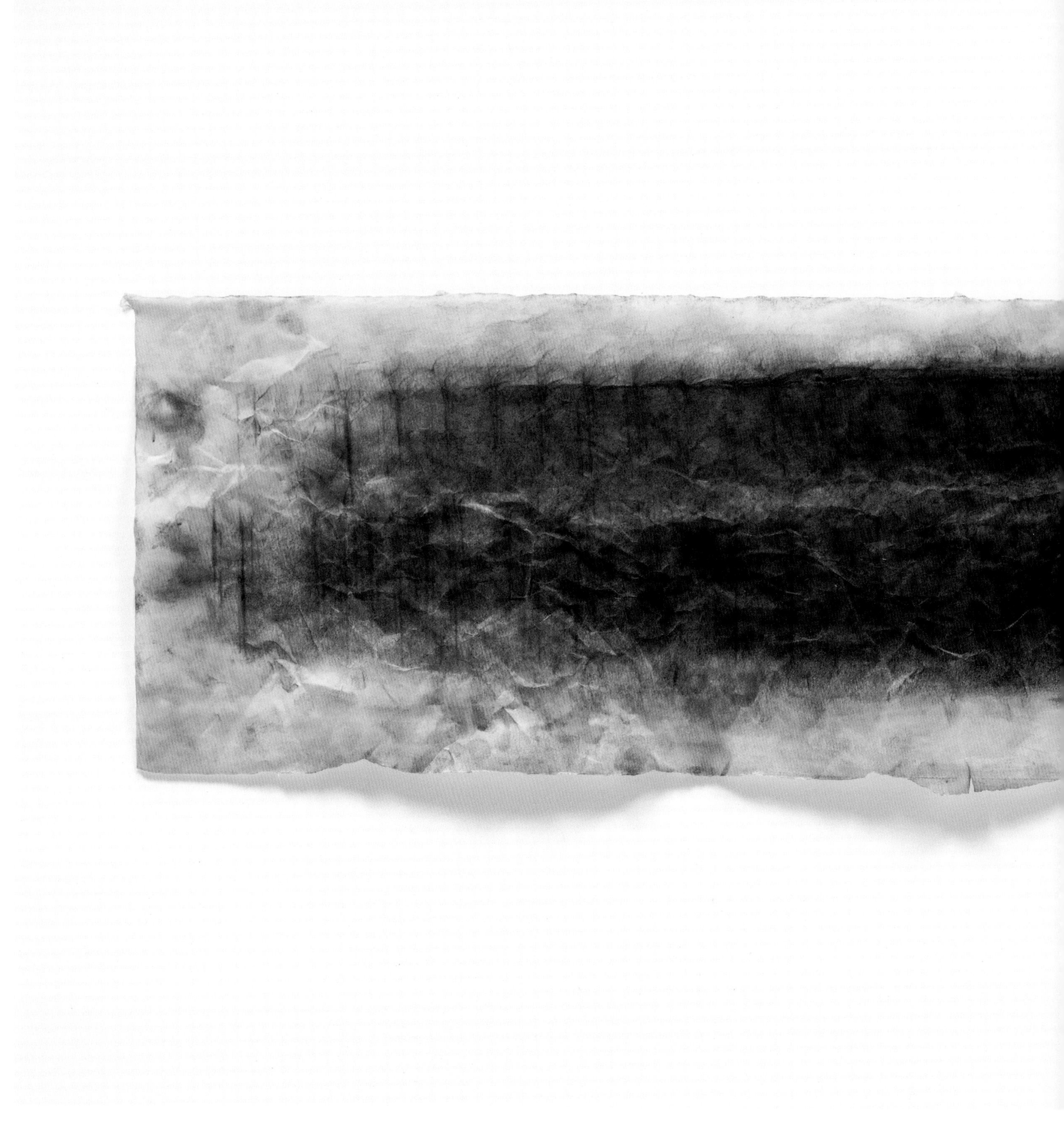

Jason Moran, *Run 6*, 2016, charcoal on paper, 10 x 36 ½ in.
(25.4 x 92.7 cm)

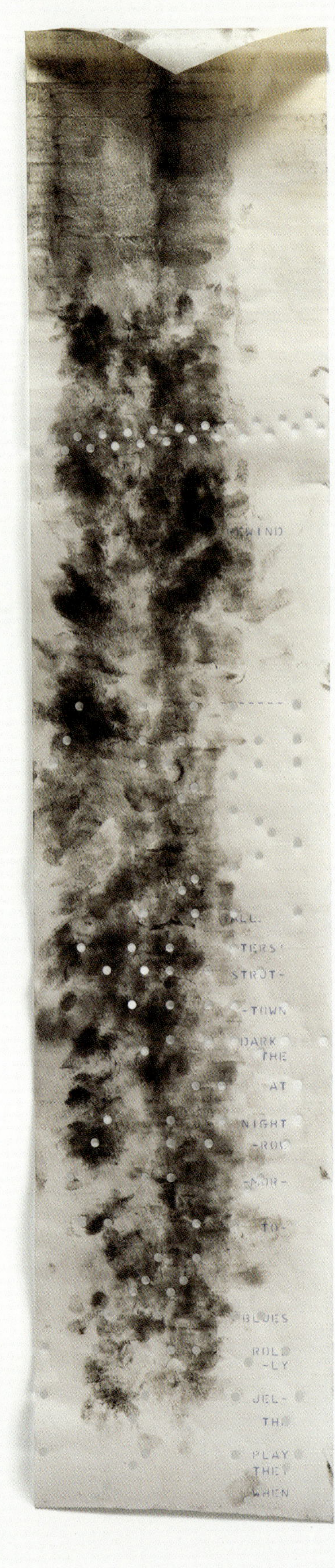
WIND
ALL.
TERS'
STRUT-
-TOWN
DARK THE
AT
NIGHT
-ROL
-MOR-
TO-
BLUES
ROL
-LY
JEL-
THE
PLAY THE
WHEN

Jason Moran, *Strutter's Ball*, 2016, charcoal on paper,
34 ½ x 6 ¾ in. (87.6 x 17.1 cm)

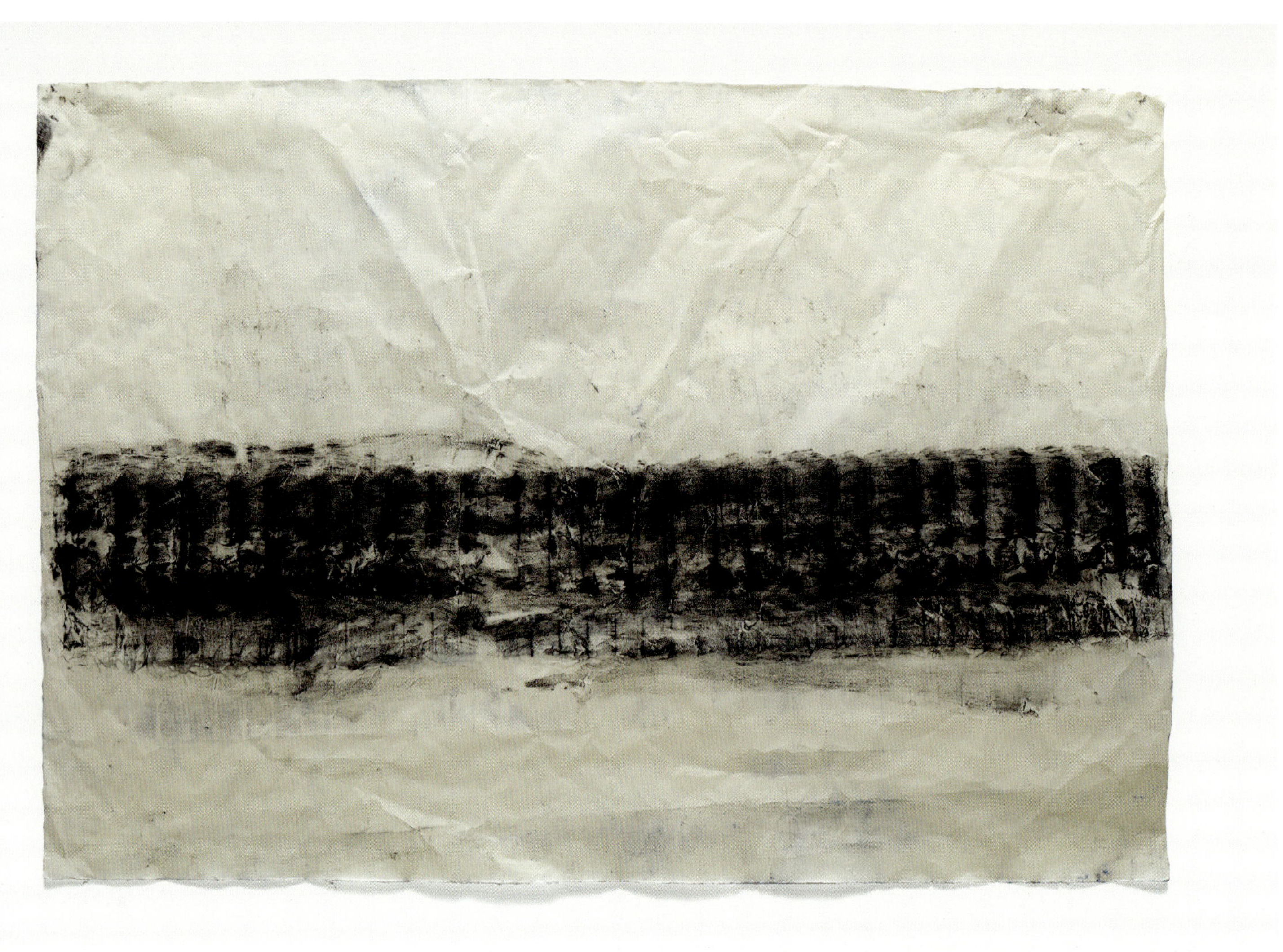

Jason Moran, *Black Run*, 2018, mixed media on paper,
25 x 36 ¾ in. (63.5 x 93.3 cm)

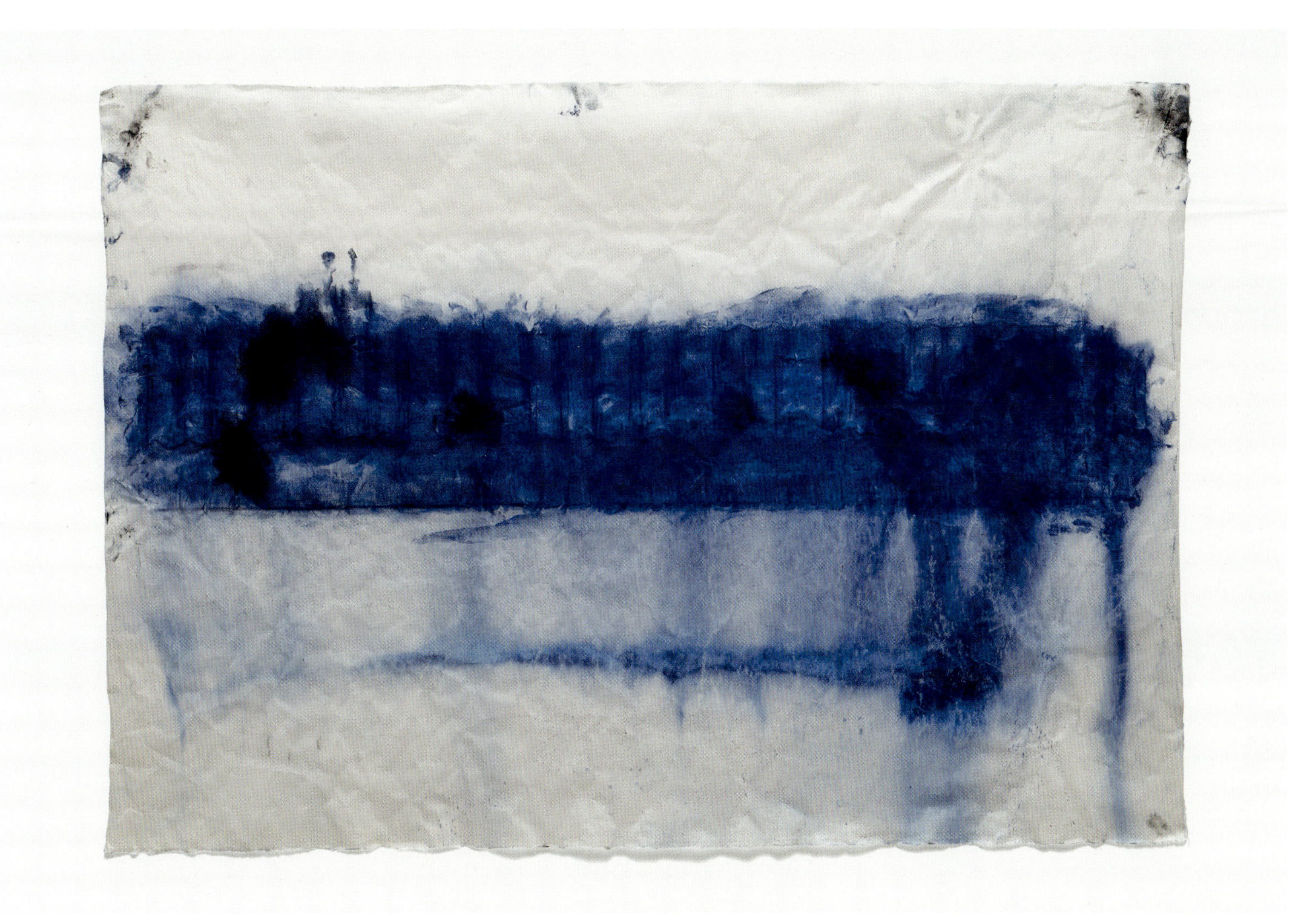

Jason Moran, *Blue (Creed) Gravity 1*, 2018, mixed media on
paper, 25 x 36 ¾ in. (63.5 x 93.3 cm)

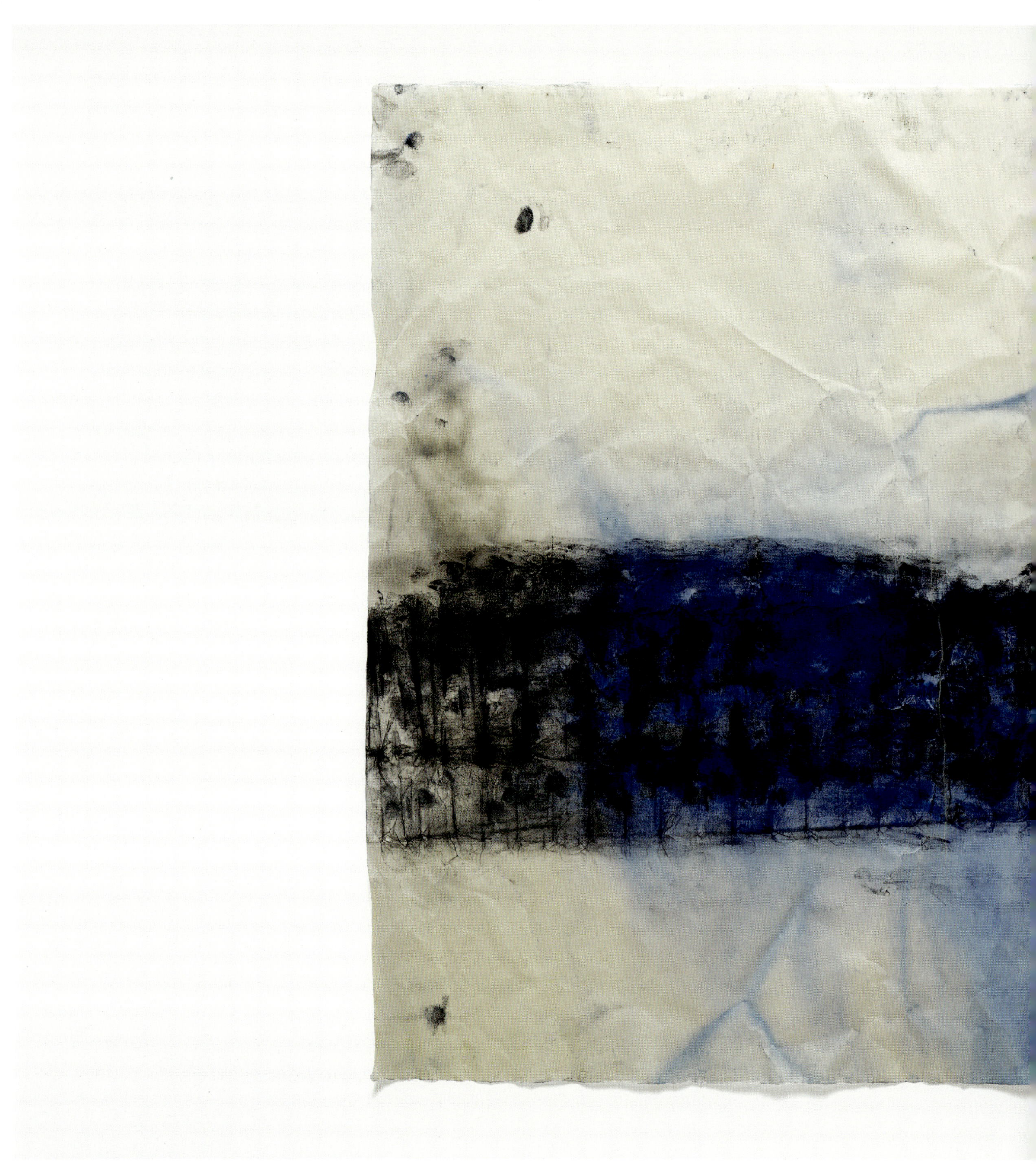

Jason Moran, *Black and Blue Gravity*, 2018,
mixed media on paper, 25 x 36 ¾ in. (63.5 x 93.3 cm)

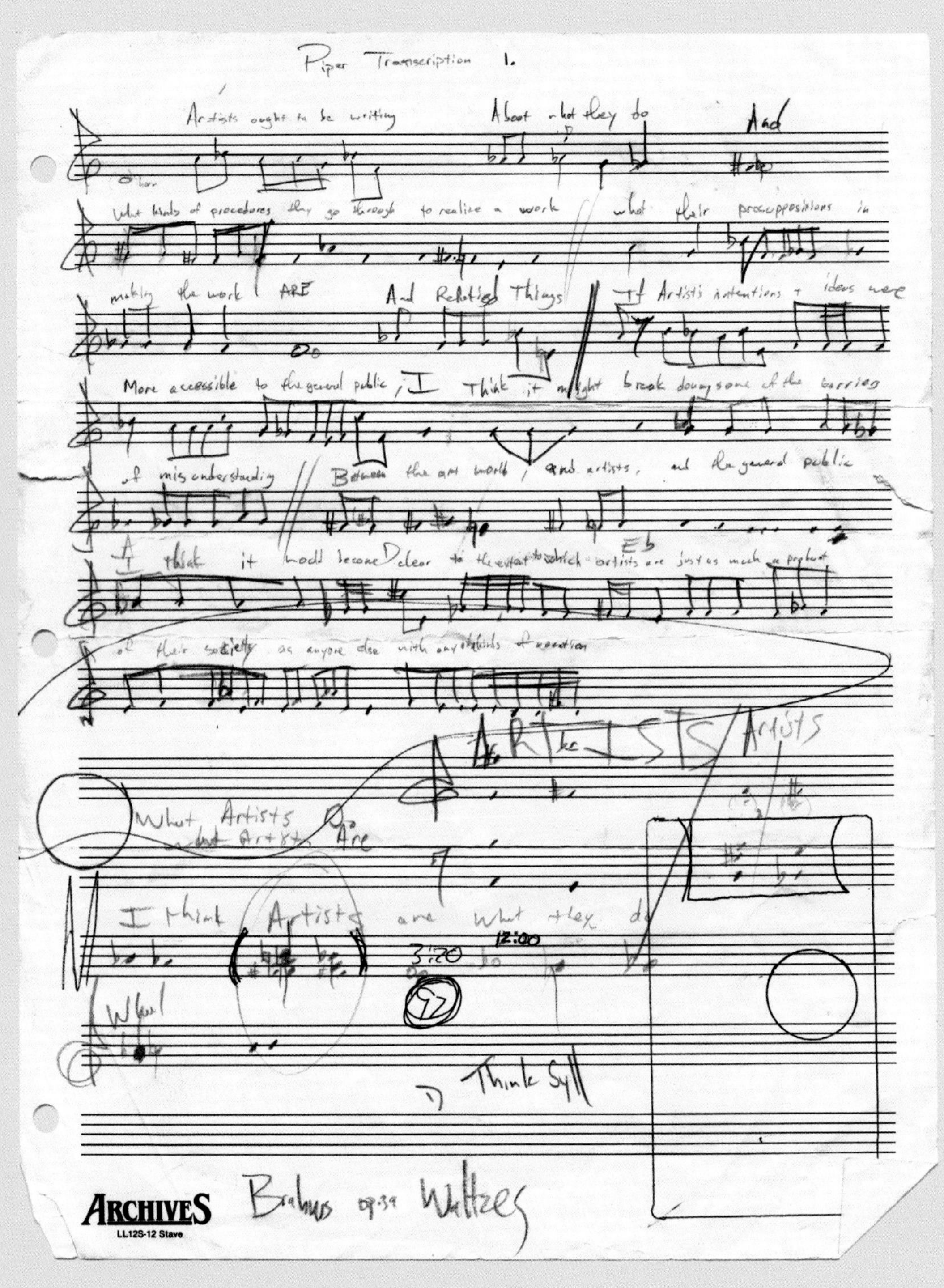

Jason Moran, *Artists Ought to Be Writing*, 2005,
score on manuscript paper, 8 ½ x 11 in. (21.6 x 27.9 cm)

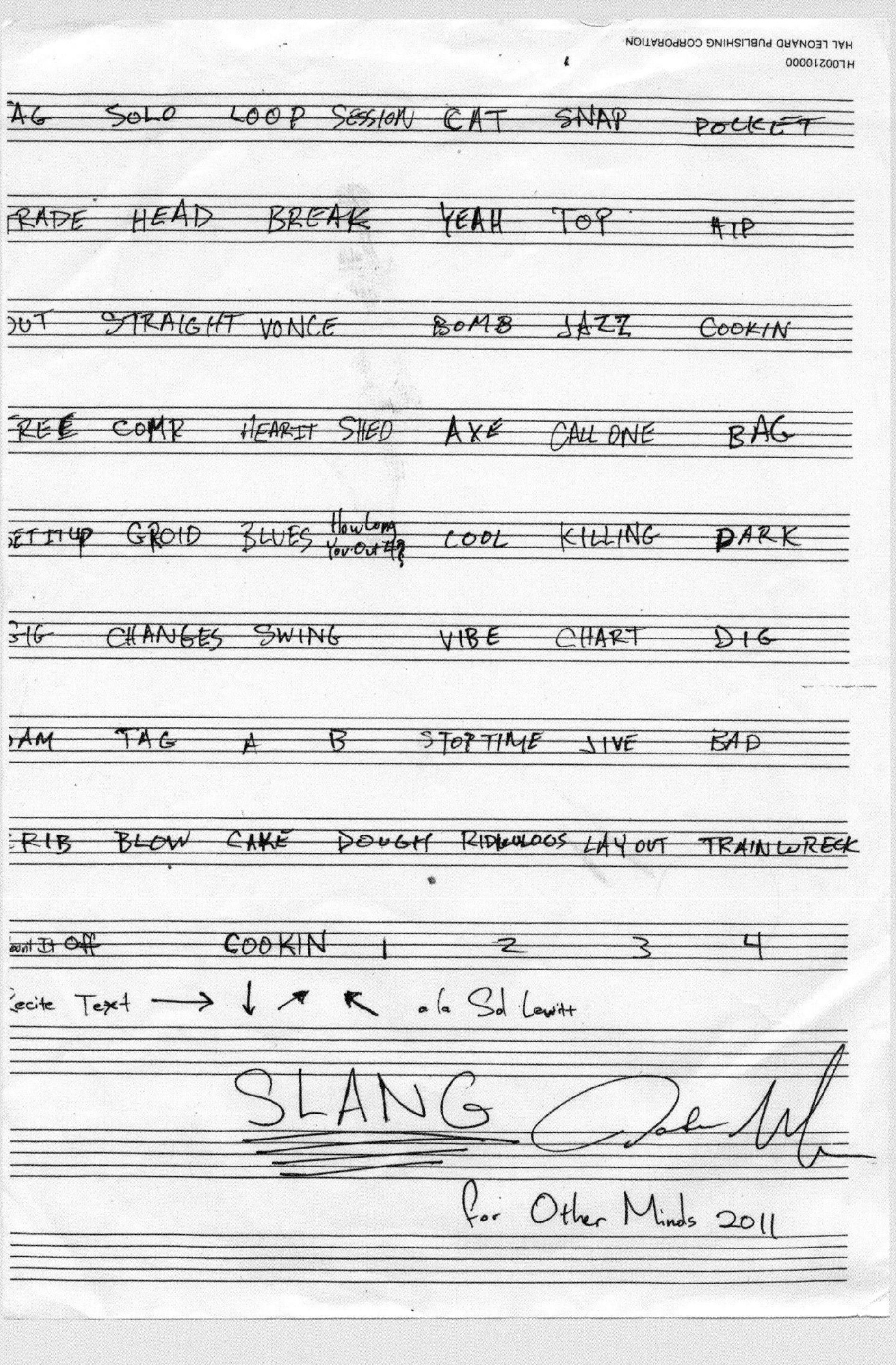

Jason Moran, *Slang*, 2011, score on manuscript paper,
8 ½ x 11 in. (21.6 x 27.9 cm)

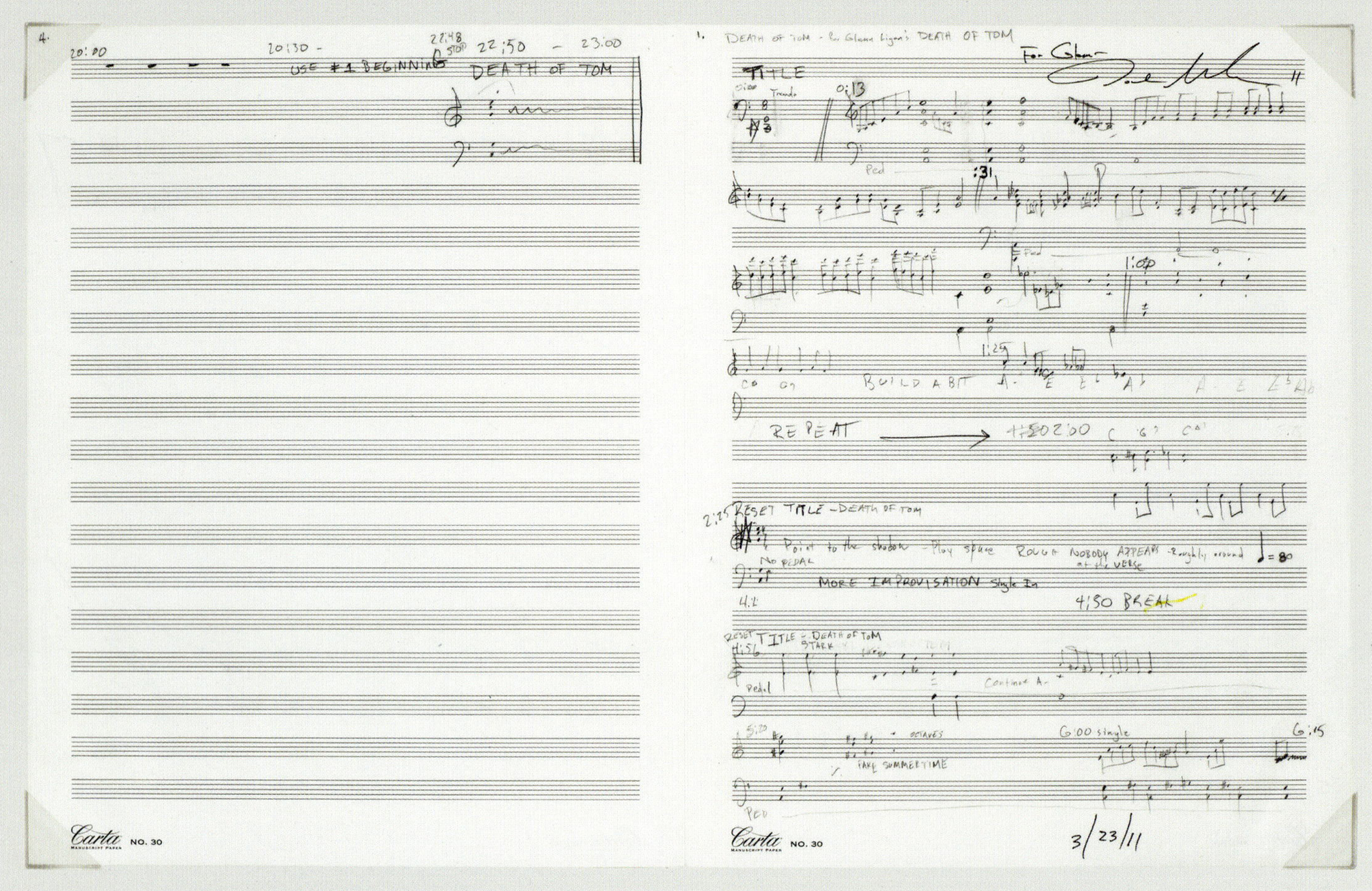

Jason Moran, *The Death of Tom*, 2011, score on manuscript paper,
13 x 21 in. (33 x 53.3 cm)

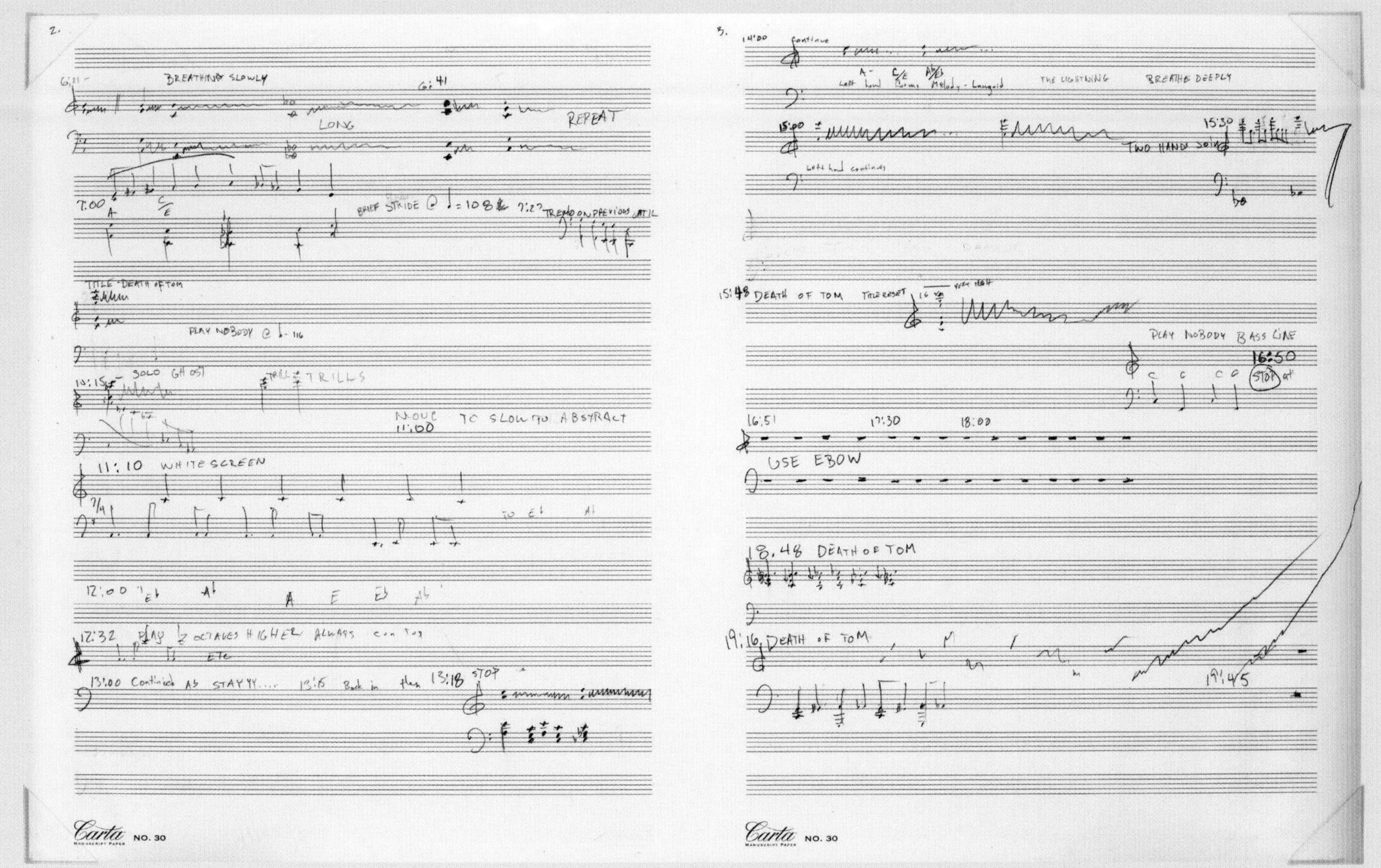
BREATHING SLOWLY
6:41
LONG
REPEAT
7:00
BRIEF STRIDE ♩ = 108 & 7:22 TREMO ON PREVIOUS UNTIL
TITLE "DEATH OF TOM
PLAY NOBODY @ ♩ = 116
10:15 SOLO GHOST TRILLS
MOVE TO SLOW TO ABSTRACT
11:00
11:10 WHITE SCREEN
TO Eb Ab
12:00 Eb Ab A E Eb Ab
12:32 PLAY 2 OCTAVES HIGHER ALWAYS etc
13:00 Continue AS STAY... 13:15 Back in then 13:18 STOP
3.
14:00 Continue
A- C/G B/D
Left hand becomes Melody - Leongold THE LIGHTNING BREATHE DEEPLY
15:00 15:30
TWO HAND SOLO
Left hand continues
15:48 DEATH OF TOM THEREOF
PLAY NOBODY BASS LINE
C C C C 16:50 STOP
16:51 17:30 18:00
USE EBOW
18:48 DEATH OF TOM
19:16 DEATH OF TOM
19:45

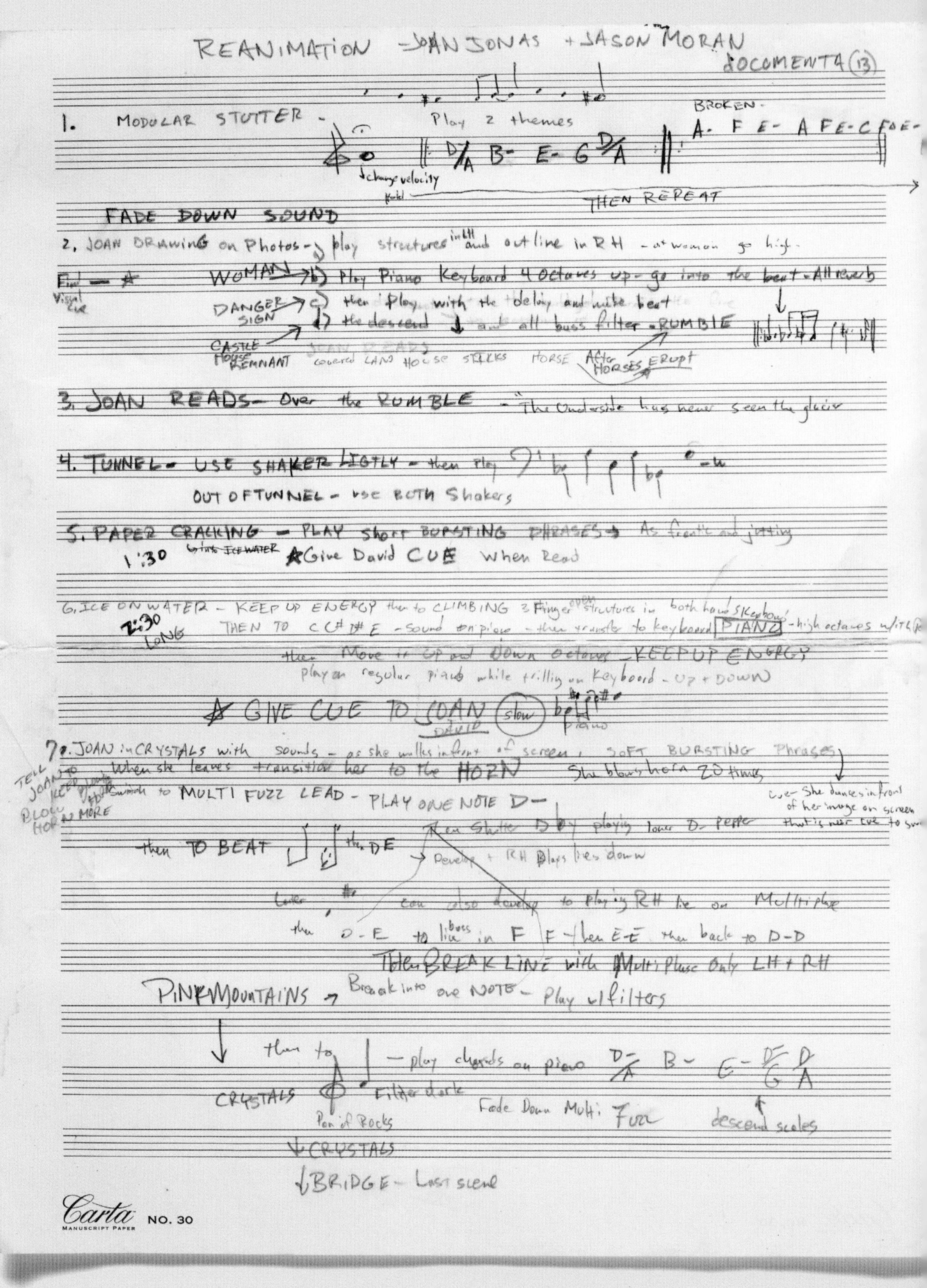

Jason Moran, *Reanimation*, 2012, score on manuscript paper,
13 x 22 in. (33 x 53.3 cm)

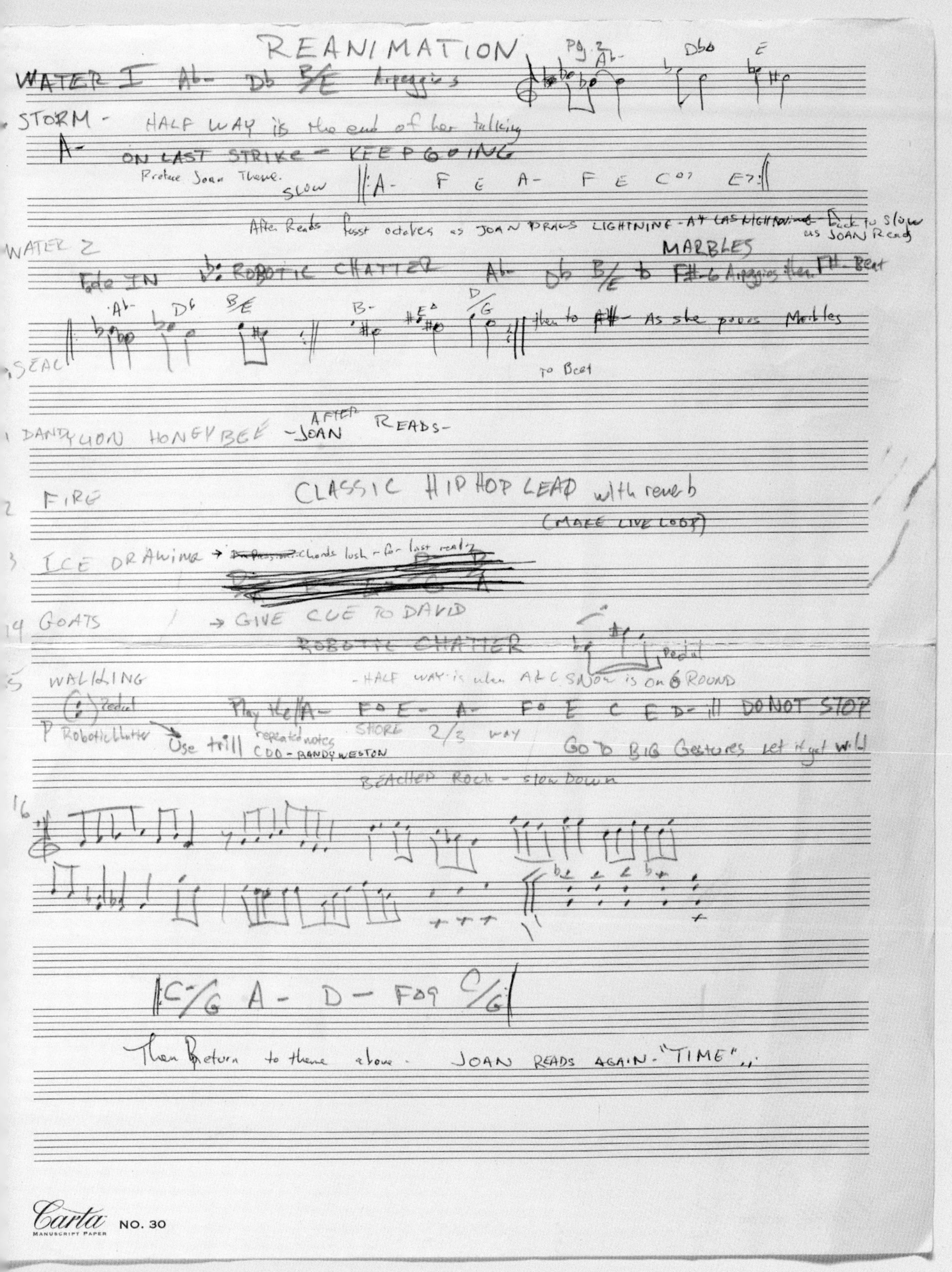
REANIMATION   Pg.2   Db   E
WATER I Ab- Db B/E   Arpeggios
STORM -   HALF WAY is the end of her talking
A-   ON LAST STRIKE - KEEP GOING
Protuce Joan Theme.   SLOW ||: A- F E A- F E C°7 E7 :||
After Reads fast octaves as JOAN DRAWS LIGHTNING - AT LAST LIGHTNING   Back to slow as JOAN Reads
WATER 2
Fade IN   Db: ROBOTIC CHATTER   Ab- Db B/E b F#-6 Arpeggios then F#-Beat   MARBLES
Ab   Db   B/E   B-   E△ D/G   then to F#- As she pours Marbles
SEAL   To Beat
DANDYLION HONEYBEE - AFTER JOAN READS-
FIRE   CLASSIC HIP HOP LEAD with reverb
                                    (MAKE LIVE LOOP)
ICE DRAWING → chords lush - for last real2
GOATS   → GIVE CUE TO DAVID
                    ROBOTIC CHATTER   pedal
WALKING
     pedal   - HALF WAY is when A & C Snow is on round
P Robotic Chatter Use trill repeated notes   Play the ||: A- F# E- A- F# E C E D- :|| DO NOT STOP
                              STORE 2/3 way   GO TO BIG Gestures Let it get wild
                    COD - RANDY WESTON
                    BEACHED ROCK - slow down
||: C/G A- D- F#°9 C/G :||
Then Return to theme above.   JOAN READS AGAIN - "TIME",.

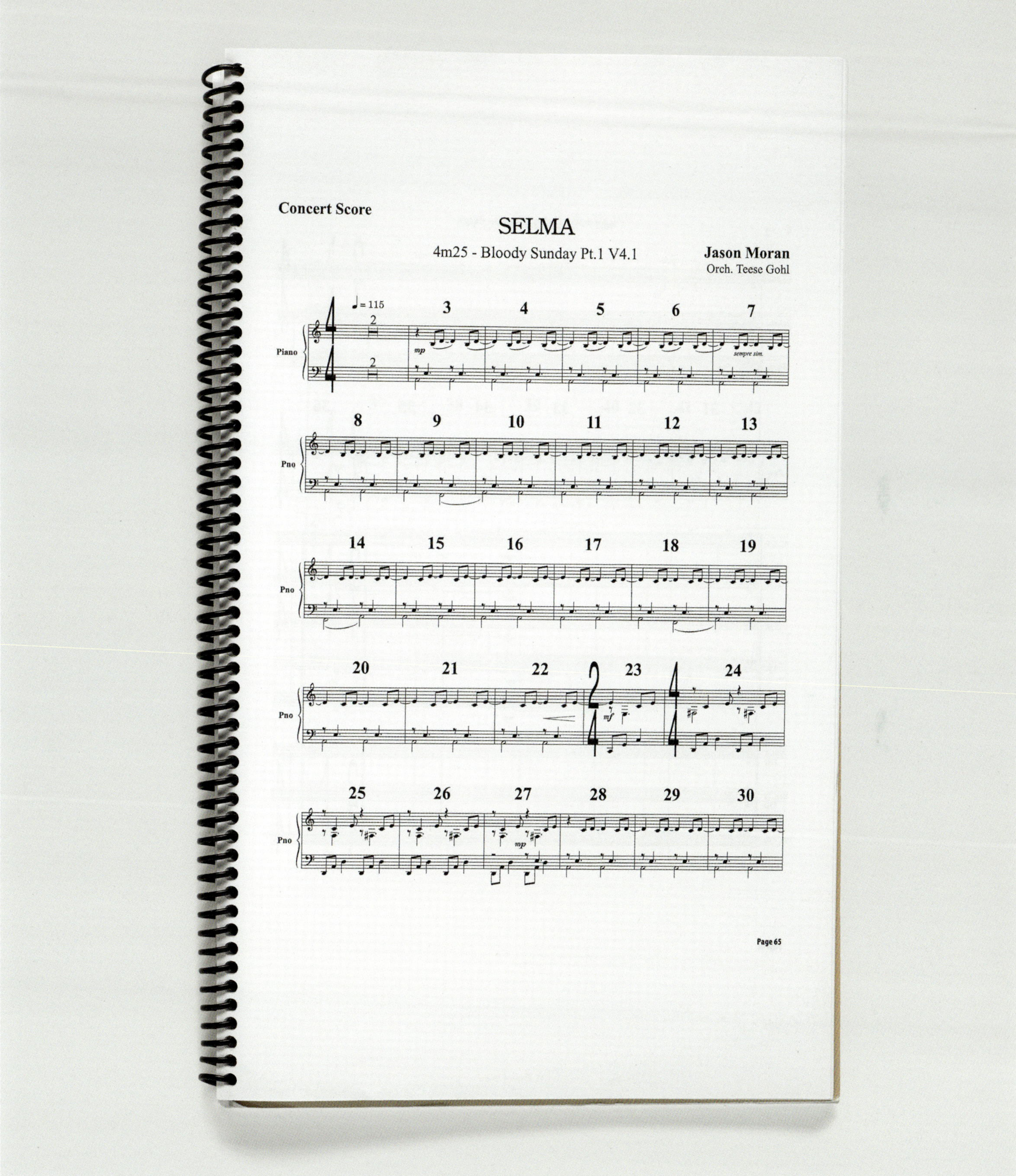

Jason Moran, "Bloody Sunday, Part 1 V4.1" for the film soundtrack *Selma*, 2014, score in booklet, 17 x 14 in. (43.1 x 35.5 cm)

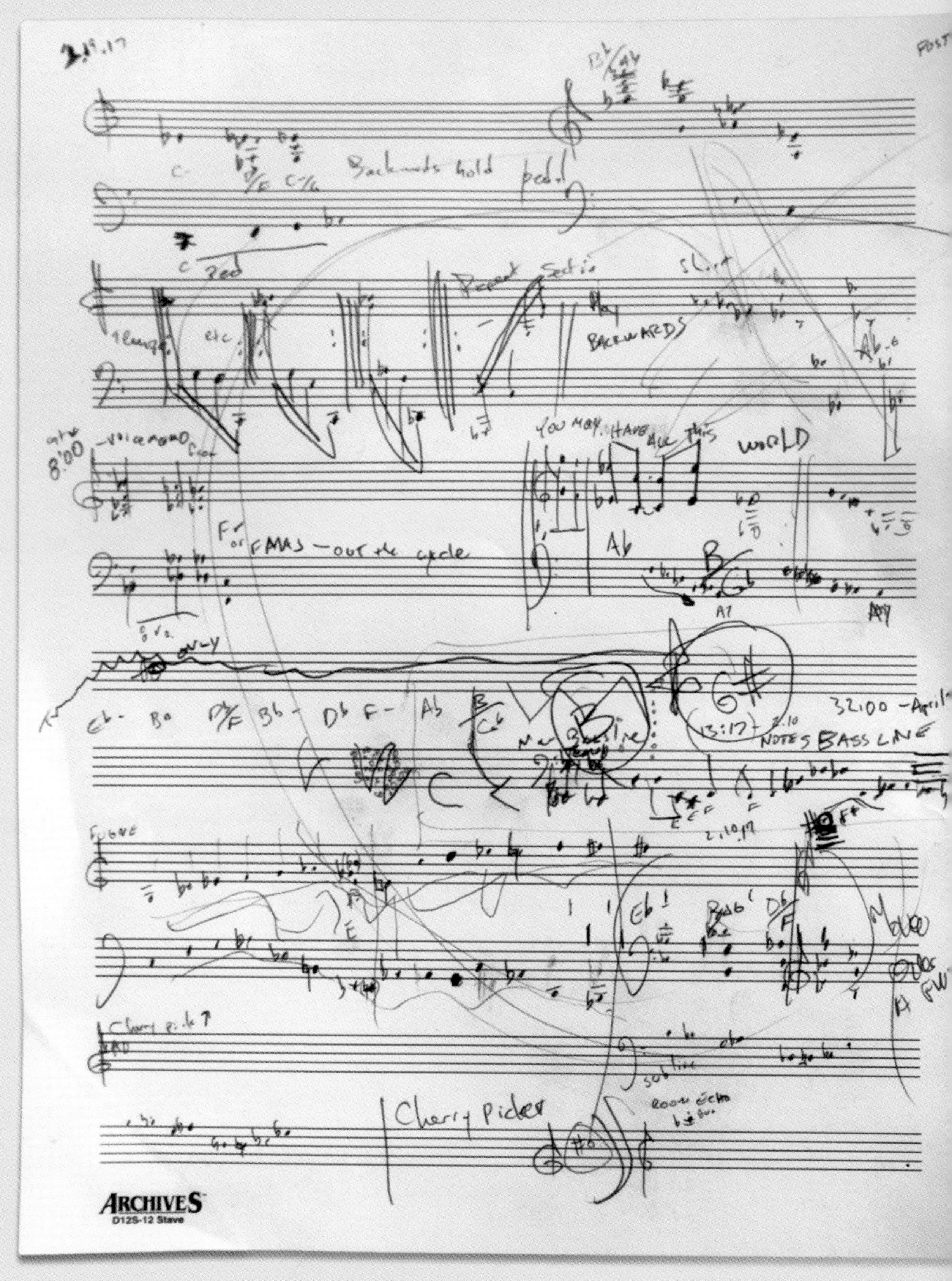

Jason Moran, *MASS (HOWL, eon)*, 2017, score on manuscript paper,
17 x 22 in. (43.2 x 55.9 cm)

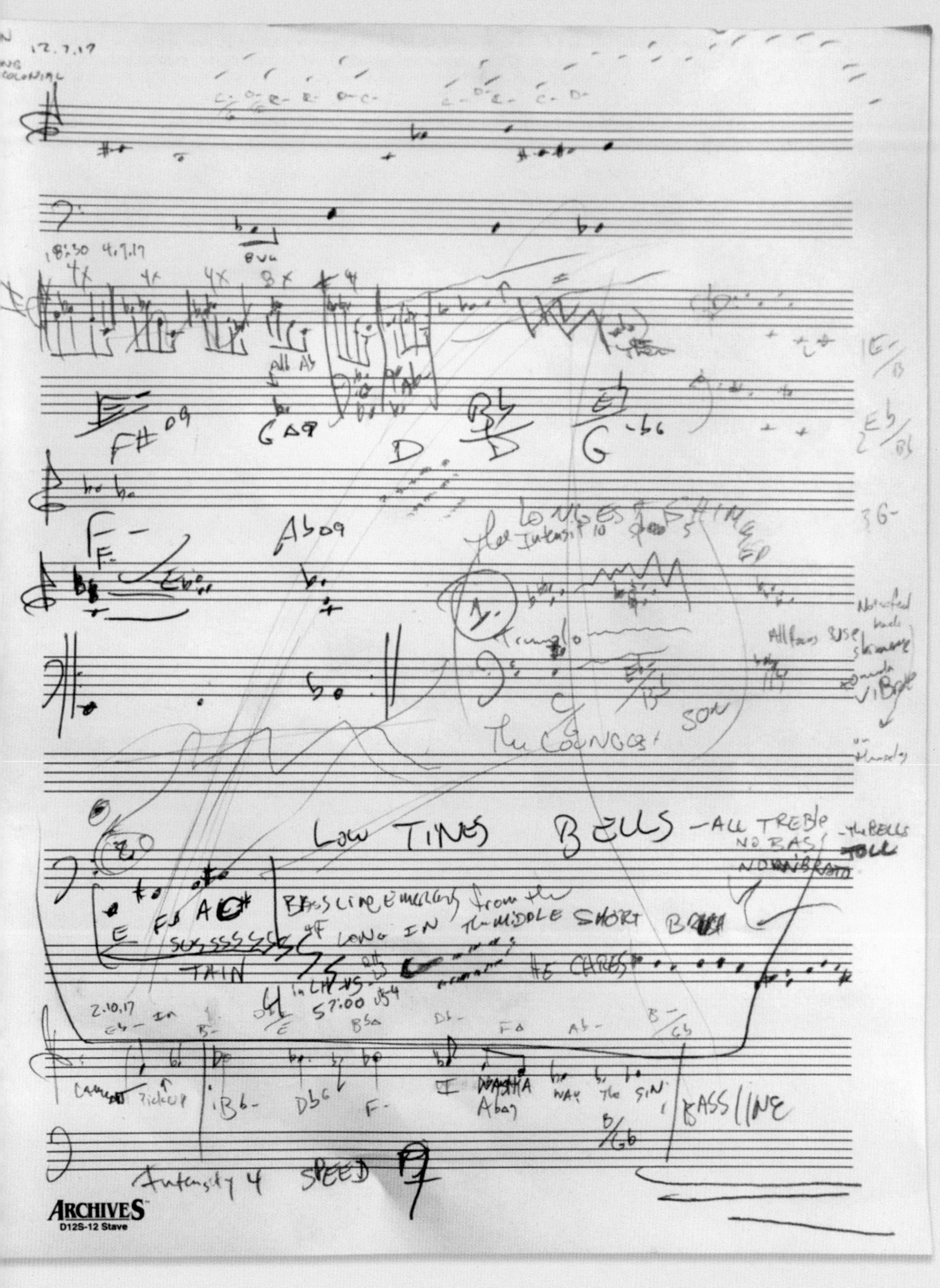
12.7.17
COLONIAL
18:30 4.7.17
4X 4X 4X 8X
F#09
GΔ9
D
B♭/D
G-♭6
F-
A♭09
LOUDEST SHIMMER
Intensity 10
Tremolo
The COLDEST SON
LOW TINES BELLS — ALL TREBLE NO BASS NO VIBRATO
THE BELLS TOLL
BASS LINE EMERGES from the
SUSSSSSSS LONG IN THE MIDDLE SHORT BOW
TAIN
HE CARES
2.10.17
in LH +5 57:00 U54
THE WAY THE SUN
BASS LINE
Intensity 4 SPEED

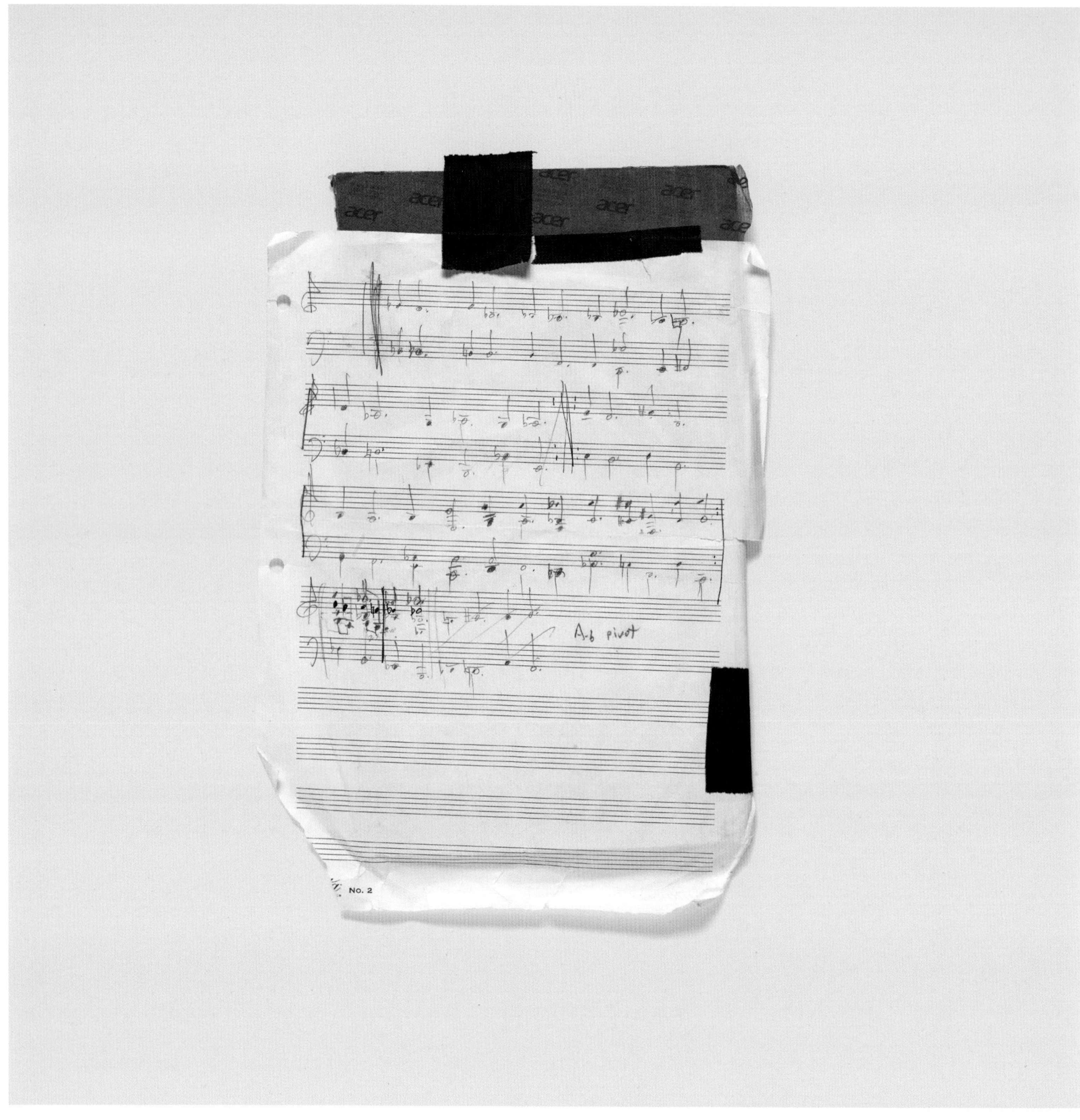

Jason Moran, *Untitled*, 2015, score on manuscript paper, cardboard, tape,
12 ⅛ x 8 ⅜ in. (30.8 x 21.3 cm)

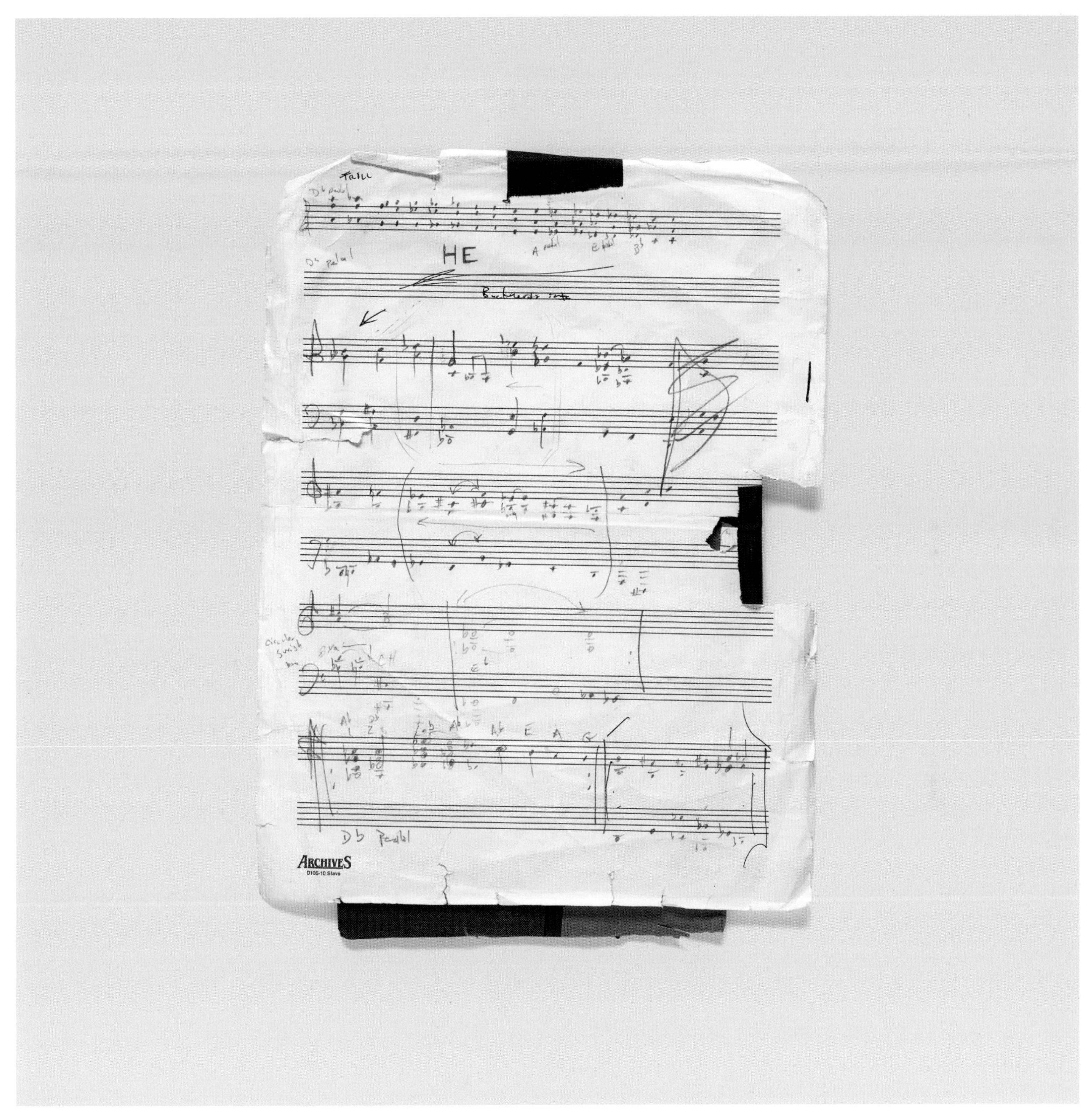

Jason Moran, *WINDS*, 2015, score on manuscript paper, cardboard, tape,
12 ⅝ x 9 ⁷⁄₁₆ in. (32.1 x 24 cm)

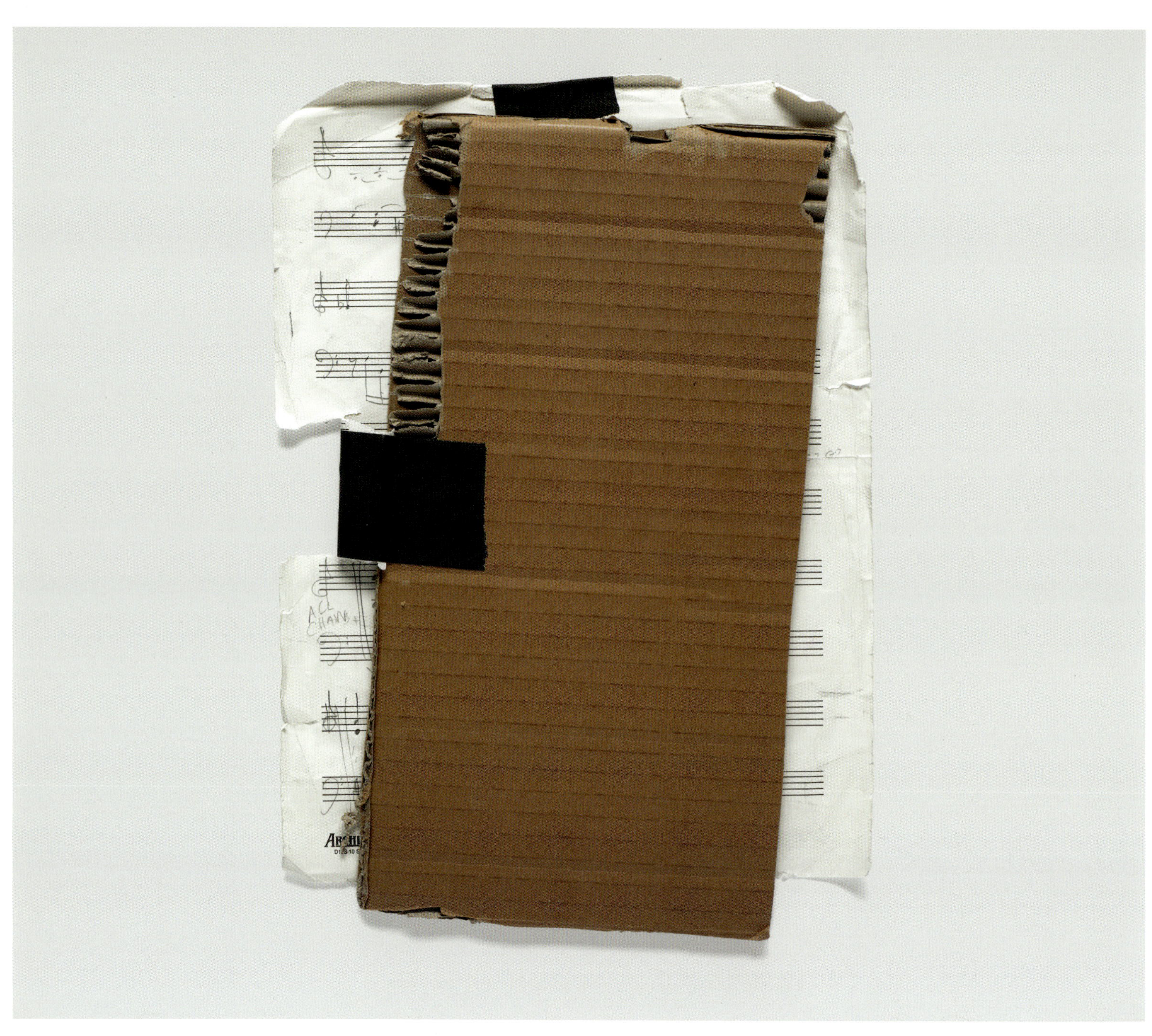

Jason Moran, *WINDS* (verso), 2015, score on manuscript paper,
cardboard, tape, 12 ⅝ x 9 ⁷⁄₁₆ in. (32.1 x 24 cm)

LINER NOTES

Following pages:
Ostia Antica archaeological site, Italy, July 2017

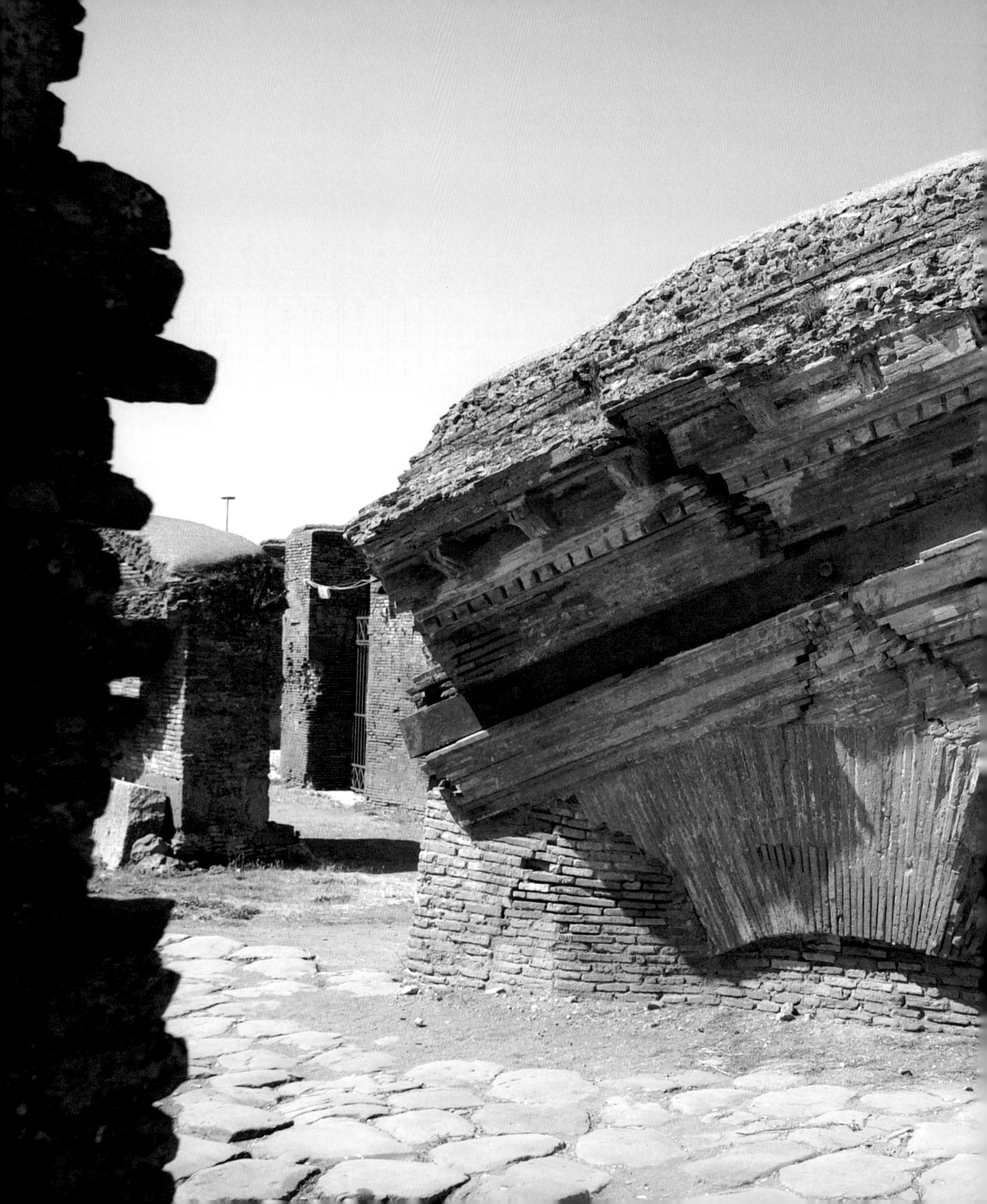

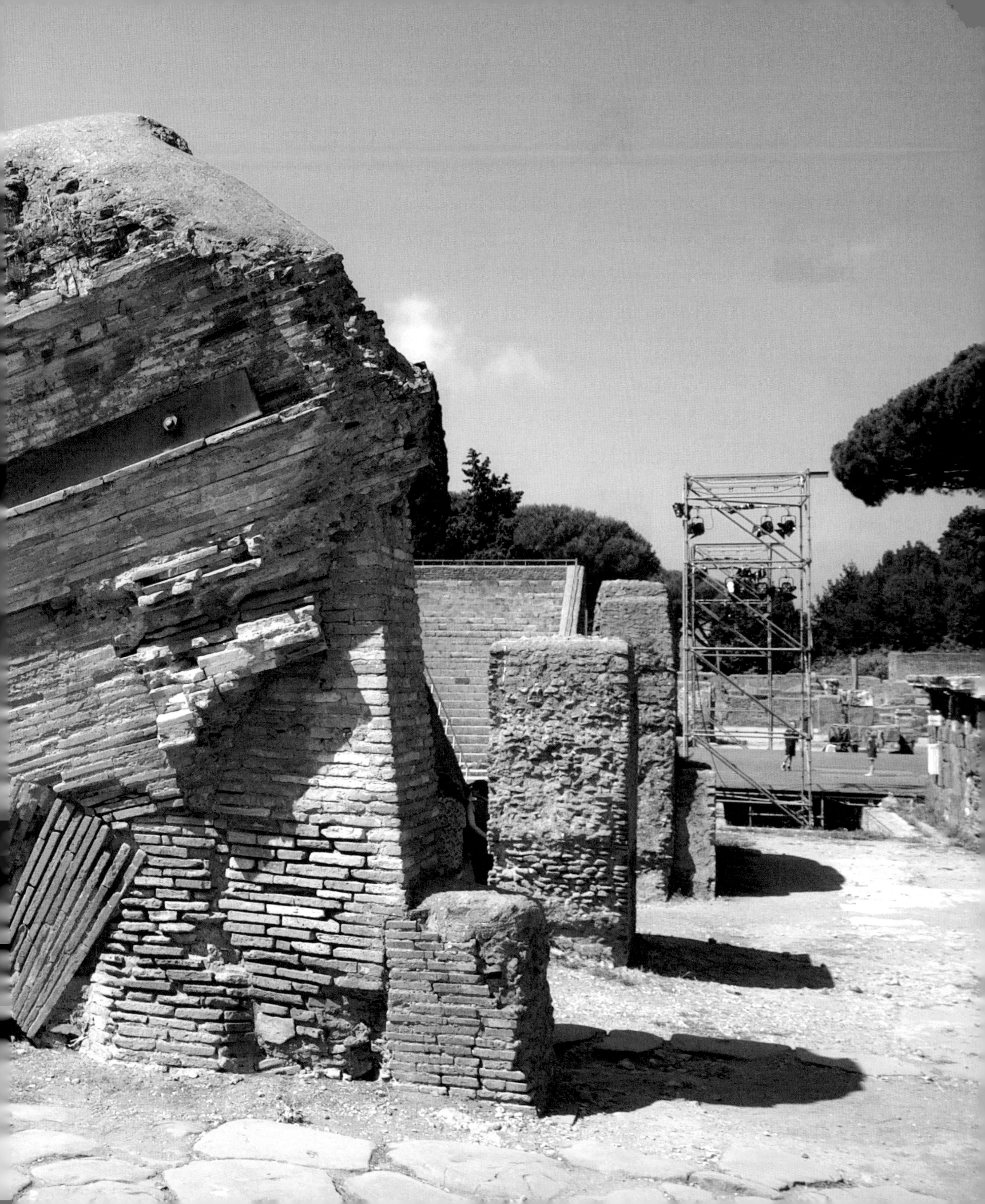

BLUE NOTE RECORDS

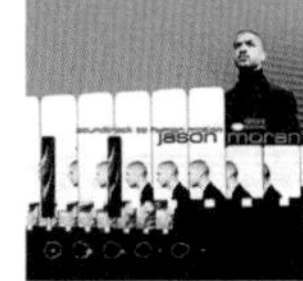

SOUNDTRACK TO HUMAN MOTION

1998

PERSONNEL
- JASON MORAN, PIANO
- GREG OSBY, ALTO SAXOPHONE
- STEFON HARRIS, VIBRAPHONE
- LONNIE PLAXICO, BASS
- ERIC HARLAND, DRUMS

TRACKLIST
01. Gangsterism on Canvas
02. Snake Stance
03. Le Tombeau de Couperin/ States of Art
04. Still Moving
05. Jamo Meets Samo
06. Kinesics
07. Aquanaut
08. Retrograde
09. Release from Suffering
10. Root Progression

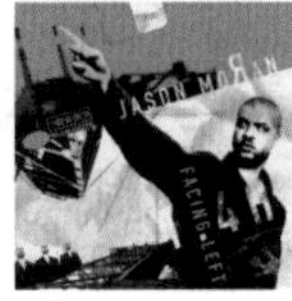

FACING LEFT

2000

PERSONNEL
- JASON MORAN, PIANO
- TARUS MATEEN, BASS
- NASHEET WAITS, DRUMS

TRACKLIST
01. Later
02. Thief Without Loot
03. Joga
04. Wig Wise
05. Yojimbo
06. Another One
07. Lies Are Sold
08. Murder of Don Fanucci
09. Twelve
10. Three of the Same from Two Different
11. Fragment of a Necklace
12. Battle of the Cattle Acts
13. Gangsterism on Wood

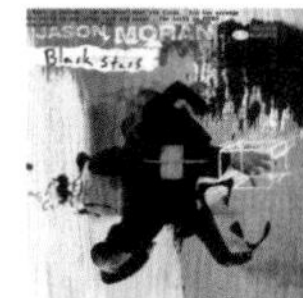

BLACK STARS

2001

PERSONNEL
- JASON MORAN, PIANO
- SAM RIVERS, TENOR SAXOPHONE, FLUTE
- TARUS MATEEN, BASS
- NASHEET WAITS, DRUMS

TRACKLIST
01. Foot Under Foot
02. Kinda Dukish
03. Gangsterism on a River
04. Earth Song
05. Summit
06. Say Peace
07. Draw the Light Out
08. Out Front
09. The Sun at Midnight
10. Skitter In
11. Sound It Out

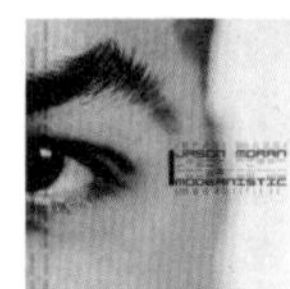

MODERNISTIC

2002

PERSONNEL
- JASON MORAN, PIANO

TRACKLIST
01. You've Got to Be Modernistic
02. Body and Soul
03. Planet Rock
04. Planet Rock Postscript
05. Time Into Space Into Time
06. Gangsterism on Irons
07. Moran Tonk Circa 1935
08. Passion
09. Gangsterism on a Lunchtable
10. Auf Einer Burg/In a Fortress
11. Gentle Shifts South

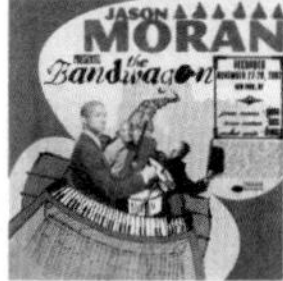

THE BANDWAGON

2003

PERSONNEL
- JASON MORAN, PIANO
- TARUS MATEEN, BASS
- NASHEET WAITS, DRUMS
- AHU GURAL, SAMPLED VOICE
- ANDREW MORAN AND CLAUDIA MORAN, SAMPLED VOICE
- BENNIE RUTH CHESTER, SAMPLED VOICE UNIDENTIFIED

TRACKLIST
01. Intro
02. Another One
03. Intermezzo, Op. 118, No. 2
04. Ringing My Phone (Straight Outta Istanbul)
05. Out Front
06. Gentle Shifts South (My Folks' Folks)
07. Gangsterism on Stages
08. Body & Soul
09. Infospace
10. Planet Rock

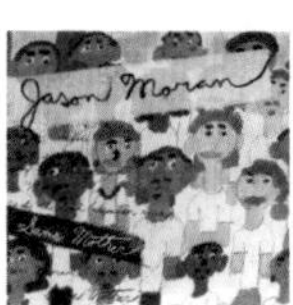

SAME MOTHER

2004

PERSONNEL
- JASON MORAN, PIANO
- MARVIN SEWELL, GUITAR
- TARUS MATEEN, BASS
- NASHEET WAITS, DRUMS

TRACKLIST
01. Gangsterism on the Rise
02. Jump Up
03. Aubade
04. G Suit Saltation
05. I'll Play the Blues for You
06. Fire Waltz
07. Field of the Dead (from Alexander Nevsky)
08. Restin'
09. The Field
10. Gangsterism on the Set

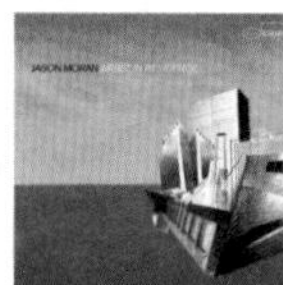

ARTIST IN RESIDENCE

2006

PERSONNEL
- JASON MORAN, PIANO
- MARVIN SEWELL, GUITAR
- TARUS MATEEN, BASS
- NASHEET WAITS, DRUMS

GUESTS
- ALICIA HALL MORAN, VOICE
- ADRIAN PIPER, SAMPLED VOICE
- JOAN JONAS, VARIOUS PERCUSSION AND TOYS
- RALPH ALESSI, TRUMPET
- ABDOU MBOUP, DJEMBE, KORA, TALKING DRUM

TRACKLIST
01. Break Down
02. Milestone
03. Refraction 2
04. Cradle Song
05. Artists Ought to Be Writing
06. Refraction 1
07. Arizona Landscape
08. RAIN
09. Lift Ev'ry Voice and Sing
10. He Puts on His Coat and Leaves

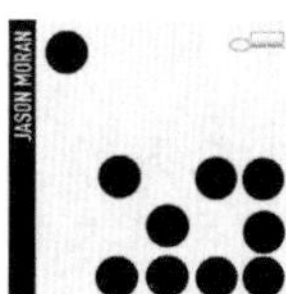

TEN

2010

PERSONNEL
- JASON MORAN, PIANO
- TARUS MATEEN, BASS
- NASHEET WAITS, DRUMS
- JONAS MORAN, VOCALS
- MALCOLM MORAN, VOCALS

TRACKLIST
01. Blue Blocks
02. RKF in the Land of Apartheid
03. Feedback Pt. 2
04. Crepuscule with Nellie
05. Study No. 6
06. Pas de Deux–Lines Ballet
07. Study No. 6
08. Gangsterism Over 10 Years
09. Big Stuff
10. Play to Live
11. The Subtle One
12. To Bob Vatel of Paris
13. Old Babies

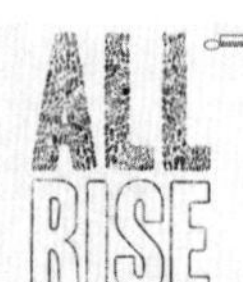

ALL RISE: A JOYFUL ELEGY FOR FATS WALLER

2014

PERSONNEL
- JASON MORAN, PIANO
- TARUS MATEEN, BASS
- NASHEET WAITS, DRUMS
- LISA E. HARRIS, VOCALS
- LERON THOMAS, TRUMPET, VOCALS
- JOSH ROSEMAN, TROMBONE
- STEPHAN LEHMAN, SAXOPHONE
- CHARLES HAYNES, DRUMS
- MESHELL NDEGEOCELLO, VOCALS

TRACKLIST
11. Put Your Hands On It
12. Ain't Misbehavin'
13. Yacht Club Swing
14. Lulu's Back in Town
15. Two Sleepy People
16. The Joint Is Jumpin'
17. Honeysuckle Rose
18. Ain't Nobody's Business
19. Fats Elegy
20. Handful of Keys
21. Jitterbug Waltz
22. Sheik of Araby / I Found a New Baby

YES RECORDS

THE ARMORY CONCERT

2016

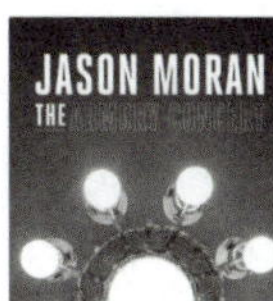

PERSONNEL
· JASON MORAN, PIANO

TRACKLIST
01. Wind
02. Reanimation
03. Big News/More News
04. Veterans
05. Trade Winds
06. South Side Digging
07. All Hammers and Chains
08. Magnet
09. Alicia
10. Winds

BANGS

2017

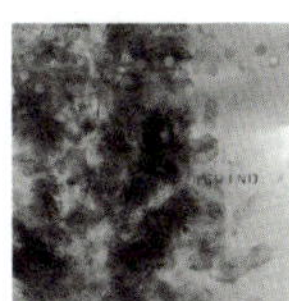

PERSONNEL
· JASON MORAN, PIANO
· MARY HALVORSON, GUITAR
· RON MILES, CORNET

TRACKLIST
01. Crops
02. Red Sky Green
03. Cupid
04. The 13th Fugue
05. They Come to Us Theme
06. Gangsterism in the Wind
07. White Space
08. My Father's House
09. Conspiracy Blue
10. Gangsterism in the Wind
    Again

*THANKSGIVING
AT THE
VANGUARD*

2017

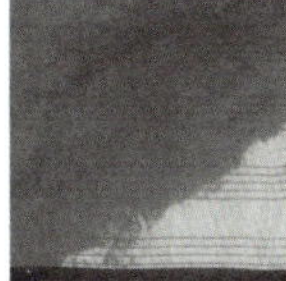

PERSONNEL
· JASON MORAN, PIANO
· TARUS MATEEN, BASS
· NASHEET WAITS, DRUMS

TRACKLIST
01. For Jaki
02. Band Intro
03. Gangsterism at The
    Vanguard
04. Winds
05. Big News/More News
06. South Side Digging
07. Blessing the Boats
08. Thelonius
09. Between Nothingness and
    Infinity
10. Wind Finale

*MASS
(HOWL, EON)*

2017

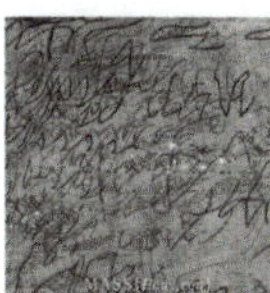

PERSONNEL
· JASON MORAN, PIANO, RHODES
  PIANO, PERCUSSION
· GRAHAM HAYNES, CORNET AND
  ELECTRONICS
· JAMIRE WILLIAMS, DRUMS

TRACKLIST
01. Invocation
02. Confession
03. Creed
04. Responsorial
05. Offertory
06. Summon
07. Benediction

LOOKS OF A LOT

2018

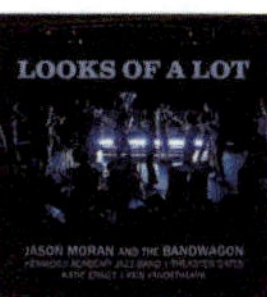

PERSONNEL
· JASON MORAN, PIANO AND MUSIC BOX
· TARUS MATEEN, BASS
· NASHEET WAITS, DRUMS
· KATIE ERNST, VOICE AND BASS
· KEN VANDERMARK, TENOR
  SAXOPHONE AND CLARINET
· THEASTER GATES, VOICE

· KENWOOD ACADEMY JAZZ BAND
· BAND DIRECTORS: GERALD POWELL
  AND BETHANY PICKENS

· SAXOPHONES: ASMINA TURNER
  (ALTO SAX/FLUTE), JARRETT
  CRENSHAW (TENOR SAX), NYREE
  MOORE (ALTO SAX), REGINALD
  MCCOY (ALTO SAX), SAMUEL
  REYNOLDS (ALTO SAX), TYLER
  BLOOMFIELD (TENOR SAX),
  WILLIAM BISHOP-GREEN (BARITONE
  SAX)

· TROMBONES: ALYSSA YOUNGER,
  BRIAN MORROW, GARRETT POWELL,
  JOSHUA WHITE, AND LORNE HUBERT

· TRUMPETS: ANDRE FRANKS,
  JORDAN GALLON, JUSTIN
  ANDERSON, KODJO ADESSU,
  MYLES HARRELL, TANITHA DALE,
  TYSON SMITH

· RHYTHM SECTION: CHARLES
  MORGAN (PIANO), TYLER SMITH
  (PIANO), STEVEN BOWMAN
  JR. (BASS GUITAR), DANIEL
  DAY (DRUMS), DANYAH HARRIS
  (CONGAS/AUX), DEAMONTE
  RUSSELL (DRUMS/CONGAS/AUX)

· DRUMLINE: DYLAN HUNTER AND
  KENDALL CURTIS (CYMBALS);
  KYNDAL PURKET (SNARE DRUM);
  NAIROBI TRIBBLE (QUINTS);
  TYLER BROWN AND WILLIAM
  BUTLER (BASS DRUM)

· CHAPERONES: KAREN ASHLEY-
  BOWMAN, HATTIE ASKEW, STEVEN
  BOWMAN, SR., AND MARIANNE
  TURNER

TRACKLIST
01. Der Doppelganger
02. Big News
03. Wasbashin'
04. Wabash Stomp
05. Easy
06. South Side Digging
07. Make Noise
08. Face Fade
09. Music Boxing More News
10. More News
11. Shoulder to Shoulder

*MUSIC FOR
JOAN JONAS*

2018

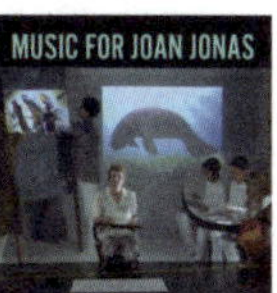

PERSONNEL
· JASON MORAN, PIANO, SYNTH
· JOAN JONAS, VOICE AND
  PERCUSSION
· JOSE LUIS BLONDET, VOICE
· ÁNDE SOMBY, VOICE

TRACKLIST
· *THE SHAPE, THE SCENT, THE
  FEEL OF THINGS*
01. Opening
02. Moths
03. Arizona
04. Snake Dance
05. Melancholia
06. Mirror Improv
07. Tree Nymph
08. Feedback Dance
09. Final Scene

· *REANIMATION*
10. Opening
11. Paper
12. Tunnel
13. Birds
14. Mountain
15. Marbles
16. Duet
17. Fish

· *THEY COME TO US WITHOUT
  A WORD*
18. Woods
19. Grass
20. Beach Dance
21. Rattles
22. Tunnel
23. Ribbons
24. Woodblock Duet
25. Oar Dance

· *BONUS TRACK*
26. Broken Symmetry

COMMISSIONS

MILESTONE

2005

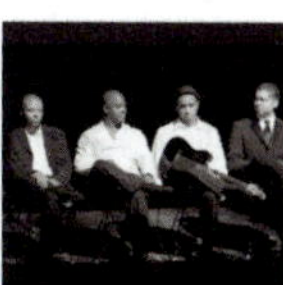

PREMIERED AT THE WALKER ART
CENTER, MINNEAPOLIS, MAY 20,
2005

PERSONNEL
· JASON MORAN, PIANO
· TARUS MATEEN, BASS
· NASHEET WAITS, DRUMS
· MARVIN SEWELL, GUITAR
· ALICIA HALL MORAN, VOICE
· BRIAN DEHLER, VIDEO DESIGN
· ADRIAN PIPER, VOICE SAMPLE,
  *THE MYTHIC BEING; I/YOU
  (HER)*, 1974

COMMISSIONED BY THE WALKER
ART CENTER, MINNEAPOLIS

*IN MY MIND:
MONK AT TOWN
HALL 1959*

2007

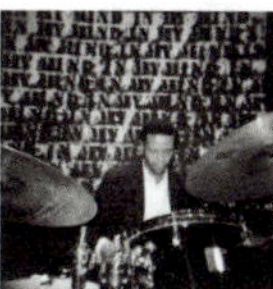

PREMIERED AT THE SYMPHONY
CENTER, CHICAGO, NOVEMBER 16,
2007

PERSONNEL
· JASON MORAN, PIANO
· TARUS MATEEN, BASS
· NASHEET WAITS, DRUMS
· GLENN LIGON, PAINTING
· DAVID DEMPEWOLF, VIDEO DESIGN

COMMISSIONED BY DUKE
UNIVERSITY, SFJAZZ, CHICAGO
SYMPHONY CENTER, AND THE
WASHINGTON PERFORMING ARTS
SOCIETY

LIVE:
TIME - THE
QUILTS
OF GEE'S BEND

2008

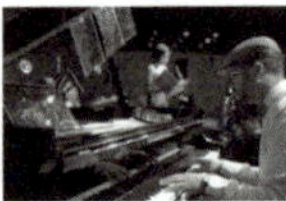

PREMIERED AT THE PHILADELPHIA
MUSEUM OF ART AS PART OF "ART
AFTER 5," DECEMBER 1, 2008

PERSONNEL
· JASON MORAN, PIANO
· BILL FRISELL, GUITAR
· ALICIA HALL MORAN, VOCALS
· TARUS MATEEN, BASS
· JAMIRE WILLIAMS, DRUMS

COMMISSIONED BY THE PHILADELPHIA
MUSEUM OF ART

LOOKS OF A LOT

2014

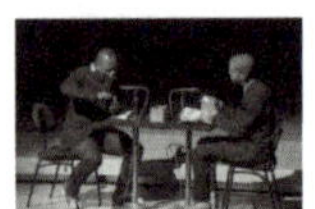

PREMIERED AT THE SYMPHONY CENTER,
CHICAGO, MAY 30, 2014

PERSONNEL
· JASON MORAN, PIANO
· TARUS MATEEN, BASS
· NASHEET WAITS, DRUMS
· KATIE ERNST, VOICE AND BASS
· KEN VANDERMARK, TENOR
  SAXOPHONE AND CLARINET
· THEASTER GATES, VOICE
· KENWOOD ACADEMY JAZZ BAND

COMMISSIONED BY THE CHICAGO
SYMPHONY ORCHESTRA

THE
RAUSCHENBERG
PROJECT:
HOLED UP

2015

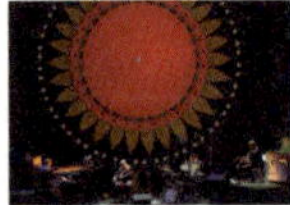

PREMIERED IN THE CULLEN THEATER
AT THE WORTHAM CENTER, HOUSTON,
FEBRUARY 7, 2015

PERSONNEL
· JASON MORAN, PIANO AND MUSIC
· TARUS MATEEN, BASS
· NASHEET WAITS, DRUMS
· MARVIN SEWELL, GUITAR
· HORACE GRIGSBY, VOCALS
· ROBERT PRUITT, VIDEO DESIGN

COMMISSIONED BY DA CAMERA OF
HOUSTON PRODUCTIONS

WIND

2016

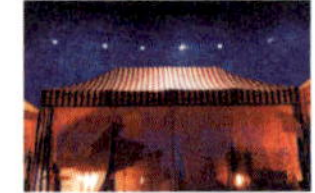

PREMIERED AT JAZZTOPAD FESTIVAL IN
WROCŁAW, POLAND, NOVEMBER 17, 2016

PERSONNEL
· JASON MORAN, PIANO
· TARUS MATEEN, DOUBLE BASS
· MARVIN SEWELL, GUITAR
· NASHEET WAITS, DRUMS

ENSEMBLE
· PIOTR DAMASIEWICZ, TRUMPET
· SZYMON KLEKOWICKI, HELICON
· DAWID LUBOWICZ, VIOLIN
· MATEUSZ SMOCYŃSKI, VIOLIN
· KRZYSZTOF LENCZOWSKI, CELLO
· MARTA NIEDŹWIECKA, POSITIVE
  ORGAN
· MICHAL TOMASZCZYK, TROMBONE

COMMISSIONED BY JAZZTOPAD

MASS
(HOWL, EON)

2017

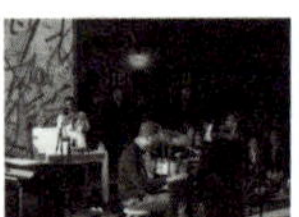

PREMIERED AT THE HARLEM PARISH,
NEW YORK, NOVEMBER 16, 2017

PERSONNEL
· JASON MORAN, PIANO AND MUSIC
· GRAHAM HAYNES, CORNET AND
  EFFECTS
· JAMIRE WILLIAMS, DRUMS
· JULIE MEHRETU, PAINTINGS

PERFORMA 17 COMMISSION

THE LAST
JAZZ FEST

2018

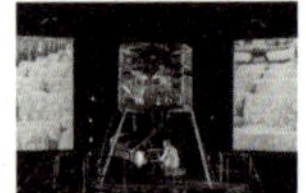

PREMIERED IN THE MCGUIRE THEATER
AT THE WALKER ART CENTER,
MINNEAPOLIS, MAY 18, 2018

PERSONNEL
· RYAN TRECARTIN, DESIGN, SET,
  VIDEO
· LIZZIE FITCH, SET, VIDEO
· DJ ASHLAND MINES (TOTAL
  FREEDOM), ELECTRONICS
· JASON MORAN, PIANO
· TARUS MATEEN, BASS
· NASHEET WAITS, DRUMS

COMMISSIONED BY THE WALKER ART
CENTER, MINNEAPOLIS, AS PART OF
THE EXHIBITION *JASON MORAN*

INSTALLATIONS, SCULPTURES, VIDEOS,
AND WORKS ON PAPER

Artist	Title	Year	Medium	Dimensions / Duration	Credit
STAN DOUGLAS Canada, b. 1960	*Luanda-Kinshasa*	2013	Video projection (color, sound)	6 hours, 1 min. (loop)	Courtesy the artist and David Zwirner, New York / Hong Kong
GLENN LIGON US, b. 1960	*The Death of Tom*	2008	16mm film (black and white, sound) transferred to video	23 min.	©Glenn Ligon; Courtesy the artist; Luhring Augustine, New York; Regen Projects, Los Angeles; and Thomas Dane Gallery, London
JASON MORAN US, b. 1975	*The Death of Tom*	2011	Score on manuscript paper	16 x 24 x 1 in. (40.6 x 61 x 2.5 cm)	Glenn Ligon Collection
JASON MORAN US, b. 1975	*STAGED: Savoy Ballroom 1*	2015	Mixed media, sound	120 x 216 x 120 in. (304.8 x 548.6 x 304.8 cm)	Courtesy the artist and Luhring Augustine, New York
JASON MORAN US, b. 1975	*STAGED: Three Deuces*	2015	Mixed media, sound	96 x 120 x 156 in. (243.8 x 304.8 x 396.2 cm)	Courtesy the artist and Luhring Augustine, New York
JASON MORAN US, b. 1975	*Atomic Count Basie*	2016	Meteorite, watch	2 ¼ x 3 ½ x 3 in. (5.7 x 8.9 x 7.6 cm)	Courtesy the artist and Luhring Augustine, New York
JASON MORAN US, b. 1975	*Run 2*	2016	Charcoal on paper	9 ½ x 37 ¾ in. (24.1 x 95.9 cm)	Walker Art Center, Minneapolis; Butler Family Fund, 2017
JASON MORAN US, b. 1975	*Run 6*	2016	Charcoal on paper	10 x 36 ½ in. (25.4 x 92.7 cm)	Walker Art Center, Minneapolis; Butler Family Fund, 2017
JASON MORAN US, b. 1975	*She Cares—Hill*	2016	Music box, wooden hat block part	5 ½ x 4 ½ x 5 ¼ in. (14.2 x 11.4 x 13.3 cm)	Courtesy the artist and Luhring Augustine, New York
JASON MORAN US, b. 1975	*She Cares—Slang*	2016	Music box, stove burner	7 ¾ x 5 ½ x 6 ½ in. (19.7 x 13.9 x 16.5 cm)	Courtesy the artist and Luhring Augustine, New York
JASON MORAN US, b. 1975	*Strutter's Ball*	2016	Charcoal on paper	34 ½ x 6 ¾ in. (87.6 x 17.1 cm)	Walker Art Center, Minneapolis; Butler Family Fund, 2017
JASON MORAN US, b. 1975	*Black and Blue Gravity*	2018	Mixed media on paper	25 x 36 ¾ in. (63.5 x 93.3 cm)	Courtesy the artist and Luhring Augustine, New York
JASON MORAN US, b. 1975	*Black Run*	2018	Mixed media on paper	25 x 36 ¾ in. (63.5 x 93.3 cm)	Courtesy the artist and Luhring Augustine, New York
JASON MORAN US, b. 1975	*Blue (Creed) Gravity 1*	2018	Mixed media on paper	25 x 36 ¾ in. (63.5 x 93.3 cm)	Courtesy the artist and Luhring Augustine, New York
JASON MORAN US, b. 1975	*STAGED: Slugs' Saloon*	2018	Mixed media, sound	120 x 254 ¼ x 199 in. (304.8 x 645.8 x 505.5 cm)	Commissioned by the Walker Art Center, Minneapolis; T. B. Walker Aquisition Fund, 2018

VIDEO COMPILATION

The works in this section — collaborative videos, audio recordings, and performance documentation — have been composed and arranged by Jason Moran into a synchronized loop displayed on screens in the galleries. The following order reflects the sequence of videos in Moran's compilation.

Artist	Title	Year	Medium	Dimensions / Duration	Credit
JASON MORAN AND THE BANDWAGON	Excerpts from *Milestone*	2005 / 2007	Video (color, sound). Performed at the Cullen Theater, Wortham Center, Houston, February 10, 2007. Conceived by Jason Moran. Performance by Jason Moran and the Bandwagon (Tarus Mateen, bass; Nasheet Waits, drums), Marvin Sewell, and Alicia Hall Moran. Direction by Alicia Hall Moran. Video design by Brian Dehler. Voice recordings by Adrian Piper.	14:46 min.	Commissioned by the Walker Art Center, Minneapolis; Courtesy the artist
JOAN JONAS US, b. 1936 JASON MORAN US, b. 1975	*Antiphony: Joan Jonas x Jason Moran*	2013	Video (color, sound). Film directed by RoundO Films (Radiclani Clytus, Gregg Conde, and Anthony Gannon).	5:18 min.	Courtesy the artists and RoundO Films LLC, New York
LORNA SIMPSON US, b. 1960	*Chess*	2013	Three-channel video (black and white, sound)	10:19 min.	©Lorna Simpson; Courtesy the artist and Hauser & Wirth, Los Angeles

Artist	Title	Year	Medium	Dimensions/Duration	Credit
THEASTER GATES US, b. 1973 JASON MORAN AND THE BANDWAGON	Excerpts from *Looks of a Lot*	2014	Video (color, sound). Performed at Symphony Center, Chicago, May 30, 2014. Performance by Jason Moran and the Bandwagon (Tarus Mateen, bass; Nasheet Waits, drums), Katie Ernst, Ken Vandermark, Theaster Gates, and the Kenwood Academy Jazz Band. Film directed by RoundO Films (Radiclani Clytus, Gregg Conde, and Anthony Gannon).	17:54 min.	Commissioned by the Chicago Symphony Orchestra. Courtesy the artists and RoundO Films, New York
KARA WALKER US, b. 1969	*National Archives Microfilm M999 Roll 34: Bureau of Refugees, Freedmen and Abandoned Lands: Six Miles from Springfield on the Franklin Road*	2009	Video (color, sound). Original score by Alicia Hall Moran and Jason Moran.	13:22 min.	©Kara Walker; Courtesy the artist and Sikkema Jenkins & Co., New York
ADAM PENDLETON US, b. 1984	Excerpts from *The Revival*	2007	Audio and digital images. Performed at Stephen Weiss Studio, New York, September 19, 2007. Musical direction by Jason Moran, Alicia Hall Moran, Vaneese Thomas, and Adam Pendleton. Testimonials by Jena Osman and Liam Gillick. Solos by Renee Neufville, Vaneese Thomas, and Clarissa Sinceno. Recorded by ARUP. Photos ©Paula Court.	4:45 min.	Performa 07 Commission; Courtesy the artist and Performa, New York
CARRIE MAE WEEMS US, b. 1953	*Lincoln, Lonnie, and Me — A Story in 5 Parts*	2012	Video (color, sound)	18:29 min.	©Carrie Mae Weems; Courtesy the artist and Jack Shainman Gallery, New York
JOAN JONAS US, b. 1936	Excerpts from *The Shape, the Scent, the Feel of Things*	2005	Video (color, sound). Performed at Dia:Beacon, New York, October 14, 2006. Conceived and directed by Joan Jonas. Video backdrops by Joan Jonas. With music composed and performed by Jason Moran.	5:29 min.	Courtesy the artist
JOAN JONAS US, b. 1936	Excerpts from *They Come to Us without a Word II*	2015	Video (color, sound). Performed at Teatro Piccolo Arsenale, Campo della Tana, Castello, Venice, July 12, 2015. Conceived and directed by Joan Jonas. Video backdrop by Joan Jonas. With music composed and performed by Jason Moran.	4:11 min.	Courtesy the artist
JULIE MEHRETU US, b. 1970 JASON MORAN US, b. 1975	Excerpts from *MASS (HOWL, eon)*	2017	Three-channel video (color, sound). Performed at Harlem Parish, New York, November 16, 2017. Cornet and effects by Graham Haynes. Drums by Jamire Williams. Piano and compositions by Jason Moran. Paintings by Julie Mehretu. Co-curated by Adrienne Edwards and RoseLee Goldberg. Produced by Esa Nickle and Raul Zbengheci (associate producer). Sound engineering by Sascha von Oertzen. Editing by Charles Cohen. Video engineering by Brendan Bercik. Light design by Wild Dogs International. Set fabrication by Standard and Supply.	8 min.	Commissioned by Performa 17 Commission as part of AFROGLOSSIA; Courtesy the artist and Performa, New York
JASON MORAN AND THE BANDWAGON	Excerpt from *The Rauschenberg Project: Holed Up*	2015	Video (color, sound). Performed at Cullen Theater, Wortham Center, Houston, February 7, 2015. Concept, direction, and original compositions by Jason Moran. Video design by Robert Pruitt. Technical direction, lighting, and set design by Clint Allen. Performance by Jason Moran and the Bandwagon (Tarus Mateen, bass; Nasheet Waits, drums), Marvin Sewell (guitar), and Horace Grigsby (vocals). Stage management by Skye Krienitz. Audio engineering by Sascha von Oertzen. Film by Carrithers Studio.	9:40 min.	Commissioned by Da Camera of Houston Productions, Sarah Rothenberg, Artistic Director

SCORES AND ARCHIVAL MATERIAL

Artist	Title	Year	Medium	Dimensions	Credit
JASON MORAN US, b. 1975	*Fourth band member*	c. 1990	Sony Minidisc Recorder, disc	recorder: 3 x 3 ½ x 2⁵⁄₃₂ in. (7.6 x 8.9 x 2 cm); disc: 2 ²⁷⁄₃₂ x 3 ⁵⁄₃₂ x ⁵⁄₁₆ in. (7.2 x 8 x .8 cm)	Courtesy the artist
JASON MORAN US, b. 1975	*Slang*	2011	Score on manuscript paper	13 x 21 in. (33 x 53.3 cm)	Courtesy the artist
JASON MORAN US, b. 1975	*Reanimation*	2012	Score on manuscript paper	13 x 21 in. (33 x 53.3 cm)	Courtesy the artist
JASON MORAN US, b. 1975	*Selma*	2014	Score booklet	17 x 14 in. (43.1 x 35.5 cm)	Courtesy the artist
JASON MORAN US, b. 1975	*Trade Winds*	2015	Score on manuscript paper, cardboard	6 ¹³⁄₁₆ x 10 ¼ in. (17.3 x 26 cm)	Courtesy the artist
JASON MORAN US, b. 1975	*Untitled*	2015	Score on manuscript paper, cardboard	12 ⅛ x 8 ⅜ in. (30.8 x 21.3 cm)	Courtesy the artist

Artist	Title	Date	Medium	Dimensions	Credit
JASON MORAN US, b. 1975	*WINDS*	2015	Score on manuscript paper, cardboard	12 ⅝ x 9 ⁷⁄₁₆ in. (32.1 x 24 cm)	Courtesy the artist
JASON MORAN US, b. 1975	*Between the World and Me*	2018	Score on manuscript paper	13 x 21 in. (33 x 53.3 cm)	Courtesy the artist
	Handbill for Slugs' Saloon	October/ November 1966	Screenprint on paper	8 ½ x 5 ½ in. (21.6 x 14 cm)	Private collection
	Sounds & Fury	December 1965	Magazine; two copies: one autographed by Charles Lloyd; published by Taylor Castell, Inc.	8 ⅜ x 10 ⅞ in. (21.27 x 27.6 cm)	Private collection
SUPERDRUPE | STUDIOS	Poster for Slugs' Saloon	March/ April 1967	Lithograph on paper	8 ½ x 11 in. (21.6 x 27.9 cm)	Private collection
	Adrian Piper and Jason Moran in Cape Cod, Massachusetts	c. 2004	Photograph	6 x 4 in. (15.2 x 10.2 cm)	Courtesy the artist
	Handwritten letter from Adrian Piper to Jason Moran	January 11, 2005		10 ⅝ x 7 ¾ in. (27 x 19.7 cm) open	Courtesy the artist
	Handwritten letter from Adrian Piper to Jason Moran	August 2005		4 x 6 in. (10.2 x 15.2 cm)	Courtesy the artist
	Cue sheet from *Milestone*	2005		8 ½ x 11 in. (21.6 x 27.9 cm)	Courtesy the artist
	Program for *Milestone*	2005		6 x 9 in. (15.2 x 22.8 cm)	Courtesy the artist
	Telephone from *Milestone*	2005		4 ¾ x 9 ½ x 9 ¹⁄₁₆ in. (12.1 x 24.1 x 23 cm)	Courtesy the artist
	Handwritten letter from Ava Duvernay to Jason Moran	2015		7 x 4 ⅞ in. (17.8 x 12.4 cm) open	Courtesy the artist

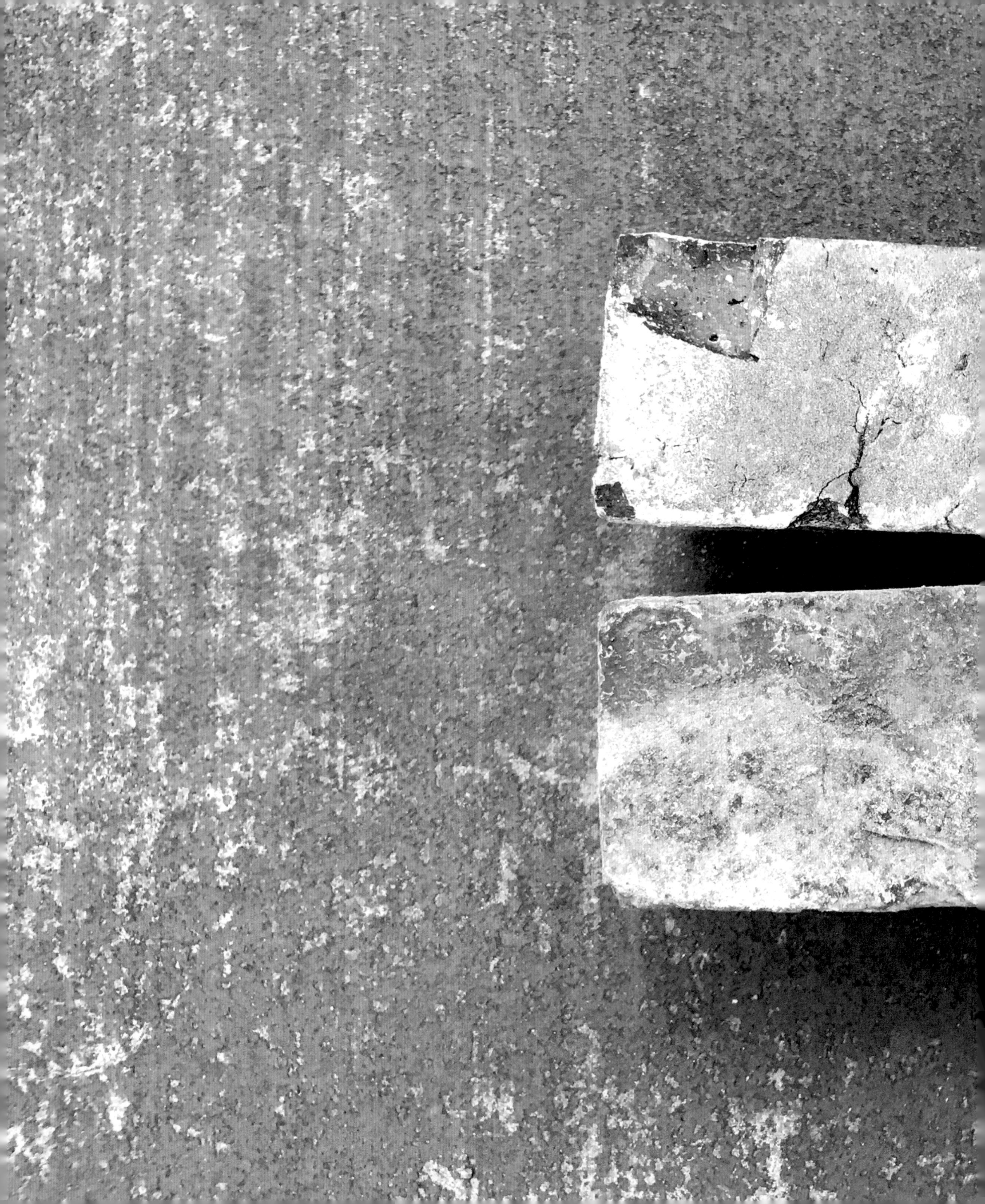

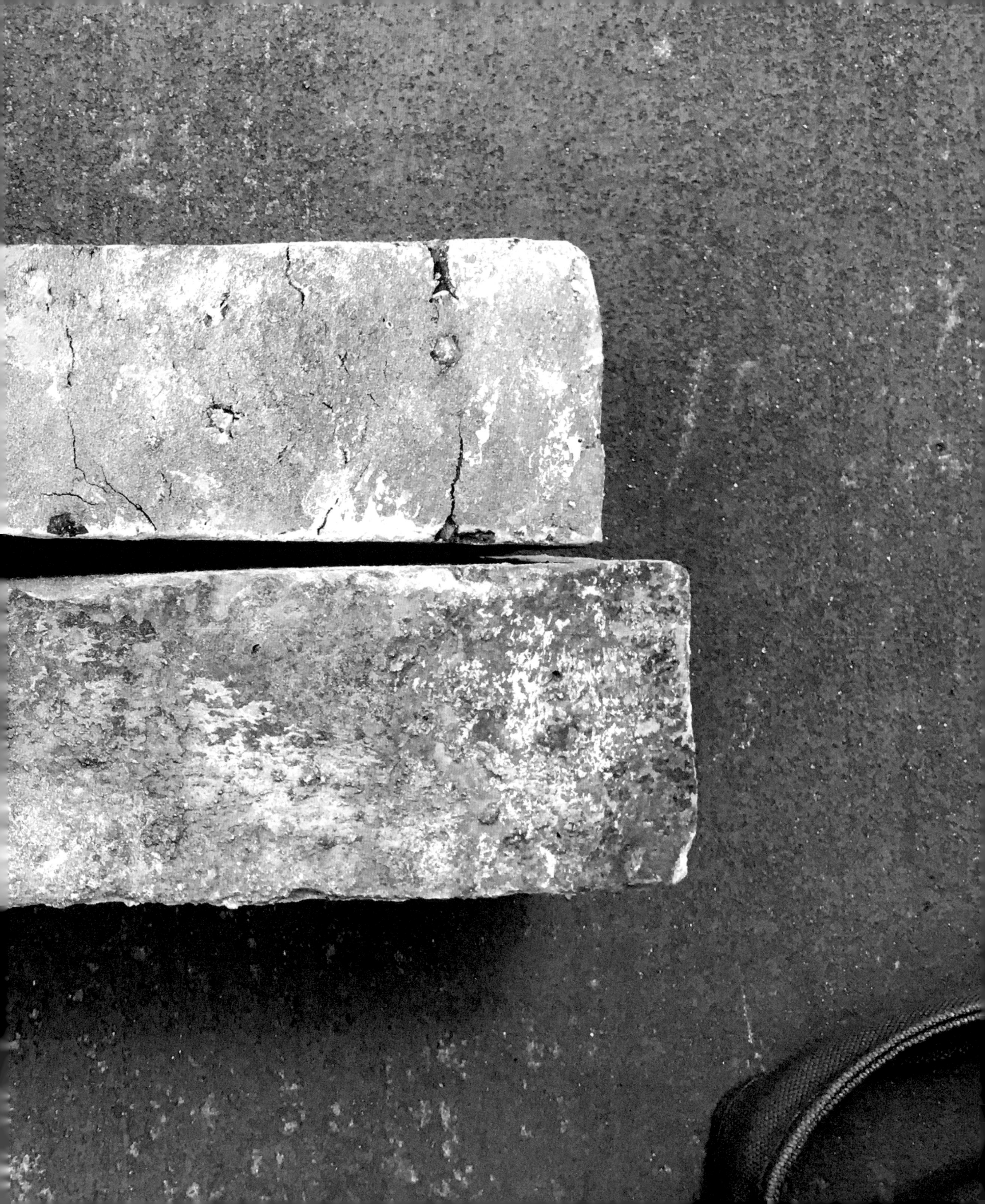

CONTRIBUTOR BIOGRAPHIES

PHILIP BITHER is the William and Nadine McGuire Director and Senior Curator of Performing Arts at the Walker Art Center, Minneapolis.

ADRIENNE EDWARDS is former curator at large for Visual Arts at the Walker Art Center, Minneapolis. She is currently the Engell Speyer Family Curator and Curator of Performance at the Whitney Museum of American Art, New York.

OKWUI ENWEZOR is former director of Haus der Kunst, Munich. In 2015 he was director of the visual arts for the 56th Venice Biennale. He has served as artistic director for several international exhibitions, including the Paris Triennale 2012, 7th Gwangju Biennale, 2nd Seville Biennial, Documenta 11 in Kassel, and the 2nd Johannesburg Biennial. Enwezor has held the positions of dean of academic affairs and senior vice president of the San Francisco Art Institute; Kirk Varnedoe Visiting Professor at the Institute of Fine Arts, New York University; Global Distinguished Professor in the Department of Art History at New York University; and visiting professor at Columbia University, New York.

ALICIA HALL MORAN mezzo-soprano, works across the genres of music, theater, and art. She has had both classical and jazz recitals at the Art Institute of Chicago, Stavanger Hall, and the Bjergsted Jazz Ensemble. She has performed at the Whitney Museum of American Art, the Museum of Modern Art, the Kitchen, and Artists Space, among other art venues. Collaborating with a diverse range of artists, Hall Moran has appeared in many productions, including Bill T. Jones/Arnie Zane Dance Company's *Chapel/Chapter* (2006), Simone Leigh and Liz Magic Laser's *Breakdown* (2011), Carrie Mae Weems's *Grace Notes* (2016), and Joan Jonas's *Reading Dante* (2008). She has created compositions with her husband, Jason Moran, for *BLEED* (2012), at the Whitney Museum of American Art, and *Work Songs* at the 56th Venice Biennale (2015). Her recent album *HEAVY BLUE* (2015) blurs the line between opera and jazz.

DANIELLE A. JACKSON is former interdisciplinary fellow, Performing Arts, at the Walker Art Center, Minneapolis.

GEORGE E. LEWIS is Edwin H. Case Professor of American Music at Columbia University, a fellow of the American Academy of Arts and Sciences, and a corresponding fellow of the British Academy. His other honors include a MacArthur Fellowship, a Guggenheim Fellowship, a United States Artists Walker Fellowship, an Alpert Award in the Arts, and fellowships from the National Endowment for the Arts. Lewis has been a member of the Association for the Advancement of Creative Musicians (AACM) since 1971, and his work in electronic and computer music, interactive installations, and notated and improvisative forms is documented on more than 150 recordings. He is the co-editor of the two-volume *Oxford Handbook of Critical Improvisation Studies* (2016), and his book *A Power Stronger Than Itself: The AACM and American Experimental Music* (University of Chicago Press, 2008) received the American Book Award and the American Musicological Society's Music in American Culture Award.

GLENN LIGON is an artist living and working in New York. He received a Bachelor of Arts from Wesleyan University and attended the Whitney Museum Independent Study Program. In 2001, *Glenn Ligon: America*, a midcareer retrospective organized by Scott Rothkopf, premiered at the Whitney Museum of American Art and traveled nationally. Ligon's work has been included in major international exhibitions, including the Venice Biennale (2015 and 1997), Berlin Biennal (2014), Istanbul Biennal (2011), Documenta XI (2002), and Gwangju Biennale (2000). Ligon curated a group exhibition titled *Blue Black* (2017) at the Pulitzer Art Foundation in St. Louis, which was inspired by Ellsworth Kelly's wall sculpture of the same name and posed questions about language, identity, and perception.

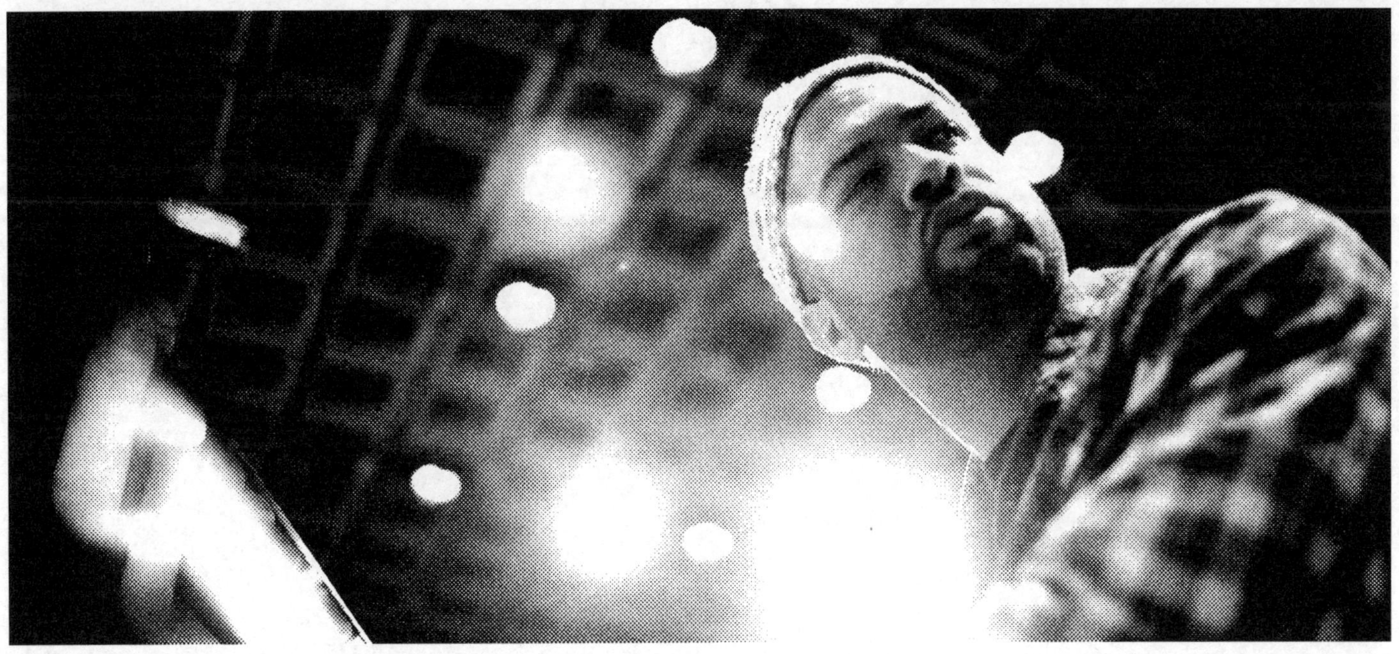

Published on the occasion of the exhibition *Jason Moran*, organized by the Walker Art Center, Minneapolis, and curated by Adrienne Edwards with Danielle A. Jackson.

Jason Moran is made possible with generous support from the Andrew W. Mellon Foundation, the National Endowment for the Arts, and the William and Nadine McGuire Commissioning Fund. Additional support provided by Mike and Elizabeth Sweeney. Piano by Steinway & Sons.

Support for the exhibition's catalogue is provided by a grant from the Andrew W. Mellon Foundation in support of Walker Art Center publications.

Walker Art Center, Minneapolis
April 26 – August 26, 2018

Institute of Contemporary Art/Boston
September 19, 2018 – January 21, 2019

Wexner Center for the Arts, Columbus, Ohio
June 1 – August 11, 2019

Whitney Museum of American Art, New York
September 20, 2019 – January 2020

EXHIBITION CURATOR	ADRIENNE EDWARDS
EXHIBITION CURATORIAL ASSISTANT AND RESEARCHER	DANIELLE A. JACKSON
DESIGN DIRECTOR	EMMET BYRNE
CATALOGUE DESIGNER	12:01 — OFFICE OF HASSAN RAHIM
EXHIBITION GRAPHIC DESIGNER	RYAN GERALD NELSON
EDITOR	CATHY LEBOWITZ
PROOFREADER	PAMELA JOHNSON
SENIOR IMAGE SPECIALIST	GREG BECKEL
DESIGN STUDIO MANAGER	ALANNA NISSEN

Library of Congress Cataloging-in-Publication Data

Edwards, Adrienne (Art critic), editor. | Walker Art Center, organizer, host institution. | Institute of Contemporary Art (Boston, Mass.), host institution. | Wexner Center for the Arts, host institution. | Whitney Museum of American Art, host institution.
Jason Moran / edited by Adrienne Edwards ; essays by Philip Bither, Adrienne Edwards, Okwui Enwezor, Alicia Hall Moran, Danielle A. Jackson, George E. Lewis, Glenn Ligon ; additional contributions by Jason Moran.
First edition. | Minneapolis: Walker Art Center, 2018. | "Published on the occasion of the exhibition Jason Moran, organized by the Walker Art Center, Minneapolis, and curated by Adrienne Edwards with Danielle A. Jackson." | Includes bibliographical references.
LCCN 2018030234 | ISBN 9781935963172 (softcover)
LCSH: Moran, Jason--Exhibitions.
LCC NX512.M64 A4 2018 | DDC 702.81--dc23
LC record available at https://lccn.loc.gov/2018030234

Available through D.A.P./Distributed Art Publishers, 155 Sixth Avenue, New York, NY 10013. www.artbook.com

Printed by Oddi Sales/Gorenjski Tisk, Kranj, Slovenia. Typefaces: Century Schoolbook Mono, Compacta, and Untitled Sans. Papers: Cyclus Print, Munken Lynx, and Omni Gloss.